The Complete Step·by·Step

COOKING CLASS
Cookbook

Copyright © 1994 by Publications International, Ltd.
All rights reserved. This publication may not be reproduced or quoted in whole or in part by mimeograph or any other printed or electronic means, or for presentation on radio, television, videotape or film without written permission from:

Louis Weber, C.E.O.
Publications International, Ltd.
7373 N. Cicero Ave.
Lincolnwood, IL 60646

Permission is never granted for commercial purposes.

All recipes that contain specific brand names are copyrighted by those companies and/or associations.

Dole is a registered trademark of the Dole Food Company, Inc.

Some of the products listed in this publication may be in limited distribution.

Photography: Sacco Productions Limited, Chicago
Pictured on the front cover: Forty-Clove Chicken Filice *(page 164)* and Savory Matchstick Carrots *(page 102)*.
Pictured on the back cover: Shrimp in Angel Hair Pasta Casserole *(page 80)*.

ISBN: 1-55185-007-9

Library of Congress Catalog Card Number: 94-66564

Printed in Canada by: St. Joseph Printing

8 7 6 5 4 3 2 1

Microwave Cooking: Microwave ovens vary in wattage. The microwave cooking times given in this publication are approximate. Use the cooking times as guidelines and check for doneness before adding more time. Consult manufacturer's instructions for suitable microwave-safe cooking dishes.

The publisher would like to thank the following companies and organizations for the use of their recipes in this publication: American Egg Board, American Spice Trade Association, Arkansas State Fair, Black Walnut Festival, Borden, Inc., Borden Kitchens, California Olive Industry, Castroville Artichoke Festival, Christopher Ranch of Gilroy, Circleville Pumpkin Festival, Delmarva Poultry Industry, Inc., Dole Food Company, Inc., Florida Tomato Committee, The HVR Company, Illinois State Fair, Kansas Department of Agriculture, Thomas J. Lipton Co., National Broiler Council, National Pasta Association, National Peanut Festival, National Sunflower Association, Nebraska State Fair, New Jersey Department of Agriculture, New Mexico State Fair, North Dakota Beef Commission, North Dakota Wheat Commission, Pace Foods, Inc., Pollio Dairy Products, The Procter & Gamble Company, The Quaker Oats Company, Southeast United Dairy Industry Association, Inc., Uncle Ben's Rice and Wisconsin Milk Marketing Board.

The Complete Step·by·Step

COOKING CLASS

Cookbook

PUBLICATIONS INTERNATIONAL, LTD.

CONTENTS

INTRODUCTION 6

APPETIZERS 8
Class Notes 10
Elegant Starters 12
Foreign Flair 22
Snack Time 32
Party Pleasers 38

PASTA 46
Class Notes 48
Salads & Soups 50
Sauces 62
Entrées 74

VEGETABLES 86
Class Notes 88
Asparagus 92
Beans, Green 94
Beans, Lima 96
Broccoli 98
Brussels Sprouts 100

Carrots 102
Cauliflower 104
Corn 106
Eggplants 110
Kohlrabies 112
Mushrooms 115
Onions 118
Parsnips 122
Peas, English 124
Peas, Snow 126
Peppers, Bell 128
Potatoes 130
Potatoes, Sweet 134
Spinach 136
Squash, Spaghetti 138
Squash, Winter 140
Tomatoes 142
Zucchini 144

CHICKEN 146
Class Notes 148
Salads 154
One-Dish Meals 162
Family Favorites 172
Elegant Entrées 184

CHINESE 194
Class Notes 196
Appetizers & Soups 198
Entrées 212
Side Dishes 230

ITALIAN 236
Class Notes 238
Appetizers & Soups 240
Pasta Dishes 250
Entrées 264
Side Dishes 274

Sesame Snow Peas

Flautas with Chicken Filling

DESSERTS 446
Class Notes 448
Perfect Pies 450
Daydream Desserts 462
Glorious Chocolate 468
Fruit Fantasies 478
Grand Finales 484

HOLIDAY RECIPES 492
Class Notes 494
Appetizers & Beverages 496
Entrées 510
Side Dishes 524
Desserts 546

Gingerbread Bears

MEXICAN 280
Class Notes 282
Appetizers 286
Tortilla Dishes 294
Entrées 308
On the Side 326
The Basics 332

CHOCOLATE COOKIES & BROWNIES 336
Class Notes 338
Quick as a Wink 340
Chips Galore 348
Family Favorites 358
Brownies 378
Extra Special 386

CAKES 402
Class Notes 404
The Classics 406
The Chocolate Collection 414
Full-o-Fruit 428
Potpourri 436

GARNISHES 560
Class Notes 562
Fruit 564
Vegetable 572
Sweet 582
Miscellaneous 590

INDEX 596

INTRODUCTION

The *Cooking Class* book series was designed to teach the novice, as well as the experienced cook, to prepare fabulous, eye-catching recipes using fresh ingredients. This collection of twelve *Cooking Class* books covers a wide variety of cooking skills and terms. From appetizers to desserts, *Cooking Class* presents a smorgasbord of great-tasting ideas, including creative ways to garnish finished dishes to enhance their appeal. As you prepare the recipes, you'll realize that you're attending a culinary course right in your own kitchen!

Each delectable recipe was created to ensure the best possible results. To guide you through preparation and cooking, the directions are written with precise step-by-step instructions. As you read through the recipes, you can see the actual techniques in the helpful how-to photographs. This aids you in the mastery of such skills as beating egg whites to stiff peaks and cutting vegetables into julienne strips. To further tantalize your creativity, each recipe is featured in a mouth-watering full-page photograph.

In addition to the wonderful recipes, each section has a Class Notes chapter that is chock-full of informative tips, hints and guidelines for preparing the recipes in that section. The Class Notes are great to use as a quick reference guide. For example, there are carving instructions for beef, pork and lamb roasts in "Holiday Recipes," a vegetable cooking chart in the Vegetable section and a glossary of Oriental ingredients in the Chinese section. This wealth of culinary information is waiting for you to explore.

Fusilli Pizzailo

"Appetizers" begins your journey of delectable creations. From finger foods for midnight munchies to enticing first courses, these recipes are designed to awaken any appetite. This section gives tips for party planning and guidelines for the number and variety of appetizers needed for various events.

"Pasta" tempts you with savory sauces, stuffed shells and manicotti, delicious casseroles and terrific salads. Nutritious, delicious and economical, it's no wonder pasta has become such a favorite food.

"Vegetables" shows you innovative ways to prepare old and soon-to-be new favorites. From asparagus to zucchini, you'll learn how to prepare, buy and store all kinds of harvest-fresh produce.

"Chicken" boasts recipes that highlight its versatility. Dress it up or keep it simple. Cook it quick or simmer it slow. Chicken adapts to any mealtime need—light lunches, busy weeknight suppers or festive occasions. Purchasing and storage tips, as well as techniques for cutting whole chicken into pieces are provided.

Ever-popular Chinese, Italian and Mexican cuisines are featured in their own sections. These appetizers, entrées and side dishes are bursting with authentic flavor. Each cuisine features a glossary, which describes ethnic ingredients and gives purchasing and storing tips.

Chicken Chow Mein

"Chocolate Cookies & Brownies" is a showcase of delectable sweets—all featuring chocolate of some type. You can choose from chocolate-flavored, chocolate-dipped, chocolate-frosted or chocolate-filled cookies. Special cookie effects, such as pinwheels, two-tone spritz and checkerboards are a cinch to do with the how-to photographs guiding your way.

"Cakes" offers taste treats from light, delicate angel food to decadently rich chocolate. You'll soon discover just how simple it is to mix and bake luscious cakes from scratch. Cake-baking basics are covered to help you abandon packaged mixes with confidence.

"Desserts" picks up where "Cakes" and "Chocolate Cookies & Brownies" leave off. Impress your family and friends with foolproof pies and luscious desserts, such as mousses, puddings and cheesecakes. Any of these treats makes a sweet ending to your meal.

"Holiday Recipes" has what it takes to make any holiday meal a pleasure to plan, a joy to cook and a delight to eat. Recipes range from delectable appetizers to heavenly desserts. Whether you plan to serve a holiday feast, or just need to bring a delectable dish to someone's home, these festive recipes are sure to be a smashing success.

"Garnishes" completes your culinary journey with the finishing touches to make any dish extra-special. Eye-catching garnishes are simple to make and generally use fruits, vegetables and other ingredients you have on hand.

So, select a few recipes that match your skill level, then experiment with some that are a little more involved. After attending this *Cooking Class*, you'll be cooking like a pro!

Caramel-Butter Pecan Cake

COOKING CLASS
APPETIZERS

10   CLASS NOTES

12   ELEGANT STARTERS

22   FOREIGN FLAIR

32   SNACK TIME

38   PARTY PLEASERS

Scampi *(page 16)*

CLASS NOTES

Appetizers, hors d'oeuvres, finger foods—whichever term you use, these tasty tidbits do much more than just tide guests over until dinner. In fact, the word *hors d'oeuvres* means "outside the main meal"—they set the stage for the meal that is to follow. These delicious appetite enhancers are versatile enough to provide party sustenance on their own at an open house, satisfy cravings for midnight munchies or just awaken the appetite in a refreshing first course. However you decide to serve them, appetizers are meant to be enjoyed by both the guests and the cook. The preparation of these menu additions need not be overwhelming. Some simple, upfront planning combined with the step-by-step instructions in this section will help to maintain the cook's composure and create a relaxed, festive atmosphere.

When serving appetizers before a meal, keep in mind they are meant to tease the appetite, not satisfy it. One or two selections should be ample, allowing five to seven servings per person. Prepare recipes that contrast in texture, temperature and flavor with the meal that follows. For example, a cold seafood hors d'oeuvre would be a refreshing opener before a main course highlighting roast beef or steak. Although, if you are planning an ethnic dinner, coordinating an appetizer from the same foreign country provides a memorable beginning. Many people prefer to serve first-course appetizers before the guests are seated at the dinner table, as this allows the cook time to make last-minute meal preparations. However, starters such as soups and marinated salads should always be served when guests are seated.

For a cocktail party or open house where appetizers are served as the main event, plan a variety of snacks and spreads, including some that are hearty and filling. Remember, too, that the longer the occasion lasts, the more your guests will eat. Plan on ten to twelve servings per person as a minimum. Cold appetizers, such as dips and marinated vegetables, should be made at least several hours to one day ahead since their flavor actually improves with time. Some hot appetizers can be cooked ahead and simply reheated just before serving, while others must be prepared at the last moment. Be sure to enlist kitchen help, if necessary, to give these final details the attention they require. If the food on your appetizer table will be sitting out for several hours, it is important, for food safety reasons, to maintain serving temperatures. Appetizers that need to remain chilled, such as shrimp cocktail, should be served on a platter set over cracked ice. Transfer hot appetizers, such as meatballs, from the oven or rangetop to a warming device, such as a chafing dish or fondue pot for serving. Prepare a balance of hot and cold appetizers that provide a range of flavors and textures, from spicy and rich to light and refreshing. And keep in mind that at a large party with limited seating, guests appreciate finger food and bite-size portions with not-too-drippy sauces.

Part of the fun in serving hors d'oeuvres is in the presentation. The beautiful color photographs of every recipe will give you some eye-catching ideas for finishing touches. A simple spray of small flowers or a handful of fresh herbs provides a colorful garnish on everything from a rustic woven basket to a formal silver platter. Another option for garnishing is to choose one of the recipe's ingredients, for example, red onion, and save a few pretty slices as a special finishing touch for the top of the dish.

Create your own appetizer menus with the delicious recipes in this publication. A fall football party or a holiday open house are just a couple of possibilities. Depending on the size and length of the party, you may wish to supplement your menu with a deli tray or a light dessert.

Clockwise from top right: Hot 'n' Honeyed Chicken Wings *(page 40)*, Scallops à la Schaller *(page 44)*, Spinach-Cheese Triangles *(page 22)* and Chilled Seafood Lasagna with Herbed Cheese *(page 18)*

Golden Tomato Soup

8 medium tomatoes
4 teaspoons (20 ml) reduced-calorie margarine
1 cup (250 ml) chopped onion (technique on page 22)
2 cloves garlic, coarsely chopped
½ cup (125 ml) chopped carrots
¼ cup (60 ml) chopped celery
6 cups (1.5 l) chicken broth
¼ cup (60 ml) uncooked rice
2 tablespoons (30 ml) tomato paste
1 tablespoon (15 ml) Worcestershire sauce
½ teaspoon (2 ml) dried thyme leaves, crushed
¼ to ½ teaspoon (1-2 ml) black pepper
5 drops hot pepper sauce
Fresh thyme sprigs for garnish

1. To easily remove tomato peels, cut a skin-deep "x" in each blossom end and place, 1 at a time, in saucepan of simmering water for 10 seconds. (Add about 30 seconds if tomato is not fully ripened.) Remove with slotted spoon; plunge immediately into bowl of cold water for another 10 seconds. (Do not add more than 1 tomato at a time to hot water, or temperature will drop rapidly and cause tomatoes to stew before their skins can be removed.)

2. Remove tomato peels with paring knife. To seed tomatoes, cut each tomato in half horizontally. Hold each half over bowl, cut side down, and squeeze to remove seeds. Chop tomatoes. Set aside.

3. Melt margarine in large Dutch oven over medium-high heat. Add onion and garlic; cook and stir 1 to 2 minutes until onion is tender. Add carrots and celery; cook and stir 7 to 9 minutes until tender.

4. Stir in tomatoes, broth, rice, tomato paste, Worcestershire sauce, dried thyme, black pepper and hot pepper sauce. Bring to a boil. Reduce heat to low. Cook about 30 minutes, stirring frequently.

5. Remove from heat. Let stand at room temperature to cool 10 minutes. Process soup in small batches in food processor or blender until smooth.

6. Return soup to Dutch oven. Bring to a boil over medium-high heat. Reduce heat to low. Simmer 3 to 5 minutes until heated through. Garnish, if desired.

Makes 8 first-course servings

Step 2. Squeezing tomato half to remove seeds.

Step 5. Processing soup in food processor until smooth.

Chilly Cucumber Soup

4 large cucumbers
2 tablespoons (30 ml) butter or
   margarine
2 tablespoons (30 ml)
   all-purpose flour
¼ cup (60 ml) finely chopped
   fresh parsley (technique on
   page 22)
¼ cup (60 ml) finely chopped
   celery leaves
1 envelope Lipton® Recipe
   Secrets™ Golden Onion
   Soup Mix
2 cups (500 ml) water
2 cups (500 ml) light cream or
   half-and-half
   Cucumber slices, celery leaves
   and lemon peel for garnish

1. Remove cucumber peels with paring knife or vegetable peeler. To seed cucumbers, cut in half lengthwise and scrape out seeds with a small spoon. Finely chop enough cucumbers to measure 3½ cups (875 ml). Set aside.

2. Melt butter in large saucepan over medium heat. Stir in flour and cook 3 minutes, stirring constantly.

3. Add chopped cucumbers, parsley and chopped celery leaves. Reduce heat to low. Cook and stir until cucumbers are tender when pierced with fork, about 8 minutes.

4. Combine soup mix and water in small bowl; add to cucumber mixture. Bring to a boil over medium-high heat. Reduce heat to low. Simmer, covered, 15 minutes. Remove from heat. Let stand at room temperature until cool.

5. Process soup in small batches in blender or food processor until smooth.

6. Transfer soup to large bowl; stir in cream. Cover; refrigerate. Serve soup cold. Garnish, if desired.

Makes about 6 first-course servings

Step 1. Seeding cucumbers.

Step 3. Testing tenderness of cucumbers.

Step 5. Processing soup in blender until smooth.

Scampi

1½ pounds (675 g) large raw
    prawns (about 16)
6 tablespoons (90 ml) butter
4 tablespoons minced garlic (60 ml)
6 green onions, thinly sliced
¼ cup (62.5 ml) dry white wine
    Juice of 1 lemon (about
    2 tablespoons /30 ml)
8 large fresh parsley sprigs,
    finely chopped (technique
    on page 22)
    Salt and black pepper to taste
    Lemon slices and fresh
    parsley sprigs for garnish

1. To remove shells from prawns, use your fingers to peel shell off the side with the legs. Lift it up and over, then back around to the leg side. Discard shells.

2. To devein prawns, use paring knife to make a small cut along the back of the prawns; lift out the dark vein with knife tip. (You may find this easier to do under cold running water.) Set prawns aside.

3. To clarify butter, melt butter in small saucepan over low heat. *Do not stir.* Skim off the white foam that forms on top. Strain clarified butter through a cheesecloth into glass measuring cup to yield ⅓ cup (75 ml). Discard milky residue in bottom of pan.

4. Heat clarified butter in large skillet over medium heat. Add garlic; cook and stir 1 to 2 minutes until softened but not brown.

5. Add prawns, green onions, wine and lemon juice; cook and stir until prawns turn pink and are firm and opaque, 1 to 2 minutes on each side. *Do not overcook.*

6. Just before serving, add chopped parsley and season with salt and pepper. Serve on individual shell-shaped or small gratin dishes. Garnish, if desired.

Makes 8 first-course servings

Step 1. Removing shells from prawns.

Step 2. Deveining prawns.

Step 3. Straining clarified butter.

Chilled Seafood Lasagna with Herbed Cheese

8 uncooked lasagna noodles
   (2 inches wide/5 cm)
2 cups (500 ml) Wisconsin
   ricotta cheese
1 ½ cups (375 ml) Wisconsin
   mascarpone cheese
2 tablespoons (30 ml) lemon
   juice
1 tablespoon (15 ml) minced
   fresh basil leaves
1 tablespoon (15 ml) minced dill
1 tablespoon (15 ml) minced
   fresh tarragon leaves
¼ teaspoon (1 ml) white pepper
1 pound (450 g) lox, divided
4 ounces (120 g) Whitefish
   caviar, gently rinsed
   Lox and fresh tarragon sprigs
   for garnish

1. Cook lasagna noodles according to package directions until tender but still firm. Drain and set aside.

2. Process the ricotta cheese, mascarpone cheese, lemon juice, basil, dill, tarragon and pepper in food processor or blender until well combined.

3. Line terrine mold* with plastic wrap, allowing wrap to extend 5 inches (12.5 cm) over sides of pan.

4. Place 1 noodle in bottom of pan. Spread ½ cup (125 ml) cheese mixture over noodle. Cover cheese mixture with 2 ounces lox (60 g); spread 2 rounded teaspoons (10 ml) caviar over lox. Repeat layers with remaining ingredients, ending with noodle. Set aside remaining 2 ounces (60 g) lox for garnish.

5. Cover; refrigerate several hours or until firm. Carefully lift lasagna from mold and remove plastic wrap.

6. Garnish with remaining strips of lox rolled to look like roses and fresh tarragon sprigs, if desired. Slice with warm knife.
Makes 24 first-course or 8 entrée servings

*Can be prepared without terrine mold. Layer lasagna on plastic wrap. Cover and wrap with foil.

Step 3. Lining terrine mold.

Step 4. Covering layer of cheese mixture with lox.

Step 6. Rolling strips of lox to look like roses.

Egg Champignons

6 eggs
¼ cup (60 ml) dry bread crumbs
¼ cup (1 ounce/30 g) crumbled
    blue cheese
2 tablespoons (30 ml) thinly
    sliced green onions with
    tops
2 tablespoons (30 ml) dry white
    wine
2 tablespoons (30 ml) butter,
    melted
1 tablespoon (15 ml) chopped
    fresh parsley (technique on
    page 22) *or* ½ tablespoon
    (7.5 ml) dried parsley
    flakes
½ teaspoon (2 ml) garlic salt
24 large fresh mushroom caps
    (about 1½ inches/4 cm in
    diameter)
    Paprika (optional)
    Green onions and tomato slices
    for garnish

1. To hard-cook eggs, place the 6 eggs in a single layer in a saucepan. Add enough water to cover eggs by at least 1 inch (2.5 cm). Cover and quickly bring water just to a boil over high heat. Turn off heat. If necessary, remove pan from burner to prevent further boiling. Let eggs stand, covered, in hot water 15 to 17 minutes. Immediately run cold water over eggs or place in ice water until completely cooled.

2. Peel eggs by tapping all around the shell with a table knife to form a network of cracks. Peel shell away under cold running water. Finely chop eggs.

3. Preheat oven to 450°F (230°C). Lightly grease baking sheet. Combine eggs, bread crumbs, blue cheese, 2 tablespoons (30 ml) green onions, wine, butter, parsley and garlic salt in medium bowl.

4. Fill each mushroom cap with 1 rounded tablespoon (15 ml) egg mixture. Place mushroom caps on prepared baking sheet.

5. Bake 8 to 10 minutes. Sprinkle with paprika. Garnish, if desired.

Makes 8 first-course servings

Step 1. Hard-cooking eggs.

Step 2. Peeling eggs.

Step 4. Filling mushroom caps.

Spinach-Cheese Triangles

1 small onion
  Fresh parsley
3 packages (10 ounces / 285 g
  each) frozen chopped
  spinach, thawed
¼ cup (62.5 ml) olive oil
2 eggs
16 ounces (1 pound / 450 g) feta
  cheese, drained and
  crumbled
1 teaspoon dried oregano leaves,
  crushed, *or* 2 tablespoons
  (30 ml) chopped fresh
  oregano leaves
  Freshly grated nutmeg to taste
  Salt and black pepper to taste
1 package (16 ounces / 450 g)
  frozen phyllo dough, thawed
  to room temperature
2 cups (500 ml) margarine,
  melted

1. To chop onion in food processor, peel and quarter onion; place in bowl. Pulse 4 to 7 times until onion is finely chopped. Scrape bowl once during chopping. Chop enough onion to measure ½ cup (125 ml). Drain onions, if needed. Set aside.*

2. To finely chop parsley, place parsley in 1-cup (250 ml) measuring cup. Snip enough parsley with kitchen scissors to measure ½ cup (125 ml). Set aside.

3. To drain spinach, place spinach, 1 package at a time, in bottom of pie plate. Place another pie plate on top; over sink squeeze plates together and tilt slightly to press excess liquid from spinach. Set spinach aside.

4. Preheat oven to 375°F (190°C).

5. Heat oil over medium-high heat in small skillet. Add onion; cook and stir until translucent and golden.

*To chop onion with knife, peel skin from onion. Cut in half through the root. Place, cut side down, on cutting board. To coarsely chop onion, hold knife horizontally. Make cuts parallel to board, almost to root end. Make vertical, lengthwise cuts of desired thickness. Slice across cuts to root end. (The closer the cuts are spaced, the finer the onion is chopped.) Set aside.

continued on page 24

Step 1. Chopping onion in food processor.

Step 2. Snipping parsley to chop.

Step 3. Draining spinach.

Spinach-Cheese Triangles, *continued*

6. Beat eggs in large bowl with electric mixer at medium-high speed until light and lemon colored.

7. Stir in onion with oil, feta cheese, parsley, oregano and spinach. Season with nutmeg, salt and pepper.

8. Remove phyllo from package; unroll and place on large sheet of waxed paper. Fold phyllo crosswise into thirds. Use scissors to cut along folds into thirds.

9. Cover phyllo with large sheet of plastic wrap and damp, clean kitchen towel. (Phyllo dries out quickly if not covered.)

10. Lay 1 strip of phyllo at a time on a flat surface and brush immediately with melted butter. Fold strip in half lengthwise. Brush with butter again. Place rounded teaspoonful (5 ml) of spinach filling on 1 end of strip; fold over 1 corner to make triangle.

11. Continue folding end to end, as you would fold a flag, keeping edges straight.

12. Brush top with butter. Repeat process until all filling is used up.

13. Place triangles in a single layer, seam-side down, on ungreased jelly-roll pan. Bake 20 minutes or until lightly browned. Serve warm.

Makes 5 dozen appetizers

Step 8. Cutting phyllo into thirds.

Step 10. Folding one corner of phyllo over filling.

Step 11. Continuing to fold the length of the phyllo strip.

Cheesy Onion Focaccia

1 large red onion
½ cup (125 ml) *plus* 3 tablespoons (45 ml) honey, divided
2⅓ cups (575 ml) warm water (105° to 115°F/50° to 55°C), divided
1½ packages active dry yeast
6 tablespoons (90 ml) olive oil, divided
⅓ cup (75 ml) cornmeal
3 cups (750 ml) whole wheat flour
1½ tablespoons (22.5 ml) coarse salt
3 to 4 cups (750 ml - 1 L) all-purpose flour, divided
1 cup (250 ml) red wine vinegar
Additional cornmeal
1 cup (250 ml) grated Parmesan cheese
½ teaspoon (2.5 ml) onion salt
Black pepper to taste

1. To slice onion, peel skin and cut onion in half through the root. Place, cut side down, on cutting board. Cut thin, vertical slices the length of the onion. Set aside.

2. To proof yeast, place 3 tablespoons (45 ml) honey in large bowl. Pour ⅓ cup (75 ml) water over honey. *Do not stir.* Sprinkle yeast over water. Let stand at room temperature about 15 minutes or until bubbly.*

3. Add remaining 2 cups (500 ml) water, 3 tablespoons (45 ml) olive oil, ⅓ cup (75 ml) cornmeal and whole wheat flour to yeast mixture; mix until well blended.

4. Stir in salt and 2 cups (500 ml) all-purpose flour. Gradually stir in enough remaining all-purpose flour until mixture clings to side of bowl.

*If yeast does not bubble, it is no longer active. Discard yeast mixture and start again. Always check the expiration date on the yeast packet. Also, water that is too hot will kill yeast; it is best to use a thermometer.

continued on page 26

Step 1. Slicing onion.

Step 2. Proofing yeast.

Step 4. Dough mixture clinging to sides of bowl.

Cheesy Onion Focaccia, continued

5. Turn dough out onto lightly floured surface. To knead in remaining flour, fold the dough in half toward you and press dough away from you with heels of hands. Give dough a quarter turn and continue folding, pushing and turning until the dough is smooth and satiny, about 10 minutes.

6. Divide dough into halves. Place each half in a large, lightly greased bowl; turn each dough half over to grease surface. Cover each with clean kitchen towel and let dough rise in warm place (85°F/40°C) until doubled in bulk. (Press two fingertips about ½ inch/1.5 cm) into dough. Dough is ready if indentations remain when fingers are removed.)

7. Meanwhile, combine onion, vinegar and remaining ½ cup (125 ml) honey in medium bowl. Marinate at room temperature at least 1 hour.

8. Grease 2 (12-inch/30-cm) pizza pans and sprinkle with additional cornmeal. Stretch dough and pat into pans; create valleys with fingertips.

9. Cover dough with greased plastic wrap; let rise for 1 hour. Dough will double in bulk.

10. Preheat oven to 400°F (200°C).

11. Drain onions and scatter them over dough. Sprinkle with remaining 3 tablespoons (45 ml) olive oil, Parmesan cheese and onion salt; season with pepper.

12. Bake 25 to 30 minutes until flatbread is crusty and golden. Cut into wedges to serve. Serve warm.
Makes 2 breads (6 to 8 servings each)

Step 5. Kneading dough.

Step 6. Testing dough that has doubled in bulk.

Step 8. Stretching and patting dough into pan.

Chinese Vegetable Rolls

¼ cup (60 ml) red wine
2 tablespoons (30 ml) teriyaki sauce
2 tablespoons (30 ml) Worcestershire sauce
1 cup (250 ml) diced zucchini
1 cup (250 ml) diced yellow squash
1 cup (250 ml) broccoli flowerets
1 cup (250 ml) cauliflower flowerets
½ cup (125 ml) diced carrots
¼ cup (60 ml) chopped red onion (technique on page 22)
¼ cup (60 ml) chopped fresh parsley (technique on page 22)
¼ teaspoon (1 ml) white pepper
¼ teaspoon (1 ml) garlic salt
⅛ teaspoon (.5 ml) ground red pepper
⅛ teaspoon (.5 ml) black pepper
1 package (16 ounces/450 g) egg roll wrappers
1 egg, beaten
   Peanut or corn oil for frying
   Sweet and sour sauce, hot mustard sauce or soy sauce for dipping

1. Combine wine, teriyaki sauce and Worcestershire sauce in large saucepan over medium heat. Stir in zucchini, squash, broccoli, cauliflower, carrots, red onion, parsley, white pepper, garlic salt, ground red pepper and black pepper. Cook and stir 5 to 6 minutes until flavors blend and vegetables are crisp-tender. *Do not overcook.*

2. Remove from heat. Immediately transfer vegetable mixture to bowl to prevent further cooking. Let stand at room temperature until cool.

3. Place about 2 tablespoons (30 ml) vegetable mixture on bottom half of 1 egg roll wrapper.

4. Moisten left and right edges of wrapper with egg. Fold bottom edge up to just cover filling.

5. Fold left and right edges over ½ inch (1.5 cm); roll up jelly-roll style.

6. Moisten top edge with egg to seal. Repeat with remaining egg roll wrappers and vegetable filling.

7. Heat ½ inch (1.5 cm) oil in large, heavy saucepan over medium-high heat until oil reaches 365°F (175°C); adjust heat to maintain temperature. Fry egg rolls, a few at a time, in hot oil 2 minutes or until golden brown, turning once. Remove with slotted spoon; drain on paper towels.

8. Serve warm with sauces for dipping.
Makes about 15 appetizers

Step 4. Folding up bottom edge of egg roll wrapper.

Step 5. Rolling up egg roll wrapper, jelly-roll fashion.

Taco Dip

12 ounces (360 g) cream cheese, softened
½ cup (125 ml) dairy sour cream
2 teaspoons (10 ml) chili powder
1½ teaspoons (7.5 ml) ground cumin
⅛ teaspoon (.5 ml) ground red pepper
½ cup (125 ml) salsa
Crisp salad greens
1 cup (4 ounces/120 g) shredded Wisconsin Cheddar cheese
1 cup (4 ounces/120 g) shredded Wisconsin Monterey Jack cheese
½ cup (125 ml) diced plum tomatoes
⅓ cup (75 ml) sliced green onions
¼ cup (60 ml) sliced pitted ripe olives
¼ cup (60 ml) sliced pimiento-stuffed green olives
Tortilla chips and blue corn chips for serving

1. Combine cream cheese, sour cream, chili powder, cumin and ground red pepper in large bowl; mix until well blended. Stir in salsa.

2. Spread dip onto greens-lined 10-inch (25 cm) serving platter.

3. Top with Cheddar cheese, Monterey Jack cheese, tomatoes, green onions, ripe olives and green olives.

4. Serve with tortilla chips and blue corn chips.   *Makes 10 servings*

Step 1. Combining cream cheese mixture and salsa.

Step 2. Spreading dip onto greens lined platter.

Step 3. Sprinkling dip with toppings.

Southwestern Snack Squares

1¼ cups (310 ml) all-purpose
    flour
1 cup (250 ml) thinly sliced
    green onions
¾ cup (175 ml) Quaker®
    Enriched Corn Meal
1 tablespoon (15 ml) firmly
    packed brown sugar
2 teaspoons (10 ml) baking
    powder
1 teaspoon (5 ml) dried oregano
    leaves, crushed
½ teaspoon (2 ml) ground cumin
¼ teaspoon (1 ml) salt (optional)
1 cup milk (250 ml)
¼ cup (60 ml) vegetable oil
1 egg
1 cup (4 ounces/120 g) shredded
    Cheddar cheese
1 can (4 ounces/120 g) chopped
    green chilies, well drained
¼ cup (60 ml) finely chopped
    red bell pepper
2 slices crisp-cooked bacon,
    crumbled

1. Preheat oven to 400°F (200°C). Grease 11 x 7-inch (27.5 cm x 17.5 cm) baking dish. Combine flour, green onions, corn meal, brown sugar, baking powder, oregano, cumin and salt in large bowl; mix well.

2. Combine milk, oil and egg in small bowl. Add to corn meal mixture; mix just until moistened.

3. Spread evenly into prepared dish.

4. Combine cheese, chilies, bell pepper and bacon in medium bowl. Sprinkle evenly over corn meal mixture.

5. Bake 25 to 30 minutes until wooden toothpick inserted into center comes out clean. Let stand at room temperature to cool 10 minutes before cutting.

Makes about 15 pieces

Note: Also great served as a side dish to fish, chicken or pork—just cut into 8 pieces.

Step 1. Combining dry ingredients.

Step 2. Combining liquid ingredients with dry ingredients.

Step 4. Sprinkling cheese mixture over corn meal mixture.

Cheesy Sun Crisps

2 cups (8 ounces/225 g)
    shredded Cheddar cheese
½ cup (125 ml) grated Parmesan
    cheese
½ cup (125 ml) sunflower oil
    margarine, softened
3 tablespoons (45 ml) water
1 cup (250 ml) all-purpose flour
¼ teaspoon (1 ml) salt (optional)
1 cup (250 ml) uncooked quick-
    cooking oats
⅔ cup (150 ml) roasted salted
    sunflower kernels

1. Beat Cheddar cheese, Parmesan cheese, margarine and water in large bowl with electric mixer at medium speed until well blended. Add flour and salt; mix well.

2. Stir in oats and sunflower kernels; mix until well combined.

3. Shape dough into 12-inch (30 cm)-long roll; wrap securely in plastic wrap.

4. Refrigerate at least 4 hours. (Dough may be stored in refrigerator up to 1 week.)

5. Preheat oven to 400°F (200°C). Lightly grease cookie sheets. Cut roll into ⅛- to ¼-inch (3 mm to 6 mm) slices; flatten each slice slightly.

6. Place on prepared cookie sheets. Bake 8 to 10 minutes until edges are light golden brown. Remove immediately to wire racks. Let stand at room temperature until cool.

Makes 4 to 5 dozen crackers

Step 2. Stirring oats and sunflower kernels into cheese mixture.

Step 3. Shaping dough into 12-inch(30 cm)-long roll.

Step 5. Cutting roll into ⅛- to ¼-inch (3 mm to 6 mm) slices.

Harvest-Time Popcorn

2 tablespoons (30 ml) vegetable
   oil
1 cup (250 ml) popcorn kernels
2 cans (1¾ ounces each/22 g)
   shoestring potatoes
   (3 cups/750 ml)
1 cup (250 ml) salted mixed
   nuts or peanuts
¼ cup (60 ml) margarine, melted
1 teaspoon (5 ml) dill weed
1 teaspoon (5 ml) Worcestershire
   sauce
½ teaspoon (2 ml) lemon-pepper
   seasoning
¼ teaspoon (1 ml) garlic powder
¼ teaspoon (1 ml) onion salt

1. Heat oil in 4-quart (4 L) saucepan over high heat until hot. Add popcorn kernels. Cover pan; shake continuously over heat until popping stops. Popcorn should measure 2 quarts (2 L). *Do not add butter or salt.*

2. Preheat oven to 325°F (160°C). Combine popcorn, shoestring potatoes and nuts in large roasting pan. Set aside.

3. Combine margarine, dill, Worcestershire sauce, lemon-pepper seasoning, garlic powder and onion salt in small bowl.

4. Pour evenly over popcorn mixture, stirring until evenly coated.

5. Bake 8 to 10 minutes, stirring once. Let stand at room temperature until cool. Store in airtight containers.
Makes 2½ quarts (2.5 L)

Step 2. Adding nuts to popcorn mixture.

Step 4. Pouring margarine mixture evenly over popcorn mixture.

Turkey-Cheese Surprises

1 pound (450 g) ground turkey
½ cup (125 ml) stuffing mix
½ cup (125 ml) finely chopped
    tart apple
½ cup (125 ml) plus 2 tablespoons
    (30 ml) grated Parmesan
    cheese, divided
½ teaspoon (2 ml) poultry
    seasoning
    Garlic salt to taste
    Black pepper to taste
1 tablespoon (15 ml) butter or
    margarine
½ cup (125 ml) finely chopped
    onion (technique on
    page 22)
2 eggs
¼ cup (60 ml) Polly-O® ricotta
    cheese
4 ounces (120 g) Polly-O®
    mozzarella cheese, cut into
    ½-inch (1.5 cm) cubes
1 cup (250 ml) dry bread
    crumbs
    Vegetable oil for frying
    Cranberry sauce for serving
    Orange twists,* orange peel
    and fresh sage sprigs for
    garnish

*To make orange twists, cut orange into thin slices. Cut slit through slices to centers. Twist slices from slits in opposite directions.

1. Combine turkey, stuffing mix, apple, 2 tablespoons (30 ml) Parmesan cheese and poultry seasoning in large bowl; season with garlic salt and pepper.

2. Heat butter in small skillet over medium-high heat. Add onion; cook and stir until onion is tender but not brown. Add onion with butter, eggs and ricotta cheese to turkey mixture; blend well. If mixture seems too dry, add a little milk.

3. For each meatball, shape small amount of turkey mixture around a cube of mozzarella cheese.

4. Mix bread crumbs and remaining ½ cup (125 ml) Parmesan cheese in large, shallow dish. Roll cheese-filled meatballs in mixture to coat well.

5. Heat ¼ inch (6 mm) oil in large, heavy saucepan over medium-high heat. Cook meatballs, a few at a time, until brown on all sides, 4 to 5 minutes. Remove with slotted spoon; drain on paper towels.

6. Serve with cranberry sauce. Garnish, if desired. *Makes about 2 dozen meatballs*

Step 2. Blending turkey mixture.

Step 3. Shaping turkey mixture around cube of mozzarella cheese.

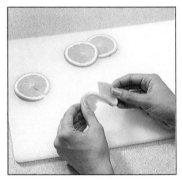
*Garnish: Making orange twists.

Hot 'n' Honeyed Chicken Wings

1 **small piece fresh gingerroot**
1 **orange**
3 **pounds (1.35 kg) chicken wings**
¾ **cup (175 ml) Pace® picante sauce**
⅔ **cup (150 ml) honey**
⅓ **cup (75 ml) soy sauce**
¼ **cup (60 ml) Dijon-style mustard**
3 **tablespoons (45 ml) vegetable oil**
  Additional Pace® picante sauce
  Fresh Italian parsley sprigs for garnish

1. To grate gingerroot, remove tough outer skin with sharp knife or vegetable peeler. Grate gingerroot using a ginger grater or the finest side of a box-shaped grater. Grate enough gingerroot to measure 2 tablespoons (30 ml). Set aside.

2. To grate orange peel, rinse orange under running water. Grate orange peel using the finest side of a box-shaped grater, being careful to remove only the outermost layer of skin and not any of the bitter, white pith. Grate enough peel to measure ½ teaspoon (2 ml). Set aside.

3. Cut off and discard wing tips from chicken. Cut each wing in half at joint.

4. Place chicken wings in 13 x 9-inch (32.5 x 22.5 cm) baking dish. Combine ¾ cup (175 ml) picante sauce, honey, soy sauce, mustard, oil, ginger and orange peel in small bowl; mix well. Pour over chicken wings.

5. Marinate, covered, in refrigerator at least 6 hours or overnight.

6. Preheat oven to 400°F (200 °C). Drain marinade; reserve. Place chicken wings in single layer on foil-lined, 15 x 10-inch (37.5 cm x 25 cm) jelly-roll pan. Pour reserved marinade evenly over chicken wings. Bake 40 to 45 minutes until brown. Serve warm with additional picante sauce. Garnish, if desired.

Makes about 34 appetizers

Step 1. Grating gingerroot.

Step 2. Grating orange peel.

Step 3. Cutting chicken wings in half at joint.

Shrimp Mold

1 can (7½ ounces/225 g) crabmeat
3 envelopes unflavored gelatin
¾ cup (175 ml) water
1 can (10¾ ounces/307 g) cream
    of shrimp soup
1 package (8 ounces/225 g)
    cream cheese, cut into
    cubes
2 cans (2½ ounces/75 g each)
    shrimp, drained
3 cups (750 ml) cooked
    Riceland® Rice
1 medium onion, chopped
    (technique on page 22)
1 red bell pepper, chopped
1 cup (250 ml) mayonnaise
¼ cup (60 ml) lemon juice
2 tablespoons (30 ml)
    Worcestershire sauce
1 tablespoon (15 ml) garlic
    powder
1 teaspoon (5 ml) black pepper
    Crisp salad greens
    Crackers for serving
    Lemon and lime slices and
      fresh mint sprig for garnish

1. Drain and discard liquid from crabmeat. Place crabmeat in small bowl; flake with fork into small pieces. Remove any bits of shell or cartilage. Set aside.

2. To soften gelatin, sprinkle gelatin over water in small bowl. Let stand 1 minute.

3. Heat soup over medium heat in large saucepan; add gelatin mixture and stir to dissolve.

4. Add cream cheese and stir until melted. Remove from heat.

5. Add crabmeat, shrimp, rice, onion, bell pepper, mayonnaise, lemon juice, Worcestershire sauce, garlic powder and black pepper; mix well.

6. Lightly spray 6-cup (1.5 L) mold with nonstick vegetable cooking spray. Pour gelatin mixture into prepared mold and refrigerate until firm.

7. To unmold, pull gelatin mixture from edge of mold with moist fingers, or run small metal spatula or pointed knife dipped in warm water around edge of gelatin mixture. (Mold can also be dipped just to the rim in warm water for 10 seconds.) Carefully invert mold onto greens-lined plate. Shake mold and plate to loosen gelatin. Gently remove mold. Serve with favorite crackers. Garnish, if desired. *Makes 1 mold*

Step 2. Softening gelatin.

Step 6. Pouring gelatin mixture into prepared mold.

Step 7. Pulling gelatin mixture away from edge of mold.

Scallops à la Schaller

Fresh parsley
1 pound (450 g) bacon, cut in
  half crosswise
2 pounds (900 g) small sea
  scallops
½ cup (125 ml) olive oil
½ cup (125 ml) dry vermouth
1 teaspoon (5 ml) garlic powder
1 teaspoon (5 ml) black pepper
½ teaspoon (2 ml) onion powder
Dash of dried oregano leaves
Crisp salad greens
Lemon peel strips for garnish

1. To chop parsley, place parsley in 1-cup (250 ml) measuring cup. Snip enough parsley with kitchen scissors to measure 2 tablespoons (30 ml). Set aside. (Photo on page 22.)

2. Wrap 1 bacon piece around each scallop; secure with wooden toothpicks if necessary. Place wrapped scallops in 13 x 9-inch (32.5 x 22.5 cm) baking dish.

3. Combine olive oil, vermouth, parsley, garlic powder, pepper, onion powder and oregano in small bowl. Pour over wrapped scallops.

4. Marinate, covered, in refrigerator at least 4 hours.

5. Remove wrapped scallops from marinade. Arrange on rack of broiler pan. Broil, 4 inches (10 cm) from heat, 7 to 10 minutes until bacon is brown. Turn over; brown other side 5 minutes or until scallops are opaque.

6. Remove wooden toothpicks. Arrange on greens-lined platter. Garnish, if desired.

Makes 8 servings

Step 2. Wrapping bacon around scallops.

Step 3. Pouring olive oil mixture over wrapped scallops.

Step 5. Arranging wrapped scallops on rack of broiler pan.

COOKING CLASS

PASTA

48   CLASS NOTES

50   SALADS & SOUPS

62   SAUCES

74   ENTRÉES

Angel Hair Pasta with
Red Chili Sauce *(page 65)*

CLASS NOTES

The recipes in this section show you how to make satisfying, delicious dishes out of versatile, economical and nutritious pasta. While there are over 150 varieties of pasta, we have featured the most popular shapes, such as fettuccine, shells, linguine and lasagna noodles. With step-by-step directions and helpful how-to photographs, you will discover how pasta makes a great addition to soups, salads, casseroles and skillet dishes. Pasta also makes a fantastic main course when topped with savory sauces.

COOKING PASTA

Dry Pasta: For every pound of dry pasta, bring 4 to 6 quarts (litres) of water to a full, rolling boil. Add 2 teaspoons (5 ml) salt, if desired. Gradually add pasta, allowing water to return to a boil. The water helps circulate the pasta so that it cooks evenly. Stir frequently to prevent the pasta from sticking. Begin testing for doneness at the minimum recommended time given on the package directions. Pasta should be "al dente"—tender, yet firm, not mushy. Immediately drain pasta to prevent overcooking. For best results, toss the pasta with sauce immediately after draining. If the sauce is not ready, toss the pasta with some butter or oil to prevent it from sticking. Store dry uncooked pasta in a cool dry place.

Fresh Pasta: Homemade pasta takes less time to cook than dry pasta. Cook fresh pasta in the same manner as dry, except begin testing for doneness after 2 minutes. Fresh pasta will last several weeks in the refrigerator or it can be frozen for up to one month. Two basic fresh pasta preparation techniques, by hand and by machine, are explained in the recipe section.

EQUIPMENT

Pasta Machine: Pasta machines with hand-turned rollers are very useful in kneading and rolling pasta dough. Cutting attachments (fettuccine and angel hair are usually included) help to cut pasta evenly. Electric machines also mix the dough, however the pasta usually lacks the resilience of hand-worked dough and the machines are more expensive.

Paring Knife: A sharp knife with a thin 3- or 4-inch-long (7.5 or 10 cm) blade used for peeling and slicing fruits and vegetables and cutting or chopping herbs.

Utility Knife: A sharp knife with a thin 6- to 8-inch-long (15 to 20 cm) blade. It is used for the same purposes as a paring knife, but the longer blade can provide better leverage.

Chef's Knife: A sharp knife with a wide 6- to 10-inch-long (15 to 25 cm) blade. It is used for chopping and slicing large, thick items.

TIME-SAVING TIPS

• Plan on preparing an extra batch of your favorite pasta soup or sauce. Pour into serving-size freezer containers and freeze. Thaw and reheat for a last minute dinner or quick lunch.

• Lasagna, manicotti and stuffed shells are perfect dishes to prepare and freeze for another time. Try freezing casseroles in single-serving portions for days when quick meals are necessary. Heat to serving temperature in the microwave or conventional oven.

• When cooking, add extra pasta to the boiling water so that you will have leftovers. If you like, toss the leftover pasta with a little olive oil to help prevent sticking. Use plain leftover pasta as a base or extender for salads, soups, side dishes and casseroles. Simply store the leftover pasta in a plastic bag in the refrigerator for up to three days. Freshen the pasta by rinsing with hot or cold water, depending on how you plan to use it. Pasta can also be frozen and then reheated in boiling water or microwaved for a fresh-cooked texture and taste.

• Combine leftover cooked meats, poultry, fish and vegetables with your favorite pasta shape and a simple sauce for a fast new meal.

• One cup of uncooked macaroni type pasta will yield 2 cups (500 ml) cooked pasta.

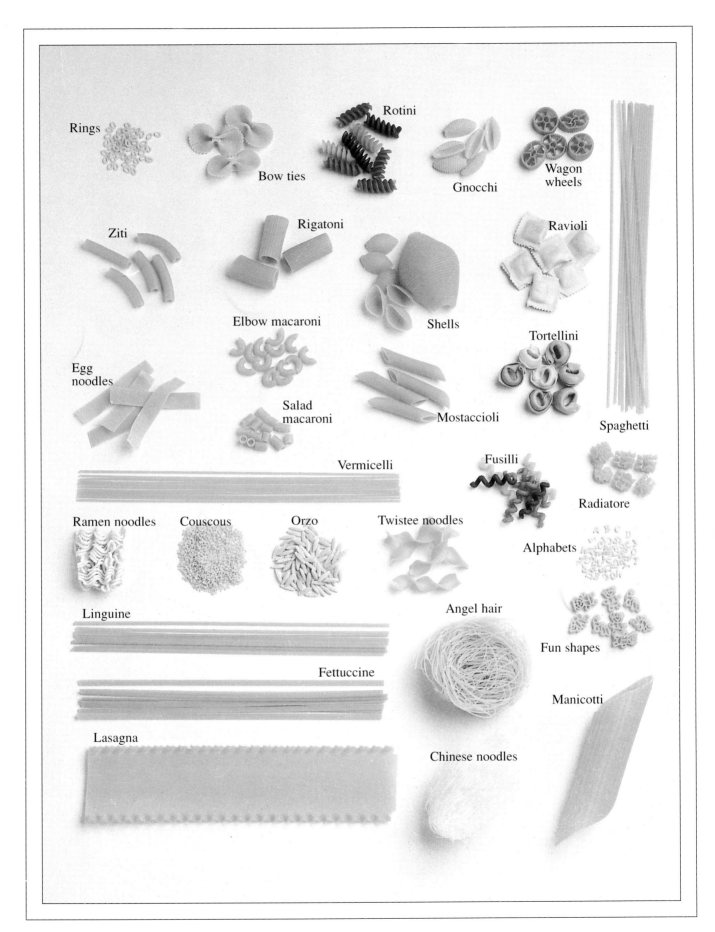

Rings

Bow ties

Rotini

Gnocchi

Wagon wheels

Ziti

Rigatoni

Ravioli

Elbow macaroni

Shells

Tortellini

Egg noodles

Salad macaroni

Mostaccioli

Spaghetti

Vermicelli

Fusilli

Radiatore

Ramen noodles

Couscous

Orzo

Twistee noodles

Alphabets

Linguine

Angel hair

Fun shapes

Fettuccine

Manicotti

Lasagna

Chinese noodles

Thai Chicken Fettuccine Salad

3 boneless skinless chicken breast
   halves (about 15 ounces/440 g)
6 ounces (180 g) fettuccine
1 cup (250 ml) PACE® Picante
   Sauce
¼ cup (60 ml) chunky peanut
   butter
2 tablespoons (30 ml) honey
2 tablespoons (30 ml) orange
   juice
1 teaspoon (5 ml) soy sauce
½ teaspoon (2 ml) ground ginger
2 tablespoons (30 ml) vegetable
   oil
   Lettuce or savoy cabbage
   leaves (optional)
¼ cup (60 ml) coarsely chopped
   cilantro (see technique for
   chopping parsley, page 68)
¼ cup (60 ml) peanut halves
¼ cup (60 ml) thin red pepper
   strips, cut into halves
   Additional PACE® Picante
   Sauce (optional)

1. Cut chicken into 1-inch (2.5 cm) pieces; set aside.

2. Cook pasta according to package directions. Drain in colander.

3. While pasta is cooking, combine 1 cup (250 ml) picante sauce, peanut butter, honey, orange juice, soy sauce and ginger in small saucepan. Cook and stir over low heat until blended and smooth. Reserve ¼ cup (60 ml) picante sauce mixture.

4. Place pasta in large bowl. Pour remaining picante sauce mixture over pasta; toss gently to coat.

5. Heat oil in large skillet over medium-high heat until hot. Cook and stir chicken in hot oil about 5 minutes until chicken is browned on the outside and no longer pink in center.

6. Add reserved ¼ cup (60 ml) picante sauce mixture; mix well.

7. Arrange pasta on lettuce-lined platter. Place chicken mixture on pasta. Top with cilantro, peanut halves and pepper strips.

8. Refrigerate until mixture is cooled to room temperature. Serve with additional picante sauce. Garnish as desired.

Makes 4 servings

Step 1. Cutting chicken breast halves into 1-inch (2.5 cm) pieces.

Step 3. Cooking and stirring picante sauce mixture.

Step 5. Cutting into chicken to test doneness.

Fresh Seafood and Linguine Salad

1½ to 3 dozen clams
    Salt
 4 pounds (1.8 kg) mussels
1½ pounds (675 g) small squid
 8 ounces (225 g) linguine
    Olive oil
¼ cup (60 ml) freshly squeezed
    lemon juice
 2 cloves garlic, minced
    (technique on page 58)
¼ teaspoon (1 ml) pepper
 1 red onion, thinly sliced and
    separated into rings for
    garnish
⅓ cup (75 ml) finely chopped
    Italian parsley for garnish
    (technique on page 68)

1. Discard any clams that remain open when tapped with fingers. To clean clams, scrub with stiff brush under cold running water. Soak clams in mixture of ⅓ cup (75 ml) salt to 1 gallon (4 L) of water for 20 minutes. Drain water; repeat 2 more times.

2. Discard any mussels that remain open when tapped with fingers. To clean mussels, scrub with stiff brush under cold running water. To debeard, pull threads from shells with fingers. Soak mussels in mixture of ⅓ cup (75 ml) salt to 1 gallon (4 L) of water for 20 minutes. Drain water; repeat 2 more times.

3. To clean each squid, hold body of squid firmly in one hand. Grasp head firmly with other hand; pull head, twisting gently from side to side. (Head and contents of body should pull away in one piece.) Set aside tubular body sac. Cut tentacles off head; set aside. Discard head and contents of body.

4. Grasp tip of pointed, thin, clear cartilage protruding from body; pull out and discard. Rinse squid under cold running water. Peel off and discard spotted outer membrane covering body sac and fins. Pull off side fins; set aside. Rinse inside of squid thoroughly under running water. Repeat with remaining squid.

continued on page 54

Step 2. Removing beards from mussels.

Step 3. Removing head from squid.

Step 4. Peeling outer membrane from squid.

***Fresh Seafood and Linguine Salad,
continued***

5. Cut squid crosswise into ¼-inch (6 mm) rings; finely chop tentacles and fins. (Rings, fins and reserved tentacles are all edible parts.) Pat pieces dry with paper towels.

6. To steam clams and mussels, place 1 cup (250 ml) water in large stockpot. Bring to a boil over high heat. Add clams and mussels. Cover stockpot; reduce heat to low. Steam 5 to 7 minutes until clams and mussels are opened. Remove from stockpot with slotted spoon. Discard any clams or mussels that remain closed.

7. Meanwhile, cook pasta according to package directions. Drain in colander. Place in large bowl and toss with 2 tablespoons (30 ml) oil.

8. Add just enough oil to large skillet to cover bottom. Heat over medium heat; add squid. Cook and stir 2 minutes until squid is opaque. Place squid in large glass bowl. Add pasta, mussels and clams.

9. Combine ½ cup (125 ml) oil, lemon juice, garlic, ½ teaspoon (2 ml) salt and pepper in small bowl; blend well. Pour over salad; toss gently to coat.

10. Cover; refrigerate at least 3 hours. Season with additional lemon juice, salt and pepper, if necessary. Garnish, if desired.

Makes 6 servings

Step 5. Cutting squid into rings.

Step 8. Removing cooked squid from skillet.

Pasta Salad in Artichoke Cups

5 cloves garlic, peeled
    (technique on page 64)
½ cup (125 ml) white wine
6 medium artichokes for cups
1 lemon, cut into halves
6 cups (1.5 L) chicken broth
1 tablespoon (15 ml) *plus* 1
    teaspoon (5 ml) olive oil,
    divided
1 package (2 ounces/60 g)
    artichoke hearts
8 ounces (225 g) corkscrew
    pasta or pasta twists
½ teaspoon (2 ml) dried basil
    leaves, crushed
  Basil Vinaigrette Dressing
    (page 56)

1. Place garlic and wine in l-quart (1 L) saucepan. Bring to a boil over high heat; reduce heat to low. Simmer 10 minutes

2. Meanwhile, prepare artichokes. Cut bottoms from artichokes with utility knife so that artichokes will sit flat. Remove outer leaves.

3. Cut 1 inch (2.5 cm) off tops of artichokes. Snip tips from remaining leaves with scissors. To help prevent discoloration, rub ends with lemon.

4. Place chicken broth in 6-quart (6 L) Dutch oven. Bring to a boil over high heat. Add artichokes, wine mixture and 1 tablespoon (15 ml) oil. Reduce heat to low. Cover; simmer 25 to 30 minutes or until leaves pull easily from base. Drain.

5. Cook artichoke hearts according to package directions. Drain well. Cut into slices to make 2 cups (500 ml). Set aside.

continued on page 56

Step 2. Cutting off bottom of artichoke.

Step 3. Snipping tips from artichoke leaves.

Step 4. Testing doneness of artichokes.

Pasta Salad in Artichoke Cups, continued

6. Cook pasta according to package directions. Drain in colander. Place pasta in large bowl. Sprinkle with remaining 1 teaspoon (5 ml) oil and basil.

7. Prepare Basil Vinaigrette Dressing.

8. Add artichoke hearts and 1 cup (250 ml) dressing to pasta; toss gently to coat.

9. Carefully spread outer leaves of whole artichokes. Remove small heart leaves by grasping with fingers, then pulling and twisting. Scoop out fuzzy choke with spoon.

10. Fill with pasta mixture. Cover; refrigerate until serving time. Serve with remaining dressing. Garnish as desired.

Makes 6 servings

Basil Vinaigrette Dressing

⅓ **cup (75 ml) white wine vinegar**
2 tablespoons (30 ml) Dijon-style mustard
3 cloves garlic, peeled (technique on page 64)
¾ **cup coarsely chopped fresh basil leaves**
1 cup (250 ml) olive oil
  Salt and pepper to taste

1. Place vinegar, mustard and garlic in blender or food processor. Cover; process using an on/off pulsing action until garlic is well mixed. Add basil; continue to pulse until mixture is blended.

2. With motor running, slowly pour in oil. Season to taste with salt and pepper.

Makes about 1½ cups (375 ml)

Step 9. Scooping out choke from artichoke with spoon.

Step 10. Filling artichoke with pasta mixture.

Basil Vinaigrette Dressing: Step 2. Slowly pouring oil into food processor.

Quick Beef Soup

1 large onion
2 cloves garlic
1½ pounds (675 g) lean ground beef
1 can (28 ounces/875 ml) whole peeled tomatoes, undrained
6 cups (1.5 L) water
6 beef bouillon cubes
¼ teaspoon (1 ml) pepper
½ cup (125 ml) uncooked orzo
1½ cups (375 ml) frozen peas, carrots and corn vegetable blend
French bread (optional)

1. To chop onion, peel skin. Cut onion in half through root with utility knife. Place cut side down on cutting board. Holding knife horizontally, make cuts parallel to board, almost to root end. Next, cut onion vertically into thin slices, holding onion with fingers to keep its shape. Turn onion and cut crosswise to root end. (The closer the cuts are spaced, the finer the onion is chopped.) Repeat with remaining onion half.

2. To mince garlic, trim ends of garlic cloves. Slightly crush clove under flat side of chef's knife blade; peel away skin. Chop garlic with chef's knife until garlic is in uniform fine pieces. Set aside.

3. Cook beef, onion and garlic in large saucepan over medium-high heat until beef is brown, stirring to separate meat; drain drippings.

4. Place tomatoes with juice in covered blender or food processor. Process until smooth.

5. Add tomatoes, water, bouillon cubes and pepper to meat mixture. Bring to a boil over high heat. Reduce heat to low. Simmer, uncovered, 20 minutes.

6. Add orzo and vegetables. Simmer 15 minutes more. Serve with French bread.

Makes 6 servings

Step 1. Chopping onion.

Step 2. Crushing garlic to remove skin.

Step 5. Stirring meat mixture.

Zucchini-Tomato-Noodle Soup

3 pounds (1.35 kg) zucchini
¾ cup (175 ml) water
½ cup (125 ml) butter
4 cups (1 L) chopped onions
    (technique on page 58)
8 cups (2 L) tomatoes, cut into
    eighths
1 can (48 ounces/1.5 L) chicken
    broth
3 cloves garlic, chopped
1 teaspoon (5 ml) Beau Monde
    seasoning
1 teaspoon (5 ml) salt
1 teaspoon (5 ml) pepper
1 pound (450 g) 100% durum
    noodles
   Garlic bread (optional)

1. Scrub zucchini with vegetable brush under cold running water. Slice lengthwise into halves with utility knife. (If zucchini is large, cut into 4 lengthwise pieces.) Cut each half into 4 to 6 lengthwise strips. Holding strips together with fingers, cut crosswise into bite-sized pieces.

2. Combine zucchini and water in stockpot; cover. Cook over medium-high heat 10 minutes until partially done, stirring twice.

3. Heat butter in large skillet over medium heat. Add onions; cook and stir in hot butter until tender.

4. Add onion mixture, tomatoes, broth, garlic, seasoning, salt and pepper to zucchini mixture; cover. Simmer 20 to 25 minutes.

5. Meanwhile, cook noodles according to package directions. Drain well.

6. Add noodles to soup; heat through. Serve with garlic bread.

Makes 8 servings

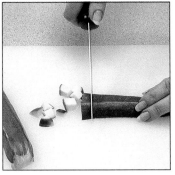

Step 1. Cutting zucchini into bite-sized pieces.

Step 2. Adding water to stockpot.

Step 6. Adding noodles to soup.

Spinach-Garlic Pasta with Garlic-Onion Sauce

½ pound (225 g) fresh spinach
6 eggs, divided
1½ cups (375 ml) all-purpose
    flour, divided
1 tablespoon (15 ml) olive oil
6 large cloves fresh garlic,
    minced (technique on
    page 58)
½ teaspoon (2 ml) salt
    Garlic-Onion Sauce (page 64)
    Grated Parmesan cheese
    (optional)

1. Separate spinach into leaves. Swish in cold water. Repeat several times with fresh cold water to remove sand and grit. Pat dry with paper towels.

2. To remove stems from spinach leaves, fold each leaf in half, then with hand pull stem toward top of leaf. Discard stem.

3. To blanch spinach, heat 1 quart (1 L) of lightly salted water in 2-quart (2 L) saucepan over high heat to a boil. Immediately add spinach. Return to a boil; boil 2 to 3 minutes until crisp-tender. Drain spinach from saucepan, then immediately plunge into cold water to stop cooking. Place in colander to drain. Let stand until cool enough to handle. Squeeze spinach between hands to remove excess moisture. Finely chop with chef's knife.

4. To separate egg yolks from whites, gently tap egg in center against hard surface, such as side of bowl. Holding shell half in each hand, transfer yolk back and forth between shell halves. Allow white to drip down between 2 halves into bowl.

5. When all white has dripped into the bowl, place yolk in another bowl. Place white in a third bowl. Repeat with 3 more eggs. Store unused egg whites in airtight container for another use. Refrigerate for about 1 week.

6. Place 1 cup (250 ml) flour on cutting board. Make well in center. Whisk 2 whole eggs, yolks and oil in small bowl until well blended. Gradually pour into well in flour mixture while mixing with fingertips or fork to form ball of dough.

continued on page 64

Step 1. Washing spinach.

Step 2. Removing stems from spinach.

Step 4. Separating egg yolk from the white.

Spinach-Garlic Pasta with Garlic-Onion Sauce, continued

7. Add spinach, garlic and salt. Mix, working in more flour as needed.

8. Place dough on lightly floured surface; flatten slightly. To knead dough, fold dough in half toward you and press dough away from you with heels of hands. Give dough a quarter turn and continue folding, pushing and turning. Continue kneading 5 minutes or until smooth and elastic, adding more flour to prevent sticking if necessary. Cover with plastic wrap. Let dough stand 15 minutes.

9. Unwrap dough and knead briefly as described in step 8 on lightly floured surface. Roll out dough to ⅛ inch (3 mm) -thick circle using lightly floured rolling pin. Gently pick up dough circle with both hands. Hold it up to the light to check for places where dough is too thick. Return to board; even out any thick spots. Let rest until dough is slightly dry but can be handled without breaking.

10. Lightly flour dough circle; roll loosely on to rolling pin. Slide rolling pin out; press dough roll gently with hand and cut into ¼-inch (6 mm) -wide strips with sharp knife. Carefully unfold strips.*

11. Prepare Garlic-Onion Sauce.

12. Cook pasta in large pot of boiling salted water 1 to 2 minutes just until tender. Drain in colander; pour into large bowl.

13. Toss sauce over pasta. Serve with cheese. Garnish as desired.

Makes 2 to 4 servings

*Fettuccine can be dried and stored at this point. Hang fettuccine strips over pasta rack or clean broom handle covered with plastic wrap and propped between 2 chairs. Dry for at least 3 hours; store in airtight container at room temperature up to 4 days. To serve, cook fettuccine in large pot of boiling salted water 3 to 4 minutes just until tender. Drain in colander.

Garlic-Onion Sauce

12 large cloves fresh garlic
½ cup (125 ml) butter
1 tablespoon (15 ml) olive oil
1 pound (450 g) Vidalia or other
    sweet onions, sliced
1 tablespoon (15 ml) honey
    (optional)
¼ cup (60 ml) Marsala wine

1. To quickly peel garlic cloves, trim ends. Drop cloves into boiling water. Boil 5 to 10 seconds. Remove with slotted spoon and plunge into cold water. Drain. The skins will slip off cloves. With chef's knife, chop garlic to equal ⅓ cup (75 ml).

2. Heat butter and oil in large skillet over medium heat. Add onions and garlic; cover and cook until soft. Add honey; reduce heat to low. Cook, uncovered, 30 minutes, stirring occasionally. Add wine; cook 5 to 10 minutes.

Makes about 2¼ cups (560 ml)

Step 8. Kneading dough.

Step 9. Checking thickness of dough.

*Hanging pasta on pasta rack to dry.

Angel Hair Pasta with Red Chili Sauce

2 cups (500 ml) all-purpose flour
¼ teaspoon (1 ml) salt
3 eggs
1 tablespoon (15 ml) milk
1 teaspoon (5 ml) olive oil
   Red Chili Sauce (page 66)
½ cup (125 ml) grated Parmesan
   cheese

1. Place flour, salt, eggs, milk and oil in food processor; process until dough forms. Shape into ball.

2. Place dough on lightly floured surface; flatten slightly. Cut dough into 4 pieces. Wrap 3 dough pieces in plastic wrap; set aside.

3. To knead by pasta machine, set rollers of pasta machine at widest setting (position 1).* Feed unwrapped dough piece through flat rollers by turning handle. (Dough may crumble slightly at first but will hold together after 2 to 3 rollings.)

4. Lightly flour dough strip; fold strip into thirds. Feed through rollers again. Continue process 7 to 10 times until dough is smooth and elastic.

5. To roll out dough by machine, reduce setting to position 3. Feed dough strip through rollers. Without folding strip into thirds, repeat on position 5 and
6. Let dough rest 5 to 10 minutes until slightly dry.

*Follow manufacturer's directions for appropriate method of rolling pasta if position settings are different. To make pasta by hand, see Spinach-Garlic Pasta with Garlic-Onion Sauce (page 62).

continued on page 66

Step 1. Preparing pasta dough in food processor.

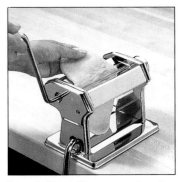

Step 3. Kneading pasta dough in a pasta machine.

Step 4. Folding dough into thirds.

Angel Hair Pasta with Red Chili Sauce, continued

6. Attach handle to angel hair pasta roller and feed dough through.** Repeat kneading and rolling with reserved dough pieces.

7. Cook pasta in large pot of boiling salted water 1 to 2 minutes just until tender; remove from heat. Drain in colander.

8. Prepare Red Chili Sauce.

9. Toss sauce over pasta. Add cheese; toss well to coat.

Makes 4 to 6 servings

**Angel hair pasta can be dried and stored at this point. Hang pasta strips over pasta rack or clean broom handle covered with plastic wrap and propped between 2 chairs. (Technique on page 64.) Or, twirl pasta into nests and place on clean kitchen towel. Dry for at least 3 hours; store in airtight container at room temperature up to 4 days. Cook pasta in large pot of boiling salted water 3 to 4 minutes just until al dente. Drain in colander.

Red Chili Sauce

2 small red hot chili peppers
6 tablespoons (90 ml) butter or margarine
4 green onions, thinly sliced
½ medium red bell pepper, minced
3 cloves garlic, minced (technique on page 58)
3 tablespoons (45 ml) minced fresh parsley (technique on page 68)
½ teaspoon (2 ml) salt
⅛ teaspoon (15 ml) black pepper

1. Rinse chili peppers; pat dry with paper towels. Cut peppers into halves with utility knife.*** Scrape out seeds. Then chop with chef's knife until peppers are in uniform small pieces.

2. Heat butter in large skillet over medium-high heat. Add chili peppers, onions, bell pepper and garlic. Cook and stir 2 minutes or until onions are soft.

3. Remove from heat. Stir in parsley, salt and black pepper.

Makes about ³/4 cup (175 ml)

***Chili peppers can sting and irritate the skin; wear rubber gloves when handling peppers and do not touch eyes. Wash your hands after handling chili peppers.

Step 6. Cutting pasta with pasta machine.

Red Chili Sauce: Step 1. Scraping seeds from chili peppers.

Crabmeat with Herbs and Pasta

1 clove garlic
  Fresh parsley
6 ounces (180 g) crabmeat
½ package (8 ounces/225 g)
    vermicelli
⅓ cup (75 ml) olive oil
3 tablespoons (45 ml) butter or
    margarine
1 small onion, minced
1 carrot, shredded
¼ cup (60 ml) chopped fresh
    basil *or* 2 teaspoons (10 ml)
    dried basil leaves, crushed
1 tablespoon (15 ml) lemon juice
½ cup (125 ml) coarsely chopped pine
    nuts (optional)
½ teaspoon (2 ml) salt

1. To mince garlic, trim ends of garlic clove. Slightly crush clove under flat side of chef's knife blade; peel away skin. Chop with chef's knife until garlic is minced. Set aside.

2. To chop parsley, place parsley in 1-cup (250 ml) measuring cup. Snip enough parsley with kitchen scissors to measure 2 tablespoons (30 ml). Set aside.

3. Pick out and discard any shell or cartilage from crabmeat. Flake with fork. Set aside.

4. Cook pasta according to package directions. Drain in colander.

5. Heat oil and butter in large skillet over medium-high heat. Cook and stir garlic, onion and carrot in hot oil mixture until vegetables are tender, but not brown.

6. Reduce heat to medium. Stir in parsley, crabmeat, basil and lemon juice. Cook 4 minutes, stirring constantly. Stir in pine nuts and salt.

7. Pour sauce over vermicelli in large bowl; toss gently to coat. Garnish as desired.

Makes 4 servings

Step 1. Crushing garlic to remove skin.

Step 2. Chopping parsley with scissors.

Step 3. Picking out shell or cartilage from crabmeat.

Pasta and Broccoli

1 bunch broccoli
1 package (16 ounces/450 g) ziti
    macaroni
2 tablespoons (30 ml) olive oil
1 clove garlic, minced
    (technique on page 58)
¾ cup (3 ounces/90 g) shredded
    American or mozzarella
    cheese
½ cup (125 ml) grated Parmesan
    cheese
¼ cup (60 ml) butter
¼ cup (60 ml) chicken broth
3 tablespoons (45 ml) white wine

1. Trim leaves from broccoli stalks. Trim ends of stalks. Cut broccoli into flowerets by removing each head to include a small piece of stem. Peel stalks, then cut into 1-inch (2.5 cm) pieces.

2. To steam broccoli, bring 2 inches (5 cm) of water in large saucepan to a boil over high heat. Place broccoli in metal steamer into saucepan. Water should not touch broccoli. Cover pan; steam 10 minutes until broccoli is tender. Add water, as necessary, to prevent pan from boiling dry.

3. Cook pasta according to package directions. Drain in colander.

4. Heat oil in large skillet over medium-high heat. Cook and stir garlic in hot oil until golden.

5. Add broccoli; cook and stir 3 to 4 minutes. Add American cheese, Parmesan cheese, butter, broth and wine; stir. Reduce heat to low. Simmer until cheese melts.

6. Pour sauce over ziti in large bowl; toss gently to coat. Garnish as desired.

Makes 6 to 8 servings

Step 1. Cutting broccoli stalk into 1-inch (2.5 cm) pieces.

Step 2. Steaming broccoli.

Step 5. Stirring broccoli mixture.

Fusilli Pizzaiolo

8 ounces (225 g) mushrooms
1 large red bell pepper
1 large green bell pepper
1 large yellow bell pepper
3 large shallots
1 package (16 ounces/450 g) fusilli or spaghetti
¼ cup (60 ml) olive oil
10 green onions, chopped
1 large onion, diced
8 cloves garlic, coarsely chopped
½ cup (125 ml) chopped fresh basil *or* 2 teaspoons (10 ml) dried basil leaves, crushed
2 tablespoons (30 ml) chopped fresh oregano *or* 1 teaspoon (5 ml) dried oregano, crushed
Dash crushed red pepper flakes
4 cups (1 L) canned or fresh tomatoes, chopped (technique on page 82)
Salt and black pepper to taste
Fresh basil sprigs and miniature plum tomatoes for garnish

1. Wipe mushrooms clean with damp paper towel. Cut thin piece from stem; discard. Cut mushrooms into slices with paring knife. Set aside.

2. Rinse bell peppers under cold running water. To seed pepper, stand on end on cutting board. Cut off sides in 3 to 4 lengthwise slices with utility knife. (Cut close to, but not through, stem.) Discard stem and seeds. Scrape out any remaining seeds. Rinse inside of pepper under cold running water, then cut into ¼-inch (6 mm) pieces. Set aside.

3. Remove papery outer skin from shallots. Cut off root end. Chop with chef's knife. Set aside.

4. Cook pasta according to package directions. Drain in colander.

5. Heat oil in large skillet over medium-high heat. Cook and stir mushrooms, bell peppers, shallots, onions, garlic, chopped basil, oregano and crushed red pepper in hot oil until vegetables are lightly browned.

6. Add tomatoes with juice; bring to a boil. Reduce heat to low; simmer, uncovered, 20 minutes. Season to taste with salt and black pepper.

7. Place fusilli on plates. Spoon sauce over fusilli. Garnish, if desired.

Makes 6 to 8 servings

Step 1. Cutting mushrooms into slices.

Step 2. Cutting off sides of bell pepper.

Step 3. Removing papery outer skin from shallot.

Beef Oriental

3 cups (750 ml) corkscrew pasta
7 green onions
2 to 3 ribs celery
8 mushrooms (optional)
1 package (20 ounces/60 g)
** frozen snow peas**
1 pound (450 g) ground beef
3 tablespoons (45 ml) soy sauce
¼ teaspoon (1 ml) ground ginger
1 can (8 ounces/225 g) tomato
** sauce**
3 fresh tomatoes, cut into wedges
1 cup (4 ounces/120 g) shredded
** Cheddar cheese, divided**
1 green pepper, cut into thin
** slices**

1. Cook pasta according to package directions. Drain in colander. Set aside.

2. Remove roots from green onions. Cut green onions diagonally into 2-inch (5 cm) pieces.

3. Place celery flat side down on cutting board. Cut celery diagonally into l-inch (2.5 cm) pieces.

4. Wipe mushrooms clean with damp paper towel. Cut thin piece from stem; discard. Cut mushrooms into slices with paring knife. (Technique on page 72.)

5. To quickly thaw snow peas, place in colander. Rinse under hot water until no ice crystals remain and pea pods are easily separated. Drain well; pat dry with paper towel.

6. Cook beef, onions, soy sauce and ginger in wok over medium-high heat until meat is brown, stirring to separate

7. Push mixture up the side of wok. Add celery and mushrooms; stir-fry 2 minutes. Push mixture up the side. Add snow peas and tomato sauce; cook 4 to 5 minutes, stirring every minute.

8. Add pasta, tomatoes and ¾ cup (175 ml) cheese. Stir gently to combine all ingredients. Cook 1 minute. Add green pepper; sprinkle remaining ¼ cup (60 ml) cheese over top. Reduce heat to low; cook until heated through.

Makes 4 servings

Step 2. Cutting green onions diagonally into 2-inch (5 cm) pieces.

Step 3. Cutting celery diagonally into l-inch (2.5 cm) pieces.

Step 7. Stir-frying vegetables.

Sunday Supper Stuffed Shells

1 package (12 ounces/360 g)
    jumbo pasta shells
1 package (10 ounces/285 g)
    frozen chopped spinach
2 tablespoons (30 ml) olive oil
3 cloves fresh garlic, peeled
    (technique on page 64)
¾ pound (335 g) ground veal
¾ pound (335 g) ground pork
1 cup (250 ml) parsley, finely
    chopped (technique on
    page 68)
1 cup (250 ml) bread crumbs
2 eggs, beaten
3 cloves fresh garlic, minced
    (technique on page 58)
3 tablespoons (45 ml) grated
    Parmesan cheese
    Salt to taste
3 cups (750 ml) spaghetti sauce
    Sautéed zucchini slices
    (optional)

1. Cook pasta according to package directions. Place in colander and rinse under warm running water. Drain well.

2. Cook spinach according to package directions. Place in colander to drain. Let stand until cool enough to handle. Squeeze spinach with hands to remove excess moisture. Set aside.

3. Heat oil in large skillet over medium heat. Cook and stir whole garlic cloves in hot oil until garlic is lightly browned. Discard garlic.

4. Add veal and pork to skillet. Cook until lightly brown, stirring to separate meat; drain drippings. Cool slightly.

5. Preheat oven to 375°F (190°C). Grease 12 x 8-inch (30 x 20 cm) baking pan.

6. Combine spinach, parsley, bread crumbs, eggs, minced garlic and cheese in large bowl; blend well. Season to taste with salt. Add cooled meat mixture; blend well. Fill shells with meat mixture using spoon.

7. Spread about 1 cup (250 ml) of spaghetti sauce over bottom of prepared pan. Arrange shells in pan. Pour remaining sauce over shells. Cover with foil.

8. Bake 35 to 45 minutes or until bubbly. Serve with zucchini. Garnish as desired.

Makes 8 to 9 servings

Step 2. Squeezing spinach with hands to remove excess moisture.

Step 4. Stirring ground meat to separate meat.

Step 6. Filling shells with meat mixture.

Sweet Garlic with Chicken Pasta

1¼ pounds (560 g) boneless
    skinless chicken breast
    halves
4 ounces (120 g) fresh plum
    tomatoes
1 package (16 ounces/450 g)
    bow tie pasta
8 ounces (225 g) garlic
5½ tablespoons (83 ml) olive oil
1½ pounds (675 g) shiitake
    mushrooms, sliced
1 cup (250 ml) chopped green
    onions
1 teaspoon (5 ml) crushed red
    pepper flakes
2 cups (500 ml) chicken broth
4 ounces (120 g) cilantro,
    chopped, divided (see
    technique for chopping
    parsley, page 68)

1. To grill chicken, heat single layer of coals in grill to medium. Oil hot grid to help prevent sticking. Grill chicken, on covered grill, 6 to 8 minutes until chicken is no longer pink in center, turning chicken over halfway through cooking.

2. Refrigerate grilled chicken until cool enough to handle. Cut chicken into ½ inch (1.25 cm) cubes. Set aside.

3. Cut tomatoes into halves. Remove stems. Scrape out seeds with spoon. Chop into small pieces to equal 2 cups (500 ml). Set aside. (Technique on page 82.)

4. Cook pasta according to package directions. Drain in colander.

5. To peel garlic cloves, trim ends. Drop cloves into boiling water. Boil 5 to 10 seconds. Remove with slotted spoon; plunge into cold water. Drain. The skins will slip off cloves. Chop with chef's knife until garlic is in very small uniform pieces.

6. Heat oil in large skillet over medium-high heat. Cook and stir garlic in hot oil until lightly browned. Add tomatoes, mushrooms, green onions and crushed red pepper. Cook and stir 2 minutes.

7. Add broth; simmer mixture to reduce slightly. Add chicken, pasta and half of cilantro; heat through. Garnish with remaining cilantro.

Makes 6 to 8 servings

Step 1. Grilling chicken.

Step 2. Cutting chicken into
½-inch (1.5 cm) pieces.

Step 6. Adding vegetables to skillet.

Shrimp in Angel Hair Pasta Casserole

1 pound (450 g) medium raw shrimp
  Fresh parsley
2 eggs
1 cup (250 ml) half-and-half
1 cup (250 ml) plain yogurt
½ cup (4 ounces/120 g) shredded
  Swiss cheese
⅓ cup (95 ml) crumbled feta
  cheese
¼ cup (60 ml) chopped fresh
  basil *or* 2 teaspoons (10 ml)
  dried basil leaves, crushed
1 teaspoon (5 ml) dried oregano
  leaves, crushed
1 package (9 ounces/270 g)
  fresh angel hair pasta
1 jar (16 ounces/450 g) mild,
  thick and chunky salsa
½ cup (4 ounces/120 g) shredded
  Monterey Jack cheese
  Snow peas and plum tomatoes
  stuffed with cottage cheese
  for garnish

1. To peel shrimp, remove the legs by gently pulling them off the shell. Loosen shell with fingers, then slide off.

2. To devein shrimp, cut a shallow slit along back of shrimp with paring knife. Lift out vein. (You may find this easier to do under cold running water.) If desired, this step may be omitted.

3. To chop parsley, place parsley in 1-cup (250 ml) measuring cup. Snip enough parsley with kitchen scissors to measure ⅓ cup (75 ml). Set aside. (Technique on page 68.)

4. Preheat oven to 350°F (180°C). Grease 12 x 8 inch (30 x 20 cm) baking pan with 1 tablespoon (15 ml) butter.

5. Combine parsley, eggs, half-and-half, yogurt, Swiss cheese, feta cheese, basil and oregano in medium bowl; mix well.

6. Spread half the pasta on bottom of prepared pan. Cover with salsa. Add half the shrimp. Cover with remaining pasta. Spread egg mixture over pasta and top with remaining shrimp. Sprinkle Monterey Jack cheese over top.

7. Bake 30 minutes or until bubbly. Let stand 10 minutes. Garnish, if desired.

Makes 6 servings

Step 1. Removing shell from shrimp.

Step 2. Deveining shrimp.

Step 6. Spreading egg mixture over pasta.

Saucy Mediterranean Frittata

Tomato Sauce (recipe follows)
1 medium tomato
1 tablespoon (15 ml) olive oil
1 small onion, chopped
    (technique on page 58)
1 teaspoon (5 ml) dried basil
    leaves, crushed
¼ teaspoon (1 ml) dried oregano
    leaves, crushed
⅓ cup (75 ml) cooked orzo
⅓ cup (75 ml) chopped pitted
    ripe olives
8 eggs
½ teaspoon (2 ml) salt
⅛ teaspoon (0.5 ml) pepper
2 tablespoons (30 ml) butter
½ cup (2 ounces/60 g) shredded
    mozzarella cheese

1. Prepare Tomato Sauce.

2. Cut tomato into halves. Remove stem. Scrape out seeds with spoon. Chop into small pieces. Set aside.

3. Heat oil in ovenproof 10-inch (25 cm) skillet over medium-high heat. Cook and stir onion in hot oil until tender. Add tomato, basil and oregano; cook and stir 3 minutes. Stir in orzo and olives; remove from skillet and set aside.

4. Beat eggs, salt and pepper in medium bowl with electric mixer at low speed. Stir in tomato mixture; set aside.

5. Melt butter in same skillet over medium heat. Add egg mixture; top with cheese. Reduce heat to low. Cook 8 to 10 minutes or until bottom and most of middle is set.

6. Place skillet on rack 4 inches (10 cm) from broiler. Broil 1 to 2 minutes or until top is browned. Cut into wedges; serve with Tomato Sauce. Garnish as desired. Cut into wedges to serve.

Makes 4 to 6 servings

Step 2. Scraping out seeds from tomatoes.

Step 5. Cooking frittata until bottom of mixture is almost set.

Tomato Sauce

1 can (8 ounces/225 g) tomato sauce
1 teaspoon (5 ml) minced dried onion
¼ teaspoon (1 ml) dried basil leaves, crushed
¼ teaspoon (1 ml) dried oregano leaves, crushed
⅛ teaspoon (0.5 ml) minced dried garlic
⅛ teaspoon (0.5 ml) pepper

Combine all sauce ingredients in small saucepan. Bring to a boil over high heat. Reduce heat to low. Simmer, uncovered, over medium-low heat 5 minutes, stirring often. Set aside; keep warm.

Makes about 1 cup (250 ml)

Spetzque

9 lasagna noodles
1 small onion
2 pounds (900 g) ground beef
1 can (4½ ounces/135 g) chopped ripe olives, drained
1 can (4 ounces/120 g) mushroom stems and pieces, drained
1 jar (16 ounces/45 g) spaghetti sauce
Dash pepper
Dash dried oregano leaves, crushed
Dash Italian seasoning
1¼ cups (310 ml) frozen corn, thawed
1¼ cups (310 ml) frozen peas, thawed
2 cups (8 ounces/225 g) shredded mozzarella cheese

1. Cook lasagna noodles according to package directions. Drain in colander.

2. To chop onion, peel skin. Cut onion in half through root with utility knife. Place cut side down on cutting board. Holding knife horizontally, make cuts parallel to board, almost to root end. Next, cut onion vertically into thin slices, holding onion with fingers to keep its shape. Turn onion and cut crosswise to root end. (The closer the cuts are, the finer the onion is chopped.) Repeat with remaining onion half.

3. Cook beef in large skillet over medium-high heat until meat is brown, stirring to separate meat; drain drippings.

4. Add olives, mushrooms and onion. Cook, stirring occasionally, until vegetables are tender. Add spaghetti sauce, pepper, oregano and Italian seasoning. Heat through, stirring occasionally; set aside.

5. Preheat oven to 350°F (180°C).

6. Place 3 noodles in bottom of 13 x 9-inch (32.5 x 22.5 cm) baking dish. Spread half the beef mixture over noodles, then half the corn and peas.

7. Repeat layers ending with noodles.

8. Bake lasagna 25 minutes. Sprinkle with cheese; bake 5 minutes more or until bubbly. Let stand 10 minutes before cutting. Garnish as desired.

Makes 6 servings

Step 2. Chopping onion.

Step 4. Stirring spaghetti sauce into meat mixture.

Step 6. Layering lasagna.

COOKING CLASS
VEGETABLES

88 CLASS NOTES

92 ASPARAGUS

94 BEANS, GREEN

96 BEANS, LIMA

98 BROCCOLI

100 BRUSSELS SPROUTS

102 CARROTS

104 CAULIFLOWER

106 CORN

110 EGGPLANTS

112 KOHLRABIES

115 MUSHROOMS

118 ONIONS

122 PARSNIPS

124 PEAS, ENGLISH

126 PEAS, SNOW

128 PEPPERS, BELL

130 POTATOES

134 POTATOES, SWEET

136 SPINACH

138 SQUASH, SPAGHETTI

140 SQUASH, WINTER

142 TOMATOES

144 ZUCCHINI

Reuben-Stuffed Kohlrabies *(page 112)*

CLASS NOTES

The produce section of today's supermarket carries an ever-growing variety of vegetables—and with good reason. Vegetables are not only nutritious, but they can be the most flavorful part of a meal. *Cooking Class Vegetables* will introduce dozens of vegetables and teach you how to prepare them. Each vegetable section includes valuable information on availability, purchasing and storage.

For a long time, vegetables have played only a supporting role at the dinner table. Vegetables were eaten, not because they tasted good, but because they were "good for you." Today, due to global growing seasons and air-freight shipping, it is possible to purchase a wide variety of vegetables throughout the year. When fresh vegetables are prepared in creative, delicious ways, they no longer stand on the sidelines but are an integral part of an enjoyable meal.

VEGETABLE PREPARATION
Preparation can make or break the appeal of a vegetable. This is why it is important to know how cooking affects a vegetable's quality by changing its texture, flavor, color and nutrient content.

TEXTURE
Most raw vegetables are hard and fibrous, which makes them appropriate for dipping or salads. But if they are to accompany an entrée, they need to be softened to be palatable.

Cooking softens the fiber in vegetables, making them more tender and easier to eat. The degree of tenderness is determined by how the vegetable is cut and how long it is cooked. Most vegetables are best when cooked to the crisp-tender stage.

FLAVOR
Some vegetable flavor is lost during cooking because flavor components leach into the water and evaporate in the steam. The best way to avoid flavor loss is to cook vegetables in as little water as possible.

With some strong-flavored vegetables, such as those in the cabbage family, it is desirable to dissolve some flavor into the cooking water or steam.

Some freshly harvested vegetables, such as corn, peas and carrots, have a high sugar content that makes them taste sweet. As they mature or sit in storage, the sugar turns to starch, causing them to lose their sweetness. For best flavor it is important to use fresh, seasonal vegetables.

COLOR
Cooking enhances the color of some vegetables. Overcooking can turn vibrant colors into dull grays and khaki greens. Because some pigments dissolve in water, such as those in beets and red cabbage, and others break down because of heat, such as those in peas and broccoli, vegetables should be cooked as quickly as possible to retain their colors.

NUTRIENT CONTENT
Vegetables are important because they supply a wide assortment of nutrients. They are major sources of vitamins A and C and are loaded with other essential vitamins and minerals. (See the Vegetable Vitamin Chart on page 94.) The larger the amount of water, the higher the temperature and the longer the cooking time, the more nutrients the vegetables lose.

USING THE VEGETABLE CHART
We have provided this handy vegetable chart to help take the guesswork out of cooking vegetables. As you refer to this chart, please keep the following in mind:

1. The times are for one pound (450 g) of vegetables unless otherwise noted.

2. The times are in minutes.

3. A range of time is given because cooking times vary due to the age and size of the vegetables. Vegetables are done when tender, but still crisp.

4. Steaming times begin when the water boils and creates steam.

5. When microwaving, some vegetables require no water except the droplets that cling to them when rinsed. If additional water is needed, the chart indicates the amount with a footnote.

6. Blanching prepares vegetables for freezing. Time begins when vegetables are dropped into boiling water. Plunge vegetables immediately into ice water, then drain and pat dry with paper towels before freezing.

7. Boiling requires covering the bottom of a pan with $\frac{1}{2}$ to 1 inch (1.5 cm to 2.5 cm) of water. More water should be used to cook whole, dense vegetables, such as beets, turnips and kohlrabies.

8. Some cooking methods are not recommended for certain vegetables, as indicated by the abbreviation "NR."

Vegetable Cooking Chart

VEGETABLE	STEAM	MICROWAVE	BLANCH	BOIL	OTHER
ARTICHOKE whole	30 to 60	4 to 5 each	NR	25 to 40	NR
ARTICHOKE hearts	10 to 15	6 to 7	8 to 12	10 to 15	Stir-fry 10
ASPARAGUS	8 to 10	4 to 6[1]	2 to 3	5 to 12	Stir-fry pieces 5
BEANS, Green	5 to 15	6 to 12[3]	4 to 5	10 to 20	Sir-fry 3 to 4
BEANS, Lima	10 to 20	8 to 12[3]	5 to 10	20 to 30	NR
BEETS (whole)	40 to 60	14 to 18[3]	NR	30 to 60	Bake 60 at 350°F (180°C)
BROCCOLI spears	8 to 15	6 to 7[1]	3 to 4	5 to 10	Blanch, then bake in sauce
BROCCOLI flowerets	5 to 6	4 to 5[1]	2 to 3	4 to 5	Stir-fry 3 to 4
BRUSSELS SPROUTS	6 to 12	7 to 8[2]	4 to 5	5 to 10	Halve; stir-fry 3 to 4
CABBAGE wedges	6 to 9	10 to 12[2]	NR	10 to 15	Blanch leaves, stuff and bake
CABBAGE shredded	5 to 8	8 to 10[2]	NR	5 to 10	Stir-fry 3 to 4
CARROTS whole	10 to 15	8 to 10[2]	4 to 5	15 to 20	Bake 30 to 40 at 350°F (180°C)
CARROTS sliced/cut	4 to 5	4 to 7[2]	3 to 4	5 to 10	Stir-fry 3 to 4
CAULIFLOWER whole	15 to 20	6 to 7	4 to 5	10 to 15	Blanch, then bake 20 at 350°F (180°C)

[1] Add 2 tablespoons (30 ml) water per pound (per 450 g).
[2] Add ¼ cup (60 ml) water per pound (per 450 g).
[3] Add ½ cup (125 ml) water per pound (per 450 g).

VEGETABLE	STEAM	MICROWAVE	BLANCH	BOIL	OTHER
CAULIFLOWER flowerets	6 to 10	3 to 4	3 to 4	5 to 8	Stir-fry 3 to 4
CORN on cob	6 to 10	3 to 4 each	3 to 4	4 to 7	Soak 10; bake at 375°F (190°C) or grill 20 to 30
CORN cut	4 to 6	2 per cup	2½ to 4	3 to 4	Stir-fry 3 to 4
EGGPLANT whole	15 to 30	7 to 10	10 to 15	10 to 15	Bake 30 at 400°F (200°C)
EGGPLANT diced/sliced	5 to 6	5 to 6[2]	3 to 4	5 to 10	Bake 10 to 15 at 425°F (220°C)
GREENS Kale, Beet	4 to 6	8 to 10[2]	4 to 5	5 to 8	Stir-fry 2 to 3
KOHLRABI whole	30 to 35	8 to 12	NR	15 to 30	Bake 50 to 60 at 350°F (180°C)
MUSHROOMS	4 to 5	3 to 4	NR[4]	3 to 4 in broth or wine	Stir-fry or broil 4 to 5
ONIONS whole	20 to 25	6 to 10	NR	20 to 30	Bake 60 at 400°F (200°C)
ONIONS Pearl	15 to 20	5 to 7[2]	2 to 3	10 to 20	Braise in broth 15 to 25
PARSNIPS	8 to 10 cut	4 to 6[2]	3 to 4	5 to 10	Bake 30 at 325°F (160°C)
PEAS, English	3 to 5	5 to 7	1 to 2	8 to 12	Stir-fry 2 to 3

[2] Add ¼ cup (60 ml) water per pound (per 450 g).
[3] Add ½ cup (125 ml) water per pound (per 450 g).
[4] Fully cook before freezing.

continued

VEGETABLE	STEAM	MICROWAVE	BLANCH	BOIL	OTHER
PEAS, Snow	2 to 3	2 to 3	1 to 2	2 to 3	Stir-fry 2 to 3
PEPPERS, Bell sliced	2 to 4	2 to 4	2 to 3 (whole 2 each)	4 to 5	Stir-fry 2 to 3
POTATOES Sweet or White whole	12 to 30	6 to 8	NR[4]	20 to 30	Bake 40 to 60 at 400°F (200°C)
POTATOES cut	10 to 12	8 to 10	NR[4]	15 to 20	Bake 25 to 30 at 400°F (200°C)
SPINACH	5 to 6	3 to 4	2 to 3	2 to 5	Stir-fry 3
SQUASH Summer, sliced	5 to 10	3 to 6	2 to 3	5 to 10	Broil halves 5
SQUASH Winter, halves	15 to 40	6 to 10	NR[4]	5 to 10	Bake 40 to 60 at 375°F (190°C)
SQUASH Spaghetti whole	NR	5 to 6 pierced	NR[4]	20 to 30	Bake 40 to 90 at 350°F (190°C)
TOMATOES	2 to 3	3 to 4	1 to 2	NR	Bake halves 8 to 15 at 400°F (200°C)
TURNIPS/ RUTABAGAS whole	20 to 25	9 to 12[2]	NR[4]	15 to 20	Bake 30 to 45 at 350°F (190°C)
TURNIPS/ RUTABAGAS cubed	12 to 15	6 to 8[2]	2 to 3	5 to 8	Stir-fry 2 to 3
ZUCCHINI	5 to 10	3 to 6	2 to 3	5 to 10	Broil halves 5

[2] Add ¼ cup (60 ml) water per pound (per 450 g).
[4] Fully cook before freezing.

Asparagus Wreath

Asparagus: *Available sporadically all year; peak March to June. Look for firm, straight spears with closed, tightly budded, compact tips. The stalks should be crisp, not wilted. Buy spears of uniform size to ensure even cooking. Avoid woody, dry stems. To help retain moisture, stand cut ends in an inch of water or wrap ends in a moist paper towel or cloth; place in a plastic bag, making sure tips stay dry. Refrigerate up to 5 days.*

1 pound (450 g) fresh asparagus
1 tablespoon (15 ml) butter or
    margarine
1 teaspoon (5 ml) lemon juice
6 thin slices pepperoni, finely
    chopped
¼ cup (60 ml) seasoned dry
    bread crumbs
    Pimiento strips for garnish

1. To prepare asparagus, snap off tough ends of spears where easily broken.

2. To ensure even cooking, peel stem ends with vegetable peeler.

3. To steam asparagus, rinse and place in steamer basket. Place steamer basket in large saucepan; add 1 inch (2.5 cm) of water. (Water should not touch bottom of basket.) Cover. Bring to a boil over high heat; steam asparagus 5 to 8 minutes until crisp-tender. Add water, as necessary, to prevent pan from boiling dry.

4. Remove spears from basket and make wreath of spears on warm, round serving platter or arrange in glass ring mold.

5. Melt butter and lemon juice in small saucepan over medium heat; pour over asparagus. Combine chopped pepperoni and bread crumbs in small bowl; sprinkle over asparagus. Garnish, if desired. Serve immediately.

Makes 4 side-dish servings

Step 1 . Snapping off tough ends of spears.

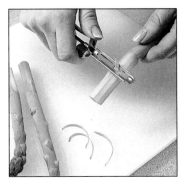

Step 2. Peeling stem ends with vegetable peeler.

Step 4. Arranging spears on serving platter.

Green Bean Bundles

Beans, Green: *Available sporadically all year; peak May to August. Look for vivid green, crisp, tender beans without scars and well shaped, slim pods with small seeds Buy beans of uniform size to ensure even cooking. Avoid bruised or large beans. Refrigerate, unwashed, in a plastic bag up to 2 days.*

8 ounces (225 g) haricot vert beans or other tiny, young green beans
1 yellow squash, about 1½ inches (4 cm) in diameter
1 tablespoon (15 ml) olive oil
1 clove garlic, minced
¼ teaspoon (1 ml) dried tarragon leaves, crushed
Salt and pepper
Fresh herb sprig and cherry tomato slices for garnish

1. Place beans in colander; rinse well. Snap off stem end from each bean. Arrange in 8 stacks, about 10 to 12 beans per stack.

2. Cut eight ½-inch-thick (1.5 cm) slices of squash; hollow out with spoon to within ¼ inch (6 mm) of rind.

3. To make bean bundles, thread stacks of beans through squash pieces as if each piece were a napkin ring.

4. To steam bean bundles, place steamer basket in large stockpot or saucepan; add 1 inch (2.5 cm) of water. (Water should not touch bottom of basket.) Place bean bundles in steamer basket. Cover. Bring to a boil over high heat; steam 4 minutes or until beans turn bright green and are crisp-tender. Add water, as necessary, to prevent pan from boiling dry.

5. Meanwhile, heat oil in small skillet over medium-high heat. Cook and stir garlic and tarragon in hot oil until garlic is soft but not brown. Transfer bean bundles to warm serving plate and pour garlic oil over top. Season with salt and pepper to taste. Garnish, if desired. Serve immediately.

Makes 8 side-dish servings

Step 1. Arranging beans in stacks.

Step 2. Hollowing out yellow squash.

Step 3. Threading stacks of beans through squash pieces.

Fresh Lima Beans in Onion Cream

Beans, Lima: *Available August and September. Look for green, shiny and pliable pods; beans should fill pods well. Avoid pods with signs of drying. Half the weight of a lima bean (the shell) is waste. Although yields vary according to size of bean, one pound when shelled will measure 1½ to 2 cups (375 to 500 ml) of beans. Buy plump-shelled beans with green to greenish-white skins. Refrigerate pods in a perforated plastic bag up to 3 days. Use as soon as possible since flavor is best when fresh. Shell beans just before using.*

1 pound (450 g) fresh lima beans*
⅔ cup (150 ml) milk
½ teaspoon (2 ml) instant minced onions
1 tablespoon (15 ml) butter or margarine
1 small onion, sliced into rings
⅓ cup (75 ml) sour cream
 Salt and pepper
2 teaspoons (10 ml) sliced pimiento
 Additional sliced pimiento and herb sprigs for garnish

*Or, use a 10-ounce (285 g) package of frozen lima beans, thawed, and omit steps 1 and 2.

1. To shell beans, open pods at seams by pinching pods between thumbs and forefingers.

2. Remove beans; discard shells.

3. Place beans in small, heavy saucepan. Add milk and minced onions. Bring *just* to a boil over medium-high heat; reduce heat to low. Simmer, uncovered, 20 to 25 minutes until tender.

4. Meanwhile, heat butter in small skillet over medium-high heat until melted and bubbly. Cook and stir onion rings in hot butter until golden. Stir sour cream into cooked beans. Add salt and pepper to taste. Gently stir in pimiento. Stir onion rings into lima bean mixture.

5. Transfer to warm serving dish. Garnish, if desired. Serve immediately.

Makes 4 side-dish servings

Step 1. Opening bean pods.

Step 2. Shelling beans.

Step 4. Stirring onion rings into lima bean mixture.

Vegetable Rings on Broccoli Spears

Broccoli: *Available all year; peak October to April. Look for tightly closed, compact, dark green to purplish-green flowerets on tender, firm stalks. Avoid those with yellow flowers, wilted leaves or thick, tough stems. Refrigerate in a plastic bag up to 4 days.*

1 small bunch broccoli (about
    12 ounces) (360 g)
1 red bell pepper
3 (¼ inch-thick/6mm) center
    slices mild white onion
2 tablespoons (30 ml) butter or
    margarine
½ teaspoon (2 ml) wine vinegar
½ teaspoon (2 ml) dried rosemary
    leaves, crushed

1. To prepare broccoli, trim leaves from broccoli stalks. Trim off tough ends of stalks. Cut broccoli into spears with large utility knife. Peel stems with vegetable peeler.

2. Rinse bell pepper under cold running water. To prepare bell pepper, make circular cut around top of pepper with paring knife. Remove stem and seeds from pepper.

3. Scrape out any remaining seeds and membrane with spoon. Rinse out pepper under running water; drain well. Thinly slice crosswise into rings with chef's knife.

4. To steam broccoli, place steamer basket in large saucepan; add 1 inch (2.5 cm) of water. (Water should not touch bottom of basket.) Place spears in steamer basket. Separate onion slices into rings; place on broccoli. Cover. Bring to a boil over high heat; steam about 8 minutes or until broccoli is crisp-tender. Add water, as necessary, to prevent pan from boiling dry.

5. Uncover; place pepper rings on top. Cover; steam briefly until pepper rings brighten in color but still hold their shape. Remove from heat; transfer vegetables with slotted spoon to warm serving dish. Melt butter in small saucepan over medium heat; stir in vinegar and rosemary. Drizzle evenly over vegetables. Serve immediately.

Makes 4 side-dish servings

Step 1. Peeling broccoli stems with vegetable peeler.

Step 2. Pulling stem and seeds from pepper.

Step 3. Slicing pepper crosswise into rings.

Broth-Simmered Brussels Sprouts

Brussels Sprouts:

Available October to March. Look for tight, vivid green heads with unblemished, compact leaves. Avoid those with loose leaves and any signs of yellowing. Refrigerate in a plastic bag up to 5 days. Use as soon as possible since flavor gets stronger with age.

1 pound (450 g) fresh Brussels sprouts
½ cup (125 ml) condensed beef broth *or* ½ cup (125 ml) water plus 2 teaspoons (10 ml) instant beef bouillon granules
1 tablespoon (15 ml) butter or margarine, softened
¼ cup (60 ml) freshly grated Parmesan cheese
Paprika

1. Cut stem from each Brussels sprout and pull off outer or bruised leaves.

2. To ensure fast, even cooking, crosshatch core by cutting an "X" deep into the stem end of each sprout with small paring knife. Refresh sprouts for 5 minutes in bowl of cold water; drain.

3. Use large enough saucepan to allow sprouts to fit in single layer. Pour broth into saucepan. Place sprouts, stem ends down, in broth. Bring to a boil over high heat; reduce heat to medium-low. Cover; simmer about 5 minutes or just until sprouts turn bright green and are crisp-tender when pierced with fork.

4. Uncover; simmer until liquid is almost evaporated. Toss cooked sprouts with butter, then cheese. Transfer to warm serving dish and sprinkle with paprika to taste. Garnish as desired. Serve immediately.

Makes 4 side-dish servings

Step 1. Pulling outer leaves from Brussels sprouts.

Step 2. Cutting "X" into core for faster cooking.

Step 3. Testing doneness of Brussels sprouts.

Savory Matchstick Carrots

Carrots: *Available all year. Look for firm, smooth, well-shaped carrots with a deep orange color. Avoid those that are flabby, soft, cracked, shriveled or show signs of mold. If leaves are attached, they should look fresh. To store, cut off leaves and refrigerate in a plastic bag up to 2 weeks. Apples produce a gas that causes a bitter flavor in carrots; therefore, store separately. Wilted carrots still have flavor and vitamin A, which makes them good for soups, stews, stocks and purées.*

½ **pound (225 g) carrots, peeled**
1 **small turnip, peeled***
½ **cup (125 ml) water**
3 **tablespoons (45 ml) butter or margarine, cut into chunks**
1½ **teaspoons (15 ml) fresh thyme leaves *or* ½ teaspoon (2 ml) dried thyme leaves, crushed**
⅛ **teaspoon (0.5 ml) salt**
⅛ **teaspoon (0.5 ml) ground black pepper**
   Green onion tops and edible flowers, such as violets, for garnish

*Or, substitute 2 extra carrots for turnip.

1. To cut carrots into julienne strips, cut lengthwise strip from carrot so that it can lie flat on cutting board. Cut carrots into 2-inch (5 cm) lengths. Place 1 carrot piece flat side down on cutting board. Cut lengthwise with utility knife into thin strips. Stack a few strips. Cut down into ¼-inch-wide (6 mm) strips. Repeat with remaining pieces.

2. To cut turnip into julienne strips, cut turnip lengthwise into quarters. Place 1 quarter flat side down on cutting board. Cut lengthwise with utility knife into thin strips. Stack a few strips. Cut down into ¼-inch-wide (6 mm) strips. Repeat with remaining quarters.

3. Place carrot and turnip strips in medium saucepan. Add water; cover. Bring to a boil over high heat; reduce heat to medium. Simmer 5 to 8 minutes until crisp-tender.

4. Drain vegetables in colander. Melt butter over medium heat in same saucepan; stir in thyme, salt and pepper. Add carrots and turnips; toss gently to coat. Transfer carrot mixture to warm serving dish. Garnish, if desired. Serve immediately.

Makes 4 side-dish servings

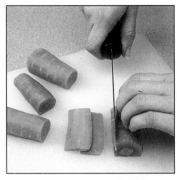

Step 1. Cutting 2-inch (5 cm) carrot pieces into thin strips.

Step 1. Cutting carrots into ¼-inch-wide (6 mm) strips.

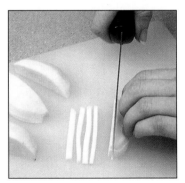

Step 2. Cutting turnip into ¼-inch-wide (6 mm) strips.

Crumb-Topped Snowball

Cauliflower: *Available all year; peak October and November. Look for a creamy-white head with tightly packed, crisp flowerets. Leaves should be bright green. Avoid heads with brown spots or dry leaves. Refrigerate in original packaging or in a plastic bag up to 4 days.*

1 large head cauliflower (about 1¼ pounds/560 g)
4 tablespoons (60 ml) butter or margarine
1 cup (250 ml) fresh bread crumbs (about 2 slices)
2 green onions, thinly sliced
2 eggs, hard cooked and finely chopped
2 tablespoons (30 ml) lemon juice
   Fresh parsley, lemon peel strips and baby sunburst squash for garnish

1. To prepare cauliflower, cut leaves from cauliflower by slicing through stem between head and leaves with chef's knife; remove and discard leaves and stem.

2. Cut around core with paring knife, being careful not to separate flowerets from head; remove and discard core. Rinse.

3. Pour 1 inch (2.5 cm) of water into large saucepan. Place cauliflower in water, stem side down; cover. Bring to a boil over high heat; reduce heat to low. Simmer 10 to 12 minutes until crisp-tender; drain. Place cauliflower in 8 x 8 inch (20 cm x 20 cm) baking dish.

4. Preheat oven to 375°F (190°C). Melt butter over medium heat in small skillet. Stir in bread crumbs and onions; cook until crumbs are lightly browned. Stir in chopped eggs and lemon juice. Press crumb mixture evenly over top of cauliflower.

5. Bake 10 minutes or until crumb mixture is crispy and lightly browned. Garnish, if desired. Serve immediately.

Makes 6 side-dish servings

Step 1. Removing leaves from cauliflower.

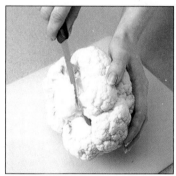

Step 2. Cutting core from cauliflower.

Step 4. Pressing crumb mixture evenly over top of cauliflower.

Cob Corn in Barbecue Butter

Corn: *Available May to September. Look for fresh, moist, green husks; cob should be well filled with bright, plump, milky kernels that pop easily when pressed with a fingernail. Kernels should be tightly packed together in even rows. Refrigerate immediately in husks; if shucked, store in plastic bags up to 2 days. Use as soon as possible since the sugar in corn begins to turn to starch as soon as it is picked.*

4 ears fresh corn
2 tablespoons (30 ml) butter or
**   margarine, softened**
½ teaspoon (2 ml) dry barbecue
**   seasoning**
¼ teaspoon (1 ml) salt
**   Cherry tomato wedges and**
**   Italian parsley for garnish**

1. To shuck corn, pull outer husks down ear to base. Snap off husks and stem at base.

2. Strip away silk from corn by hand.

3. Remove any remaining silk with dry vegetable brush. Trim any blemishes from corn and rinse under cold running water.

4. Pour 1 inch (2.5 cm) of water into large saucepan or skillet. (Do *not* add salt, as it will make corn tough.) Bring to a boil over medium-high heat. Add ears; cover. Cook 4 to 7 minutes until kernels are slightly crisp when pierced with fork.*

5. Remove corn with tongs to warm serving platter. Blend butter, barbecue seasoning and salt in small bowl until smooth. Serve immediately with corn. Garnish, if desired.

Makes 4 side-dish servings

*Length of cooking time depends on size and age of corn.

Step 1. Removing outer husks.

Step 2. Stripping away silk from corn.

Step 3. Removing remaining silk with dry vegetable brush.

Corn and Tomatillo Salsa

4 ears fresh corn
2 jalapeño peppers
½ pound (225 g) tomatillos* or
    tomatoes
½ red or green bell pepper,
    cored, membranes removed
    (technique on page 98)
    and chopped**
2 green onions, thinly sliced
2 tablespoons (30 ml) lime or
    lemon juice
2 tablespoons (30 ml) water
½ teaspoon (2 ml) ground
    coriander
2 tablespoons (30 ml) chopped
    fresh cilantro leaves
    Tortilla chips
    Lime slices, red chili pepper
    slices and fresh cilantro
    leaves for garnish

*Despite its name and appearance, the tomatillo is not a variety of tomato. Native to Mexico, it resembles a green tomato encased in a papery husk, but its flavor is lemony.

**Use red bell pepper if using tomatillos and green bell pepper if using tomatoes for variety in color.

1. Shuck corn by removing husk and silk from corn. (Technique on page 106.) Rinse under cool running water.

2. Holding tip of 1 ear, stand upright on stem end in large skillet. Cut down sides of cob with paring knife, releasing kernels without cutting into cob.

3. Press down along each cob with dull edge of utility knife to release remaining corn and liquid.

4. Jalapeño peppers can sting and irritate the skin; wear plastic disposable gloves when handling peppers and do not touch eyes. Cut peppers in half lengthwise. Remove seeds, membranes and stems with small paring knife; discard. Chop peppers finely and add to corn.

5. Remove husks from tomatillos. Wash off sticky residue; core and chop.

6. Add tomatillos, bell pepper, onions, lime juice, water and coriander to corn mixture; cover. Bring to a boil over high heat; reduce heat to medium-low. Simmer 5 minutes, stirring halfway through cooking. Cool; stir in cilantro. Store in refrigerator. Serve with tortilla chips. Garnish, if desired.

Makes 3 cups (750 ml) salsa

Step 2. Cutting down sides of cob to release kernels.

Step 3. Pressing down along edge of cob to release remaining corn and liquid.

Step 5. Removing husks from tomatillos.

Caponata-Style Fettuccine

Eggplants: *Available all year; peak August and September. Look for firm eggplants with smooth skin and a uniform color. Avoid those that are soft, shriveled or have cuts or scars. Usually, the smaller the eggplant is the sweeter and more tender it is. Eggplants bruise easily. Handle gently and store at room temperature up to 2 days. Or, refrigerate in a plastic bag up to 4 days. Use as soon as possible since eggplant becomes bitter with age.*

1 medium eggplant (about 1 pound/450g)
1¼ teaspoons (6 ml) salt, divided
3 medium tomatoes (about 1 pound/450g)
⅓ cup (75 ml) olive oil, divided
1 small green bell pepper, cored, membrane removed (technique on page 98), cut into strips
1 medium onion, coarsely chopped (technique on page 115)
2 cloves garlic, minced
⅓ cup (75 ml) *each* halved pitted green olives and raisins
¼ cup (60 ml) balsamic or red wine vinegar
2 tablespoons (30 ml) capers (optional)
¼ teaspoon (1 ml) *each* ground cinnamon and black pepper
10 ounces (285 g) fresh spinach fettuccine, hot cooked and drained
Fresh basil leaves for garnish

1. Rinse eggplant. To prepare eggplant, trim off cap and stem. Cut eggplant into ¼-inch-thick (6 mm) slices with chef's knife. Place in large colander over bowl; sprinkle with 1 teaspoon (5 ml) salt. Drain 1 hour.

2. To seed tomatoes, cut in half. Remove stems and seeds; discard. Coarsely chop tomatoes.

3. Move oven rack to lowest position. Preheat oven to 450°F (230°C). Place eggplant slices in single layer on baking sheet or jelly-roll pan; brush both sides lightly with some of oil.

4. To roast eggplant slices, bake 10 minutes or until lightly browned on bottoms. Turn slices over with tongs; roast about 5 minutes more or until tops are lightly browned and slices are softened; set aside.

5. Heat remaining oil in large skillet over medium-high heat. Cook and stir bell pepper in hot oil about 5 minutes or until pepper turns bright green. Transfer pepper strips to plate; set aside.

6. Add onion and garlic to same skillet; cook and stir 5 minutes or until onion is soft. Add tomatoes, olives, raisins, vinegar, capers, cinnamon, black pepper and remaining ¼ teaspoon (1 ml) salt. Cook until most of liquid has evaporated.

7. Cut roasted eggplant slices into quarters; add to tomato mixture. Add reserved bell pepper; cook until heated through. Serve over fettuccine. Garnish, if desired.
Makes 4 main-dish or 8 appetizer servings

Note: Caponata is a Sicilian eggplant dish that may be served cold as an appetizer or on lettuce as a salad. Here it is made into a vegetarian sauce for pasta.

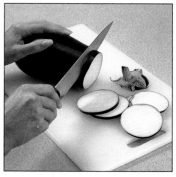

Step 1. Cutting eggplant into ¼-inch-thick (6 mm) slices.

Step 2. Seeding tomatoes.

Step 4. Turning eggplant slices while browning.

Reuben-Stuffed Kohlrabies

Kohlrabies: *Available sporadically all year; peak May to July. Look for small to medium, smooth bulbs. Leaves should be firm and green. Avoid kohlrabies with cracks or yellowing leaves. Separate leaves from bulbs. Refrigerate bulbs in a plastic bag up to 1 week and leaves up to 2 days.*

4 kohlrabies (each about 2½ inches/6.25 cm) in diameter)
2 tablespoons (30 ml) butter or margarine
¼ cup (60 ml) chopped onion (technique on page 115)
¼ teaspoon (1 ml) dry mustard
¼ teaspoon (1 ml) caraway seeds
2 slices pumpernickel bread, crumbled to make 1 cup (250 ml) crumbs
¼ cup (60 ml) chopped corned beef
2 tablespoons (30 ml) mayonnaise
¼ cup (1 ounce/30g) shredded Swiss cheese
Green onion tops
Raspberry leaves for garnish

1. Detach 1 leaf from kohlrabi and finely chop; set aside. Cut off slice from bottom of each kohlrabi and cut off stems with utility knife; discard.

2. Peel each kohlrabi vertically from top to bottom with vegetable peeler or paring knife.

3. To hollow out kohlrabies, scoop out pulp with melon baller, leaving ¼-inch (6 mm) thick shells; reserve pulp.

4. Fill large saucepan halfway with water. Bring to a boil over high heat; add kohlrabi shells. Boil about 15 minutes or until crisp-tender. Remove shells with slotted spoon; drain upside down on paper towels.

continued on page 114

Step 1. Cutting off kohlrabi stems with utility knife.

Step 2. Peeling kohlrabies with vegetable peeler.

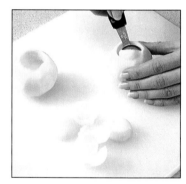

Step 3. Hollowing out kohlrabies with melon baller.

Reuben-Stuffed Kohlrabies, *continued*

5. Chop reserved kohlrabi pulp. Heat butter in small skillet over medium-high heat until melted and bubbly. Add chopped kohlrabi, onion, mustard and caraway seeds to skillet; cook and stir until onion is soft. Stir in bread crumbs and corned beef. Remove from heat; stir in reserved kohlrabi leaf, mayonnaise and cheese.

6. Fill hollowed kohlrabies with crumb mixture. Spread remaining mixture in buttered round baking dish. Place kohlrabies in dish.*

7. Preheat oven to 350°F (180°C). Bake, uncovered, 20 to 30 minutes until kohlrabies are heated through and fork-tender. Meanwhile, immerse green onion tops in boiling water over high heat 1 minute. Remove with tongs; set aside. Tie 1 green onion piece around each kohlrabi. Serve immediately with additional filling. Garnish, if desired.

Makes 4 side-dish servings

*This dish may be prepared to this point up to 1 day before serving. Cover with plastic wrap and refrigerate.

Note: Kohlrabi means "cabbage turnip" and its bulb tastes like a broccoli stem. The leaves taste like kale or spinach.

Step 5. Stirring kohlrabi mixture.

Step 6. Filling kohlrabi with crumb mixture.

Step 6. Spreading remaining crumb mixture in baking dish.

Exotic Mushroom Soup

Mushrooms: *Available all year for most fresh and dried varieties; some exotics peak in fall or spring. Look for firm, fleshy mushrooms with no discoloration or bruises. Avoid limp or dehydrated specimens; button mushrooms should not have gills showing. Refrigerate, unwashed, in a paper bag, ventilated package or plastic bag punched with holes up to 5 days. If damp, wrap mushrooms in paper towels before storing. Use as soon as possible for best flavor.*

1 small onion
6 tablespoons (90 ml) butter or margarine, divided
4 cups (1 L) water, divided
3 teaspoons (15 ml) instant chicken bouillon granules
8 ounces (225 g) fresh assorted exotic mushrooms, such as cèpes, shiitakes, oysters, portobellos, criminis, morels or chanterelles *or* 8 ounces (225 g) button mushrooms
1 teaspoon (5 ml) lemon juice
4 tablespoons (60 ml) all-purpose flour
¼ teaspoon (1 ml) white pepper
1 cup (250 ml) half-and-half or heavy cream
Pink oyster mushrooms and small spinach leaves, cleaned, for garnish

1. To chop onion, peel skin. Cut onion in half through the root with utility knife. Place onion half, cut side down, on cutting board. Holding knife horizontally, make cuts parallel to board, almost to root end. Cut onion vertically into thin slices, holding onion with fingers to keep its shape. Turn onion and cut crosswise to root end. (The closer the cuts are spaced, the finer the onion is chopped.) Repeat with remaining onion half.

2. Heat 2 tablespoons (30 ml) butter in 2-quart (2 L) saucepan over medium-high heat until melted and bubbly. Cook and stir onion in hot butter until soft. Add 3½ cups (875 ml) water and bouillon; cover. Bring mixture to a boil over high heat; reduce heat to medium-low.

3. To prepare mushrooms, cut thin slice from base of each mushroom stem with paring knife; discard. Clean mushroom caps by wiping with damp paper towel.

4. If using shiitake, chanterelle or morel mushrooms, slice stems and caps; add to broth mixture. Slice other types of mushroom *stems* thinly and add to broth mixture; reserve caps.* Simmer broth mixture 10 minutes.

continued on page 116

Step 1. Chopping onion.

Step 3. Slicing bases from mushrooms.

Step 3. Wiping mushroom caps with damp paper towel.

Exotic Mushroom Soup, continued

5. Slice reserved mushroom caps. Heat 2 tablespoons (30 ml) butter in medium skillet over medium-high heat until melted and bubbly. Cook and stir mushrooms briefly in hot butter until softened. Remove with slotted spoon to broth mixture.

6. Melt remaining 2 tablespoons (30 ml) butter with lemon juice in same skillet. Stir in flour and pepper, then remaining ½ cup (125 ml) water; blend well. Add to broth mixture and blend in with wire whisk. Cook until mixture thickens, stirring constantly. Stir in half-and-half.

7. Ladle into 6 bowls. Garnish, if desired.

Makes 6 appetizer servings

*If using button mushrooms, slice lengthwise through caps and stems; add to broth mixture.

Note: The mushroom is one of the most primitive foods eaten today. Technically, it is a plant of the fungus family, but it is used as a vegetable.

Step 5. Slicing mushroom caps.

Step 5. Cooking and stirring mushrooms in hot butter.

Creamed Pearl Onions

Onions: *Available all year. Pearl onions (immature dry onions) peak in fall and winter and sweet onions peak in late summer and fall. Look for firm, well-shaped onions with dry skins. Avoid sooty or sprouting onions. Green onions should be crisp and tender with fresh tops and medium-size necks. Store onions in a cool, dark, dry place up to a month, preferably hung where air can circulate around them. Onions can give off an odor in the refrigerator and affect the flavor of other foods. Refrigerate green onions in a plastic bag up to 1 week.*

1 pint pearl onions
    (about 10 ounces/285 g)
2 tablespoons (30 ml) butter or
    margarine
2 tablespoons (30 ml) all-purpose
    flour
1 cup (250 ml) half-and-half
¼ teaspoon (1 ml) salt
¼ teaspoon (1 ml) ground black
    pepper
¼ cup (60 ml) dry bread crumbs
    Red onion slices and fresh
    sage leaves for garnish

1. To peel onions easily, blanch onions first. To blanch onions, bring 1 quart (1 L) of water in 2-quart (2 L) saucepan to a boil over high heat. Drop onions into boiling water; boil 2 minutes. Drain onions and immediately plunge into a bowl of cold water to stop cooking.

2. Cut stem end off 1 onion; squeeze onion between thumb and forefinger to loosen skin. Remove skin; discard. Repeat with remaining onions.

3. Place peeled onions in same saucepan with ½ inch (1.25 cm) of water; cover. Bring to a boil over high heat; reduce heat to medium-low. Simmer 15 to 20 minutes until fork-tender. Drain; set aside.

4. To make cream sauce, melt butter in small saucepan over medium heat. Blend in flour with wire whisk. Heat until mixture bubbles. Whisk in half-and-half. Cook until mixture thickens, whisking constantly. Add salt and pepper. Stir in cooked onions. When completely coated, transfer creamed onions to warm serving bowl. Sprinkle with dry bread crumbs. Garnish, if desired. Serve immediately.
Makes 4 side-dish servings

Step 1. Blanching onions.

Step 2. Squeezing onion to loosen skin.

Step 4. Whisking cream sauce.

Onions Baked in Their Papers

4 medium-size yellow onions (about 2½ inches/6.25 cm) in diameter)*

1½ teaspoons (7 ml) mixed herbs, such as dried thyme, sage and tarragon leaves, crushed

1 teaspoon (5 ml) sugar

½ teaspoon (2 ml) salt

Dash crushed red pepper flakes

¼ cup (60 ml) butter or margarine, melted

½ cup (125 ml) fresh bread crumbs

Fresh tarragon sprigs, yellow squash strips, red bell pepper strips and chives for garnish

*Choose onions with skins intact.

1. Preheat oven to 400°F (200°C). Line square baking pan with aluminum foil; set aside. Slice off stem and root ends of onions.

2. Cut 1½ x 1½-inch (3.75 x 3.75 cm) cone-shaped indentation in top of each onion with paring knife. Place onions in prepared pan on root ends.

3. Stir herbs, sugar, salt and red pepper into melted butter. Add bread crumbs; mix until blended. Spoon equal amounts of crumb mixture into indentations.

4. Bake about 1 hour or until fork-tender. Garnish, if desired. Serve immediately.

Makes 4 side-dish servings

Tip: Onions, which make people cry, contain an enzyme called alliinase. When this enzyme is exposed to air, it bonds with sulphur, which stimulates tear ducts. To minimize exposure to this enzyme, chill or run water over onions before cutting.

Step 1. Slicing root ends of onions.

Step 2. Cutting cone-shaped indentation in top of each onion.

Step 3. Spooning crumb mixture into onion.

Parsnip Patties

Parsnips: *Available all year; peak October to March. Look for straight, small (5- to 10-inch; 12.5- to 25-cm), smooth-skinned roots. Large parsnips might have woody cores. Avoid parsnips that are limp, shriveled or have splits or brown spots. Refrigerate in a plastic bag up to 10 days.*

1 pound (450 g) fresh parsnips
4 tablespoons (60 ml) butter or margarine, divided
¼ cup (60 ml) chopped onion (technique on page 115)
¼ cup (60 ml) all-purpose flour
⅓ cup (75 ml) milk
2 teaspoons (10 ml) chopped chives
Salt and pepper
¾ cup (175 ml) fresh bread crumbs
2 tablespoons (30 ml) vegetable oil

1. To prepare parsnips, peel with vegetable peeler. Trim ends and cut into ¾-inch (2 cm) chunks.

2. Pour 1 inch (2.5 cm) of water into medium saucepan. Bring to a boil over high heat; add parsnip chunks. Cover; boil 10 minutes or until parsnips are fork-tender. Drain. Place in large bowl. Coarsely mash with fork; set aside.

3. To make parsnip mixture, heat 2 tablespoons (30 ml) butter in small skillet over medium-high heat until melted and bubbly. Cook and stir onion in hot butter until onion is transparent. Stir in flour with wire whisk; heat until bubbly and lightly browned. Whisk in milk; heat until thickened. Stir onion mixture into mashed parsnips with chives; season with salt and pepper to taste.

4. Form parsnip mixture into 4 patties. Spread bread crumbs on plate. Dip patties in bread crumbs to coat sides evenly. Press crumbs firmly into patties. Place on waxed paper and refrigerate 2 hours.

5. Heat remaining 2 tablespoons (30 ml) butter and oil in 12-inch (30 cm) skillet over medium-high heat until butter is melted and bubbly. Add patties; cook about 5 minutes on each side or until browned. Transfer to warm dish. Garnish as desired.

Makes 4 side-dish servings

Step 1. Cutting parsnips into ¾-inch (2 cm) chunks.

Step 2. Mashing parsnips with fork.

Step 4. Dipping patties in bread crumbs.

Peas with Cukes 'n' Dill

Peas, English: *Available all year; peak January to August. Look for fresh, light green, plump, velvety young pods filled with developed peas. Avoid wilted, yellow or flat pods. Refrigerate pods, unwashed, in a plastic bag up to 2 days.*

2 pounds (900 g) fresh peas*
**½ medium cucumber
   (sliced crosswise)**
**2 tablespoons (30 ml) butter or
   margarine**
**1 teaspoon (5 ml) dried dill
   weed**
   Salt and pepper
   **Fresh dill, pineapple sage
   leaves and edible flowers,
   such as pansies, for garnish**

*Or, substitute 1 (10-ounce/285 g) package frozen peas, thawed, for fresh peas.

1. To prepare peas, press each pea pod between thumbs and forefingers to open.

2. Push peas out with thumb into colander; discard pods. Rinse peas under running water. Drain well; set aside.

3. Peel cucumber with vegetable peeler and halve lengthwise with utility knife. Scrape out seeds with spoon and discard. Cut cucumber into ¼-inch (6 mm) slices.

4. Heat butter in medium skillet over medium-high heat until melted and bubbly. Cook and stir peas and cucumber in hot butter 5 minutes or until vegetables are crisp-tender.

5. Stir in dill weed and season with salt and pepper to taste. Transfer to warm serving dish. Garnish, if desired. Serve immediately.

Makes 4 side-dish servings

Step 1. Opening pea pods.

Step 2. Shelling peas.

Step 3. Scraping seeds from cucumber.

Sesame Snow Peas

Peas, Snow: *Available all year; peak fall and spring. Look for bright green pods that are firm, crisp, small and flat with immature seeds. Avoid peas which are drying along the seam. Refrigerate, unwashed, in a plastic bag up to 2 days.*

½ **pound (225 g) snow peas (Chinese pea pods)**
1 **tablespoon (5 ml) sesame seeds**
2 **teaspoons (10 ml)** *each* **sesame and vegetable oils**
2 **green onions, cut into ¼-inch (6 mm) slices**
½ **teaspoon (2 ml) grated fresh gingerroot** *or* ¼ **teaspoon (1 ml) ground ginger**
1 **medium carrot, julienned (technique on page 102)**
1 **teaspoon (5 ml) soy sauce**

1. To de-stem peas decoratively, pinch off 1 stem end from each pod, pulling strings off if present. (Young, tender pods might not have strings.)

2. Make a "V"-shaped cut at opposite end of pod with utility knife.

3. To toast sesame seeds, heat small skillet over medium heat. Add sesame seeds; cook and stir about 5 minutes or until golden. Set aside.

4. To stir-fry, place wok or large skillet over high heat. (Test hot pan by placing drop of water in pan; if water sizzles, pan is sufficiently hot.) Add sesame and vegetable oils, swirling to coat sides. Heat oils until hot, about 30 seconds. Add onions, gingerroot, peas and carrot; briskly toss and stir with wok utensil or spoon, keeping vegetables in constant motion about 4 minutes or until peas are bright green and crisp-tender.

5. Stir in soy sauce. Transfer to warm serving dish; sprinkle with reserved sesame seeds. Serve immediately.

Makes 4 side-dish servings

Step 1. Removing strings from pea pods.

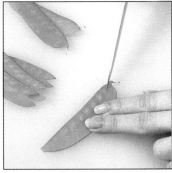

Step 2. Making "V"-shaped cut in pod.

Step 4. Stir-frying pea and carrot mixture in wok.

Ratatouille-Stuffed Pepper Halves

Peppers, Bell: *Available all year; peak August and September. Look for shiny, crisp peppers with smooth skins. Peppers should feel heavy for their size. Avoid those with soft spots or shriveled areas. Refrigerate in a plastic bag up to 5 days.*

3 large bell peppers (1 red, 1 yellow and 1 green *or* any combination)
¼ cup (60 ml) olive oil
1 small eggplant (¾ pound/335 g), unpeeled, cut into ½-inch cubes
1 small onion, thinly sliced
1 clove garlic, minced
1 large tomato, seeded and coarsely chopped (technique on page 110)
1 cup (250 ml) sliced fresh mushrooms
½ teaspoon (2 ml) *each* dried basil and oregano leaves, crushed
½ teaspoon (2 ml) salt
Dash ground black pepper
Dash ground red pepper
1 zucchini, quartered and cut into ½-inch (1.5 cm) chunks
Plum tomato slices and fresh basil leaves for garnish

1. Cut bell peppers (including stems) in half lengthwise with chef's knife.

2. Scrape out seeds and membrane with spoon, being careful not to cut through shell. Rinse out pepper halves under running water; drain.

3. To steam pepper halves, place steamer basket in large saucepan or stockpot; add 1 inch (2.5 cm) of water. (Water should not touch bottom of basket.) Place pepper halves, cut sides up, in steamer basket; cover. Bring to a boil; steam 5 minutes or until peppers are crisp-tender. Add water, as necessary, to prevent pan from boiling dry. Plunge pepper halves into ice water to stop cooking. Place pepper halves in 13 x 9-inch (32.5 x 22.5 cm) baking dish.

4. Heat oil in large skillet over medium heat. Cook eggplant and onion in hot oil 10 minutes or until vegetables are soft, stirring occasionally. Add garlic, tomato, mushrooms, basil, oregano, salt, ground black pepper and ground red pepper. Bring to a boil over medium-high heat; reduce heat to medium-low. Simmer about 5 minutes, stirring occasionally. Add zucchini; simmer 5 minutes more or until mixture thickens slightly.

5. Preheat oven to 350°F (180°C). Spoon mixture evenly into pepper halves.* Bake 15 minutes or until heated through. Garnish, if desired. Serve immediately.
Makes 6 side-dish servings

*Pepper halves may be refrigerated up to 4 days at this point.

Step 1. Cutting peppers in half lengthwise.

Step 2. Scraping out seeds and membrane with spoon.

Step 3 Steaming peppers until crisp-tender.

Scalloped Red Skin Potatoes

Potatoes: *Available all year. Look for firm, somewhat smooth, clean, well-shaped potatoes. Avoid wilted, sprouted or green-tinged potatoes. Store, unwashed, in a cool, dark, dry place up to 3 weeks. Do not refrigerate as starch will turn to sugar.*

**2 pounds (900 g) red skin potatoes
2 tablespoons (30 ml) all-purpose flour
4 tablespoons (60 ml) butter or margarine, divided
Salt, pepper and paprika
1¼ cups (312 ml) milk
Fresh thyme sprig for garnish**

1. Preheat oven to 350°F (180°C). To prepare potatoes, scrub potatoes under running water with soft vegetable brush; rinse well. Cut potatoes into ¼-inch (6 mm) slices with chef's knife. Place slices on waxed paper and sprinkle with flour; toss gently to coat.

2. Grease 9-inch (22.5 cm) round baking dish with 1 tablespoon (15 ml) butter. Place ⅓ of potatoes in dish; sprinkle with salt, pepper and paprika to taste. Dot with 1 tablespoon (15 ml) butter. Repeat layers twice.

3. Heat milk in small saucepan over medium heat until hot. *Do not boil.* Pour over potatoes; sprinkle with salt, pepper and paprika to taste. Cover with lid or foil.

4. Bake 35 minutes. Uncover; bake 20 minutes more or until potatoes are fork-tender. Garnish, if desired. Serve immediately.

Makes 6 side-dish servings

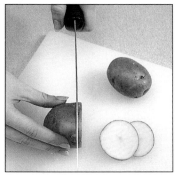

Step 1. Cutting potatoes into ¼-inch (6 mm) slices.

Step 2. Layering potatoes in baking dish.

Step 3. Pouring milk over potatoes.

Swiss Rösti Potatoes

4 **large Russet potatoes (about 6 ounces/180 g *each*)***
4 **tablespoons (60 ml) butter or margarine**
  Salt and pepper
  Cherry tomato wedges and fresh rosemary sprigs for garnish

*Prepare potatoes several hours or up to 1 day in advance.

1. Preheat oven to 400°F (200°C). To prepare potatoes, scrub potatoes with soft vegetable brush under running water; rinse well. Pierce each potato in several places with fork. Bake 1 hour or until fork-tender. Cool completely, then refrigerate.

2. When potatoes are cold, peel with paring knife. Grate potatoes by hand with large section of metal grater or use food processor with large grater disk.

3. Heat butter in 10-inch (25 cm) skillet over medium-high heat until melted and bubbly. Press grated potatoes evenly into skillet. (Do not stir or turn potatoes.) Season with salt and pepper to taste. Cook 10 to 12 minutes until golden brown.

4. Turn off heat; invert serving plate over skillet. Turn potatoes out onto plate. Garnish, if desired. Serve immediately.

Makes 4 side-dish servings

Step 2. Grating potatoes.

Step 3. Pressing grated potatoes evenly into skillet.

Step 4. Inverting serving plate over skillet.

Sweet Potato and Apple Casserole

Potatoes, Sweet: *Available all year; peak October to December. Look for firm, blemish-free potatoes of uniform shape. Avoid those that have cracks, mold or soft spots. Store in paper or perforated plastic bag in a cool, well-ventilated spot up to 1 week. Do not refrigerate.*

2 pounds (900 g) fresh sweet potatoes
4 tablespoons (60 ml) butter, divided
½ cup (125 ml) packed dark brown sugar
½ teaspoon (2 ml) ground cinnamon
¼ teaspoon (1 ml) ground mace or nutmeg
Salt to taste
2 Granny Smith apples, peeled, cored and quartered
½ cup (125 ml) granola cereal
Apple wedges for garnish

1. Preheat oven to 375°F (190°C). To prepare sweet potatoes, peel with vegetable peeler. Cut in half lengthwise, then cut into ½-inch (1.25 cm) slices.

2. Grease 2-quart (2 L) casserole or baking pan with 1 tablespoon (15 ml) butter. Mix brown sugar, cinnamon and mace in small bowl. Place ⅓ of potato slices in prepared casserole. Sprinkle with salt. Crumble half the sugar mixture over potatoes and dot with 1 tablespoon (15 ml) butter.

3. Slice each apple quarter into 4 wedges. Layer half the apples on top of potatoes in casserole. Repeat layers. Top with remaining potatoes and 1 tablespoon (15 ml) butter. Cover with lid or foil.

4. Bake 25 minutes. Uncover; spoon pan liquid over potatoes. Sprinkle with granola; bake 35 minutes more or until potatoes are fork-tender. Garnish, if desired. Serve immediately.

Makes 6 side-dish servings

Step 1. Cutting potato half into ½-inch (1.25 cm) slices.

Step 2. Crumbling sugar mixture over potatoes.

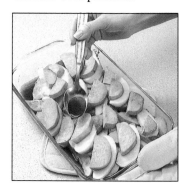

Step 4. Spooning pan liquid over potatoes.

Wilted Spinach Mandarin

Spinach: *Available all year; peak March to June. Look for dark green, fresh leaves. Avoid yellow, wilted, bruised or mushy leaves. Refrigerate, unwashed, in a plastic bag up to 3 days.*

½ **pound (225 g) fresh spinach**
1 **tablespoon (15 ml) vegetable oil**
1 **cup (250 ml) bean sprouts**
1 **can (11 ounces/330 g) mandarin oranges, drained**
2 **tablespoons (30 ml) reduced-sodium soy sauce**
2 **tablespoons (30 ml) orange juice**
Quartered orange slices for garnish

1. Separate spinach into leaves. Swish in cold water. Repeat several times with fresh cold water to remove sand and grit. Pat dry with paper towels.

2. To remove stems from spinach leaves, fold each leaf in half lengthwise. Pull stem toward top of leaf; discard stem. Blot any moisture from leaves with paper towels.

3. Heat oil in wok or large skillet over medium-high heat. To stir-fry spinach, quickly place spinach, bean sprouts and mandarin oranges in wok. Cook and stir 1 to 2 minutes *just* until spinach wilts. Transfer to serving dish. Heat soy sauce and orange juice in wok; pour over spinach and toss gently to coat. Garnish, if desired. Serve immediately.

Makes 4 side-dish servings

Step 1. Swishing spinach leaves in cold water.

Step 2. Removing stems from spinach leaves.

Step 3. Stir-frying spinach mixture in wok.

Neptune's Spaghetti Squash

Squash, Spaghetti:

Available all year; peak December to February. Look for hard, smooth, even-colored squash without ridges or bumps. Avoid those that are green or have spots. Store, uncut, in a cool, dry place up to 3 days; refrigerate up to 1 week.

1 spaghetti squash (about 3 pounds/1.35 kg)
½ pound (225 g) medium raw shrimp
1 clove garlic
4 tablespoons (60 ml) olive oil
½ pound (225 g) bay scallops
½ cup (125 ml) fresh or frozen peas
¼ cup (60 ml) sun-dried tomatoes in oil, drained and chopped*
½ teaspoon (2 ml) dried basil leaves, crushed
¼ cup (60 ml) freshly grated Parmesan cheese
Fresh basil leaves and tarragon flowers for garnish

*Or, substitute 2 plum tomatoes, seeded and chopped, for sun-dried tomatoes. (To seed tomatoes, cut in half. Remove seeds with spoon; discard.)

1. Preheat oven to 375°F (190°C). To bake squash, pierce in several places with long-handled fork to vent steam.

2. Place squash in large foil-lined baking dish; bake 20 minutes. Turn squash over; cook 25 minutes more or until easily depressed with finger.** Cut in half immediately to prevent further cooking.

3. Meanwhile, to peel shrimp, remove legs by gently pulling them off shell. Loosen shell with fingers, then slide off. To devein shrimp, cut shallow slit along back of shrimp with paring knife. Lift out and discard vein. (You might find this easier to do under cold running water.)

4. To slice garlic, trim ends of garlic clove. Slightly crush clove. Peel away skin. Cut into slices with paring knife.

5. Heat oil over medium-high heat in large skillet. Cook and stir garlic in hot oil *just* until it begins to brown. Remove garlic; discard. Add shrimp, scallops, peas, tomatoes and basil. Cook and stir 1 to 2 minutes until shrimp turn pink and scallops are opaque. Set aside.

6. Scoop out seeds from squash.

7. To remove spaghetti strands from squash, "comb" strands from each half of rind with 2 forks. Transfer to warm serving platter. Top with cooked seafood mixture; toss gently to coat. Sprinkle with cheese. Garnish, if desired. Serve immediately.

Makes 4 main-dish servings

**Larger squash may take longer to cook.

Step 1. Piercing squash to vent steam.

Step 6. Scooping seeds from squash.

Step 7. "Combing" squash strands from rind with forks.

Chutney-Squash Circles

Squash, Winter: *Available all year; peak December to February. Look for hard, firm skins. Avoid those with signs of softness, mushiness or bruises. Store, uncut, in a dark, dry, cool (50° to 55°F/ 32° to 35°C) place up to 2 months. Refrigerate cut squash wrapped in plastic wrap up to 1 week.*

2 acorn squash (1 pound/450 g
    each)
2 tablespoons (30 ml) butter or
    margarine
½ cup (125 ml) prepared
    chutney
2 tablespoons (30 ml) water
    Purple kale and scented
    geranium leaves for
    garnish*

*Be sure to use only nontoxic leaves.

1. Preheat oven to 400°F (200°C). Slice tip and stem ends from squash with chef's knife; cut squash crosswise into ¾-inch (1.8 cm) circles.

2. Scoop out seeds with spoon.

3. Tear off 18-inch (45 cm) square of heavy-duty foil. Center foil in 13 x 9-inch (32.5 x 22.5 cm) baking dish. Dot foil with butter and place squash on butter, slightly overlapping circles. Spoon chutney over slices and sprinkle with water.

4. Bring foil edges on long sides of pan together in center, folding over to make tight seam. Crimp ends to form tight seal.

5. Bake 20 to 30 minutes until squash is fork-tender. Transfer with spatula to warm serving plate. Pour pan drippings over squash. Garnish, if desired. Serve immediately.

Makes 4 side-dish servings

Step 1. Cutting squash into ¾-inch (1.8 cm) circles.

Step 2. Scooping out seeds with spoon.

Step 4. Folding foil to make tight seam.

Tabbouleh in Tomato Cups

Tomatoes: *Available all year; peak May to August. Look for well-shaped, heavy tomatoes with uniform full color. Avoid those with bruises and mushy centers. Vine-ripened tomatoes are better than those picked while green, which are often treated with ethylene gas to force reddening. Store ripe tomatoes at room temperature for 1 day or refrigerate up to 3 days. Underripe tomatoes should be left in a warm spot until ripe. Never refrigerate tomatoes until fully ripe.*

4 large firm, ripe tomatoes
    (about 8 ounces/225 g *each*)
4 green onions
2 tablespoons (30 ml) olive oil
1 cup (250 ml) bulgur wheat
1 cup (250 ml) water
2 tablespoons (30 ml) lemon
    juice
1 tablespoon (15 ml) chopped
    fresh mint leaves *or* ½
    teaspoon (2 ml) dried mint
    leaves, crushed
Salt and pepper
Lemon peel and mint leaves
    for garnish

1. To prepare tomato cups, remove stems. Cut tomatoes in half crosswise with sharp paring knife. Carefully loosen pulp from shell with spoon. Scoop pulp and seeds out of tomatoes into medium bowl, leaving shells intact.

2. Invert tomatoes on paper towel-lined plate; drain 20 minutes. Meanwhile, chop tomato pulp. Set aside.

3. Cut off green onion roots. Clean onions thoroughly. Thinly slice green onion tops on the diagonal with utility knife; set aside. Thinly slice white parts of onions on the diagonal.

4. Heat oil in 2-quart (2 L) saucepan over medium-high heat. Cook and stir white parts of onions in hot oil 1 to 2 minutes until wilted. Add bulgur; cook 3 to 5 minutes until browned.

5. Add reserved tomato pulp, water, lemon juice and mint to bulgur mixture. Bring to a boil over high heat; reduce heat to medium-low. Cover; simmer gently 15 to 20 minutes until liquid is absorbed.

6. Reserve a few sliced green onion tops for garnish; stir remaining green onions into bulgur mixture. Add salt and pepper to taste. Spoon mixture into tomato cups.*

7. Preheat oven to 400°F (200°C). Place filled cups in 13 x 9-inch (32.5 x 22.5 cm) baking dish; bake 15 minutes or until heated through. Top with reserved onion tops. Garnish, if desired. Serve immediately.
Makes 4 main-dish or 8 side-dish servings

*Tomato cups may be covered and refrigerated at this point up to 24 hours.

Step 1. Scooping pulp and seeds from tomatoes.

Step 4. Browning bulgur.

Step 6. Spooning bulgur mixture into tomato cups.

Crisp Zucchini Ribbons

Zucchini: *Available all year; peak June through August. Look for glossy, dark green skin and firm flesh. Zucchini should be heavy for its size. Avoid zucchini longer than 8 inches (20 cm) and with any brown or yellow spots. Refrigerate in a perforated plastic bag up to 4 days.*

3 small zucchini (about ¾ pound/338 g *total*)
2 tablespoons (30 ml) olive oil
1 tablespoon (15 ml) white wine vinegar
2 teaspoons (10 ml) chopped fresh basil leaves *or* ½ teaspoon (2 ml) dried basil leaves, crushed
½ teaspoon (2 ml) crushed red pepper flakes
¼ teaspoon (1 ml) ground coriander
Salt and freshly ground black pepper
Green onion top and julienne carrot strips (technique on page 102) for garnish

1. To make zucchini ribbons, cut tip and stem ends from zucchini with paring knife. Using vegetable peeler, begin at stem end and make continuous ribbons down length of each zucchini.

2. To steam zucchini ribbons, place steamer basket in large saucepan; add 1 inch (2.5 cm) of water. (Water should not touch bottom of basket.) Place zucchini ribbons in steamer basket; cover. Bring to a boil over high heat. When pan begins to steam, check zucchini for doneness. (Zucchini should be crisp-tender.) Transfer zucchini to warm serving dish with slotted spatula or tongs.

3. Combine oil, vinegar, basil, red pepper and coriander in small glass bowl, whisking until thoroughly blended.

4. Pour dressing mixture over zucchini ribbons; toss gently to coat. Season with salt and pepper to taste. Garnish, if desired. Serve immediately or refrigerate up to 2 days.

Makes 4 side-dish servings

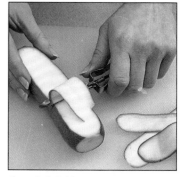

Step 1. Making zucchini ribbons with vegetable peeler.

Step 2. Steaming zucchini ribbons.

Step 3. Whisking oil mixture.

COOKING CLASS
CHICKEN

148   CLASS NOTES

154   SALADS

162   ONE-DISH MEALS

172   FAMILY FAVORITES

184   ELEGANT ENTRÉES

Pollo alla Firènze *(page 186)*

CLASS NOTES

Chicken is highly regarded by cooks for its universal appeal. Economical, versatile and readily available, chicken is the perfect ingredient for everyday cooking. Plus, chicken is high in protein and low in fat and cholesterol. Its delicious flavor makes it a winning choice for healthy eating.

The vast selection of chicken products available can make choosing the right ones a challenge. Knowing the differences between types of chicken can help you make the most of this popular ingredient.

CHICKEN BASICS

Chickens are classified by age and weight. Young chickens are tender and cook quickly; older chickens need slow cooking to make them tender. For best results, it's important to know which type of chicken to buy.

Broiler-fryers are young chickens weighing from 1½ to 3½ pounds (775 g to 1.57 kg). Only 7 to 10 weeks old, they yield tender, mildly flavored meat and are best when broiled, fried or roasted.

Roasters are 4- to 6-pound (1.8 to 2.7 kg) chickens that are 16 weeks old. As the name implies, they are perfect for roasting and rotisserie cooking.

Capons are young castrated roosters that weigh from 5 to 7 pounds (2.25 to 3.15 kg). These richly flavored birds have a higher fat content and yield more meat than roasters.

Stewing hens are adult chickens from 1 to 1½ years old. They weigh from 4½ to 7 pounds (2 to 3.15 kg) and have tough, stringy meat. Stewing hens are excellent for stocks, soups or stews, since moist-heat preparation tenderizes them and enhances their chicken-y flavor.

Supermarkets fulfill a constant demand for chicken with a variety of chicken cuts and products. Here are some of the more popular choices:

Whole chickens of every type are available with the neck and giblets wrapped separately and stuffed inside. Look for **livers** and **giblets** packaged separately for use in stuffings, soups and specialty dishes.

Cut-up chickens, usually broiler-fryers, are disjointed whole chickens consisting of two breast halves, two thighs, two wings and two drumsticks. Small broiler-fryers are also available in **halves** and **quarters**.

Chicken pieces are available to suit many needs. **Chicken legs** are whole broiler-fryer legs with thighs and drumsticks attached. **Thighs** and **drumsticks** are also packaged separately.

Packaged **chicken wings** are a popular choice for appetizer recipes. **Drumettes** are disjointed wing sections.

Chicken breasts are popular because of their tender, meaty, sweet character. They are available whole or split into halves. (*Note:* One *whole* breast is comprised of two *half* breasts. Recipes in this book that call for *one whole breast* require *both* breast halves.)

Boneless skinless chicken has become a favorite choice for today's busy cook because of its convenience and quick-cooking appeal. Boneless breasts, also called **cutlets** or **supremes**, plus **chicken tenders** and boneless thighs are some of the cuts of boneless chicken available.

Ground chicken is a recent addition to the poultry case; its most popular use is as a low-fat replacement for ground beef or pork. Processed chicken includes **canned chunk chicken**, newly introduced chicken **sausage**, chicken **franks** and traditional **deli** and **luncheon meats**.

SHOPPING TIPS

Once you have determined the kind of chicken you wish to buy, check out these important tips on inspecting and purchasing chicken.

• Check the package for the U.S.D.A. Grade A rating; chicken in most supermarkets should be government inspected. Look for secure, unbroken packaging, as well as a "sell-by" date stamp that indicates the last day the chicken should be sold.

• Physically inspect the chicken before purchasing. Its skin should be creamy white to deep yellow; meat should never look gray or pasty. Odors could signal spoilage. If you notice a strong, unpleasant odor after opening a package of chicken, leave it open on the counter for a few minutes. Sometimes oxidation takes place inside the package, resulting in a slight, but harmless odor. If the odor remains, return the chicken in its original package to the store for a refund.

• The key to purchasing chicken is knowing what you plan to use it for and then buying according to your needs. After all, chicken is both economical and convenient. If you purchase whole chickens on sale and cut them apart at home, you can save money (see Helpful Preparation Techniques, pages 150-153). Save time by stocking the freezer with ready-to-use boneless skinless chicken. Store the chicken in efficient, meal-size portions; they defrost and cook quickly and eliminate leftovers.

• To make sure you buy enough chicken to meet your family's needs, follow this guide: One broiler-fryer (2 to 3 pounds/900 g to 1.35 kg), cut up, yields 3 to 5 servings; one roaster (3 to 6 pounds/1.35 to 2.7 kg) yields 4 to 8 servings. One whole chicken breast or two chicken breast halves (about 12 ounces/360 g total) yields 2 servings; one pound (450 g) of chicken thighs or drumsticks yields about 2 servings.

• As a rule, two whole chicken breasts (about 12 ounces/360 g each) yield about 2 cups (500 ml) chopped cooked chicken; one broiler-fryer (about 3 pounds/1.35 kg) yields about 2½ cups (625 ml) chopped cooked chicken.

PROPER CHICKEN STORAGE

Fresh, raw chicken can be stored in its original wrap for up to two days in the coldest part of the refrigerator. However, freeze chicken immediately if you do not plan to use it within two days after purchasing. You can freeze most chicken in its original packaging safely for up to two months; if you plan to freeze it longer, consider double-wrapping or rewrapping with freezer paper, aluminum foil or plastic wrap. Airtight packaging is the key to freezing chicken successfully.

When freezing whole chickens, remove and rinse giblets (if any) and pat dry with paper towels. Trim away any excess fat from chicken. Tightly wrap, label, date and freeze both chicken and giblets in separate freezer-strength plastic, paper or foil wraps.

Thaw frozen chicken, wrapped, in the refrigerator for best results. Thawing times for frozen chicken vary depending on how thoroughly frozen the chicken is and whether the chicken is whole or cut up. A general guideline is to allow 24 hours thawing time for a 5-pound (2.25 kg) whole chicken; allow about 5 hours per pound (450 g) for thawing chicken pieces. Never thaw chicken on the kitchen counter; this promotes bacterial growth.

A WORD ABOUT HANDLING CHICKEN

When handling raw chicken, you must keep everything that comes into contact with it clean. Raw chicken should be rinsed and patted dry with paper towels before cooking; cutting boards and knives must be washed in hot sudsy water after using and hands must be scrubbed thoroughly before and after handling. Why? Raw chicken can harbor harmful salmonella bacteria. If bacteria are transferred to work surfaces, utensils or hands, they could contaminate other foods as well as the cooked chicken and cause food poisoning. With careful handling and proper cooking, this is easily prevented.

Chicken should always be cooked completely before eating. You should never cook chicken partially, then store it to be finished later, since this promotes bacterial growth as well.

IS IT DONE YET?

There are a number of ways to determine if chicken is thoroughly cooked and ready to eat. For whole chickens, a meat thermometer inserted into the thickest part of the thigh, but not near bone or fat, should register 180° to 185°F (115° to 118°C) before removing from the oven. If a whole chicken is stuffed, insert the thermometer into the center of the body cavity; when the stuffing registers 160°F (105°C), the chicken should be done. (*Note:* Chicken should only be stuffed *just before* roasting; *never* stuff a chicken ahead of time.) Roasted whole chicken breasts are done when they register 170°F (108°C) on a meat thermometer.

To test bone-in chicken pieces, you should be able to insert a fork into the chicken with ease and the juices should run clear; however, the meat and juices nearest the bones might still be a little pink even though the chicken is cooked thoroughly. Boneless chicken pieces are done when the centers are no longer pink; you can determine this by simply cutting into the chicken with a knife.

HELPFUL PREPARATION TECHNIQUES

Flattening Uncooked Boneless Chicken Breasts

Place one chicken breast half between two sheets of waxed paper. Using flat side of meat mallet or rolling pin, gently pound chicken from center to outside of chicken to desired thickness.

Skinning Uncooked Chicken

Freeze chicken until firm, but not hard. (However, do not refreeze thawed chicken.) Grasp skin with clean cotton kitchen towel and pull away from meat; discard skin. When finished skinning chicken, launder towel before using again.

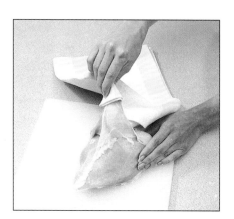

Disjointing a Whole Chicken

1. Place chicken, breast side up, on cutting board. Cut between thigh and body to hip joint. Bend leg back slightly to free hip joint from socket; cut through hip joint and remove leg. Repeat to remove other leg.

2. Place leg, skin side down, on cutting board. Locate joint by moving thigh back and forth with one hand while holding drumstick with other hand. Cut completely through joint.

3. Place chicken on side. Pull one wing out from body; cut through shoulder joint. Turn chicken over and repeat to remove other wing.

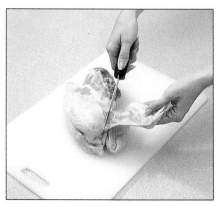

4. Working from tail to neck, cut breast from backbone, cutting through small rib bones and along outside of collarbone.

5. Turn chicken over and repeat on other side. Cut through any remaining connective tissue; pull breast away from backbone.

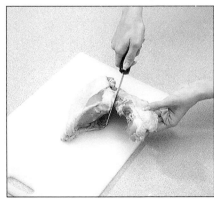

6. Place breast, skin side up, on cutting board. Split breast into halves by cutting along one side of breastbone. If desired, you may debone the whole breast before splitting (see Skinning and Deboning a Whole Chicken Breast, pages 152-153, steps 2–8).

Cutting a Whole Chicken into Halves and Quarters

1. Place chicken, breast side down, on cutting board with neck end away from you. Working from neck to tail, cut along one side of backbone, cutting as close to bone as possible. Cut down other side of backbone; remove backbone.

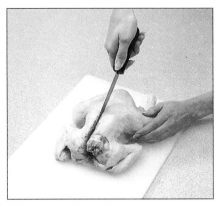

2. Remove breastbone (see Skinning and Deboning a Whole Chicken Breast, pages 152-153, steps 2–7).

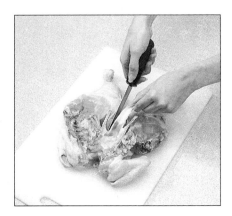

3. Turn chicken, skin side up. Cut lengthwise down center of chicken to split into halves.

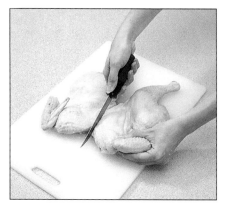

4. To cut into quarters, cut through skin separating thighs from breast.

Skinning and Deboning a Whole Chicken Breast

1. Freeze chicken breast until firm, but not hard. (However, do not refreeze thawed chicken.) Grasp skin with clean cotton kitchen towel and pull away from meat; discard skin. When finished skinning chicken breast, launder towel before using again.

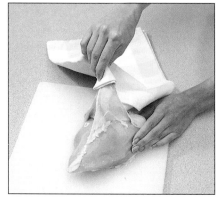

2. Place breast, meaty side down, on cutting board. Cut small slit through membrane and cartilage at the V of the neck end.

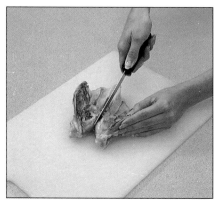

3. Grasp breast with both hands and gently bend both sides backward to snap breastbone.

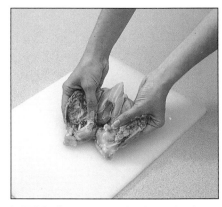

4. With fingers, work along both sides of breastbone to loosen triangular keel bone; pull out bone.

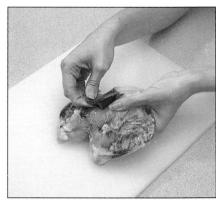

5. With tip of sharp knife, cut along both sides of cartilage at end of breastbone. Remove cartilage.

6. Slip point of knife under long rib bone on one side of breast. Cut and scrape meat from rib bones, pulling bones away from meat.

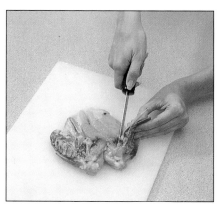

7. Cut meat away from collarbone. Remove bones. Repeat procedure to debone other side of breast.

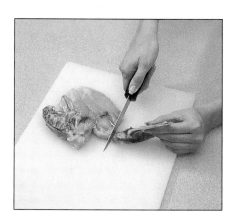

8. Remove wishbones of chicken breasts that have been cut from whole chickens in your home kitchen. Cut meat away from wishbone at neck end of breast. Grasp wishbone and pull it out of breast.

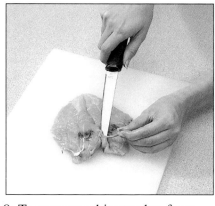

9. To remove white tendon from each side of breast, cut enough meat away from each tendon so you can grasp it (use paper towel for firmer grasp). Remove tendon.

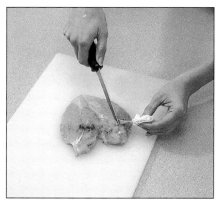

10. Turn breast, meaty side up. If desired, remove chicken tenders from thickest edge of each breast half and reserve for another use. Trim any loosened remaining connective tissue, if needed. Cut whole chicken breast lengthwise into halves, if desired.

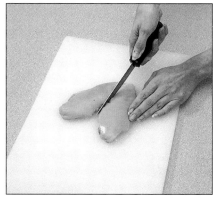

Shredding Cooked Chicken

Place cooked boneless skinless chicken on cutting board. Pull meat into long shreds with two forks or fingers.

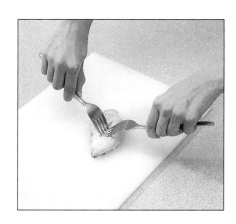

Hot Chinese Chicken Salad

8 boneless skinless chicken thighs
1 large tomato
¼ cup (62.5 ml) cornstarch
¼ cup (62.5 ml) vegetable oil
1 can (4 ounces/120 g) water chestnuts, drained and sliced
1 can (4 ounces/120 g) sliced mushrooms, drained
1 cup (250 ml) coarsely chopped green onions
1 cup (250 ml) diagonally sliced celery
¼ cup (62.5 ml) soy sauce
⅛ teaspoon (0.5 ml) garlic powder
2 cups (500 ml) finely shredded iceberg lettuce
  Orange slices for garnish
  Hot cooked rice

1. Cut chicken into bite-size pieces on cutting board; set aside.

2. To prepare tomato, with paring knife, make circular cut around stem end using sawing motion. Remove stem end. Cut tomato in half on cutting board; cut each half into bite-size pieces. Set aside.

3. Place cornstarch in shallow dish.

4. Place chicken, one piece at a time, in cornstarch. Coat evenly, shaking off excess; set aside.

5. Place wok or large skillet over high heat. (Test hot pan by adding drop of water to pan; if water sizzles, pan is sufficiently hot.) Add oil to wok, swirling to coat all sides. Heat oil until hot, about 30 seconds.

6. Add chicken to wok; stir-fry chicken with wok utensil or wooden spoon, keeping chicken in constant motion, 3 minutes or until chicken is no longer pink in center.

7. Stir in tomato, water chestnuts, mushrooms, green onions, celery, soy sauce and garlic powder. Cover; simmer 5 minutes.

8. Place chicken mixture on lettuce-lined serving platter. Garnish, if desired. Serve with rice.

Makes 4 servings

Step 2. Removing stem from tomato.

Step 4. Coating chicken with cornstarch.

Step 6. Stir-frying chicken.

Lagoon Chicken Salad

1½ cups (375 ml) unsweetened
    apple juice
2 whole chicken breasts (about
    1½ pounds/1.12 kg)
1 medium apple
3 cups (750 ml) cooled cooked
    rice (1 cup/250 ml
    uncooked)
1½ cups (375 ml) seedless green
    grapes, halved
½ cup (125 ml) chopped celery
¾ cup (180 ml) slivered
    almonds, divided
½ cup (125 ml) chopped water
    chestnuts
1 cup (250 ml) mayonnaise
½ teaspoon (2 ml) seasoned salt
¼ teaspoon (1 ml) ground
    cinnamon
    Spinach leaves
    Apple slices for garnish

1. To poach chicken, simmer apple juice in deep saucepan over medium heat; add chicken. Cover; simmer about 30 minutes or until chicken is tender. Remove chicken from saucepan to cool; discard liquid.

2. When chicken is cool enough to handle, carefully remove and discard skin and bones.

3. Dice chicken on cutting board. Place in large bowl; set aside.

4. To prepare apple, cut lengthwise into quarters on cutting board; remove stem, core and seeds with paring knife. Chop apple quarters into ½-inch (1.25 cm) pieces. Toss with chicken in bowl.

5. Gently toss chicken, apple, rice, grapes, celery, ½ cup (125 ml) almonds and water chestnuts; set aside.

6. Combine mayonnaise, seasoned salt and cinnamon in small bowl.

7. Add mayonnaise mixture to chicken mixture; toss lightly. Cover; refrigerate chicken salad at least 30 minutes.

8. Spoon chicken salad onto spinach-lined serving platter. Sprinkle with remaining ¼ cup (62.5 ml) almonds. Garnish, if desired.

Makes 4 to 6 servings

Step 2. Removing bones from chicken.

Step 3. Dicing chicken.

Step 4. Removing stem, core and seeds from apple.

Larry's Pineapple Hula Salad

1 papaya
2 whole chicken breasts, split,
    skinned, boned (technique
    on pages 152-153) and
    cooked
1 large rib celery
2 cans (8 ounces/225 g *each*)
    Dole® Pineapple Chunks,
    drained
½ cup (125 ml) macadamia nuts
    or peanuts
1 cup (250 ml) mayonnaise
2 teaspoons (10 ml) curry
    powder
    Salad greens
    Chives and sliced kumquats
    for garnish

1. To prepare papaya, slice papaya lengthwise in half on cutting board. With large spoon, scoop out seeds; discard. Remove peel from papaya using vegetable peeler or paring knife.

2. Dice enough papaya to measure 1 cup (250 ml). Reserve remainder for other use.*

3. Dice chicken on cutting board; set aside.

4. To prepare celery, trim stem end and leaves from celery rib on cutting board. Slice celery diagonally.

5. Combine papaya, chicken, celery, pineapple and nuts in large bowl.

6. Blend mayonnaise and curry in small bowl.

7. Spoon mayonnaise mixture over chicken mixture; blend thoroughly. Cover; refrigerate salad at least 1 hour.

8. Serve salad mounded on salad-green-lined serving platter. Garnish, if desired.

Makes 4 servings

*For best results, store leftover papaya tightly wrapped in the refrigerator. Cut papaya should be eaten within two days.

Step 1. Removing peel from papaya.

Step 2. Dicing papaya.

Step 3. Dicing chicken.

Chicken and Walnut Salad Athena

½ cup (125 ml) extra virgin olive
   oil
½ cup (125 ml) lemon juice
1 tablespoon (15 ml) light
   brown sugar
1 package (1 ounce/30 g)
   Hidden Valley Ranch®
   Salad Dressing Mix
2 cups (500 ml) diced cooked
   chicken
¼ cup (62.5ml) loosely packed
   fresh parsley, minced
1 green onion, thinly sliced
4 ounces (225 g) fresh feta
   cheese
   Cold water
2 tablespoons (30 ml)
   margarine
½ teaspoon (2 ml) dried
   rosemary leaves, crushed
1 cup (250 ml) walnut halves
3 small ripe tomatoes
6 radishes, thinly sliced
12 California ripe olives, sliced
   Crisp salad greens
   Rosemary sprigs and radish
   slices for garnish

1. Combine oil, lemon juice, sugar and salad dressing mix in glass jar with tightly fitting lid. Cover; shake until dressing is well blended.

2. Pour dressing into large bowl. Add chicken, turning to coat with dressing. Stir in parsley and green onion. Cover; marinate in refrigerator at least 1 hour or overnight.

3. Remove feta from package; drain. Place feta in small bowl; cover with cold water and soak 5 minutes to remove excess salt.

4. Meanwhile, melt margarine with ½ teaspoon (2 ml) rosemary in small, heavy skillet over low heat. Add walnuts; cook 5 minutes or until walnuts are lightly toasted, stirring occasionally. Remove skillet from heat; cool walnuts.

5. Remove feta from water; pat dry. Discard water. Using fingers, crumble feta into small chunks. Return feta to bowl; set aside.

6. To prepare tomato, with paring knife, make circular cut around stem end using sawing motion. Remove stem end. Cut each stemmed tomato lengthwise into halves on cutting board; cut each half lengthwise into three or four wedges.

7. To serve, stir feta, walnuts, radishes and olives into chicken mixture; toss until well mixed. Arrange chicken mixture and tomatoes on salad-green-lined plates. Garnish, if desired.

Makes 6 servings

Step 4. Toasting walnuts.

Step 5. Crumbling feta.

Step 6. Removing stem from tomato.

Apple Curry Chicken

2 whole chicken breasts, split, skinned and boned (technique on pages 152-153)
1 cup (250 ml) apple juice, divided
¼ teaspoon (1 ml) salt
Dash of pepper
1 medium apple
1 medium onion
1½ cups (375 ml) plain croutons
¼ cup (62.5 ml) raisins
2 teaspoons (10 ml) brown sugar
1 teaspoon (5 ml) curry powder
¾ teaspoon (3.75 ml) poultry seasoning
⅛ teaspoon (0.5 ml) garlic powder
2 apple slices and fresh thyme sprigs for garnish

1. Preheat oven to 350°F (180°C). Lightly grease 1 quart (1 L) round baking dish.

2. Arrange chicken breasts in single layer in prepared dish.

3. Combine ¼ cup (62.5 ml) apple juice, salt and pepper in small bowl. Brush all of juice mixture over chicken.

4. To prepare apple, cut lengthwise into quarters on cutting board; remove stem, core and seeds with paring knife. Chop apple quarters into ½-inch (1.25 cm) pieces; place in large bowl.

5. To prepare onion, peel skin from onion; cut in half through the root. Place, cut side down, on cutting board. To coarsely chop onion, hold knife horizontally. Make cuts parallel to board, almost to root end. Next, make vertical, lengthwise cuts, then slice across cuts to root end. (The closer the cuts are spaced, the finer the onion is chopped.) Toss chopped onion with apples in bowl.

6. Stir croutons, raisins, brown sugar, curry, poultry seasoning and garlic powder into apple-onion mixture. Toss with remaining ¾ cup (187 ml) apple juice.

7. Spread crouton mixture over chicken.

8. Cover with foil or lid; bake 45 minutes or until chicken is tender. Garnish, if desired.

Makes 4 servings

Step 3. Brushing chicken with juice mixture.

Step 4. Removing stem, core and seeds from apple.

Step 7. Spreading crouton mixture over chicken.

Forty-Clove Chicken Filice

1 (3-pound/1.35 kg) frying
    chicken, cut into serving
    pieces (technique on pages
    150-151)
40 cloves garlic (about 2 heads*)
1 lemon
½ cup (125 ml) dry white wine
¼ cup (62.5 ml) dry vermouth
¼ cup (62.5 ml) olive oil
4 ribs celery, thickly sliced
2 tablespoons (30 ml) finely
    chopped parsley
2 teaspoons (10 ml) dried basil
    leaves, crushed
1 teaspoon (5 ml) dried oregano
    leaves, crushed
    Pinch of crushed red pepper
    flakes
    Salt and black pepper to taste

*The whole garlic bulb is called a
head.

1. Preheat oven to 375°F (190°C). Place chicken, skin side up, in single layer in shallow baking pan; set aside.

2. To peel whole heads of garlic, drop garlic heads into enough boiling water in small saucepan to cover for 5 to 10 seconds. Immediately remove garlic with slotted spoon. Plunge garlic into cold water; drain. Peel away skins; set aside.

3. To prepare lemon, hold lemon in one hand. With other hand, remove colored portion of peel with citrus zester or vegetable peeler into small bowl.

4. To juice lemon, cut lemon in half on cutting board; with tip of knife, remove visible seeds.

5. Using citrus reamer or squeezing tightly with hand, squeeze juice from lemon into small glass or dish; remove any remaining seeds from juice.

6. Combine garlic, wine, vermouth, oil, celery, parsley, basil, oregano and red pepper flakes in medium bowl; mix thoroughly. Sprinkle garlic mixture over chicken. Place zest over and around chicken in pan; pour lemon juice over top of chicken. Season with salt and black pepper.

7. Cover pan with foil. Bake 40 minutes.

8. Remove foil; bake 15 minutes or until chicken is tender and juices run clear. Garnish as desired.

Makes 4 to 6 servings

Step 2. Placing whole head of garlic into boiling water.

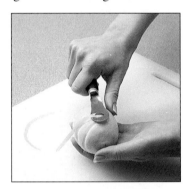
Step 3. Removing peel from lemon.

Step 5. Squeezing juice from lemon.

Olympic Seoul Chicken

2 tablespoons (30 ml) peanut oil
8 chicken thighs, skinned
    (technique on page 150)
10 cloves garlic
¼ cup (62.5 ml) white vinegar
3 tablespoons (45 ml) soy sauce
2 tablespoons (30 ml) honey
¼ teaspoon (1 ml) ground ginger
½ to 1 teaspoon (2 to 5 ml)
    crushed red pepper flakes
2 ounces (55 g) Chinese rice
    stick noodles
    Snow peas, steamed
    Diagonally sliced yellow
    squash, steamed

1. Heat oil in large skillet over medium-high heat. Add chicken to skillet in single layer. Cook 10 minutes or until chicken is evenly browned and no longer pink in center, turning once.

2. Meanwhile, to prepare garlic, trim ends of cloves on cutting board. Slightly crush garlic under flat side of knife blade; peel away skins.

Step 2. Crushing garlic.

3. Arrange garlic together in small pile; chop coarsely.

4. Combine vinegar, soy sauce, honey and ginger in small bowl; set aside.

Step 3. Chopped garlic.

5. When chicken is browned, add garlic and red pepper flakes to skillet; cook and stir 2 to 3 minutes.

6. Spoon off excess fat from skillet. Add vinegar mixture. Cover; reduce heat and simmer 15 minutes or until chicken is tender and juices run clear.

7. Meanwhile, to prepare rice stick noodles, cut noodle bunches in half; gently pull each half apart into smaller bunches. Heat 3 inches (7.5 cm) oil in wok or large skillet over medium-high heat until deep-fry thermometer registers 375°F (190°C). Using tongs or slotted spoon, lower 1 bunch of noodles into hot oil. Cook until noodles rise to the top, 3 to 5 seconds. Remove noodles immediately to paper towels using slotted spoon; drain. Repeat with remaining bunches; keep warm.

Step 7. Lowering noodles into hot oil.

8. Uncover skillet; cook chicken 2 minutes or until sauce is reduced and thickened. Place chicken on individual serving plates; spoon sauce over chicken. Serve with rice stick noodles, peas and squash. Garnish as desired.

Makes 4 servings

Chicken Picante

1 medium lime
½ cup (125 ml) medium-hot
    chunky taco sauce
¼ cup (62.5 ml) Dijon-style
    mustard
3 whole chicken breasts, split,
    skinned and boned
    (technique on pages
    152-153)
2 tablespoons (30 ml) butter
    Plain yogurt
    Chopped fresh cilantro and
    lime slices for garnish

1. To juice lime, cut lime in half on cutting board; with tip of knife, remove any visible seeds.

2. Using citrus reamer or squeezing tightly with hand, squeeze juice from lime into small glass or dish; remove any remaining seeds from juice.

3. Combine lime juice, taco sauce and mustard in large bowl. Add chicken, turning to coat with marinade. Cover; marinate in refrigerator at least 30 minutes.

4. Melt butter in large skillet over medium heat until foamy.

5. Drain chicken, reserving marinade. Add chicken to skillet in single layer. Cook 10 minutes or until chicken is lightly browned on both sides.

6. Add reserved marinade to skillet; cook 5 minutes or until chicken is tender and glazed with marinade.

7. Remove chicken to serving platter; keep warm.

8. Boil marinade in skillet over high heat 1 minute; pour over chicken. Serve with yogurt. Garnish, if desired.

Makes 6 servings

Step 1. Removing seeds from lime.

Step 2. Squeezing juice from lime.

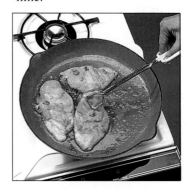

Step 5. Browning chicken.

Rick's Good-as-Gold Chili

½ cup (125 ml) vegetable oil
2 whole chicken breasts, split, skinned and boned (technique on pages 152-153)
⅓ cup (83 ml) water
¼ cup (62.5 ml) instant minced onion
2 teaspoons (10 ml) instant minced garlic
1 can (15 ounces/420 g) tomato sauce
¾ cup (187 ml) beer
½ cup (125 ml) chicken broth
2 tablespoons (30 ml) chili powder
2 teaspoons (10 ml) ground cumin
1 teaspoon (5 ml) dried oregano leaves, crushed
1 teaspoon (5 ml) soy sauce
1 teaspoon (5 ml) Worcestershire sauce
¾ teaspoon (3.75 ml) salt
½ teaspoon (2 ml) paprika
½ teaspoon (2 ml) ground red pepper
¼ teaspoon (1 ml) ground turmeric
⅛ teaspoon (0.5 ml) rubbed sage
⅛ teaspoon (0.5 ml) dried thyme leaves, crushed
⅛ teaspoon (0.5 ml) dry mustard
   Jalapeño pepper slices for garnish

l. Heat oil in large skillet over medium-high heat. Add chicken to skillet in single layer. Cook 10 minutes or until chicken is golden brown and no longer pink in center, turning once.

2. Meanwhile, to soften instant onion and garlic, stir together water, onion and garlic in small bowl; let stand 10 minutes.

3. When chicken is browned, remove from skillet and drain on paper towels.

4. When chicken cools slightly, cut into ¼-inch (6 mm) cubes on cutting board; set aside.

5. Drain drippings from skillet, reserving 2 tablespoons (30 ml). Heat reserved drippings in skillet over medium-high heat. Add softened instant onion and garlic; cook and stir 5 minutes or until onion and garlic are golden.

6. Add cubed chicken and remaining ingredients except jalapeños; stir well. Bring chili to a boil; reduce heat and simmer 20 minutes, stirring occasionally, until chili thickens slightly. Garnish, if desired.

Makes 4½ cups (1.125 L)

Step 2. Softened instant onion and garlic.

Step 5. Reserving 2 tablespoons (30 ml) drippings.

Fresh Gazpacho Chicken

¼ cup (62.5 ml) all-purpose flour
1½ teaspoons (17 ml) salt, divided
½ teaspoon (2 ml) paprika
¼ teaspoon (1 ml) black pepper, divided
2 whole chicken breasts, split (technique on page 151)
¼ cup (62.5 ml) vegetable oil
1 medium tomato, seeded and chopped
1 medium onion, chopped (technique on page 182)
1 medium green bell pepper, chopped
1 small cucumber
2 cloves garlic, minced (technique on page 184)
2½ cups (625 ml) tomato juice
½ cup (125 ml) finely chopped carrots
½ cup (125 ml) finely chopped celery
½ cup (125 ml) red wine vinegar
¼ cup (62.5 ml) olive oil
5 teaspoons (25 ml) Worcestershire sauce
5 dashes hot pepper sauce
Hot cooked rice

1. Combine flour, 1 teaspoon (5 ml) salt, paprika and ⅛ teaspoon (0.5 ml) black pepper in shallow dish. Coat chicken, one piece at a time, in flour mixture, shaking off excess.

2. Heat vegetable oil in large skillet over medium heat; add chicken to skillet in single layer. Cook 10 minutes or until chicken is lightly browned on both sides.

3. Remove chicken to paper-towel-lined baking sheets, using tongs or slotted spoon; keep warm in preheated 200°F (128°C) oven.

4. Drain oil from skillet.

5. Place tomato, onion and bell pepper in large bowl; set aside.

6. To prepare cucumber, carefully peel skin from cucumber with paring knife. Cut peeled cucumber in half lengthwise on cutting board; remove seeds. Chop cucumber; place in bowl with tomato mixture and set aside.

7. Stir garlic, tomato juice, carrots, celery, vinegar, olive oil, Worcestershire sauce, pepper sauce, remaining ½ teaspoon (2 ml) salt and ⅛ teaspoon (0.5 ml) black pepper into vegetables.

8. Reserve 1 cup (250 ml) tomato mixture; cover and refrigerate.

9. Return chicken to skillet. Pour remaining tomato mixture over chicken. Cover; cook over medium heat, turning occasionally, 30 minutes or until tender.

10. Arrange chicken on serving platter; spoon sauce over chicken. Serve with chilled tomato mixture and rice. Garnish, if desired.

Makes 4 servings

Step 3. Transferring chicken to prepared baking sheets.

Step 6. Peeling cucumber.

Chicken Avocado Boats

3 large ripe avocados
6 tablespoons (90 ml) lemon juice
¾ cup (187 ml) mayonnaise
1½ tablespoons (22.5 ml) grated onion
¼ teaspoon (1 ml) celery salt
¼ teaspoon (1 ml) garlic powder
Salt and pepper to taste
2 cups (500 ml) diced cooked chicken
½ cup/125 ml (2 ounces/57 g) shredded sharp Cheddar cheese
Snipped chives for garnish

1. To prepare avocados, on cutting board, insert knife into stem end of each avocado; slice in half lengthwise to the pit turning avocado while slicing.

2. Remove knife blade; twist both halves to pull apart.

3. Press knife blade into pit; twist knife to pull pit from avocado. Sprinkle each avocado half with 1 tablespoon (15 ml) lemon juice; set aside.

4. Preheat oven to 350°F (180°C).

5. Combine mayonnaise, onion, celery salt, garlic powder, salt and pepper in medium bowl. Stir in chicken; mix well.

6. Drain any excess lemon juice from avocado halves.

7. Fill avocado halves with chicken mixture; sprinkle with cheese.

8. Arrange filled avocado halves in single layer in baking dish. Pour water into same dish to depth of ½ inch (1.25 cm).

9. Bake filled avocado halves 15 minutes or until cheese melts. Garnish, if desired.

Makes 6 servings

Step 1. Slicing avocado in half.

Step 2. Twisting avocado halves apart.

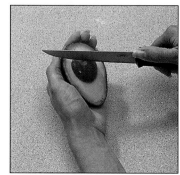

Step 3. Removing pit from avocado.

Calorie-Wise Dill Chicken

Nonstick cooking spray
1 cup (250 ml) plain yogurt
½ cup (125 ml) almonds
1½ cups (375 ml) natural wheat germ
2 teaspoons (10 ml) dried dill weed, crushed
½ teaspoon (2 ml) salt
¼ teaspoon (1 ml) pepper
12 chicken drumsticks

1. Preheat oven to 350°F (180°C).

2. Line baking sheet with foil; spray foil with nonstick cooking spray. Set aside.

3. Place yogurt in shallow bowl.

4. Process almonds in small batches with on/off pulses in food processor until almost all the almonds are a fine powder. Place ground almonds in shallow dish; set aside.

5. Combine wheat germ, almonds, dill weed, salt and pepper in another shallow bowl.

6. Coat drumsticks, one at a time, in yogurt, shaking off excess.

7. Coat drumsticks in wheat germ mixture, shaking off excess.

8. Arrange chicken in single layer on prepared baking sheet.

9. Bake 50 minutes or until chicken is tender and juices run clear. Garnish as desired.

Makes 4 servings

Step 2. Preparing baking sheet.

Step 6. Coating drumsticks in yogurt.

Step 7. Coating drumsticks in wheat germ mixture.

Bittersweet Farm Chicken

½ cup (125 ml) all-purpose flour
1 teaspoon (5 ml) salt
¼ teaspoon (1 ml) pepper
1 (3½- to 4-pound/1.57 to 1.8 kg) frying chicken, cut into serving pieces (technique on pages 150-151)
8 tablespoons (120 ml) butter or margarine, divided
1 orange
¼ cup (62.5 ml) lemon juice
¼ cup (62.5 ml) orange-flavored liqueur
¼ cup (62.5 ml) honey
1 tablespoon (15 ml) soy sauce
Whole cooked baby carrots
Kumquat slices and lettuce leaves for garnish

1. Preheat oven to 350°F (180°C).

2. Combine flour, salt and pepper in large resealable plastic bag.

3. Add chicken to bag; shake to coat completely with flour mixture, shaking off excess.

4. Melt 4 tablespoons (60 ml) butter in large baking pan in oven.

5. Remove pan from oven; roll chicken in butter to evenly coat. Arrange chicken, skin side down, in single layer in pan. Bake chicken 30 minutes.

6. Meanwhile, melt remaining 4 tablespoons (60 ml) butter in small saucepan over medium heat.

7. To prepare orange, hold orange in one hand. With other hand, remove colored portion of peel with zester or vegetable peeler into small bowl.

8. Stir orange zest, lemon juice, liqueur, honey and soy sauce into melted butter in saucepan; reserve 2 tablespoons (30 ml) honey mixture.

9. Remove chicken from oven; turn pieces over with tongs.

10. Pour remaining honey mixture over chicken. Continue baking, basting occasionally with pan drippings, 30 minutes or until chicken is glazed and tender.

11. Toss reserved 2 tablespoons (30 ml) honey mixture with desired amount of carrots; serve with chicken. Garnish, if desired.

Makes 4 servings

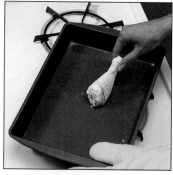

Step 5. Rolling chicken in melted butter.

Step 7. Removing peel from orange.

Step 9. Turning chicken.

Laguna Beach Pecan Chicken Breasts

6 tablespoons (90 ml) unsalted
    butter
¼ cup (62.5 ml) plus 2
    tablespoons (30 ml) Dijon-
    style mustard, divided
2 cups (500 ml) pecan halves
4 whole chicken breasts, split,
    skinned and boned
    (technique on pages
    152-153)
    Pepper to taste
1½ to 2 cups (375 to 500 ml) plain
    yogurt
1 cup (250 ml) California sliced
    pitted ripe olives
1 package (1 ounce/28 g)
    Hidden Valley Ranch®
    Original Ranch® Salad
    Dressing Mix
    Fresh green beans and
    pattypan squash, steamed
    Mint sprig for garnish

1. Preheat oven to 400°F (200°C).

2. Melt butter in small saucepan over low heat; remove from heat.

3. Whisk in ¼ cup (62.5 ml) mustard; set aside.

4. To grind pecans, process pecan halves in small batches with on/off pulses in food processor to fine powder. Place ground pecans in shallow dish; set aside.

5. Flatten chicken breasts to ¼-inch (6 mm) thickness. (Technique on page 150.) Sprinkle chicken with pepper.

6. Dip chicken into mustard mixture, then roll in ground pecans to coat, shaking off excess.

7. Arrange chicken in single layer in lightly greased baking pan. Bake 15 minutes or until chicken is golden and tender.

8. Meanwhile, thoroughly combine yogurt, olives, salad dressing mix and remaining 2 tablespoons (30 ml) mustard in medium saucepan; set aside.

9. When chicken is done, remove from pan and set aside. Stir drippings from pan into yogurt mixture in saucepan. Simmer mixture over low heat 2 minutes.

10. Place 2 tablespoons (30 ml) yogurt sauce on each serving plate. Top sauce with one chicken breast; top chicken with spoonful of sauce. Serve with steamed vegetables and remaining sauce. Garnish, if desired.

Makes 8 servings

Step 4. Ground pecans.

Step 9. Stirring drippings into yogurt mixture.

Curried Chicken Rolls

½ medium onion
1 tablespoon (15 ml) butter or
  margarine
¾ cup (187 ml) hot cooked rice
¼ cup (62.5 ml) raisins
1 tablespoon (15 ml) chopped
  fresh parsley
1 teaspoon (5 ml) curry powder
1 teaspoon (5 ml) brown sugar
½ teaspoon (2 ml) poultry
  seasoning
  Pinch of garlic powder
2 whole chicken breasts, split,
  skinned and boned
  (technique on pages
  152-153)
½ teaspoon (2 ml) salt
⅛ teaspoon (0.5 ml) pepper
1 tablespoon (15 ml) vegetable
  oil
½ cup (125 ml) dry white wine
1 teaspoon (5 ml) instant
  chicken bouillon granules
  Apple quarters, orange slices
  and parsley sprigs for
  garnish

1. To prepare onion, peel skin from onion; cut in half through the root. Reserve one half for another use. Place other half, cut side down, on cutting board. To coarsely chop onion, hold knife horizontally. Make cuts parallel to board, almost to root end. Next, make vertical, lengthwise cuts, then slice across cuts to root end. (The closer the cuts are spaced, the finer the onion is chopped.)

2. Melt butter in large skillet over medium heat until foamy. Add onion; cook and stir about 3 minutes or until onion is soft. Remove from heat.

3. Stir rice, raisins, parsley, curry, brown sugar, poultry seasoning and garlic powder into skillet; mix well and set aside.

4. Flatten chicken breasts to ⅜-inch (9 mm) thickness. (Technique on page 150.) Sprinkle with salt and pepper.

5. Divide rice mixture evenly among chicken breasts; spread to within 1 inch (2.5 cm) of edges.

6. Roll up each chicken breast from short end, jelly-roll style; secure with wooden toothpicks, making sure filling is entirely enclosed.

7. Heat oil in large skillet over medium heat; add chicken rolls to skillet in single layer. Cook 15 minutes or until rolls are brown on all sides. Add wine and bouillon to skillet; carefully stir until granules are dissolved. Cover; simmer 30 minutes or until chicken is tender. Garnish, if desired.

Makes 4 servings

Serving Suggestion: Additional rice stuffing may be prepared and served alongside the chicken rolls. Bake in covered casserole at 350°F (180°C) until heated through.

Step 1. Chopping onion.

Step 5. Spreading rice mixture on chicken breasts.

Step 6. Rolling up filled chicken breast.

Coconut Chicken with Fresh Chutney

1 can (15 ounces/420 g) cream
    of coconut, divided
2 tablespoons (30 ml) soy sauce
2 whole chicken breasts, split
    (technique on page 151) *or*
    8 chicken thighs
½ lemon
1 small piece fresh ginger
    (1 x ¾ inch/2.5 x 1.87 cm)
1 clove garlic
3 cups (750 ml) chopped
    nectarines or apples
½ cup (125 ml) raisins
⅓ cup (83 ml) packed light
    brown sugar
¼ cup (62.5 ml) cider vinegar
½ teaspoon (2 ml) curry powder
¼ cup (62.5 ml) flaked coconut

1. To prepare coconut marinade, combine ¾ cup (187 ml) cream of coconut and soy sauce in small bowl.

2. Arrange chicken in single layer in 12 x 7-inch (30 x 17.5 cm) glass baking dish. Pour coconut marinade over chicken, turning chicken to coat with marinade. Cover; marinate in refrigerator overnight.

3. Meanwhile, to prepare chutney mixture, with tip of knife, remove any visible seeds from lemon half.

4. Chop lemon to measure ¼ cup (62.5 ml); set aside.

5. Peel ginger; chop until minced.

6. To prepare garlic, trim ends of clove on cutting board. Slightly crush garlic under flat side of knife blade; peel away skin. Chop garlic until minced.

7. Combine lemon, ginger, garlic, nectarines, raisins, brown sugar, vinegar and curry in medium saucepan; mix well. Bring to a boil; boil 2 minutes, stirring occasionally. Cool chutney mixture.

8. Add flaked coconut and remaining cream of coconut; mix well. Cover chutney mixture; refrigerate overnight to allow flavors to blend.

9. Preheat oven to 350°F (180°C). Bake chicken in dish with coconut marinade 45 minutes to 1 hour or until chicken is tender, basting frequently with coconut marinade.

10. Place chicken on individual serving plates. Spoon equal amounts of the chutney mixture alongside chicken. Garnish as desired.

Makes 4 servings

Step 3. Removing seeds from lemon half.

Step 4. Chopping lemon.

Step 6. Minced garlic.

Pollo alla Firènze

2 cups (500 ml) *plus* 2 tablespoons (30 ml) dry sherry, divided
3 whole chicken breasts, split and boned (technique on pages 152-153)
2 cloves garlic
3 tablespoons (45 ml) olive oil
3 cups (750 ml) fresh spinach leaves, washed and shredded
2 cups (500 ml) coarsely chopped mushrooms
1 cup (250 ml) grated carrots
⅓ cup (83 ml) sliced green onions
Salt and pepper to taste
1½ cups (375 ml) prepared Italian salad dressing
1 cup (250 ml) Italian seasoned dry bread crumbs
⅓ cup (83 ml) grated Romano cheese
Steamed fresh asparagus
Parsley sprigs and carrot strips for garnish

1. Pour 2 cups (500 ml) sherry into large, shallow dish. Add chicken, turning to coat. Cover; marinate in refrigerator 3 hours.

2. Chop garlic until minced. (Technique on page 184.) Heat oil in large skillet over medium heat. Add garlic, spinach, mushrooms, grated carrots, green onions, salt, pepper and remaining 2 tablespoons (30 ml) sherry. Cook and stir 3 to 5 minutes or until spinach is completely wilted; cool spinach mixture.

3. Place dressing in another shallow dish; set aside. Combine bread crumbs with Romano cheese in shallow dish; set aside. Preheat oven to 375°F (190°C).

4. Remove chicken from marinade; discard marinade. Slice a pocket into side of each chicken breast where breasts were originally attached.

5. Fill pockets in chicken with spinach mixture.

6. Secure pockets with wooden toothpicks to enclose mixture.

7. Coat each filled chicken breast with dressing, shaking off excess. Place each chicken breast in bread crumb mixture; spoon bread crumb mixture over chicken to coat.

8. Place chicken in single layer in greased 13 x 9-inch (32.5 x 22.5 cm) baking pan. Drizzle with remaining dressing. Cover; bake 15 minutes. Uncover; bake 10 minutes or until chicken is tender. Serve with asparagus. Garnish, if desired.

Makes 6 servings

Step 4. Slicing pocket into chicken breast.

Step 5. Filling pocket with spinach mixture.

Step 6. Enclosing filling with toothpicks.

Elegant Entrées • CHICKEN

Chicken with Fruit and Mixed Mustards

½ cup (125 ml) Dijon-style
    mustard
½ cup (125 ml) Bavarian or
    other German mustard
1 tablespoon (15 ml) Chinese
    mustard
⅓ cup (83 ml) honey
⅓ cup (83 ml) light cream
2 whole chicken breasts, split,
    skinned and boned
    (technique on pages
    152-153)
½ teaspoon (2 ml) salt
¼ teaspoon (1 ml) pepper
2 tablespoons (30 ml) butter
1 honeydew melon
1 cantaloupe
4 kiwifruit
¼ cup (62.5 ml) mayonnaise
    Mint sprigs for garnish

1. Combine mustards, honey and cream in medium bowl. Spoon half of the mustard sauce into large glass bowl. Reserve remainder in medium bowl.

2. Sprinkle chicken with salt and pepper; add to large glass bowl with mustard marinade, turning to coat with mustard marinade. Cover; marinate in refrigerator 30 minutes.

3. Heat butter in large skillet over medium heat until foamy. Remove chicken from mustard marinade, shaking off excess; discard mustard marinade. Add chicken to skillet in single layer. Cook 10 minutes or until chicken is brown and no longer pink in center, turning once.

5. To prepare melon balls, cut melons crosswise in half on cutting board. Remove seeds with spoon; discard. Make melon balls by scooping out equal amounts of melon flesh from each melon to total 2 cups (500 ml) using melon baller or half-teaspoon measuring spoon. To prepare kiwifruit, remove peel from kiwifruit with vegetable peeler or paring knife. Cut kiwifruit into thin slices; set aside.

6. Arrange chicken, melon balls and kiwifruit on serving platter; set aside.

7. Place reserved mustard sauce in small saucepan. Whisk in mayonnaise. Heat thoroughly over medium heat.

8. Drizzle some mustard sauce over chicken. Garnish, if desired. Pass remaining sauce.

Makes 4 servings

Step 2. Coating chicken with mustard sauce marinade.

Step 4. Cutting chicken into thin slices.

Step 5. Scooping out melon balls.

Chicken Breasts Sautéed with Sun-Dried Tomatoes

Nonstick cooking spray
8 to 10 pieces sun-dried
   tomatoes
1 egg, beaten
1 container (15 ounces/420 g)
   Polly-O® ricotta cheese
1 package (4 ounces/112 g)
   Polly-O® shredded
   mozzarella cheese
   (1 cup/125 ml)
⅓ cup (83 ml) Polly-O® grated
   Parmesan or Romano
   cheese
2 tablespoons (30 ml) chopped
   fresh parsley
½ teaspoon (2 ml) garlic powder
¼ teaspoon (1 ml) pepper
4 whole chicken breasts, split,
   skinned and boned
   (technique on pages
   152-153)
2 tablespoons (30 ml) pine nuts
2 tablespoons (30 ml) currants
⅓ cup (83 ml) butter
⅔ cup (167 ml) sliced shallots
1 cup (250 ml) chicken broth
½ cup (125 ml) dry white wine
   Sliced plum tomatoes, fresh
      thyme sprigs and additional
      pine nuts for garnish

1. To chop tomatoes, spray blade of chef's knife with nonstick cooking spray. Arrange tomatoes in single layer on cutting board; chop enough tomatoes to measure ⅓ cup (83 ml), spraying knife blade with nonstick cooking spray as needed to prevent sticking. Slice remaining tomatoes into strips; reserve and set aside.

2. Combine chopped tomatoes, egg, cheeses, parsley, garlic powder and pepper in medium bowl. Stir to mix well; set aside.

3. Flatten chicken breasts to ¼-inch (6 mm) thickness. (Technique on page 150.) Set aside.

4. Divide cheese mixture evenly among chicken breasts; spread to within 1 inch (2.5 cm) of edges. Sprinkle pine nuts and currants over cheese mixture.

5. Roll up chicken from short end, jelly-roll style; enclose filling and secure with wooden toothpicks.

6. Melt butter in large skillet over medium-high heat until foamy. Add chicken to skillet; cook until golden on all sides. Remove chicken; set aside.

7. Add shallots and reserved tomato strips to drippings in skillet; cook over low heat 2 minutes. Add broth and wine; cook 3 minutes.

8. Return chicken to skillet. Cover; simmer 15 to 20 minutes or until tender, turning once and basting often with sauce. Place chicken on platter; pour sauce over chicken. Garnish, if desired.

Makes 8 servings

Step 1. Chopping tomatoes.

Step 5. Rolling up filled chicken breast.

Stuffed Chicken with Apple Glaze

1 (3½- to 4-pound/1.57 to 1.8
  kg) whole frying chicken
½ teaspoon (2 ml) salt
¼ teaspoon (1 ml) pepper
2 tablespoons (30 ml) vegetable
  oil
1 package (6 ounces/168 g)
  chicken-flavored stuffing
  mix *plus* ingredients to
  prepare mix
1 large apple
½ teaspoon (2 ml) grated lemon
  peel
¼ cup (62.5 ml) chopped
  walnuts
¼ cup (62.5 ml) raisins
¼ cup (62.5 ml) thinly sliced
  celery
½ cup (125 ml) apple jelly
1 tablespoon (15 ml) lemon
  juice
½ teaspoon (2 ml) ground
  cinnamon
  Celery leaves and lemon peel
  twists for garnish

1. Preheat oven to 350°F (180°C).

2. Rinse chicken under cold running water; pat dry with paper towels. Sprinkle inside of chicken with salt and pepper; rub outside with oil.

3. Prepare stuffing mix according to package directions in large bowl.

4. To prepare apple, cut lengthwise into quarters on cutting board; remove stem, core and seeds with paring knife. Chop apple quarters into ½-inch (1.25 cm) pieces.

5. Add apple, lemon peel, walnuts, raisins and celery to prepared stuffing; mix thoroughly.

6. Stuff body cavity loosely with stuffing.

7. Place chicken in shallow baking pan. Cover loosely with foil; roast chicken 1 hour.

8. Combine jelly, lemon juice and cinnamon in small saucepan. Simmer over low heat 3 minutes, stirring often, until jelly dissolves and mixture is well blended.

9. Remove foil from chicken; brush with jelly glaze.

10. Roast chicken, uncovered, brushing frequently with jelly glaze, 30 minutes or until meat thermometer inserted into thickest part of thigh, not touching bone, registers 185°F (118°C). Let chicken stand 15 minutes before carving. Garnish, if desired.

Makes 4 servings

Step 4. Removing stem, core and seeds from apple.

Step 6. Stuffing chicken.

Step 9. Brushing chicken with jelly glaze.

COOKING CLASS
CHINESE

196   CLASS NOTES

198   APPETIZERS & SOUPS

212   ENTRÉES

230   SIDE DISHES

Two-Onion Pork Shreds *(page 216)*

CLASS NOTES

TECHNIQUES FOR CHINESE COOKING

Preparing tasty and attractive Chinese dishes can be a rewarding experience that is easy to accomplish. There are just a few rules to keep in mind for successfully cooking most recipes: 1) Preparation and cooking are two separate procedures. 2) All ingredients should be prepared *before* any cooking is begun. 3) Paying attention to the cooking process is crucial because many of the foods are cooked over intense heat in a matter of minutes.

The Chinese have perfected a variety of cooking techniques, including stir-frying, deep-frying, braising, stewing, steaming, roasting, barbecuing and preserving. All of these techniques are probably familiar to you. But in order to stir-fry correctly, an understanding of its basic principles is necessary.

Stir-frying—a rapid-cooking method invented by the Chinese— is the brisk cooking of small pieces of ingredients in hot oil over intense heat for a short time, usually just for a few minutes. During cooking, the ingredients must be kept in constant motion by stirring or tossing vigorously. Once cooking is completed, the food should be removed immediately from the heat.

When stir-frying, all of the ingredients must be well organized and prepared *before the cooking is started*. They should be measured or weighed, cleaned, chopped, sliced, combined or the like. Meat, poultry, fish and vegetables should be cut into pieces of approximately the same size for even cooking. Otherwise, one ingredient may be overcooked while others remain undercooked. The stir-frying is accomplished so quickly that there is usually not time to complete any preparation steps once cooking is begun.

The intensity of the heat used for stir-frying is important. In most cases, easily controlled high heat is needed. For this reason, a gas range with its ability for instant heat control is generally more efficient for stir-frying than is an electric range.

The kind of oil used is also crucial. A vegetable oil that can be heated to a high temperature without smoking is essential. Peanut oil, corn oil, cottonseed oil and soybean oil all work well. Other kinds of fats, such as olive oil, sesame oil, butter or lard cannot be used because they have low burning points.

Due to the variables involved in stir-frying, such as kinds of foods, type of heat and the kind of cooking equipment used, cooking times given in this publication should be used as guidelines—not as absolutes. Most of the recipes, for example, were tested on a gas range. Cooking times needed when using a wok on an electric range, or when using an electric wok, may vary somewhat.

INGREDIENTS IN CHINESE CUISINE

When preparing Chinese foods, you will come across many ingredients that are familiar. You will also encounter some that may be unfamiliar such as bean threads, oyster sauce or Chinese five-spice powder. Some of the items— seasonings in particular—may be available only in Chinese food markets. Before you search for an out-of-the-way specialty store, however, check your local supermarket. Many supermarkets now stock good inventories of Chinese ingredients. In addition to canned, bottled or packaged goods, many carry fresh items such as Chinese cabbage (napa or bok choy), bean sprouts, wonton and egg-roll wrappers, bean curd and Chinese-style thin egg noodles. A check of the frozen-food cases will yield additional Chinese items.

The glossary that follows describes many of the Chinese foods used in the recipes in this publication.

GLOSSARY OF CHINESE INGREDIENTS

Bamboo shoots: tender, ivory-colored shoots of tropical bamboo plants, used separately as a vegetable and to add crispness and a slight sweetness to dishes. They are available in cans—whole or sliced— and should be rinsed with water before using.

Bean curd (also called tofu): puréed soybeans pressed to form a white custard-like cake, used as a vegetable and as an excellent source of protein. Bean curd can be used in all kinds of recipes because it readily absorbs the flavor of other foods. Bean curd is available fresh or in cans. If fresh, cover with water and store in refrigerator until ready to use.

Bean sauce (also called yellow bean sauce or brown bean sauce): a Chinese seasoning made from soybeans, flour, vinegar, salt and hot chilies.

Bean sprouts: small white shoots of the pea-like mung bean plant, used separately as a vegetable and included in a wide variety of dishes. They are available fresh or in cans. Canned sprouts should be rinsed before use to eliminate any metallic taste. Fresh or opened, unused canned sprouts should be covered with water and stored in the refrigerator.

Bean threads (also called Chinese rice vermicelli, transparent or cellophane noodles): dry, hard, white, fine noodles made from powdered mung beans. They have little flavor of their own, but readily absorb the flavors of other foods. Bean threads can be used in numerous steamed, simmered, deep-fried or stir-fried dishes. They are available in packets or small bundles.

Cabbage, Chinese: there are two types of Chinese cabbages generally available in American markets. One is bok choy, which has white stalks and green, crinkled leaves. The other is napa cabbage, which has elongated tightly furled leaves with wide white ribs and soft pale green tips. Both varieties need very little

cooking and are often included in soups and stir-fried dishes.

Chili oil (also called chili pepper oil or hot pepper oil): reddish-colored, fiery hot oil made from peanut oil infused with dried red chili peppers. Use sparingly for flavoring. Store in cool, dark place.

Chili sauce, Chinese: a bright red, extremely spicy sauce made from crushed fresh chili peppers and salt. It is available in cans or bottles and should be used sparingly.

Chives, Chinese (also called garlic chives): thin, slender, flat green leaves give a distinctive garlic flavor to many Chinese dishes.

Egg noodles, Chinese-style: thin pasta usually made of flour, egg, water and salt. The noodles can be purchased fresh, frozen or dehydrated. They can be boiled, braised, stir-fried or deep-fried; the time and method of cooking vary with the type of noodle. Check the package for specific instructions.

Five-spice powder, Chinese: cocoa-colored, ready-mixed blend of five ground spices, usually anise seeds, fennel, clove, cinnamon and ginger or pepper. It has a slightly sweet, pungent flavor and should be used sparingly.

Ginger: (also called ginger root): a knobby, gnarled root, having a brown skin and whitish or light green interior. It has a fresh, pungent flavor and is used as a basic seasoning in many Chinese recipes. Ginger is available fresh or in cans. It will keep for weeks in the refrigerator wrapped in plastic, or for months if kept in salted water

or dry sherry. Always remove the outer brown skin from fresh ginger before using in any recipe.

Mushrooms, dried: dehydrated black or brown mushrooms from the Orient, having caps from 1 to 3 inches (2.5 to 7.5 cm) in diameter. They have a strong, distinctive flavor and are included in many different kinds of recipes. Chinese dried mushrooms must be soaked in hot water before using; they are usually thinly sliced prior to combining them with other foods. Dried mushrooms are available in cellophane packages.

Oyster sauce: a thick, brown, concentrated sauce made of ground oysters, soy sauce and brine. It imparts very little fish flavor and is used as a seasoning to intensify other flavors. Oyster sauce is included in a variety of recipes, especially in stir-fried Cantonese dishes.

Sesame oil: an amber-colored oil pressed from toasted sesame seeds. It has a strong, nutlike flavor and is best used sparingly. Sesame oil is generally used as a flavoring, not as a cooking oil, because of its low smoking point. It is available in bottles.

Szechuan (Sichuan) peppercorns: a reddish-brown pepper with a strong, pungent aroma and flavor with a time-delayed action—its potent flavor may not be noticed immediately. It should be used sparingly. It is usually sold whole or crushed in small packages.

Wonton wrappers: commercially prepared dough that is rolled thinly and cut into 3- to 4 inch (7.5 to 10 cm) squares. They are available fresh or frozen.

Shrimp Toast

12 large shrimp, shelled and
    deveined, leaving tails
    intact
1 raw egg
2½ tablespoons (37 ml)
    cornstarch
¼ teaspoon (1 ml) salt
    Dash of pepper
3 slices white sandwich bread,
    crusts removed and
    quartered
1 slice cooked ham, cut into
    ½-inch (1.25 cm) pieces
1 hard-cooked egg yolk, cut
    into ½-inch (1.25 cm)
    pieces
1 green onion with top, finely
    chopped
    Vegetable oil for frying
    Hard-cooked egg half and
    Green Onion Curls
    (page 206) for garnish

1. Cut deep slit down back of each shrimp; press gently with fingers to flatten.

2. Beat raw egg, cornstarch, salt and pepper in large bowl until blended. Add shrimp; toss to coat well.

3. Place 1 shrimp, cut-side down, on each bread piece; press shrimp gently into bread.

4. Brush small amount of egg mixture over each shrimp.

5. Place 1 piece *each* of ham and egg yolk and a scant ¼ teaspoon (1 ml) onion on top of each shrimp.

6. Heat about 2 inches (5 cm) oil in wok or large skillet over medium-high heat to 375°F (190°C). Add 3 or 4 bread pieces at a time; cook until golden, 1 to 2 minutes on each side. Drain on paper towels. Garnish, if desired.

Makes 1 dozen

Step 1. Flattening shrimp.

Step 4. Brushing egg mixture over shrimp.

Step 5. Placing egg yolk on shrimp.

Pot Stickers

2 cups (500 ml) all-purpose
    flour
¾ cup (187 ml) *plus* 2
    tablespoons (30 ml) boiling
    water
½ cup (125 ml) very finely
    chopped napa cabbage
8 ounces (225 g) lean ground
    pork
1 green onion with top, finely
    chopped
2 tablespoons (30 ml) finely
    chopped water chestnuts
1½ teaspoons (7 ml) soy sauce
1½ teaspoons (7 ml) dry sherry
1½ teaspoons (7 ml) cornstarch
½ teaspoon (2 ml) minced fresh
    ginger
½ teaspoon (2 ml) sesame oil
¼ teaspoon (1 ml) sugar
2 tablespoons (30 ml) vegetable
    oil, divided
⅔ cup (167 ml) chicken broth,
    divided
    Soy sauce, vinegar and chili oil

1. Place flour in large bowl; make well in center. Pour in boiling water; stir with wooden spoon until mixture forms dough.

2. Place dough on lightly floured surface; flatten slightly. To knead dough, fold dough in half toward you and press dough away from you with heel of hand. Give dough a quarter turn and continue folding, pushing and turning. Continue kneading 5 minutes or until smooth and elastic, adding additional flour to prevent sticking if necessary. Wrap dough in plastic wrap; let stand 30 minutes.

3. For filling, squeeze cabbage to remove as much moisture as possible; place in large bowl. Add pork, onion, water chestnuts, soy sauce, sherry, cornstarch, ginger, sesame oil and sugar; mix well.

4. Unwrap dough and knead briefly (as described in step 2) on lightly floured surface; divide into 2 equal pieces. Cover 1 piece with plastic wrap or clean towel while working with other piece.

5. Using lightly floured rolling pin, roll out dough to ⅛-inch (3 mm) thickness on lightly floured surface.

6. Cut out 3-inch (7.5 cm) circles with round cookie cutter or top of clean empty can.

7. Place 1 rounded teaspoon (5 ml) filling in center of each dough circle.

continued on page 202

Step 1. Stirring flour mixture to form dough.

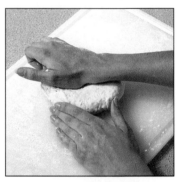

Step 2. Kneading dough.

Step 6. Cutting out dough circles.

Pot Stickers, *continued*

8. To shape each pot sticker, lightly moisten edge of 1 dough circle with water; fold in half.

9. Starting at 1 end, pinch curled edges together making 4 pleats along edge; set pot sticker down firmly, seam-side up. Cover finished pot stickers with plastic wrap while shaping remaining pot stickers.

10. Pot stickers may be cooked immediately or covered securely and stored in refrigerator up to 4 hours. Pot stickers may also be frozen. To freeze, place pot stickers on cookie sheet or shallow pan; place in freezer 30 minutes to firm slightly. Remove from freezer; place in freezer-weight resealable plastic bag. Freeze up to 3 months. (Frozen pot stickers do not need to be thawed before cooking.)

11. To cook pot stickers, heat 1 tablespoon (15 ml) vegetable oil in large nonstick skillet over medium heat. Place ½ of pot stickers in skillet, seam-side up. Cook until bottoms are golden brown, 5 to 6 minutes.

12. Pour in ⅓ cup (83 ml) chicken broth; cover tightly. Reduce heat to low. Simmer until all liquid is absorbed, about 10 minutes (15 minutes if frozen). Repeat with remaining vegetable oil, pot stickers and chicken broth.

13. Place pot stickers on serving platter. Serve with soy sauce, vinegar and chili oil for dipping.

Makes about 3 dozen

Step 8. Shaping pot stickers.

Step 9. Pleating pot stickers.

Step 11. Browning pot stickers.

Hors d'Oeuvre Rolls

Sweet and Sour Sauce
(page 204), optional
8 ounces (225 g) deveined
shelled shrimp
1 package (17¼ ounces/483 g)
frozen ready-to-bake puff
pastry sheets *or* 40 wonton
wrappers
½ cup (125 ml) egg noodles or
Chinese-style thin egg
noodles, broken into 1-inch
(2.5 cm) pieces
2 tablespoons (30 ml) butter or
margarine
4 ounces (112 g) boneless lean
pork, finely chopped
6 fresh medium mushrooms,
finely chopped
6 green onions with tops, finely
chopped
1 hard-cooked egg, finely
chopped
1½ tablespoons (7 ml) dry sherry
½ teaspoon (2 ml) salt
⅛ teaspoon (0.5 ml) pepper
1 egg, lightly beaten
Vegetable oil for frying
Vegetable bundle* for garnish

*To make vegetable bundle, cut 6- to
8 inch (15 to 20 cm) length off top of
green onion. Place in salted water; let
stand at least 15 minutes. Tie around
small bundle of fresh vegetables.

1. Prepare Sweet and Sour Sauce.

2. Place enough water to cover shrimp in
medium saucepan. Bring to a boil over
medium-high heat. Add shrimp. Reduce
heat to low. Simmer 5 to 10 minutes or
until shrimp curl and turn pink. (Do not
overcook shrimp as they will become
tough.) Drain and set aside to cool.

3. Remove puff pastry from freezer. Let
stand, uncovered, at room temperature
until ready to use, about 20 minutes.

4. Meanwhile, cook noodles according to
package directions just until tender but
still firm, 2 to 3 minutes. Drain and rinse
under cold running water; drain again.
Chop noodles finely.

5. Heat butter in wok or large skillet over
medium-high heat. Add pork; stir-fry until
no longer pink in center, about 5 minutes.

6. Add mushrooms and onions; stir-fry 2
minutes.

7. Remove wok from heat. Finely chop
shrimp. Add to wok with noodles, hard-
cooked egg, sherry, salt and pepper; mix
well.

8. If using puff pastry, gently unfold each
pastry sheet. If pastry is too soft, place it
in refrigerator for a few minutes to chill.
(For ease in handling, pastry should be
cold to the touch.) Place pastry on lightly
floured surface. With lightly floured
rolling pin, roll and trim each sheet to
15 x 12-inch (37.5 x 30 cm) rectangle; cut
into 20 (3-inch/7.5 cm) squares.

Step 4. Chopping noodles.

Step 5. Stir-frying pork.

Step 8. Cutting out dough
squares.

continued on page 204

Hors d'Oeuvre Rolls, *continued*

9. Spoon 1 tablespoon (15 ml) pork mixture across center of each pastry square or wonton wrapper.

10. Brush edges lightly with beaten egg. Roll up tightly around filling; pinch edges slightly to seal.

11. Heat oil in wok or large skillet to 375°F (190°C). Add 4 to 6 rolls at a time; cook until golden and crisp, 3 to 5 minutes. Drain on paper towels. Garnish, if desired. Serve with Sweet and Sour Sauce.

Makes 40 rolls

Sweet and Sour Sauce

4 teaspoons (20 ml) cornstarch
1 cup (250 ml) water
½ cup (125 ml) distilled white vinegar
½ cup (125 ml) sugar
¼ cup (62.5 ml) tomato paste

Combine all ingredients in small saucepan. Bring to a boil over medium heat, stirring constantly. Boil 1 minute, stirring constantly. Set aside until ready to use or cover and refrigerate up to 8 hours.

Step 9. Spooning filling onto dough.

Step 10. Rolling up dough.

Step 11. Cooking rolls.

Barbecued Pork

¼ cup (62.5 ml) soy sauce
2 tablespoons (30 ml) dry red
   wine
1 tablespoon (15 ml) packed
   brown sugar
1 tablespoon (15 ml) honey
2 teaspoons (10 ml) red food
   coloring (optional)
½ teaspoon (2 ml) ground
   cinnamon
1 green onion with top, cut in
   half
1 clove garlic, minced
2 whole pork tenderloins (about
   12 ounces/335 g *each*),
   trimmed
   Green Onion Curls (recipe
   follows) for garnish

1. Combine soy sauce, wine, sugar, honey, food coloring, cinnamon, onion and garlic in large bowl. Add meat; turn to coat completely. Cover and refrigerate 1 hour or overnight, turning meat over occasionally.

2. Preheat oven to 350°F (180°C). Drain meat, reserving marinade. Place meat on wire rack over baking pan. Bake 45 minutes or until no longer pink in center, turning and basting frequently with reserved marinade.

3. Remove meat from oven; cool. Cut into diagonal slices. Garnish with Green Onion Curls, if desired.

Makes about 8 appetizer servings

Green Onion Curls: Step 1.
Trimming onions.

Green Onion Curls: Step 2.
Cutting onion stems into strips.

Green Onion Curls

6 to 8 medium green onions with tops
Cold water
10 to 12 ice cubes

1. Trim bulbs (white part) from onions; reserve for another use. Trim remaining stems (green part) to 4-inch (10 cm) lengths.

2. Using sharp scissors, cut each section of green stems lengthwise into very thin strips down to beginning of stems, cutting 6 to 8 strips in each stem section.

3. Fill large bowl about ½ full with cold water. Add green onions and ice cubes. Refrigerate until onions curl, about 1 hour; drain.

Makes 6 to 8 curls

Green Onion Curls: Step 3.
Soaking onions.

Wonton Soup

½ cup (125 ml) finely chopped
    cabbage
8 ounces (225 g) ground pork
4 ounces (112 g) deveined
    shelled shrimp, finely
    chopped
3 green onions with tops, finely
    chopped
1 egg, lightly beaten
1½ tablespoons (22 ml)
    cornstarch
2 teaspoons (10 ml) soy sauce
2 teaspoons (10 ml) sesame oil,
    divided
1 teaspoon (5 ml) oyster sauce
48 wonton wrappers (about 1
    pound/450 g)
1 egg white, lightly beaten
¾ pound (337 g) bok choy *or*
    napa cabbage
6 cups (1.5 L) chicken broth
1 cup (250 ml) thinly sliced
    Barbecued Pork (page 206)
3 green onions with tops, thinly
    sliced
    Edible flowers for garnish

1. For filling, squeeze cabbage to remove as much moisture as possible. Place cabbage in large bowl. Add pork, shrimp, chopped onions, whole egg, cornstarch, soy sauce, 1½ teaspoons (7 ml) sesame oil and oyster sauce; mix well.

2. For wontons, work with about 12 wrappers at a time, keeping remaining wrappers covered with plastic wrap. Place 1 wonton wrapper on work surface with 1 point facing you. Place 1 teaspoon (5 ml) filling in bottom corner; fold bottom corner over filling.

3. Moisten side corners of wonton wrapper with egg white. Bring side corners together, overlapping slightly; pinch together firmly to seal. Cover finished wontons with plastic wrap while filling remaining wontons. (Cook immediately, refrigerate up to 8 hours or freeze in resealable plastic bag.)

4. Add wontons to large pot of boiling water; cook until filling is no longer pink, about 4 minutes (6 minutes if frozen); drain. Place in bowl of cold water to prevent wontons from sticking together.

5. Cut bok choy stems into 1-inch (2.5 cm) slices; cut leaves in half crosswise. Set aside.

6. Bring chicken broth to a boil in large saucepan. Add bok choy and remaining ½ teaspoon (2 ml) sesame oil; simmer 2 minutes. Drain wontons; add to hot broth. Add slices of Barbecued Pork and sliced onions. Ladle into soup bowls. Serve immediately. Garnish, if desired.

Makes 6 servings

Step 2. Folding wonton
wrapper over filling.

Step 3. Shaping wontons.

Long Soup

¼ **of small head of cabbage
(4 to 6 ounces/112 to 168 g)**
1½ **tablespoons (22 ml) vegetable
oil**
8 **ounces (225 g) boneless lean
pork, cut into thin strips**
6 **cups (1.5 L) chicken broth**
2 **tablespoons (30 ml) soy sauce**
½ **teaspoon (2 ml) minced fresh
ginger**
8 **green onions with tops,
diagonally cut into ½-inch
(1.25 cm) slices**
4 **ounces (112 g) Chinese-style
thin egg noodles**

1. Remove core from cabbage; discard.

2. Shred cabbage.

3. Heat oil in wok or large skillet over medium-high heat. Add cabbage and pork; stir-fry until pork is no longer pink in center, about 5 minutes.

4. Add chicken broth, soy sauce and ginger. Bring to a boil. Reduce heat to low; simmer 10 minutes, stirring occasionally. Stir in onions.

5. Add noodles.

6. Cook just until noodles are tender, 2 to 4 minutes.

Makes 4 servings

Step 1. Removing core from cabbage.

Step 5. Adding noodles to wok.

Step 6. Cooking noodles.

Beef with Cashews

1 piece fresh ginger (about
    1-inch/2.5 cm square)
1 pound (450 g) beef rump
    steak
4 tablespoons (60 ml) vegetable
    oil, divided
4 teaspoons (20 ml) cornstarch
½ cup (125 ml) water
4 teaspoons (20 ml) soy sauce
1 teaspoon (5 ml) sesame oil
1 teaspoon (5 ml) oyster sauce
1 teaspoon (5 ml) Chinese chili
    sauce
8 green onions with tops, cut
    into 1-inch (2.5 cm) pieces
2 cloves garlic, minced
⅔ cup (167 ml) unsalted roasted
    cashews (about 3 ounces/
    85 g)
   Fresh carrot slices and thyme
    leaves for garnish

1. Peel and finely chop ginger; set aside.

2. Trim fat from meat; discard. Cut meat across grain into thin slices, each about 2 inches (5 cm) long.

3. Heat 1 tablespoon (15 ml) vegetable oil in wok or large skillet over high heat. Add ½ of meat; stir-fry until browned, 3 to 5 minutes. Remove from wok; set aside. Repeat with 1 tablespoon (15 ml) vegetable oil and remaining meat.

4. Combine cornstarch, water, soy sauce, sesame oil, oyster sauce and chili sauce in small bowl; mix well.

5. Heat remaining 2 tablespoons (30 ml) vegetable oil in wok or large skillet over high heat. Add ginger, onions, garlic and cashews; stir-fry 1 minute.

6. Stir cornstarch mixture; add to wok with meat. Cook and stir until liquid boils and thickens. Garnish, if desired.

Makes 4 servings

Step 1. Chopping peeled ginger.

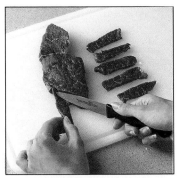

Step 2. Cutting meat.

Step 5. Adding cashews to wok.

Beef with Peppers

1 ounce (28 g) dried
    mushrooms
    Water
1 teaspoon (5 ml) cornstarch
1 teaspoon (5 ml) instant beef
    bouillon granules
1 tablespoon (15 ml) soy sauce
1 teaspoon (5 ml) sesame oil
1 pound (450 g) beef tenderloin,
    trimmed
2½ tablespoons (37 ml) vegetable
    oil
1 clove garlic, minced
¼ teaspoon (1 ml) Chinese
    five-spice powder
2 small onions, cut into wedges
1 green pepper, thinly sliced
1 red pepper, thinly sliced
8 ounces (225 g) Chinese-style
    thin egg noodles, cooked
    and drained (optional)

1. Place mushrooms in medium bowl; add enough warm water to cover mushrooms completely. Let stand 30 minutes; drain.

2. Squeeze excess water from mushrooms. Remove and discard stems. Slice caps into thin strips.

3. Combine cornstarch, bouillon granules, additional ¼ cup (62.5 ml) water, soy sauce and sesame oil in small bowl; mix well. Set aside.

4. Cut meat into thin slices, each about 1 inch (2.5 cm) long.

5. Heat vegetable oil in wok or large skillet over high heat. Add garlic and five-spice powder; stir-fry 15 seconds.

6. Add meat to wok; stir-fry until browned, about 5 minutes. Add onions; stir-fry 2 minutes. Add mushrooms and peppers; stir-fry until peppers are crisp-tender, about 2 minutes.

7. Stir cornstarch mixture; add to wok. Cook and stir until liquid boils and thickens. Serve over hot cooked noodles.

Makes 4 servings

Step 2. Removing stems from mushrooms.

Step 4. Slicing meat.

Step 6. Adding mushrooms and peppers to wok.

Two-Onion Pork Shreds

½ teaspoon (2 ml) Szechuan
  peppercorns
1 teaspoon (5 ml) cornstarch
4 teaspoons (20 ml) soy sauce,
  divided
4 teaspoons (20 ml) dry sherry,
  divided
7½ teaspoons (37.5 ml) vegetable
  oil, divided
8 ounces (225 g) boneless lean
  pork
2 teaspoons (10 ml) red wine
  vinegar
½ teaspoon (2 ml) sugar
2 cloves garlic, minced
½ small yellow onion, cut into
  ¼-inch (6 mm) slices
8 green onions with tops, cut
  into 2-inch (5 cm) pieces
½ teaspoon (2 ml) sesame oil

1. For marinade, place peppercorns in small skillet. Cook over medium-low heat, shaking skillet frequently, until fragrant, about 2 minutes. Let cool.

2. Crush peppercorns* with mortar and pestle (or place between paper towels and crush with hammer).

Step 2. Crushing peppercorns.

3. Transfer peppercorns to medium bowl. Add cornstarch, 2 teaspoons (10 ml) soy sauce, 2 teaspoons (10 ml) sherry and 1½ teaspoons (7 ml) vegetable oil; mix well.

4. Slice meat ⅛ inch (3 mm) thick; cut into 2 x ½-inch (5 x 1.25 cm) pieces. Add to marinade; stir to coat well. Cover and refrigerate 30 minutes, stirring occasionally.

Step 4. Adding meat to marinade.

5. Combine remaining 2 teaspoons (10 ml) soy sauce, 2 teaspoons (10 ml) sherry, vinegar and sugar in small bowl; mix well.

6. Heat remaining 6 teaspoons (30 ml) vegetable oil in wok or large skillet over high heat. Stir in garlic. Add meat mixture; stir-fry until no longer pink in center, about 2 minutes. Add yellow onion; stir-fry 1 minute. Add green onions; stir-fry 30 seconds.

7. Add soy-vinegar mixture; cook and stir 30 seconds. Stir in sesame oil.

Makes 2 to 3 servings

*Szechuan peppercorns are deceptively potent. Wear rubber or plastic gloves when crushing them and do not touch your eyes or lips when handling.

Step 6. Adding green onions to wok.

Asparagus Chicken with Black Bean Sauce

5 teaspoons (25 ml) cornstarch, divided
4 teaspoons (20 ml) soy sauce, divided
1 tablespoon (15 ml) dry sherry
1 teaspoon (5 ml) sesame oil
3 boneless skinless chicken breast halves, cut into bite-sized pieces
1 tablespoon (15 ml) fermented, salted black beans
1 teaspoon (5 ml) minced fresh ginger
1 clove garlic, minced
½ cup (125 ml) chicken broth
1 tablespoon (15 ml) oyster sauce
1 medium-size yellow onion
3 tablespoons (45 ml) vegetable oil, divided
1 pound (450 g) fresh asparagus spears, trimmed and diagonally cut into 1-inch (2.5 cm) pieces
2 tablespoons (30 ml) water
Fresh cilantro leaves for garnish

1. Combine 2 teaspoons (10 ml) cornstarch, 2 teaspoons (10 ml) soy sauce, sherry and sesame oil in large bowl; mix well. Add chicken; stir to coat well. Let stand 30 minutes.

2. Place beans in sieve; rinse under cold running water. Finely chop beans. Combine with ginger and garlic; set aside.

3. Combine remaining 3 teaspoons (15 ml) cornstarch, remaining 2 teaspoons (10 ml) soy sauce, chicken broth and oyster sauce in small bowl; mix well. Set aside.

4. Peel onion; cut into 8 wedges. Separate wedges; set aside.

5. Heat 2 tablespoons (30 ml) vegetable oil in wok or large skillet over high heat. Add chicken mixture; stir-fry until chicken is no longer pink in center, about 3 minutes. Remove from wok; set aside.

6. Heat remaining 1 tablespoon (15 ml) vegetable oil in wok. Add onion and asparagus; stir-fry 30 seconds.

7. Add water; cover. Cook, stirring occasionally, until asparagus is crisp-tender, about 2 minutes. Return chicken to wok.

8. Stir chicken broth mixture; add to wok with bean mixture. Cook until sauce boils and thickens, stirring constantly. Garnish, if desired.

Makes 3 to 4 servings

Step 4. Separating onion wedges.

Step 6. Stir-frying onion and asparagus.

Almond Chicken

2½ tablespoons (37 ml)
    cornstarch, divided
1½ cups (375 ml) water
4 tablespoons (60 ml) dry
    sherry, divided
4 teaspoons (20 ml) soy sauce
1 teaspoon (5 ml) instant
    chicken bouillon granules
1 egg white
½ teaspoon (2 ml) salt
4 whole boneless skinless
    chicken breasts, cut into
    1-inch (2.5 cm) pieces
    Vegetable oil for frying
½ cup (125 ml) blanched whole
    almonds (about 3 ounces/
    85 g)
1 large carrot, finely chopped
1 teaspoon (5 ml) minced fresh
    ginger
6 green onions with tops, cut
    into 1-inch (2.5 cm) pieces
3 ribs celery, diagonally cut into
    ½-inch (1.25 cm) pieces
½ cup (125 ml) sliced bamboo
    shoots (½ of 8-ounce/225 g
    can), drained
8 fresh mushrooms, sliced Fried
    Noodles (page 234), optional
    Carrot strips and fresh
    cilantro leaves for garnish

1. Combine 1½ tablespoons (22 ml) cornstarch, water, 2 tablespoons (30 ml) sherry, soy sauce and bouillon granules in small saucepan. Cook and stir over medium heat until mixture boils and thickens, about 5 minutes; keep warm.

2. Beat egg white in medium bowl until foamy.

3. Add remaining 1 tablespoon (15 ml) cornstarch, 2 tablespoons (30 ml) sherry and salt to egg white; mix well. Add chicken pieces; stir to coat well.

4. Heat about 2 inches (5 cm) oil in wok or large skillet over high heat to 375°F (190°C). Add ⅓ of chicken pieces, 1 at a time; cook until no longer pink in center, 3 to 5 minutes. Drain chicken pieces on paper towels. Repeat with remaining chicken.

5. Remove all but 2 tablespoons (30 ml) oil from wok. Add almonds; stir-fry until golden brown, about 2 minutes. Remove almonds from wok; set aside.

6. Add carrot and ginger to wok; stir-fry 1 minute. Add onions, celery, bamboo shoots and mushrooms; stir-fry until celery is crisp-tender, about 3 minutes. Stir in chicken, almonds and cornstarch mixture; cook and stir until thoroughly heated. Serve with Fried Noodles and garnish, if desired.

Makes 4 to 6 servings

Step 1. Cooking sauce.

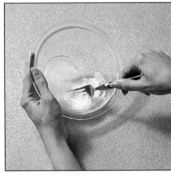

Step 2. Beating egg white.

Step 4. Cooking chicken.

Chicken Chow Mein

Fried Noodles (page 234)
2 whole chicken breasts
8 ounces (225 g) boneless lean
  pork
3 teaspoons (15 ml) cornstarch,
  divided
2½ tablespoons (37 ml) dry
  sherry, divided
2 tablespoons (30 ml) soy sauce,
  divided
½ cup (125 ml) water
2 teaspoons (10 ml) instant
  chicken bouillon granules
2 tablespoons (30 ml) vegetable
  oil
1 piece fresh ginger (1 inch/2.5
  cm square), peeled and
  finely chopped
1 clove garlic, minced
8 ounces (225 g) deveined
  shelled shrimp
2 medium-size yellow onions,
  chopped
1 red or green pepper, thinly
  sliced
2 ribs celery, diagonally cut into
  1-inch (2.5 cm) slices
8 green onions with tops,
  chopped
4 ounces (112 g) cabbage (¼ of
  small head), shredded

1. Prepare Fried Noodles; set aside.

2. Remove skin and bones from chicken breasts.

3. Cut chicken and pork into 1-inch (2.5 cm) pieces.

4. Combine 1 teaspoon (5 ml) cornstarch, 1½ teaspoons (7 ml) sherry and 1½ teaspoons (7 ml) soy sauce in large bowl. Add chicken and pork; toss to coat well. Cover and refrigerate 1 hour.

5. Combine remaining 2 teaspoons (10 ml) cornstarch, 2 tablespoons (30 ml) sherry, 1½ tablespoons (22 ml) soy sauce, water and boullion granules in small bowl; set aside.

6. Heat oil in wok or large skillet over high heat. Add ginger and garlic; stir-fry 1 minute. Add chicken and pork; stir-fry until no longer pink in center, about 5 minutes. Add shrimp; stir-fry until shrimp turn pink, about 3 minutes.

7. Add vegetables to wok; stir-fry until crisp-tender, 3 to 5 minutes. Add bouillon-soy sauce mixture. Cook and stir until sauce boils and thickens; cook and stir an additional minute.

8. Arrange Fried Noodles on serving plate; top with chicken mixture.

Makes 6 servings

Step 2. Removing chicken bones.

Step 3. Cutting chicken and pork.

Step 6. Stir-frying shrimp and chicken mixture.

Lo Mein Noodles with Shrimp

12 ounces (335 g) egg noodles or
    Chinese style thin egg
    noodles
2 teaspoons (10 ml) sesame oil
    Chinese chives*
1½ tablespoons (22 ml) oyster
    sauce
1½ tablespoons (22 ml) soy sauce
½ teaspoon (2 ml) sugar
¼ teaspoon (1 ml) salt
¼ teaspoon (1 ml) ground white
    or black pepper
2 tablespoons (30 ml) vegetable
    oil
1 teaspoon (5 ml) minced fresh
    ginger
1 clove garlic, minced
8 ounces (225 g) medium
    shrimp, shelled and
    deveined
1 tablespoon (15 ml) dry sherry
8 ounces (225 g) bean sprouts

*Or, substitute ¼ cup (62.5 ml)
domestic chives cut into 1-inch (2.5
cm) pieces and 2 green onions with
tops, cut into 1-inch (2.5 cm) pieces,
for the Chinese chives.

1. Add noodles to boiling water; cook according to package directions until tender but still firm, 2 to 3 minutes.

2. Drain noodles; rinse under cold running water. Drain again.

3. Combine noodles and sesame oil in large bowl; toss lightly to coat.

4. Cut enough chives into 1-inch (2.5 cm) pieces to measure ½ cup (125 ml); set aside.

5. Combine oyster sauce, soy sauce, sugar, salt and pepper in small bowl.

6. Heat vegetable oil in wok or large skillet over high heat. Add ginger and garlic; stir-fry 10 seconds. Add shrimp; stir-fry until shrimp begin to turn pink, about 1 minute. Add chives and sherry; stir-fry until chives begin to wilt, about 15 seconds. Add ½ of bean sprouts; stir-fry 15 seconds. Add remaining bean sprouts; stir-fry 15 seconds.

7. Add oyster sauce mixture and noodles. Cook and stir until thoroughly heated, about 2 minutes.

Makes 4 servings

Step 1. Adding noodles to boiling water.

Step 2. Rinsing cooked noodles.

Step 4. Snipping chives.

Fish Rolls with Crab Sauce

1 pound (450 g) sole fillets, ¼ to
⅜ inch (6 to 9 mm) thick
(about 4 ounces/112 g *each*)
1 tablespoon (15 ml) dry sherry
2 teaspoons (10 ml) sesame oil
1 green onion with top, finely
chopped
1 teaspoon (5 ml) minced fresh
ginger
½ teaspoon (2 ml) salt
Dash of ground white pepper

Crab Sauce
1½ tablespoons (22 ml)
cornstarch
2 tablespoons (30 ml) water
1 tablespoon (15 ml) vegetable
oil
1 teaspoon (5 ml) minced fresh
ginger
2 green onions with tops, thinly
sliced
1 tablespoon (5 ml) dry sherry
6 ounces (165 g) fresh
crabmeat, flaked
1¼ cups (312.5 ml) chicken broth
¼ cup (62.5 ml) milk
Scored cucumber slices,*
lemon wedges and fresh
tarragon leaves for garnish

*To score cucumber, run tines of fork
lengthwise down all sides of cucumber
before slicing.

1. If fillets are large, cut in half crosswise
(each piece should be 5 to 6 inches/12.5 to
15 cm long).

2. Combine 1 tablespoon (15 ml) sherry,
sesame oil, chopped green onion, 1
teaspoon (5 ml) ginger, salt and white
pepper in small bowl. Brush each piece of
fish with sherry mixture; let stand 30
minutes.

3. Fold fish into thirds; place in rimmed
heatproof dish that will fit inside a
steamer.

4. Place dish on rack in steamer; cover
steamer. Steam over boiling water until
fish turns opaque and flakes easily with
fork, 8 to 10 minutes. Meanwhile,
combine cornstarch and water in small
cup.

5. Heat vegetable oil in 2-quart (2 L)
saucepan over medium heat. Add 1
teaspoon (5 ml) ginger; cook and stir 10
seconds. Add sliced green onions, 1
tablespoon (15 ml) sherry and crabmeat;
stir-fry 1 minute. Add chicken broth and
milk; bring to a boil. Stir cornstarch
mixture; add to saucepan. Cook, stirring
constantly, until sauce boils and thickens
slightly.

6. Using slotted spoon, transfer fish to
serving platter; top with Crab Sauce.
Garnish, if desired.

Makes 4 to 6 servings

Step 2. Brushing fish with
sherry mixture.

Step 3. Placing fish in rimmed
dish.

Step 4. Placing fish in
steamer.

Entrées • CHINESE 227

Ma Po Bean Curd

1 tablespoon (15 ml) Szechuan
    peppercorns (optional)
12 to 14 ounces (335 to 390 g)
    bean curd, drained
¾ cup (187 ml) chicken broth
1 tablespoon (15 ml) soy sauce
1 tablespoon (15 ml) dry sherry
1½ tablespoons (22 ml)
    cornstarch
3 tablespoons (45 ml) water
2 tablespoons (30 ml) vegetable
    oil
4 ounces (112 g) ground pork
2 teaspoons (10 ml) minced
    fresh ginger
2 cloves garlic, minced
1 tablespoon (15 ml) hot bean
    sauce
2 green onions with tops, thinly
    sliced
1 teaspoon (5 ml) sesame oil
    Fresh chives for garnish

1. Place peppercorns in small dry skillet. Cook and stir over medium-low heat until fragrant, about 2 minutes; let cool.

2. Place peppercorns* between paper towels; crush with hammer. Set aside.

3. Cut bean curd into ½-inch (1.25 cm) cubes. Set aside.

4. Combine chicken broth, soy sauce and sherry in small bowl; set aside. Combine cornstarch and water in small cup; mix well. Set aside.

5. Heat vegetable oil in wok or large skillet over high heat. Add meat, cook until no longer pink, about 2 minutes, stirring occasionally. Add ginger, garlic and hot bean sauce. Stir-fry 1 minute.

6. Add chicken broth mixture and bean curd; simmer, uncovered, 5 minutes. Stir in onions. Stir cornstarch mixture; add to wok. Cook until sauce boils and thickens slightly, stirring constantly. Stir in sesame oil. Sprinkle with ground peppercorns and garnish, if desired.

Makes 3 to 4 servings

*Szechuan peppercorns are deceptively potent. Wear rubber or plastic gloves when crushing them and do not touch eyes or lips when handling.

Step 1. Cooking peppercorns.

Step 2. Crushing peppercorns.

Step 3. Cutting bean curd into cubes.

Zucchini Shanghai Style

4 dried mushrooms
  Water
1 large tomato
½ cup (125 ml) chicken broth
2 tablespoons (30 ml) ketchup
2 teaspoons (10 ml) soy sauce
1 teaspoon (5 ml) dry sherry
¼ teaspoon (1 ml) sugar
⅛ teaspoon (0.5 ml) salt
1 teaspoon (5 ml) red wine
  vinegar
1 teaspoon (5 ml) cornstarch
2 tablespoons (15 ml) vegetable
  oil, divided
1 teaspoon (5 ml) minced fresh
  ginger
1 clove garlic, minced
1 green onion with top, finely
  chopped
1 pound (450 g) zucchini,
  diagonally cut into 1-inch
  (2.5 cm) pieces
½ small yellow onion, cut into
  wedges and separated

1. Place mushrooms in small bowl; add enough warm water to cover mushrooms completely. Let stand 30 minutes. Drain, reserving ¼ cup (62.5 ml) liquid. Squeeze out excess water.

2. Cut stems off mushrooms; discard. Cut caps into thin slices.

3. To loosen skin from tomato, add tomato to small saucepan of boiling water. Let stand 30 to 45 seconds. Rinse immediately under cold running water. Gently peel skin from tomato.

4. Cut tomato in half. Remove stem and seeds; discard.

5. Coarsely chop tomato; set aside.

6. Combine reserved ¼ cup (62.5 ml) mushroom liquid, chicken broth, ketchup, soy sauce, sherry, sugar, salt and vinegar in small bowl; set aside.

7. Combine cornstarch and 1 tablespoon (15 ml) water in small cup; mix well. Set aside.

8. Heat 1 tablespoon (15 ml) oil in wok or large skillet over medium-high heat. Add ginger and garlic; stir-fry 10 seconds. Add mushrooms, tomato and green onion; stir-fry 1 minute. Stir in chicken broth mixture. Bring to a boil. Reduce heat to low; simmer 10 minutes, stirring occasionally. Remove from wok; set aside.

9. Add remaining 1 tablespoon (15 ml) oil to wok; heat over medium-high heat. Add zucchini and yellow onion; stir-fry 30 seconds. Add 3 tablespoons (45 ml) water; cover. Cook, stirring occasionally, until vegetables are crisptender, 3 to 4 minutes. Stir cornstarch mixture. Add to wok with mushroom mixture. Cook and stir until sauce boils and thickens.

Makes 4 to 6 servings

Step 3. Peeling tomato.

Step 4. Removing tomato seeds.

Fried Rice

3 cups (750 ml) water
1½ teaspoons (7 ml) salt
1½ cups (375 ml) uncooked
    long-grain rice
4 slices uncooked bacon,
    chopped
3 eggs
⅛ teaspoon (0.5 ml) pepper
9 teaspoons (45 ml) vegetable
    oil, divided
2 teaspoons (10 ml) minced
    fresh ginger
8 ounces (225 g) Barbecued
    Pork (page 206), cut into
    thin strips
8 ounces (225 g) shelled
    deveined shrimp, cooked
    and coarsely chopped
8 green onions with tops, finely
    chopped
1 to 2 tablespoons (15 to 30 ml)
    soy sauce
    Fresh chervil leaves for
    garnish

1. Combine water and salt in 3-quart (3 L) saucepan; cover. Bring to a boil over medium-high heat. Stir in rice. Reduce heat to low; cover. Simmer until rice is tender, 15 to 20 minutes; drain.

2. Cook bacon in wok or large skillet over medium heat, stirring frequently, until crisp; drain.

3. Remove all but 1 tablespoon (15 ml) bacon drippings from wok.

4. Beat eggs with pepper in small bowl. Pour ⅓ of egg mixture into wok, tilting wok slightly to cover bottom.

5. Cook over medium heat until eggs are set, 1 to 2 minutes. Remove from wok.

6. Roll up omelet; cut into thin strips.

7. Pour 1½ teaspoons (7 ml) oil into wok. Add ½ of remaining egg mixture, tilting wok to cover bottom. Cook until eggs are set. Remove from wok; roll up and cut into thin strips. Repeat with another 1½ teaspoons (7 ml) oil and remaining eggs.

8. Heat remaining 6 teaspoons (30 ml) oil in wok over medium-high heat. Add ginger; stir-fry 1 minute. Add rice; cook 5 minutes, stirring frequently. Stir in omelet strips, bacon, Barbecued Pork, shrimp, onions and soy sauce. Cook and stir until heated through. Garnish, if desired.

Makes 6 to 8 servings

Step 2. Cooking bacon.

Step 4. Tilting wok to cover bottom with egg mixture.

Step 6. Cutting omelet into strips.

Fried Noodles

8 ounces (225 g) Chinese-style
    thin egg noodles
Vegetable oil for frying

1. Cook noodles according to package directions until tender but still firm, 2 to 3 minutes; drain. Rinse under cold running water; drain again.

2. Place several layers of paper towels over jelly-roll pans or cookie sheets. Spread noodles over paper towels; let dry 2 to 3 hours.

3. Heat about 2 inches (5 cm) oil in wok or large skillet over medium-high heat to 375°F (190°C). Using slotted spoon or tongs, lower a small portion of noodles into hot oil. Cook noodles until golden brown, about 30 seconds.

4. Drain noodles on paper towels. Repeat with remaining noodles.

Makes 4 servings

Step 3. Frying noodles.

Step 4. Draining fried noodles.

Steamed Rice

1 cup (250 ml) uncooked
    long-grain rice
2 cups (500 ml) water
1 tablespoon (15 ml) oil
1 teaspoon (5 ml) salt

1. Place rice in strainer; rinse under cold running water to remove excess starch. Combine rice, 2 cups (500 ml) water, oil and salt in medium saucepan.

2. Cook over medium-high heat until water comes to a boil. Reduce heat to low; cover. Simmer until rice is tender, 15 to 20 minutes. Remove from heat; let stand 5 minutes. Uncover; fluff rice lightly with fork.

Makes 3 cups (750 ml)

Step 2. Fluffing rice.

Vermicelli

**8 ounces (225 g) Chinese rice
vermicelli *or* bean threads
Vegetable oil for frying**

1. Cut bundle of vermicelli in half. Gently pull each half apart into small bunches.

2. Heat about 2 inches (5 cm) oil in wok or large skillet over medium-high heat to 375°F (190°C). Using slotted spoon or tongs, lower a small bunch of vermicelli into hot oil.

3. Cook until vermicelli rises to top, 3 to 5 seconds; remove immediately.

4. Drain vermicelli on paper towels. Repeat with remaining vermicelli.
Makes about 4 servings

Step 1. Separating vermicelli.

Step 2. Adding vermicelli to hot oil.

Step 3. Cooking vermicelli.

COOKING CLASS
ITALIAN

238   CLASS NOTES

240   APPETIZERS & SOUPS

250   PASTA DISHES

264   ENTRÉES

274   SIDE DISHES

Four-Meat Ravioli *(page 255)*

CLASS NOTES

In the last decade, Italian cuisine has gone from the usual spaghetti and meatballs to becoming a favorite in America's kitchens with diverse dishes like tortellini in cream sauce and seafood marinara. In fact, Americans eat more than 4 billion pounds (1.8 billion kg) of pasta each year. That comes to more than 17 pounds (7.65 kg) per person. With pasta popularity at an all-time high, more than 150 different shapes are available!

But Italian food is clearly more than just pasta. A true Italian meal is very different from the single, large plate of pasta many of us associate with Italian cooking. In Italy, there is a series of courses rather than a main course as we know it. *Antipasto,* which literally translated means "before the pasta," is the appetizer course and can be served either hot or cold. Soup may sometimes follow or replace the antipasto. The next course— *I Primi* or first course—usually consists of a pasta dish. *I Secondi* is the second course and features meat, poultry or fish. The pasta and meat courses are sometimes combined. The salad course or *Insalata* is served after the main portion of the meal to perk up tired tastebuds. *I Dolci,* which translates to "the sweets," is the dessert course and is usually served with an espresso or cappuccino.

The recipes in this section include many traditional dishes of Italy and illustrate the variety of this delicious cuisine.

COOKING PASTA

Dry Pasta: For every pound (450 g) of dry pasta, bring 4 to 6 quarts (4 to 6 L) of water to a full, rolling boil. Add 2 teaspoons (10 ml) salt, if desired. Gradually add pasta, allowing water to return to a boil. The boiling water helps circulate the pasta so that it cooks evenly. Stir frequently to prevent the pasta from sticking. Begin testing for doneness after 5 minutes of cooking. Pasta that is "al dente"— meaning "to the tooth"—is tender, yet firm. Draining the pasta as soon as it is done stops the cooking action and helps prevent overcooking. For best results, toss the pasta with sauce immediately after draining and serve within minutes. If the sauce is not ready, toss the pasta with some butter or oil to prevent it from becoming sticky. Pasta in its dry, uncooked form can be stored almost indefinitely in a cool dry place.

Fresh Pasta: Homemade pasta takes less time to cook than dry pasta. Cook fresh pasta in the same manner as dry, except begin testing for doneness after 2 minutes. Many of the recipes in this section show you how to make homemade pasta. Making pasta is fun and easy, but when time is short, dry pasta is a good substitute. What's important is that the pasta is never overcooked. Fresh pasta will last several weeks in the refrigerator or can be frozen for up to 1 month.

EQUIPMENT

Pastry Board: A slab made of marble or granite that is well suited for rolling dough and pastry because it is smooth and stays cool. A floured countertop or acrylic cutting board can also be used.

Pasta Machine: Pasta machines with hand-turned rollers are very useful in kneading and rolling pasta dough. Cutting attachments (fettuccine and angel hair are usually included) help to cut pasta evenly. Electric machines also mix the dough; however, the pasta usually lacks the resilience of hand-worked dough and the machines are expensive. Methods of making pasta by hand are also included in this publication.

Pastry Wheel: A straight or scalloped wheel with a handle that speeds the cutting of pastry or pasta shapes, such as ravioli. A sharp utility knife or pizza cutter can be substituted.

ITALIAN INGREDIENTS

These ingredients are normally available in Italian groceries. Many can be found in supermarkets and gourmet food stores.

Arborio Rice: Italian-grown short-grain rice that has large, plump grains with a delicious nutty taste. Arborio rice is traditionally used for risotto dishes because its high starch content produces a creamy texture and it can absorb more liquid than regular- or long-grain rice.

Cannellini Beans: Large, white Italian kidney beans available both in dry and canned forms. Dried beans need to be soaked in water several hours or overnight to rehydrate before cooking; canned beans should be rinsed and drained to freshen the beans. Cannellini beans are often used in Italian soups, such as Minestrone. Great Northern beans make a good substitute.

Capers: Flower buds of a bush native to the Mediterranean. The buds are sun-dried, then pickled in a vinegar brine. Capers should be rinsed and drained before using to remove excess salt.

Eggplant: A cousin of the tomato, the eggplant is actually a fruit, though commonly thought of as a vegetable. Eggplants come in various shapes and sizes and their color can vary from deep purple to creamy ivory. However, these varieties are similar in taste and should be salted to remove their bitter flavor. Choose firm, unblemished eggplants with smooth, glossy skin. They should feel heavy for their size. Store in a cool, dry place and use within a day or two of purchase. Do not cut in advance as the flesh discolors rapidly.

Fennel: An anise-flavored, bulb-shaped vegetable with celerylike stems and feathery leaves. Both the base and stems can be eaten raw in salads or sautéed, and the seeds and leaves can be used for seasoning food.

Italian Plum Tomatoes: A flavorful egg-shaped tomato that comes in red and yellow varieties. As with other tomatoes, they are very perishable. Choose firm tomatoes that are fragrant and free of blemishes. Ripe tomatoes should be stored at room temperature and used within a few days. Canned tomatoes are a good substitute when fresh ones are out of season.

Olive Oil: Extracted oil from tree-ripened olives used for both salads and cooking. Olive oils are graded by the level of acidity they contain. The best are cold-pressed and produce a low level of acidity. The highest grade is extra virgin olive oil, which contains a maximum of 1 percent acidity. Virgin olive oil contains up to a 3½ percent acidity level, and pure olive oil is a blend of virgin olive oil and refined residue. Olive oil does not improve with age; exposure to air and heat turns oil rancid. Store olive oil in a cool, dark place for up to 6 months or refrigerate for up to 1 year. Olive oil becomes cloudy when chilled; bring chilled olive oil to room temperature before using.

Parmesan Cheese: A hard, dry cheese made from skimmed cow's milk. This cheese has a straw-colored interior with a rich, sharp flavor. The imported Italian Parmigiano-Reggiano has been aged at least 2 years, whereas domestic renditions are only aged 14 months. Parmesan cheese is primarily used for grating. While pre-grated cheese is available, it does not compare with freshly grated. Store Parmesan cheese pieces loosely in plastic and refrigerate for up to 1 week. Refrigerate freshly grated Parmesan cheese in an airtight container for up to 1 week.

Pine Nuts (also called Pignolias): These nuts are inside pine cones. Italian pine nuts come from the stone pine tree. Pine nuts have a light, delicate flavor and are a well known ingredient in the classic Italian pesto sauce. Store in an air-tight container in the refrigerator for up to 3 months or freeze for up to 9 months.

Prosciutto: The Italian word for "ham," prosciutto is seasoned, salt-cured and air-dried (not smoked). Although the imported Parma can now be purchased in America, the less expensive domestic prosciutto is a good substitute. It is usually sold in very thin slices and eaten as a first course with melon slices and figs. It also can be added at the last minute to cooked foods, such as pasta and vegetables. Wrap tightly and refrigerate slices for up to 3 days or freeze for up to 1 month.

Radicchio: Mainly used as a salad green, this red-leafed Italian chicory has burgundy red leaves with white ribs and a slightly bitter flavor. Choose crisp heads with no sign of browning; refrigerate in a plastic bag for up to 1 week. It may also be grilled, sautéed or baked.

Ricotta Cheese: A white, moist cheese with a slightly sweet flavor. It is rich, fresh and slightly grainy, but smoother than cottage cheese. Ricotta, which translated means "recooked," is made from heating the whey from another cooked cheese, such as mozzarella or provolone. Ricotta cheese is often used in lasagna and manicotti. Cottage cheese makes a good substitute, but with creamier results. When purchasing cheese, check the expiration date; store tightly covered in the refrigerator.

Venetian Canapés

12 slices firm white bread
 5 tablespoons (75 ml) butter or
    margarine, divided
 2 tablespoons (30 ml)
    all-purpose flour
½ cup (125 ml) milk
 3 ounces (85 g) fresh
    mushrooms (about 9
    medium), finely chopped
 6 tablespoons (90 ml) grated
    Parmesan cheese, divided
 2 teaspoons (10 ml) anchovy
    paste
¼ teaspoon (1 ml) salt
⅛ teaspoon (0.5 ml) black
    pepper
    Green and ripe olive slices,
    red and green bell pepper
    strips and rolled anchovy
    fillets for garnish

l. Preheat oven to 350°F (180°C). Cut circles out of bread slices with 2-inch (5 cm) round cutter. Melt 3 tablespoons (45 ml) butter in small saucepan. Brush both sides of bread circles lightly with butter. Bake bread circles on ungreased baking sheet 5 to 6 minutes per side until golden. Remove to wire rack. Cool completely. *Increase oven temperature to 425°F (220°C).*

2. Melt remaining 2 tablespoons (30 ml) butter in same small saucepan. Stir in flour; cook and stir over medium heat until bubbly. Whisk in milk; cook and stir 1 minute or until sauce thickens and bubbles. (Sauce will be very thick.) Place mushrooms in large bowl; stir in sauce, 3 tablespoons (45 ml) cheese, anchovy paste, salt and black pepper until well blended.

3. Spread heaping teaspoonful mushroom mixture on top of each toast round; place on ungreased baking sheet. Sprinkle remaining 3 tablespoons (45 ml) cheese over canapés, dividing evenly. Garnish, if desired.

4. Bake 5 to 7 minutes until tops are light brown. Serve warm.
    Makes 8 to 10 servings (about 2 dozen)

Step 1. Brushing bread circles with butter.

Step 2. Stirring thickened sauce into mushrooms.

Step 3. Spreading mushroom mixture on toast rounds.

Antipasto with Marinated Mushrooms

1 recipe Marinated Mushrooms
   (page 244)
4 teaspoons (20 ml) red wine
   vinegar
1 clove garlic, minced
½ teaspoon (2 ml) dried basil
   leaves, crushed
½ teaspoon (2 ml) dried oregano
   leaves, crushed
   Generous dash freshly ground
   black pepper
¼ cup (62.5 ml) olive oil
4 ounces (112 g) mozzarella
   cheese, cut into ½-inch
   (1.25 cm) cubes
4 ounces (112 g) prosciutto or
   cooked ham, thinly sliced
4 ounces (112 g) Provolone
   cheese, cut into 2-inch
   (5 cm) sticks
1 jar (10 ounces/280 g)
   pepperoncini peppers,
   drained
8 ounces (225 g) hard salami,
   thinly sliced
2 jars (6 ounces/165 g *each*)
   marinated artichoke
   hearts, drained
1 can (6 ounces/165 g) pitted
   ripe olives, drained
   Lettuce leaves (optional)
   Fresh basil leaves and chives
   for garnish

1. Prepare Marinated Mushrooms; set aside.

2. Combine vinegar, garlic, basil, oregano and black pepper in small bowl. Add oil in slow steady stream, whisking until oil is thoroughly blended. Add mozzarella cubes; stir to coat.

3. Marinate, covered, in refrigerator at least 2 hours.

4. Wrap ½ of prosciutto slices around Provolone sticks; roll up remaining slices separately.

5. Drain mozzarella cubes; reserve marinade.

6. Arrange mozzarella cubes, prosciutto-wrapped Provolone sticks, prosciutto rolls, marinated mushrooms, pepperoncini, salami, artichoke hearts and olives on large platter lined with lettuce, if desired.

7. Drizzle reserved marinade over pepperoncini, artichoke hearts and olives. Garnish, if desired. Serve with small forks or wooden toothpicks.

Makes 6 to 8 servings

continued on page 244

Step 2. Whisking oil into vinegar mixture.

Step 4. Wrapping prosciutto around Provolone sticks.

Antipasto with Marinated
Mushrooms, continued

Marinated Mushrooms

   3 tablespoons (45 ml) lemon juice
   2 tablespoons (30 ml) chopped
      fresh parsley
   ½ teaspoon (2 ml) salt
   ¼ teaspoon (1 ml) dried tarragon
      leaves, crushed
      Generous dash freshly ground
      black pepper
   ½ cup (125 ml) olive oil
   1 clove garlic
   ½ pound (225 g) small or medium
      fresh mushrooms

1. To make marinade, combine lemon juice, parsley, salt, tarragon and pepper in medium bowl. Add oil in slow steady stream, whisking until oil is thoroughly blended.

2. Lightly crush garlic with flat side of chef's knife or mallet.

3. Spear garlic with small wooden toothpick and add to marinade.

4. Slice stems from mushrooms; reserve for another use. Wipe mushroom caps clean with damp kitchen towel.

5. Add mushrooms to marinade; mix well. Marinate, covered, in refrigerator 4 hours or overnight, stirring occasionally.

6. To serve, remove and discard garlic. Serve mushrooms on antipasto tray or as relish. Or, add mushrooms to tossed green salad, using marinade as dressing.

Makes about 2 cups (500 ml)

Marinated Mushrooms: Step 1. Whisking oil into lemon juice mixture.

Marinated Mushrooms: Step 2. Crushing garlic.

Marinated Mushrooms: Step 4. Cleaning mushrooms.

Cioppino

6 to 8 hard-shell clams
1 quart (1 L) *plus* 2 tablespoons (30 ml) water, divided
1 cup (250 ml) dry white wine
2 onions, thinly sliced
1 rib celery, chopped
3 sprigs parsley
1 bay leaf
¾ pound (337 g) ocean perch or snapper fillets
1 can (14½ ounces/405 g) whole peeled tomatoes, undrained
1 tablespoon (15 ml) tomato paste
1 clove garlic, minced
1 teaspoon (5 ml) dried oregano leaves, crushed
1 teaspoon (5 ml) salt
½ teaspoon (2 ml) sugar
⅛ teaspoon (0.5 ml) pepper
2 large ripe tomatoes
2 large potatoes
1 pound (450 g) fresh halibut or haddock fillets
½ pound (225 g) fresh medium shrimp
2 tablespoons (30 ml) chopped fresh parsley
Celery leaves for garnish

1. Scrub clams with stiff brush under cold running water. Soak clams in large bowl of cold salt water 30 minutes. (Use ⅓ cup/83 ml salt dissolved in 1 gallon of water/4 L). Remove clams with slotted spoon; discard water.

2. Repeat soaking 2 more times.

3. To make fish stock, combine 1 quart (1 L) water, wine, onions, celery, parsley sprigs and bay leaf in 6-quart (6 L) stockpot or Dutch oven. Bring to a boil over high heat; reduce heat to low. Add perch; uncover and gently simmer 20 minutes.

4. Strain fish stock through sieve into large bowl. Remove perch to plate with slotted spatula; set aside. Discard onions, celery, parsley sprigs and bay leaf.

5. Return stock to stockpot; press canned tomatoes and juice through sieve into stockpot. Discard seeds. Stir in tomato paste, garlic, oregano, salt, sugar and pepper. Simmer, uncovered, over medium-low heat 20 minutes.

continued on page 246

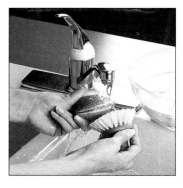

Step 1. Scrubbing clams.

Step 3. Simmering fish stock.

Step 4. Straining fish stock.

Cioppino, continued

6. Combine clams and remaining 2 tablespoons (30 ml) water in large stockpot or saucepan. Cover and cook over medium heat 5 to 10 minutes until clams open; remove clams immediately with metal tongs as they open.

7. Discard any clams with unopened shells. Rinse clams; set aside.

8. Cut fresh tomatoes in half. Remove stems and seeds; discard. Coarsely chop tomatoes.

9. Peel potatoes; cut into ¾-inch (1.8 cm) cubes. Skin halibut; cut into 1½ x 1-inch (3.75 x 2.5 cm) pieces.

10. Add fresh tomatoes, potatoes and halibut to soup mixture in stockpot. Bring to a boil over high heat; reduce heat to medium-low. Cover and cook 12 to 15 minutes until potatoes are fork-tender.

11. Remove shells from shrimp under cold running water. To devein, cut shallow slit down back of shrimp; pull out and discard vein. Add shrimp to soup mixture in stockpot.

12. Cook over medium heat 1 to 2 minutes just until shrimp turn opaque and are cooked through.

13. Flake reserved perch with fork; stir perch, reserved clams and chopped parsley into soup. Garnish, if desired. Serve immediately.

Makes 6 to 8 servings
(about 10 cups/2.5 L)

Step 6. Removing opened clams.

Step 8. Seeding tomatoes.

Step 11. Deveining shrimp.

Minestrone alla Milanese

¼ pound (112 g) green beans
2 medium zucchini
1 large potato
½ pound (225 g) cabbage
⅓ cup (83 ml) olive oil
3 tablespoons (45 ml) butter or
    margarine
2 medium onions, chopped
3 medium carrots, coarsely
    chopped
3 ribs celery, coarsely chopped
1 clove garlic, minced
1 can (28 ounces/785 g) Italian
    plum tomatoes, undrained
3½ cups (875 ml) beef broth
1½ cups (375 ml) water
½ teaspoon (2 ml) salt
½ teaspoon (2 ml) dried basil
    leaves, crushed
¼ teaspoon (1 ml) dried
    rosemary leaves, crushed
¼ teaspoon (1 ml) pepper
1 bay leaf
1 can (16 ounces/450 g)
    cannellini beans
    Freshly grated Parmesan
    cheese (optional)

1. Trim green beans; cut into 1-inch (2.5 cm) pieces. Trim zucchini; cut into ½-inch (1.25 cm) cubes. Peel potato; cut into ¾-inch (1.8 cm) cubes. Coarsely shred cabbage.

2. Heat oil and butter in 6-quart (6 L) stockpot or Dutch oven over medium heat. Add onions; cook and stir 6 to 8 minutes until onions are soft and golden but not brown. Stir in carrots and potato; cook and stir 5 minutes. Stir in celery and green beans; cook and stir 5 minutes. Stir in zucchini; cook and stir 3 minutes. Stir in cabbage and garlic; cook and stir 1 minute more.

3. Drain tomatoes, reserving juice. Add broth, water and reserved juice to stockpot. Chop tomatoes coarsely; add to stockpot. Stir in salt, basil, rosemary, pepper and bay leaf. Bring to a boil over high heat; reduce heat to low. Cover and simmer 1½ hours, stirring occasionally.

4. Rinse and drain cannellini beans; add beans to stockpot. Uncover and cook over medium-low heat 30 to 40 minutes more until soup thickens, stirring occasionally. Remove bay leaf. Serve with cheese.

Makes 8 to 10 servings
(about 12 cups/3 L)

Step 1. Shredding cabbage with chef's knife.

Step 2. Cooking and stirring vegetables.

Step 4. Adding drained beans to stockpot.

Classic Pesto with Linguine

Homemade Linguine *or* ¾
    pound (338 g) dry
    uncooked linguine, hot
    cooked and drained
2 tablespoons (30 ml) butter or
    margarine
¼ cup (62.5 ml) *plus* **1**
    tablespoon (15 ml) olive oil,
    divided
2 tablespoons (30 ml) pine nuts
1 cup (250 ml) tightly packed
    fresh (not dried) basil
    leaves, rinsed, drained and
    stemmed
2 cloves garlic
¼ teaspoon (1 ml) salt
¼ cup (62.5 ml) freshly grated
    Parmesan cheese
1½ tablespoons (22 ml) freshly
    grated Romano cheese
    Fresh basil leaves for garnish

1. To prepare Homemade Linguine, make dough following steps 1 and 2 of Homemade Fettuccine (page 252). In step 3, roll out dough to ¹⁄₁₆-inch-thick (1.5 mm) circle. In step 5, cut dough into ⅛-inch (3 mm) wide strips. Proceed as directed in step 6. Add butter to cooked and drained pasta, tossing to coat evenly.

2. To toast pine nuts, heat 1 tablespoon (15 ml) oil in small saucepan or skillet over medium-low heat. Add pine nuts; cook and stir 30 to 45 seconds until light brown, shaking pan constantly. Remove with slotted spoon; drain on paper towels.

3. Place toasted pine nuts, basil leaves, garlic and salt in food processor or blender. With processor running, add remaining ¼ cup (62.5 ml) oil in slow steady stream until evenly blended and pine nuts are finely chopped.

4. Transfer basil mixture to small bowl. Stir in Parmesan and Romano cheeses.*

5. Combine hot, buttered linguine and pesto sauce in large serving bowl; toss until well coated. Garnish, if desired. Serve immediately.

*Makes 4 servings
(about ¾ cup/167 ml pesto sauce)*

*Pesto sauce can be stored at this point in airtight container; pour thin layer of olive oil over pesto and cover. Refrigerate up to 1 week. Bring to room temperature. Proceed as directed in step 5.

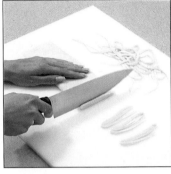

Step 1. Cutting dough into strips.

Step 2. Toasting pine nuts.

Step 3. Adding oil through feed tube while processing.

Classic Fettuccine Alfredo

1 recipe Homemade Fettuccine
   (recipe follows) *or* ¾ pound
   (337 g) uncooked dry
   fettuccine
6 tablespoons (90 ml) unsalted
   butter
⅔ cup (167 ml) heavy or
   whipping cream
½ teaspoon (2 ml) salt
   Generous dash ground white
   pepper
   Generous dash ground
   nutmeg
1 cup (250 ml) freshly grated
   Parmesan cheese (about 3
   ounces/85 g)
2 tablespoons (30 ml) chopped
   fresh parsley
   Fresh Italian parsley sprig for
   garnish

1. Prepare and cook Homemade
Fettuccine or cook dry fettuccine in large
pot of boiling salted water 6 to 8 minutes
just until al dente; remove from heat.
Drain well; return to dry pot.

2. Place butter and cream in large, heavy
skillet over medium-low heat. Cook and
stir until butter melts and mixture bubbles.
Cook and stir 2 minutes more. Stir in salt,
pepper and nutmeg. Remove from heat.
Gradually stir in cheese until thoroughly
blended and smooth. Return briefly to
heat to completely blend cheese if
necessary. (Do not let sauce bubble or
cheese will become lumpy and tough.)

3. Pour sauce over fettuccine in pot. Stir
and toss with 2 forks over low heat 2 to 3
minutes until sauce is thickened and
fettuccine is evenly coated. Sprinkle with
chopped parsley. Garnish, if desired.
Serve immediately.

Makes 4 servings

Step 2. Stirring cheese into
sauce.

Homemade Fettuccine: Step 1.
Mixing egg mixture into flour
with fork to form dough.

Homemade Fettuccine

2 cups (500 ml) all-purpose flour
¼ teaspoon (1 ml) salt
3 eggs
1 tablespoon (15 ml) milk
1 teaspoon (5 ml) olive oil

1. Combine flour and salt on pastry board,
cutting board or countertop; make well in
center. Whisk eggs, milk and oil in small
bowl until well blended; gradually pour
into well in flour mixture while mixing
with fork or fingertips to form ball of
dough.

continued on page 254

Classic Fettuccine Alfredo, continued

2. Place dough on lightly floured surface; flatten slightly. To knead dough, fold dough in half toward you and press dough away from you with heels of hands. Give dough a quarter turn and continue folding, pushing and turning. Continue kneading 5 minutes or until smooth and elastic, adding more flour to prevent sticking if necessary. Wrap dough in plastic wrap; let stand 15 minutes.

3. Unwrap dough and knead briefly (as described in step 2) on lightly floured surface. Using lightly floured rolling pin, roll out dough to ⅛-inch- (3 mm) thick circle on lightly floured surface. Gently pick up dough circle with both hands. Hold it up to the light to check for places where dough is too thick. Return to board; even out any thick spots. Let rest until dough is slightly dry but can be handled without breaking.

4. Lightly flour dough circle; roll loosely on rolling pin.

5. Slide rolling pin out; press dough roll gently with hand and cut into ¼-inch- (6 mm) wide strips with sharp knife. Carefully unfold strips.*

6. Cook fettuccine in large pot of boiling salted water 1 to 2 minutes just until al dente. Drain well.
Makes about ¾ pound (337 g)

*Fettuccine can be dried and stored at this point. Hang fettuccine strips over pasta rack or clean broom handle covered with plastic wrap and propped between two chairs. Dry at least 3 hours; store in airtight container at room temperature up to 4 days. To serve, cook fettuccine in large pot of boiling salted water 3 to 4 minutes just until al dente. Drain well.

Homemade Fettuccine: Step 2. Kneading dough.

Homemade Fettuccine: Step 4. Rolling dough loosely on rolling pin.

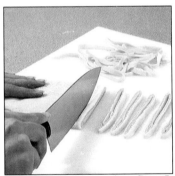
Homemade Fettuccine: Step 5. Cutting dough into strips.

Four-Meat Ravioli

Four-Meat Filling (page 256)
Plum Tomato Sauce (page 256)
4 cups (1 L) all-purpose flour
¼ teaspoon (1 ml) salt
2 eggs
1 tablespoon (15 ml) olive oil
⅔ to 1 cup (167 to 250 ml) water
1 egg yolk
1 teaspoon (5 ml) milk
1 tablespoon (15 ml) chopped
  fresh parsley
  Freshly grated Parmesan
  cheese
  Fresh rosemary sprig for
  garnish

1. Prepare Four-Meat Filling; refrigerate.

2. Prepare Plum Tomato Sauce; set aside.

3. For dough, mix flour and salt in large bowl. Combine 2 eggs, oil and ⅔ cup (167 ml) water in small bowl; whisk thoroughly. Gradually stir egg mixture into flour mixture with fork. Add enough of remaining ⅓ cup (83 ml) water, 1 tablespoon (15 ml) at a time, to form firm but pliable dough.

4. Place dough on lightly floured surface; flatten slightly. To knead dough, fold dough in half toward you and press dough away from you with heels of hands. Give dough a quarter turn and continue folding, pushing and turning. Continue kneading 5 minutes or until smooth and elastic, adding more flour to prevent sticking if necessary. Wrap dough in plastic wrap; let rest 30 minutes.

5. Unwrap dough and knead briefly (as described in step 4) on lightly floured surface; divide into 4 pieces. Using lightly floured rolling pin, roll out 1 dough piece to ¹⁄₁₆-inch (1.5 mm) thickness on lightly floured surface. (Keep remaining dough pieces wrapped in plastic wrap to prevent drying.) Cut dough into 4-inch-wide (10 cm) strips. Place teaspoonfuls of Four-Meat Filling along top half of each strip at 2-inch (5 cm) intervals.

6. Whisk egg yolk and milk in small bowl. Brush dough on long edge and between filling with egg-milk mixture.

Step 3. Mixing egg mixture into flour with fork to form dough.

Step 4. Kneading dough.

Step 5. Placing filling on rolled out dough.

continued on page 256

Four-Meat Ravioli, continued

7. Fold dough over filling; press firmly between filling and along long edge to seal, making sure all air has been pushed out.

8. Cut ravioli apart with fluted pastry wheel. Repeat with remaining 3 dough pieces, filling and egg-milk mixture.

9. Cook ravioli, ¼ at a time, in large pot of boiling salted water 3 to 5 minutes just until al dente. Remove with slotted spoon; drain well. Add ravioli to reserved sauce. Bring sauce and ravioli to a boil over medium-high heat; reduce heat to medium-low. Simmer, uncovered, 6 to 8 minutes until heated through. Sprinkle with parsley and cheese. Garnish, if desired. Serve immediately.

Makes 6 servings

Four-Meat Filling

- 5 ounces (140 g) fresh spinach
- 2 small boneless skinless chicken breast halves (about 4 ounces/112 g each), cooked
- 3 ounces (85 g) prosciutto or cooked ham
- 1½ ounces (42 g) hard salami
- 1 clove garlic
- 6 ounces (165 g) ground beef
- ½ cup (125 ml) chopped fresh parsley
- 2 eggs
- ¼ teaspoon (1 ml) ground allspice
- ¼ teaspoon (1 ml) salt

1. To steam spinach, rinse spinach thoroughly in large bowl of water; drain but do not squeeze dry. Trim and discard stems. Place spinach in large saucepan over medium heat. Cover and steam 4 minutes or until tender, stirring occasionally. Let stand until cool enough to handle; squeeze dry.

2. Mince spinach, chicken, prosciutto, salami and garlic; combine in medium bowl with beef, parsley, eggs, allspice and salt. Mix well.

Plum Tomato Sauce

- ⅓ cup (83 ml) butter or margarine
- 1 clove garlic, minced
- 1 can (28 ounces/785 g) Italian plum tomatoes, undrained
- 1 can (8 ounces/225 g) tomato sauce
- ¾ teaspoon (3.75 ml) salt
- ½ teaspoon (2 ml) ground allspice
- ½ teaspoon (2 ml) dried basil leaves, crushed
- ½ teaspoon (2 ml) dried rosemary leaves, crushed
- ⅛ teaspoon (0.5 ml) pepper

1. Heat butter in large saucepan over medium heat until melted and bubbly; cook and stir garlic in hot butter 30 seconds. Press tomatoes and juice through sieve into garlic mixture; discard seeds. Stir in tomato sauce, salt, allspice, basil, rosemary and pepper.

2. Cover and simmer 30 minutes. Uncover and simmer 15 minutes more or until sauce thickens, stirring occasionally.

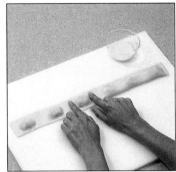

Step 7. Pressing dough over filling.

Step 8. Cutting ravioli apart with pastry wheel.

Homemade Angel Hair Pasta with Classic Tomato Sauces

2 cups (500 ml) *plus* 2
    tablespoons (30 ml)
    all-purpose flour
¼ teaspoon (1 ml) salt
3 eggs
1 tablespoon (15 ml) milk
1 teaspoon (5 ml) olive oil
    Neapolitan Sauce (page 260)
    Pizzaiola Sauce (page 260)
½ cup (125 ml) freshly grated
    Parmesan cheese (optional)
    Fresh marjoram sprigs for
    garnish

1. Place flour, salt, eggs, milk and oil in food processor; process until dough forms. Shape into a ball.

2. Place dough on lightly floured surface; flatten slightly. Cut dough into 4 pieces. Wrap 3 dough pieces in plastic wrap; set aside.

3. To knead dough by pasta machine,* set rollers of pasta machine at widest setting (position 1). Feed unwrapped dough piece through flat rollers by turning handle. (Dough may crumble slightly at first but will hold together after 2 to 3 rollings.)

4. Lightly flour dough strip; fold strip into thirds. Feed through rollers again. Continue process 7 to 10 times until dough is smooth and elastic.

5. To roll out dough by machine, reduce setting to position 3. Feed dough strip through rollers. Without folding strip into thirds, repeat on positions 5 and 6. Let dough stand 5 to 10 minutes until slightly dry.

*Follow manufacturer's directions for appropriate method of rolling pasta if position settings are different. To make pasta by hand, see Homemade Fettuccine (page 252).

continued on page 260

Step 1. Processing dough.

Step 3. Kneading dough with pasta machine.

Step 4. Folding dough into thirds.

Homemade Angel Hair Pasta with Classic Tomato Sauces, continued

6. Attach handle to angel hair pasta roller and feed dough through.** Repeat kneading and rolling with reserved dough pieces.

7. Cook angel hair pasta in large pot of boiling salted water 1 to 2 minutes just until al dente; remove from heat. Drain well; divide angel hair pasta into 2 large bowls.

8. Prepare Neapolitan Sauce and Pizzaiola Sauce. Pour hot Neapolitan Sauce over ½ of angel hair pasta; toss until well coated. Pour hot Pizzaiola Sauce over remaining angel hair pasta; toss until well coated. Serve with cheese. Garnish, if desired.

Makes 4 to 6 servings

**Angel hair pasta can be dried and stored at this point. Hang pasta strips over pasta rack or clean broom handle covered with plastic wrap and propped between two chairs. (Or, twirl pasta into nests and place on clean kitchen towel.) Dry at least 3 hours; store in airtight container at room temperature up to 4 days. To serve, cook angel hair pasta in large pot of boiling salted water 3 to 4 minutes just until al dente. Drain well; proceed as directed in step 8.

Neapolitan Sauce

- **2 tablespoons (30 ml) butter or margarine**
- **1 tablespoon (15 ml) olive oil**
- **1 can (28 ounces/785 g) Italian plum tomatoes, undrained**
- **1 teaspoon (5 ml) dried basil leaves, crushed**
- **½ teaspoon (2 ml) salt**
- **⅛ teaspoon (0.5 ml) pepper**
- **3 tablespoons (45 ml) chopped fresh parsley**

Heat butter and oil in 2-quart (2 L) saucepan over medium heat. Press tomatoes and juice through sieve into hot butter mixture; discard seeds. Stir in basil, salt and pepper. Bring to a boil over high heat; reduce heat to medium-low. Cook, uncovered, 30 to 40 minutes until sauce is reduced to 2 cups (500 ml), stirring frequently. Stir in parsley.

Pizzaiola Sauce

- **1 tablespoon (15 ml) olive oil**
- **2 cloves garlic**
- **1 can (28 ounces/785 g) Italian plum tomatoes, undrained**
- **¾ teaspoon (3.7 ml) dried marjoram leaves, crushed**
- **½ teaspoon (2 ml) salt**
- **⅛ teaspoon (0.5 ml) pepper**
- **2 tablespoons (30 ml) minced fresh parsley**

Heat oil in 2-quart (2 L) saucepan over medium heat. Cut garlic in half. Cook and stir garlic in hot oil 2 to 3 minutes until garlic is golden but not brown. Remove and discard garlic. Press tomatoes and juice through sieve into garlic-flavored oil; discard seeds. Stir in marjoram, salt and pepper. Bring to a boil over high heat; reduce heat to medium-low. Cook, uncovered, 30 to 40 minutes until sauce is reduced to 2 cups (500 ml), stirring frequently. Stir in parsley.

Step 6. Feeding dough through angel hair pasta roller.

Neapolitan Sauce: Pressing tomatoes and juice through sieve.

Pizzaiola Sauce: Cooking sauce.

Spinach Lasagna

1 pound (450 g) ground beef
¼ pound (112 g) fresh
    mushrooms, thinly sliced
1 medium onion, chopped
1 clove garlic, minced
1 can (28 ounces/785 g) Italian
    plum tomatoes, undrained
1¼ teaspoons (6 ml) salt, divided
¾ teaspoon (3.7 ml) dried
    oregano leaves, crushed
¾ teaspoon (3.7 ml) dried basil
    leaves, crushed
¼ teaspoon (1 ml) pepper,
    divided
9 uncooked lasagna noodles
¼ cup (62.5 ml) *plus* 1
    tablespoon (30 ml) butter
    or margarine, divided
¼ cup (62.5 ml) all-purpose
    flour
⅛ teaspoon (0.5 ml) ground
    nutmeg
2 cups (500 ml) milk
1½ cups (375 ml) shredded
    mozzarella cheese (about
    6 ounces/165 g), divided
½ cup (125 ml) grated Parmesan
    cheese, divided
1 package (10 ounces/280 g)
    frozen chopped spinach,
    thawed and squeezed dry

1. For meat sauce, crumble ground beef into large skillet over medium-high heat. Brown 8 to 10 minutes, stirring to separate meat, until meat loses its pink color. Spoon off and discard fat.

2. Stir in mushrooms, onion and garlic; cook over medium heat 5 minutes or until onion is soft.

3. Press tomatoes and juice through sieve into meat mixture; discard seeds.

4. Stir in ¾ teaspoon (3.7 ml) salt, oregano, basil and ⅛ teaspoon (0.5 ml) pepper. Bring to a boil over medium-high heat; reduce heat to low. Cover and simmer 40 minutes, stirring occasionally. Uncover and simmer 15 to 20 minutes more until sauce thickens. Set aside.

5. Add lasagna noodles to large pot of boiling salted water, 1 at a time, allowing noodles to soften and fit into pot. Cook 10 minutes or just until al dente.

6. Drain noodles; rinse with cold water. Drain again; hang individually over pot rim to prevent sticking. Set aside.

continued on page 262

Step 3. Pressing tomatoes and juice through sieve.

Step 5. Adding lasagna noodles to boiling water.

7. For cheese sauce, melt ¼ cup (62.5 ml) butter in medium saucepan over medium heat. Stir in flour, remaining ½ teaspoon (2 ml) salt, remaining ⅛ teaspoon (0.5 ml) pepper and nutmeg; cook and stir until bubbly. Whisk in milk; cook and stir until sauce thickens and bubbles. Cook and stir 1 minute more. Remove from heat. Stir in 1 cup (250 ml) mozzarella and ¼ cup (62.5 ml) Parmesan cheeses. Stir until smooth. Set aside.

8. Preheat oven to 350°F (180°C). Spread remaining 1 tablespoon (15 ml) butter on bottom and sides of 12 x 8-inch (30 x 20 cm) baking dish with waxed paper. Spread noodles in single layer on clean kitchen (not paper) towel. Pat noodles dry.

9. Arrange 3 lasagna noodles in single layer, overlapping slightly, in bottom of baking dish.

10. Top with ½ of reserved meat sauce; spread evenly. Spread ½ of reserved cheese sauce over meat sauce in even layer.

11. Repeat layers once, using 3 noodles, remaining meat sauce and remaining cheese sauce. Sprinkle spinach over cheese sauce in even layer; pat down lightly. Arrange remaining 3 lasagna noodles over spinach.

12. Mix remaining ½ cup (125 ml) mozzarella and remaining ¼ cup (62.5 ml) Parmesan cheeses in cup. Sprinkle cheeses evenly on top of lasagna to completely cover lasagna noodles.

13. Bake 40 minutes or until top is golden and edges are bubbly. Let lasagna stand 10 minutes before serving. Garnish as desired.

Makes 6 servings

Step 8. Greasing baking dish with butter.

Step 10. Spreading cheese sauce over meat sauce.

Step 12. Sprinkling cheeses over top of lasagna.

Veal Parmesan

4 veal cutlets, cut ⅜ inch
    (9 mm) thick (about
    4 ounces/112 g each)
4 tablespoons (60 ml) olive oil,
    divided
1 small red bell pepper, finely
    chopped
1 medium onion, finely chopped
1 rib celery, finely chopped
1 clove garlic, minced
1 can (14½ ounces/405 g) whole
    peeled tomatoes, undrained
    and finely chopped
1 cup (250 ml) chicken broth
1 tablespoon (15 ml) tomato
    paste
1 tablespoon (15 ml) chopped
    parsley
1 teaspoon (5 ml) sugar
¾ teaspoon (3.7 ml) dried basil
    leaves, crushed
½ teaspoon (2 ml) salt
⅛ teaspoon (0.5 ml) ground
    black pepper
1 egg
¼ cup (62.5 ml) all-purpose
    flour
⅔ cup (167 ml) fine dry bread
    crumbs
2 tablespoons (30 ml) butter or
    margarine
1½ cups (375 ml) shredded
    mozzarella cheese (about
    6 ounces/165 g)
⅔ cup (167 ml) freshly grated
    Parmesan cheese (about 2
    ounces/56 g)
Fresh basil leaves for garnish
Hot cooked pasta (optional)

1. Place each veal cutlet between sheets of waxed paper on wooden board. Pound veal with meat mallet to ¼-inch (6 mm) thickness. Pat dry with paper towels; set aside.

2. To make tomato sauce, heat 1 tablespoon (15 ml) oil in medium saucepan over medium heat. Cook and stir bell pepper, onion, celery and garlic in hot oil 5 minutes. Stir in tomatoes and juice, broth, tomato paste, parsley, sugar, dried basil, salt and black pepper. Cover and simmer over low heat 20 minutes. Uncover and cook over medium heat 20 minutes more or until sauce thickens, stirring frequently; set aside.

3. Beat egg in shallow bowl; spread flour and bread crumbs on separate plates. Dip reserved veal cutlets to coat both sides evenly, first in flour, then in egg, then in bread crumbs. Press crumb coating firmly onto veal.

4. Heat butter and 2 tablespoons (30 ml) oil in large skillet over medium-high heat. Add veal. Cook 3 minutes per side or until browned.

5. Preheat oven to 350°F (180°C). Remove veal with slotted spatula to ungreased 13 x 9-inch (32.5 x 22.5 cm) baking dish. Sprinkle mozzarella cheese evenly over veal. Spoon reserved tomato sauce evenly over cheese. Sprinkle Parmesan cheese over tomato sauce.

6. Drizzle remaining 1 tablespoon (15 ml) oil over top. Bake, uncovered, 25 minutes or until veal is tender and cheese is golden. Garnish, if desired. Serve with pasta.

Makes 4 servings

Step 1. Pounding veal to ¼-inch (6 mm) thickness.

Step 3. Coating veal with bread crumbs.

Step 5. Sprinkling cheese over tomato sauce.

Classic Chicken Marsala

2 tablespoons (30 ml) unsalted butter

1 tablespoon (15 ml) vegetable oil

4 boneless skinless chicken breast halves (about 1¼ pounds/560 g total)

4 slices mozzarella cheese (1 ounce/28 g each)

12 capers, drained

4 flat anchovy fillets, drained

1 tablespoon (15 ml) chopped fresh parsley

1 clove garlic, minced

3 tablespoons (45 ml) marsala

⅔ cup (167 ml) heavy or whipping cream

Dash salt

Dash pepper

Hot cooked pasta (optional)

1. Heat butter and oil in large skillet over medium-high heat until melted and bubbly. Add chicken; reduce heat to medium. Cook, uncovered, 5 to 6 minutes per side until chicken is tender and golden brown. Remove chicken with slotted spatula to work surface. Top each chicken piece with 1 cheese slice, 3 capers and 1 anchovy fillet.

2. Return chicken to skillet. Sprinkle with parsley. Cover and cook over low heat 3 minutes or until cheese is semi-melted and juices from chicken run clear. Remove chicken with slotted spatula to heated serving platter; keep warm.

3. Add garlic to drippings remaining in skillet; cook and stir over medium heat 30 seconds. Stir in marsala; cook and stir 45 seconds, scraping up any brown bits in skillet.

4. Stir in cream. Cook and stir 3 minutes or until sauce thickens slightly. Stir in salt and pepper. Spoon sauce over chicken. Serve with pasta. Garnish as desired.

Makes 4 servings

Step 1. Topping chicken with cheese, capers and anchovies.

Step 2. Removing chicken with slotted spatula.

Step 3. Stirring marsala into garlic mixture.

Fried Calamari with Tartar Sauce

1 pound (450 g) fresh or thawed
    frozen squid
1 egg
1 tablespoon (15 ml) milk
¾ cup (187 ml) fine dry
    unseasoned bread crumbs
    Vegetable oil for frying
    Tartar Sauce (page 270)
    Lemon wedges (optional)

1. To clean each squid, hold body of squid firmly in one hand. Grasp head firmly with other hand; pull head, twisting gently from side to side. (Head and contents of body should pull away in one piece.) Set aside tubular body sac.

2. Cut tentacles off head; set aside. Discard head and contents of body.

3. Grasp tip of pointed, thin, clear cartilage protruding from body; pull out and discard.

4. Rinse squid under cold running water. Peel off and discard spotted outer membrane covering body sac and fins. Pull off side fins; set aside.

5. Rinse inside of squid body thoroughly under running water. Repeat with remaining squid.

6. Cut each squid body crosswise into ¼-inch (6 mm) rings. Cut reserved fins into thin slices. (Body rings, fins and reserved tentacles are all edible parts.) Pat pieces thoroughly dry with paper towels.

continued on page 270

Step 1. Removing head and contents of body from body sac.

Step 4. Peeling off membrane covering body sac.

Step 6. Cutting squid body into rings.

Fried Calamari with Tartar Sauce, continued

7. Beat egg with milk in small bowl. Add squid pieces; stir to coat well. Spread bread crumbs in shallow bowl. Dip squid pieces in bread crumbs; place on plate or waxed paper. Let stand 10 to 15 minutes before frying.

8. To deep fry squid, heat 1½ inches (3.75 cm) oil in large saucepan to 350°F (180°C). (*Caution:* Squid will pop and spatter during frying; do not stand too close to pan.) Adjust heat to maintain temperature. Fry 8 to 10 pieces of squid at a time in hot oil 45 to 60 seconds until light brown. Remove with slotted spoon; drain on paper towels. Repeat with remaining squid pieces.

9. Or, to shallow fry squid, heat about ¼-inch (6 mm) oil in large skillet over medium-high heat; reduce heat to medium. Add pieces of squid in single layer, without crowding, to hot oil. Cook, turning once with 2 forks, 1 minute per side or until light brown. Remove with slotted spoon; drain on paper towels. Repeat with remaining squid. (This method uses less oil but requires slightly more hand work.)

10. Serve hot with Tartar Sauce and lemon wedges. Garnish as desired.

Makes 2 to 3 servings

Tartar Sauce

1 green onion
1 tablespoon (15 ml) drained capers
1 small sweet gherkin or pickle
2 tablespoons (30 ml) chopped fresh parsley
1⅓ cups (333 ml) mayonnaise

1. Thinly slice green onion. Mince capers and gherkin.

2. Fold green onion, capers, gherkin and parsley into mayonnaise. Cover and refrigerate until ready to serve.

Makes about 1⅓ cups (333 ml)

Step 7. Coating squid with bread crumbs.

Step 8. Deep frying squid.

Step 9. Turning squid with forks when shallow frying.

Homemade Pizza

½ tablespoon (8 ml) active dry
  yeast
1 teaspoon (5 ml) sugar, divided
½ cup (125 ml) warm water
  (105° to 115°F/67° to 73°C)
1¾ cups (437 ml) all-purpose
  flour, divided
¾ teaspoon (3.7 ml) salt, divided
2 tablespoons (30 ml) olive oil,
  divided
1 can (14½ ounces/405 g) whole
  peeled tomatoes, undrained
1 medium onion, chopped
1 clove garlic, minced
2 tablespoons (30 ml) tomato
  paste
1 teaspoon (5 ml) dried oregano
  leaves, crushed
½ teaspoon (2 ml) dried basil
  leaves, crushed
⅛ teaspoon (0.5 ml) ground
  black pepper
½ small red bell pepper, cored
  and seeded
½ small green bell pepper, cored
  and seeded
4 fresh medium mushrooms
1 can (2 ounces/56 g) flat
  anchovy fillets
1¾ cups (437 ml) shredded
  mozzarella cheese (about 7
  ounces/195 g)
½ cup (125 ml) freshly grated
  Parmesan cheese
⅓ cup (83 ml) pitted ripe olives,
  halved

1 . To proof yeast, sprinkle yeast and ½ teaspoon (2 ml) sugar over warm water in small bowl; stir until yeast is dissolved. Let stand 5 minutes or until mixture is bubbly.*

2. Place 1½ cups (375 ml) flour and ¼ teaspoon (1 ml) salt in medium bowl; stir in yeast mixture and 1 tablespoon (15 ml) oil, stirring until a smooth, soft dough forms. Place dough on lightly floured surface; flatten slightly.

3. To knead dough, fold dough in half toward you and press dough away from you with heels of hands. Give dough a quarter turn and continue folding, pushing and turning. Continue kneading, using as much of remaining ¼ cup (62.5 ml) flour as needed to form a stiff, elastic dough.

4. Shape dough into a ball; place in large greased bowl. Turn to grease entire surface. Cover with clean kitchen towel and let dough rise in warm place 30 to 45 minutes until doubled in bulk.

5. Press two fingertips about ½-inch (1.5 cm) into dough. Dough is ready if indentations remain when fingertips are removed.

*If yeast does not bubble, it is no longer active. Always check expiration date on yeast packet. Also, water that is too hot will kill yeast; it is best to use a thermometer.

continued on page 272

Step 1. Proofing yeast.

Step 3. Kneading dough.

Step 5. Pressing fingertips into dough to test if ready.

6. For sauce, finely chop tomatoes; reserve juice. Heat remaining 1 tablespoon (15 ml) oil in medium saucepan over medium heat. Add onion; cook 5 minutes or until soft. Add garlic; cook 30 seconds more. Add tomatoes and juice, tomato paste, oregano, basil, remaining ½ teaspoon (2 ml) sugar, ½ teaspoon (2 ml) salt and black pepper. Bring to a boil over high heat; reduce heat to medium-low. Simmer, uncovered, 10 to 15 minutes until sauce thickens, stirring occasionally. Pour into small bowl; cool.

7. Punch dough down. Knead briefly (as described in step 3) on lightly floured surface to distribute air bubbles; let dough stand 5 minutes more. Flatten dough into circle on lightly floured surface. Roll out dough, starting at center and rolling to edges, into 10-inch (25 cm) circle. Place circle in greased 12-inch (30 cm) pizza pan; stretch and pat dough out to edges of pan. Cover and let stand 15 minutes.

8. Preheat oven to 450°F (230°C). Cut bell peppers into ¾-inch (1.8 cm) pieces. Trim mushroom stems; wipe clean with damp kitchen towel (technique on page 244) and thinly slice. Drain anchovies. Mix mozzarella and Parmesan cheeses in small bowl.

9. Spread sauce evenly over pizza dough. Sprinkle with ⅔ of cheeses. Arrange bell peppers, mushrooms, anchovies and olives over cheeses.

10. Sprinkle remaining cheeses on top of pizza. Bake 20 minutes or until crust is golden brown. To serve, cut into wedges.

Makes 4 to 6 servings

Step 7. Rolling out dough.

Step 9. Spreading sauce over dough.

Spinach Gnocchi

2 packages (10 ounces/280 g
   each) frozen chopped
   spinach
1 cup (250 ml) ricotta cheese
2 eggs
⅔ cup (167 ml) freshly grated
   Parmesan cheese (about 2
   ounces/56 g), divided
1 cup (250 ml) *plus* 3
   tablespoons (45 ml)
   all-purpose flour, divided
½ teaspoon (2 ml) salt
⅛ teaspoon (0.5 ml) pepper
⅛ teaspoon (0.5 ml) nutmeg
3 tablespoons (45 ml) butter or
   margarine, melted

1. Cook spinach according to package directions. Drain well; let cool. Squeeze spinach dry; place in medium bowl. Stir in ricotta cheese. Add eggs; mix well. Add ⅓ cup (83 ml) Parmesan cheese, 3 tablespoons (45 ml) flour, salt, pepper and nutmeg; mix well. Cover and refrigerate 1 hour.

2. Spread remaining 1 cup (250 ml) flour in shallow baking pan. Press a heaping tablespoonful of spinach mixture between a spoon and your hand to form oval gnocchi; place on flour. Repeat with remaining spinach mixture.

3. Roll gnocchi lightly in flour to coat evenly; discard excess flour. Drop 8 to 12 gnocchi into large pot of boiling salted water; reduce heat to medium.

4. Cook, uncovered, 5 minutes or until gnocchi are slightly puffed and slightly firm to the touch. Remove gnocchi with slotted spoon; drain on paper towels. Immediately transfer to greased *broilerproof* shallow baking dish. Reheat water to boiling. Repeat with remaining gnocchi in batches of 8 to 12. Arrange gnocchi in single layer in baking dish.

5. Preheat broiler. Spoon butter over gnocchi; sprinkle with remaining ⅓ cup (83 ml) Parmesan cheese. Broil gnocchi 5 inches (12.5 cm) from heat source 2 to 3 minutes until cheese melts and browns lightly. Serve immediately. Garnish as desired.

Makes 4 to 6 servings (about 24 gnocchi)

Step 2. Shaping gnocchi.

Step 3. Boiling flour-coated gnocchi.

Step 4. Removing gnocchi with slotted spoon to paper towels.

Risotto alla Milanese

¼ teaspoon (1 ml) saffron
    threads
3½ to 4 cups (875 ml to 1 L)
    chicken broth, divided
7 tablespoons (105 ml) butter or
    margarine, divided
1 large onion, chopped
1½ cups (375 ml) uncooked
    Arborio or short-grain
    white rice
½ cup (125 ml) dry white wine
½ teaspoon (2 ml) salt
    Dash pepper
¼ cup (62.5 ml) freshly grated
    Parmesan cheese
    Chopped fresh parsley, fresh
    parsley sprig and tomato
    slices for garnish

1. Crush saffron to a powder using mortar and pestle. Transfer to small bowl.

2. Bring broth to a boil in saucepan over medium heat; reduce heat to low. Stir ½ cup (125 ml) broth into saffron to dissolve; set aside. Keep remaining broth hot.

3. Heat 6 tablespoons (90 ml) butter in large, heavy skillet or 2½-quart (2.5 L) saucepan over medium heat until melted and bubbly. Cook and stir onion in hot butter 5 minutes or until onion is soft. Stir in rice; cook and stir 2 minutes. Stir in wine, salt and pepper. Cook, uncovered, over medium-high heat 3 to 5 minutes until wine has evaporated, stirring occasionally.

4. Measure ½ cup (125 ml) hot broth; stir into rice. Reduce heat to medium-low, maintaining a simmer throughout steps 4 and 5. Cook and stir until broth has absorbed. Repeat, adding ½ cup (125 ml) broth 3 more times, cooking and stirring until broth has absorbed.

5. Add saffron-flavored broth to rice and cook until absorbed. Continue adding remaining broth, ½ cup (125 ml) at a time, and cooking until rice is tender but firm and mixture has slightly creamy consistency. (Not all the broth may be necessary. Total cooking time of rice will be about 20 minutes.)

6. Remove risotto from heat. Stir in remaining 1 tablespoon (15 ml) butter and cheese. Garnish, if desired. Serve immediately.

Makes 6 to 8 servings

Step 1. Crushing saffron threads.

Step 3. Stirring rice into onion mixture.

Step 4. Stirring broth into rice until absorbed.

Classic Polenta

6 cups (1.5 L) water
2 teaspoons (10 ml) salt
2 cups (250 ml) yellow
    cornmeal
¼ cup (62.5 ml) vegetable oil

1. Bring water and salt to a boil in large, heavy saucepan over medium-high heat. Stirring water vigorously, add cornmeal in very thin but steady stream (do not let lumps form). Reduce heat to low.

2. Cook polenta, uncovered, 40 to 60 minutes until very thick, stirring frequently. Polenta is ready when spoon will stand upright by itself in center of mixture. Polenta can be served at this point.*

3. For fried polenta, spray 11 x 7-inch (27.5 x 17.5 cm) baking pan with nonstick cooking spray. Spread polenta mixture evenly into baking pan. Cover and let stand at room temperature at least 6 hours or until completely cooled and firm.

4. Unmold polenta onto cutting board. Cut polenta crosswise into 1¼-inch-wide (3 cm) strips. Cut strips into 2- to 3-inch-long (5 to 7.5 cm) pieces.

5. Heat oil in large, heavy skillet over medium-high heat; reduce heat to medium. Fry polenta pieces, ½ at a time, 4 to 5 minutes until golden on all sides, turning as needed. Garnish as desired.

Makes 6 to 8 servings

*Polenta is an important component of Northern Italian cooking. The basic preparation presented here can be served in two forms. Hot freshly made polenta, prepared through step 2, can be mixed with ⅓ cup (83 ml) butter and ⅓ cup (83 ml) grated Parmesan cheese and served as a first course. Or, pour onto a large platter and top with Neapolitan Sauce (page 260) or your favorite spaghetti sauce for a main dish. Fried polenta, as prepared here, is appropriate as an appetizer or as a side dish with meat.

Step 1. Stirring cornmeal into boiling water.

Step 3. Spreading polenta into baking pan.

Step 5. Frying polenta.

COOKING CLASS
MEXICAN

282   CLASS NOTES

286   APPETIZERS

294   TORTILLA DISHES

308   ENTRÉES

326   ON THE SIDE

332   THE BASICS

Baked Shrimp with
Chili-Garlic Butter *(page 324)*

CLASS NOTES

Tacos, burritos, enchiladas–once considered exotic foods, they are now as familiar as earlier imports of pizza, quiche and egg rolls. Due to their vibrant flavors, enticing textural contrasts and eye-catching colors these Mexican dishes have been readily accepted into our menus.

Mexican cuisine is more diverse than the taco lover might suspect. Based on foods such as corn, tomatoes, chilies and beans, this cuisine has developed over centuries and was shaped by unique geography, climate, indigenous foods and the native Indian culture. Mexican cuisine was also enhanced, but not overshadowed, by the Spanish introduction of their cooking techniques and domestic animals.

The recipes in this section were chosen to illustrate the variety of this wonderful cuisine; they range from subtle to spicy, simple to complex, rustic to sophisticated. Using authentic ingredients and cooking techniques, and presented with clear instructions and how-to photos, these dishes are sure to be a success even for the novice cook.

EQUIPMENT
Mexican cuisine requires very little in the way of specialized equipment, but a few items call for some discussion.

Bean Masher: A solid wooden block or perforated metal disk attached to a handle, this tool is very useful for the proper stirring and mashing needed to make refried beans. If necessary, a potato masher can be substituted.

Mortar and Pestle: Used to grind whole spices, herbs and nuts into a powder. The mortar is a bowl-shaped container and the pestle is a rounded-bottomed utensil. The mortar and pestle come as a set and are made out of marble, hardwood, porcelain or stoneware.

Spice or Coffee Grinder, Electric: A small appliance that effectively and quickly grinds whole spices. It can be used to prepare pure fresh chili powder from whole dried chilies. It is also used to grind seeds and nuts into the fine powder that is needed for some sauces, a function neither the blender nor food processor performs as well.

Tortilla Press: The press consists of two flat metal disks (usually 6 inches/15 cm in diameter) that are hinged on one side and have a pressing handle attached at the opposite side. It is readily available in cookware shops and Mexican markets. A tortilla press is essential for speed and accuracy if you plan to make corn tortillas on a regular basis. However, you can improvise pressing the dough with the bottom of a heavy skillet or pie plate.

MEXICAN INGREDIENTS
These ingredients are normally available in Mexican groceries. Many can be found in supermarkets and gourmet food stores and some can be purchased in other Latin American, Caribbean and even Oriental food stores.

Annatto Seeds (also called achiote): Small, hard crimson-colored seeds used primarily in the Mayan-based cooking of the Yucatan. The seeds impart a deep yellow color and mild but distinctive flavor. They are soaked to soften or ground to a fine powder before using.

Chayote: A pear-shaped, pale green, soft-skinned squash with a delicious delicate flavor. It is also called mirliton or christophene. Chayote is generally available in the winter months and can be eaten raw, sautéed or baked. Store it in a plastic bag in the refrigerator for up to one month.

Chilies: See the descriptions on pages 283-284.

Chorizo: An orange- or red-colored, coarse-textured pork sausage sold bulk-style or stuffed into casings. The flavor ranges from highly seasoned to quite hot. Always remove the casing before using.

Cilantro (also called fresh coriander or Chinese parsley): A pungent herb with green delicate leaves, similar in appearance, but not flavor, to flat-leaf parsley. Used extensively in Mexican cooking, there is no substitute. Store it in the refrigerator for up to one week with the stems in a glass of water; cover the leaves with a plastic bag.

Jícama: A root vegetable with thin tan-brown skin and crisp, sweetish, white flesh. Shaped like a large turnip, jícama is most often used raw in salads or eaten as a refreshing snack. It should be peeled before using. Store it in the refrigerator for up to five days.

Masa Harina: A specially prepared flour used to make corn tortillas, tamales and other corn-based doughs. It is commonly available in 5-pound (2.25 kg) bags.

Mexican Chocolate: A mixture of chocolate, almonds, sugar and sometimes cinnamon and vanilla, ground together and formed into octagonal tablets. It is used in desserts, frothy chocolate beverages and, in small amounts, to add a subtle flavor enrichment to some mole sauces.

Onions: White onions with a sharp bite are used in Mexican cooking and are necessary for flavor balance and authenticity. Yellow onions are too mild and impart an undesirable sweetness when cooked.

Queso Chihuahua: A rich semi-soft cheese with a creamy color, mild flavor and good melting qualities. Mild Cheddar, Monterey Jack or Muenster can be used as substitutes.

Tomatillo (also called tomate verde or Mexican tomato): A small hard, green fruit with a papery outer husk that is pulled off before using. Tomatillos have a distinct acidic flavor and are used extensively in cooked sauces. They are available fresh or canned (often labeled tomatillo entero). There is no substitute.

Tortillas: The mainstay of Mexican cuisine. These thin, flat breads are made of corn or wheat flour. Nothing can compare with the taste and texture of freshly made tortillas, but making them at home (see recipes on pages 333 and 334) requires some practice and skill. Tortillas are readily available in the supermarket and these may be substituted for homemade tortillas. Corn tortillas usually measure between 5 and 6 inches (12.5 and 15 cm) in diameter; flour tortillas are available in many sizes, ranging from 7 to 12 inches (17.5 and 30 cm) in diameter.

CHILIES
The subject of chilies can be very confusing for beginning and experienced cooks alike. There are over 100 varieties of chilies in Mexico, each with its own unique characteristics. They are used both fresh and dried and either type can be whole or ground. The same chili can even be found under different names depending upon its region of origin. Chilies range in degree of heat from very mild to incendiary, and the heat can vary within a variety.

Due to increasing interest in Mexican foods, chilies that were once available only in Mexican grocery stores are now readily available in gourmet food stores and many local supermarkets. However, not all chilies will be available in all areas at all times. The following descriptions of the more common varieties will provide you with a basic knowledge of individual chili traits. With this knowledge, you can substitute one chili for another with similar traits. The character of the dish may change slightly, but it will still be delicious and enjoyable.

A Note of Caution: The heat of chilies comes from the seeds, the veins (the thin inner membranes to which the seeds are attached) and in the parts nearest the veins. For milder dishes, the veins and seeds are removed and discarded. The oils from the seeds and veins can be very irritating to the skin and can cause painful burning of the hands, eyes and lips. Do not touch your face while handling chilies and wash your hands well in warm soapy water after handling. Wear rubber gloves if your skin is especially sensitive or if you are handling a number of chilies.

Fresh Chilies
Fresh chilies will keep for several weeks refrigerated in a plastic bag lined with paper towels. (The towels absorb any moisture.) When purchasing fresh chilies, select those that have firm, unblemished skin.

Anaheim (also called California green chili): A light green chili that has a mild flavor with a slight bite. They are 4 to 6 inches (10 to 15 cm) long.

From left to right: Anaheim, Jalapeño, Poblano and Serrano chilies.

about 1½ inches (3.75 cm) wide and have a rounded tip. Anaheims are also sold canned. For a spicier flavor, poblano chilies can be substituted.

Jalapeño: A small, dark green chili, 2 to 3 inches (5 to 7.5 cm) long and about ¾ inch (1.8 cm) wide with a blunt or slightly tapered end. Their flavor varies from hot to very hot. They are also sold canned and pickled. Serranos or other small, hot, fresh chilies can be substituted.

Poblano: A very dark green, large triangular-shaped chili with a pointed end. Poblanos are usually 3½ to 5 inches (8.75 to 12.5 cm) long. Their flavor ranges from mild to quite hot. For a milder flavor, Anaheims can be substituted.

Serrano: A medium green, very small chili with a very hot flavor. It usually ranges from 1 to 1½ inches (2.5 to 3.75 cm) in length and is about ⅜ inch (9 mm) wide with a pointed end. Serranos are also available pickled. Jalapeños or any other small, hot, fresh chilies can be substituted.

Dried Chilies

Dried red (ripe) chilies are usually sold in cellophane packages of various weights. They will keep indefinitely if stored in a tightly covered container in a cool, dark, dry place.

From left to right: Pasilla, Pequín, Mulato, De árbol and Ancho chilies.

Ancho: A fairly large, triangular-shaped chili, slightly smaller than the mulato chili. It has wrinkled, medium to dark reddish-brown skin. Anchos are full-flavored, ranging from mild to medium-hot.

Chipotle: A smoked and dried jalapeño chili. It has wrinkled, medium-brown skin and a rich, smoky, very hot flavor. Chipotles are also commonly available canned in adobo sauce.

De árbol: A very small, slender, almost needle-shaped chili with smooth, bright red skin and a very hot flavor.

Mulato: A triangular-shaped, large chili that has wrinkled, blackish-brown skin. Its flavor is rich, pungent and medium-hot.

Pasilla: A long, slender, medium-sized chili with wrinkled, blackish-brown skin. It has a pungent flavor, ranging from mild to quite hot. (Pasillas are sometimes labeled "negro chilies.")

Pequín (also spelled piquín): A very tiny chili shaped like an oval bead. It has a slightly wrinkled, orangish-red skin. Use pequín chilies with caution as their flavor is very, very hot. (These are sometimes labeled "tepin chilies.")

HELPFUL PREPARATION TECHNIQUES

Roasting Fresh Chilies: Using tongs to hold the chili, place it directly in the medium flame of a gas burner; roast, turning as needed, until the chili is evenly blistered and charred.

Immediately place the roasted chili into a plastic bag; close the bag. Repeat with the remaining chilies. To roast in the broiler, place the chilies on a foil-lined broiler rack; roast them 2 to 3 inches (5 to 7.5 cm) from the heat until they are evenly blistered and charred, turning as needed. Place the roasted chilies in a plastic bag; close the bag.

Let the roasted chilies stand in the closed plastic bag 20 minutes. Peel each chili under cold running water, rubbing and pulling off the charred

skin. Slit the chili open lengthwise using scissors or a knife.

Carefully pull out and discard the seeds and veins. Rinse the chilies well and drain; pat them dry with paper towels.

Toasting Dried Chilies: Heat an ungreased griddle or heavy skillet over medium heat; place the chilies on the griddle in a single layer. Cook the chilies 1 to 3 minutes until the color changes slightly *(but do not burn)* and the chilies become fragrant *(but not to the point of emitting a harsh aroma)*, pressing them down with a spatula and turning over occasionally. If you are toasting a large number of dried chilies, place them in a single layer on a baking sheet in a 350°F (180°C) oven 3 to 5 minutes until the chilies are hot to the touch and fragrant. When the chilies are cool enough to handle but still pliable, cut each one open lengthwise with scissors; carefully pull out the

seeds and the veins. Only if the recipe specifies, rinse and rub chilies under cold running water.

Broiling Tomatoes: Place whole tomatoes on a foil-lined broiler rack. Broil the tomatoes 4 inches (10 cm) from the heat 15 to 20 minutes until the tomatoes are evenly blistered and dark brown *(not black)* on the outside and soft throughout, turning as needed. Use the entire tomato; do not skin, seed or core.

Softening and Warming Tortillas: Stack the tortillas and wrap in foil. Heat the tortillas in a 350°F (180°C) oven 10 minutes until the tortillas are warm. Or, warm them in a microwave oven. Stack the tortillas and wrap them in plastic wrap; microwave on HIGH ½ to 1 minute, turning them over and rotating ¼ turn once during heating.

Cheesy Chorizo Wedges

Red & Green Salsa (recipe
  follows) (optional)
8 ounces (225 g) chorizo
1 cup/250 ml (4 ounces/112 g)
  shredded mild Cheddar
  cheese
1 cup/250 ml (4 ounces/112 g)
  shredded Monterey Jack
  cheese
3 flour tortillas (10-inch/25 cm
  diameter)

1. Prepare Red & Green Salsa.

2. Remove and discard casing from
chorizo. Heat medium skillet over high
heat until hot. Reduce heat to medium.
Crumble chorizo into skillet. Brown 6 to 8
minutes, stirring to separate meat. Remove
with slotted spoon; drain on paper towels.

3. Preheat oven to 450°F (230°C). Mix
cheeses in bowl.

4. Place tortillas on baking sheets. Divide
chorizo evenly among tortillas, leaving ½
inch (1.25 cm) of edges of tortillas
uncovered. Sprinkle cheese mixture over
top.

5. Bake 8 to 10 minutes until edges are
crisp and golden and cheese is bubbly and
melted.

6. Transfer to serving plates; cut each
tortilla into 6 wedges. Sprinkle Red &
Green Salsa on wedges, if desired.
Makes 6 to 8 servings

Step 2. Removing casing from
chorizo.

Step 2. Browning chorizo.

Step 4. Sprinkling cheese
mixture over tortilla.

Red & Green Salsa

1 small red bell pepper
¼ cup (62.5 ml) coarsely chopped
  cilantro
3 green onions, cut into thin slices
2 fresh jalapeño chilies, seeded,
  minced
2 tablespoons (30 ml) fresh lime juice
1 clove garlic, minced
¼ teaspoon (1 ml) salt

Cut bell pepper lengthwise in half; remove
and discard seeds and veins. Cut halves
lengthwise into thin slivers; cut slivers
crosswise into halves. Mix all ingredients
in bowl. Let stand, covered, at room
temperature 1 to 2 hours to blend flavors.
Makes 1 cup (250 ml)

Nachos Olé

1½ cups (375 ml) **Refried Beans (page 332) or canned refried beans**

6 dozen **Corn Tortilla Chips (page 335) or packaged corn tortilla chips**

1½ cups/375 ml (6 ounces/165 g) **shredded Monterey Jack cheese**

1½ cups/375 ml (6 ounces/165 g) **shredded Cheddar cheese**

1 large **tomato**

½ cup (125 ml) **thinly sliced pickled jalapeño chilies**

1. Prepare Refried Beans.

2. Prepare Corn Tortilla Chips.

3. Preheat oven to 400°F (200°C). Combine cheeses in small bowl. Reheat beans, if necessary.

4. Cut tomato crosswise in half. Gently squeeze each half to remove and discard seeds. Chop tomato.

5. Spread 1 teaspoon (5 ml) beans on each tortilla chip.

6. Arrange chips in single layer with edges overlapping slightly on 2 to 3 baking sheets or large ovenproof plates.

7. Sprinkle chips evenly with tomato and chilies; sprinkle with cheese mixture.

8. Bake 5 to 8 minutes until cheese is bubbly and melted.

Makes 4 to 6 servings

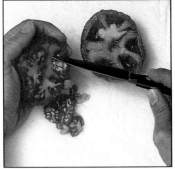

Step 4. Gently squeezing tomato half to remove seeds.

Step 5. Spreading beans on tortilla chips.

Step 7. Sprinkling chips with cheese mixture.

Classic Guacamole

4 tablespoons (60 ml) finely
    chopped white onion,
    divided
1½ tablespoons (22 ml) coarsely
    chopped cilantro, divided
1 or 2 fresh serrano or jalapeño
    chilies, seeded, finely
    chopped
¼ teaspoon (1 ml) chopped
    garlic (optional)
2 large, soft-ripe avocados
1 medium, very ripe tomato
    Boiling water
1 to 2 teaspoons (5 to 10 ml)
    fresh lime juice
¼ teaspoon (1 ml) salt
    Corn Tortilla Chips
    (page 335) or packaged
    corn tortilla chips
    Chilies and cilantro sprig for
    garnish

1. Combine 2 tablespoons (30 ml) onion, 1 tablespoon (15 ml) cilantro, chilies and garlic in large mortar. Grind with pestle until almost smooth. (Mixture can be processed in blender, if necessary, but it will become more watery than desired.)

2. Cut avocados lengthwise into halves; remove and discard pits. Scoop avocado flesh out of shells; place in bowl. Add chili mixture. Mash roughly with wooden spoon, bean masher or potato masher, leaving avocado slightly chunky.

3. To loosen skin from tomato, place tomato in small saucepan of boiling water 30 to 45 seconds. Rinse immediately under cold running water. Peel tomato; cut crosswise in half. Gently squeeze each half to remove and discard seeds. Chop tomato.

4. Add tomato, lime juice, salt and remaining 2 tablespoons (30 ml) onion and ½ tablespoon (2 ml) cilantro to avocado mixture; mix well. Serve immediately or cover and refrigerate up to 4 hours. Serve with Corn Tortilla Chips. Garnish, if desired.

Makes about 2 cups (500 ml)

Step 2. Scooping avocado flesh out of shells.

Step 3. Gently squeezing tomato half to remove seeds.

Step 4. Adding tomato to avocado mixture.

Gazpacho

6 large, very ripe tomatoes (about 3 pounds/1.3 kg), divided
1½ cups (375 ml) tomato juice
1 small clove garlic
2 tablespoons (30 ml) fresh lime juice
2 tablespoons (30 ml) olive oil
1 tablespoon (15 ml) white wine vinegar
1 teaspoon (5 ml) sugar
½ to 1 teaspoon (2 to 5 ml) salt
½ teaspoon (2 ml) dried oregano leaves, crushed
6 green onions, cut into thin slices
¼ cup (62.5 ml) finely chopped celery
¼ cup (62.5 ml) finely chopped, seeded, unpared cucumber
1 or 2 fresh jalapeño chilies, seeded, minced
Garlic Croutons (recipe follows) or packaged croutons
1 cup (250 ml) diced avocado
1 red or green bell pepper, seeded, chopped
2 tablespoons (30 ml) cilantro
Lime wedges (optional)
Sour Cream (optional)

1. Seed and finely chop 1 tomato. (Technique on page 288.) Set aside.

2. Coarsely chop remaining 5 tomatoes; process half of tomatoes, ¾ cup (187 ml) tomato juice and garlic in blender until smooth. Press through sieve into large bowl; discard seeds. Repeat with remaining coarsely chopped tomatoes and ¾ cup (187 ml) tomato juice.

3. Whisk lime juice, oil, vinegar, sugar, salt and oregano into tomato mixture. Stir in finely chopped tomato, onions, celery, cucumber and chilies. Cover; refrigerate at least 4 hours or up to 24 hours.

4. Prepare Garlic Croutons.

5. Stir soup; ladle into chilled bowls. Add croutons, avocado, pepper, cilantro, lime wedges and sour cream according to taste.

Makes 2 servings

Step 2. Pressing tomatoes through sieve.

Step 3. Whisking lime juice into tomato mixture.

Garlic Croutons

5 slices firm white bread
2 tablespoons (30 ml) olive oil
1 clove garlic, minced
¼ teaspoon (1 ml) paprika

1. Preheat oven to 300°F (150°C). Trim crusts from bread; cut into ½-inch (1.25 cm) cubes.

2. Heat oil in skillet over medium heat. Stir in garlic and paprika. Add bread; cook and stir 1 minute just until bread is evenly coated with oil.

3. Spread bread on baking sheet. Bake 20 to 25 minutes until crisp and golden. Cool.

Makes about 2 cups (500 ml)

Flautas with Chicken Filling

3 chicken breast halves (about
    1½ pounds/675 g)
1 can (4 ounces/112 g) diced
    green chilies, drained
½ cup (125 ml) water
⅛ teaspoon (0.5 ml) salt
    (optional)
½ teaspoon (2 ml) ground cumin
    Fresh Tomato Salsa (page 300)
1 cup (250 ml) Classic
    Guacamole (page 290) or
    prepared guacamole
12 corn tortillas (6-inch/15 cm
    diameter)
    Vegetable oil
4 cups (1 L) shredded iceberg
    lettuce
1 cup/250 ml (4 ounces/112 g)
    shredded Monterey Jack
    cheese
½ cup (125 ml) sour cream
    Tomato wedges and cilantro
    sprigs for garnish

1. Combine chicken, chilies, water, salt and cumin in medium skillet. Bring to a boil over medium-high heat. Reduce heat to low. Cover; simmer 15 to 20 minutes until chicken is tender. Remove chicken; let stand until cool enough to handle. Drain chilies and reserve.

2. Prepare Fresh Tomato Salsa and Classic Guacamole.

3. Remove and discard bones and skin from chicken. With fingers, tear chicken into long, thin shreds. Warm corn tortillas. (Technique on page 285.)

4. For each flauta: Overlap 2 tortillas by about half of each tortilla. Spoon ⅛ of chicken mixture down center. Top with ⅛ of reserved chilies. Roll up as tightly as possible.

5. Preheat oven to 250°F (120°C). Heat 1 inch (2.5 cm) oil in deep, heavy skillet over medium-high heat to 375°F (190°C); adjust heat to maintain temperature. Line baking sheet with paper towels.

6. Fry flautas, 1 or 2 at a time, in oil, holding closed with tongs during first 30 seconds to prevent flautas from unrolling. Fry 2 minutes or until crisp and golden on all sides, turning occasionally. Drain on paper towels. Keep warm in oven on prepared baking sheet.

7. To serve, place 2 to 3 flautas on each lettuce-lined plate. Top each serving with some of the cheese, Classic Guacamole and sour cream. Garnish, if desired. Serve with Fresh Tomato Salsa.

Makes 4 to 6 servings

Step 1. Adding water to skillet.

Step 4. Forming flauta.

Step 6. Frying flautas.

Chicken Tostadas

2 cups (500 ml) Refried Beans
   (page 332) or canned
   refried beans
  Fresh Tomato Salsa (page 300)
  Lime-Cumin Dressing (recipe
   follows)
4 flour tortillas (10-inch/25 cm
   diameter) *or* 8 corn
   tortillas (6-inch/15 cm
   diameter)
  Vegetable oil
3 cups (750 ml) shredded
   cooked chicken
4 cups (1 L) shredded iceberg
   lettuce
1 small carrot, shredded
1 cup/250 ml (4 ounces/112 g)
   shredded mild Cheddar
   cheese, divided
1 large, firm-ripe avocado,
   pared, pitted, sliced
½ cup (125 ml) sour cream

1. Prepare Refried Beans, mashing coarsely.

2. Prepare Fresh Tomato Salsa and Lime-Cumin Dressing.

3. Preheat oven to 250°F (120°C). Heat 1 inch (2.5 cm) oil in deep, heavy, large skillet over medium-high heat to 375°F (190°C); adjust heat to maintain temperature. Line baking sheet with paper towels.

4. Fry tortillas, 1 at a time, in oil 1 minute or until crisp and light brown, turning once. Drain on paper towels. Keep warm in oven on prepared baking sheet.

5. Reheat beans, if necessary. Combine chicken, lettuce and carrot in large bowl. Add dressing; toss to mix.

6. To serve, place 1 flour or 2 corn tortillas on each plate. Spread beans to within ½ inch (1.25 cm) of edge of each tortilla. Sprinkle ¾ cup (187 ml) cheese evenly over tostadas. Top with chicken mixture and avocado. Garnish with remaining cheese. Serve with Fresh Tomato Salsa and sour cream.

Makes 4 servings

Step 4. Frying tortilla.

Step 6. Sprinkling cheese over tostada.

Lime-Cumin Dressing

 2 tablespoons (30 ml) fresh lime juice
¼ teaspoon (1 ml) grated lime peel
¼ teaspoon (1 ml) salt
¼ teaspoon (1 ml) ground cumin
¼ cup (62.5 ml) vegetable oil

Combine lime juice, lime peel, salt and cumin in small bowl. Gradually add oil, whisking continuously, until thoroughly blended. Store in refrigerator.

Makes about 1⅓ cup (333 ml)

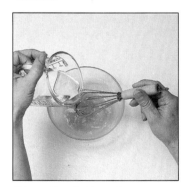

Lime-Cumin Dressing: Whisking oil into lime juice mixture.

Beef Chimichangas

Fresh Tomato Salsa (page 300)
6 ounces (165 g) chorizo
1 pound (450 g) ground beef
½ cup (125 ml) finely chopped
    white onion
1 clove garlic, minced
½ teaspoon (2 ml) ground cumin
1 can (8 ounces/225 g) tomato
    sauce
¼ cup (62.5 ml) sliced pitted
    ripe olives
12 flour tortillas (8-inch/20 cm
    diameter)
1 cup/250 ml (4 ounces/112 g)
    shredded Monterey Jack
    cheese
    Vegetable oil
1 cup (250 ml) sour cream
    Cilantro sprigs and radishes
    for garnish

1. Prepare Fresh Tomato Salsa.

2. Remove and discard casing from chorizo. Heat large skillet over high heat until hot. Reduce heat to medium. Crumble chorizo into skillet. Brown 6 to 8 minutes, stirring to separate meat.

3. Crumble beef into skillet. Brown over medium-high heat 6 to 8 minutes, stirring to separate meat. Add onion, garlic and cumin; cook and stir 4 minutes or until onion is softened. Spoon off and discard fat.

4. Stir in tomato sauce. Bring to a boil over high heat. Reduce heat to low. Cover and simmer 15 minutes. Uncover skillet; increase heat to medium. Cook and stir 5 minutes or until most of liquid has evaporated and meat is moistly coated with sauce. Stir in olives.

5. If not freshly made, soften and warm tortillas. (Technique on page 285.)

6. Place ¼ cup (62.5 ml) meat mixture on bottom half of 1 tortilla; spread to within 1½ inches (3.75 cm) of bottom and side edges. Sprinkle with slightly rounded tablespoon cheese.

continued on page 300

Step 2. Removing casing from chorizo.

Step 3. Spooning off and discarding fat from skillet.

Step 4. Cooking meat mixture until most of liquid has evaporated.

Beef Chimichangas, continued

7. To form, fold bottom edge of tortilla up over filling; fold in side edges, then roll up to completely enclose filling. Secure top with wooden toothpick.

8. Repeat steps 6 and 7 with remaining tortillas, meat mixture and cheese to make 11 more chimichangas.

9. Preheat oven to 250°F (120°C). Heat 1 inch (2.5 cm) oil in deep, heavy skillet over medium-high heat to 375°F (190°C); adjust heat to maintain temperature. Line baking sheet with paper towels.

10. Fry 2 to 3 chimichangas at a time in oil 2 to 3 minutes until golden on all sides, turning occasionally. Remove with tongs; drain on paper towels. Keep warm in oven on prepared baking sheet.

11. Remove toothpicks before serving. Serve with sour cream and Fresh Tomato Salsa. Garnish, if desired.

Makes 6 servings

Fresh Tomato Salsa

1 medium tomato, finely chopped
¼ cup (62.5 ml) coarsely chopped cilantro
2 tablespoons (30 ml) finely chopped white onion
1 fresh jalapeño chili, seeded, finely chopped
1 tablespoon (15 ml) fresh lime juice

Combine all ingredients in small bowl; mix well. Let stand, covered, at room temperature 1 to 2 hours to blend flavors.

Makes about ¾ cup (187 ml)

Step 7. Forming chimichanga.

Step 10. Frying chimichangas.

Beef Enchiladas

Red Chili Sauce (page 302)
1½ pounds (675 g) lean boneless
    beef chuck
½ teaspoon (2 ml) salt
2 tablespoons (30 ml) vegetable
    oil
½ cup (125 ml) finely chopped
    white onion
¾ cup (187 ml) beef broth
¼ cup (62.5 ml) raisins
1 clove garlic, minced
½ teaspoon (2 ml) ground cloves
¼ teaspoon (1 ml) anise seeds,
    crushed
12 corn tortillas (6-inch/15 cm
    diameter)
1 cup/250 ml (4 ounces/112 g)
    shredded mild Cheddar
    cheese
¾ cup (187 ml) sour cream
⅓ cup (83 ml) sliced pitted ripe
    olives
    Basil sprig and tomato wedge
    for garnish

1. Prepare Red Chili Sauce

2. Cut meat lengthwise with utility knife into l-inch (2.5 cm) strips. Then cut crosswise at l-inch (2.5 cm) intervals to form l-inch (2.5 cm) cubes.

3. Sprinkle beef with salt. Brown half of beef in hot oil in large skillet over medium-high heat 10 to 12 minutes, turning frequently. Remove with slotted spoon to plate. Repeat with remaining beef.

4. Reduce heat to medium. Add onion; cook and stir 4 minutes or until onion is softened. Return beef to skillet. Stir in broth, raisins, garlic, cloves, anise seeds and ¼ cup (62.5 ml) Red Chili Sauce. Bring to a boil over medium-high heat. Reduce heat to low. Cover and simmer 1½ to 2 hours until beef is very tender. Using 2 forks, pull beef into coarse shreds in skillet. Remove from heat.

5. Preheat oven to 375°F (190°C). Heat remaining Red Chili Sauce in medium skillet over medium heat until hot; remove from heat.

6. Dip 1 tortilla in sauce with tongs a few seconds or until limp. Remove, draining off excess sauce.

continued on page 302

Step 3. Removing beef from skillet with slotted spoon.

Step 4. Pulling beef into coarse shreds.

Step 6. Dipping tortilla in sauce.

7. Spread about 3 tablespoons (45 ml) meat filling down center of tortilla. Roll up; place in 13 x 9-inch (32.5 x 22.5 cm) baking dish. Repeat with remaining tortillas, sauce and meat filling. Pour remaining sauce over enchiladas.

8. Sprinkle cheese over top. Bake 25 minutes or until bubbly and cheese is melted. To serve, spoon sour cream down center of enchiladas. Sprinkle with olives. Garnish, if desired.

Makes 4 to 6 servings

Red Chili Sauce

3 ounces (85 g) dried ancho chilies (about 5), toasted, seeded, deveined, rinsed (technique on page 285)
2½ cups (625 ml) boiling water
2 tablespoons (30 ml) vegetable oil
2 tablespoons (30 ml) tomato paste
1 clove garlic, minced
½ teaspoon (2 ml) salt
½ teaspoon (2 ml) dried oregano leaves, crushed
¼ teaspoon (1 ml) ground cumin
¼ teaspoon (1 ml) ground coriander

1. Place chilies in medium bowl; cover with boiling water. Let stand 1 hour.

2. Place chilies along with soaking water in blender; process until smooth.

3. Pour into 2-quart (2 L) saucepan; whisk in remaining ingredients. Bring to a boil over medium-high heat. Reduce heat to very low. Cover and simmer 10 minutes, stirring occasionally.

Makes about 2½ cups (583 ml)

Note: Sauce can be refrigerated, covered, up to 3 days or frozen up to 1 month.

Step 7. Forming enchilada.

Red Chili Sauce: Step 1. Covering chilies with boiling water.

Red Chili Sauce: Step 3. Whisking remaining ingredients into chili mixture.

Spicy Beef Tacos

1 pound (450 g) boneless beef chuck, cut into 1-inch (2.5 cm) cubes
Vegetable oil
1 to 2 teaspoons (5 to 10 ml) chili powder
1 clove garlic, minced
½ teaspoon (2 ml) salt
½ teaspoon (2 ml) ground cumin
1 can (14½ ounces/405 g) whole peeled tomatoes, undrained, chopped
12 corn-tortillas (6-inch/15 cm diameter)*
1 cup/250 ml (4 ounces/112 g) shredded mild Cheddar cheese
2 to 3 cups (500 to 750 ml) shredded iceberg lettuce
1 large fresh tomato, seeded, chopped (technique on page 288)
Cilantro for garnish

*Or, substitute packaged taco shells for the corn tortillas. Omit steps 4 and 5. Warm taco shells according to package directions.

1. Brown beef in 2 tablespoons (30 ml) hot oil in large skillet over medium-high heat 10 to 12 minutes, turning frequently. Reduce heat to low. Stir in chili powder, garlic, salt and cumin. Cook and stir 30 seconds.

2. Add undrained tomatoes. Bring to a boil over high heat. Reduce heat to low. Cover and simmer 1½ to 2 hours until beef is very tender.

3. Using 2 forks, pull beef into coarse shreds in skillet. Increase heat to medium. Cook, uncovered, 10 to 15 minutes until most of liquid has evaporated and beef is moistly coated with sauce. Keep warm.

4. Heat 4 to 5 inches (10 to 12.5 cm) of oil in deep fat fryer or deep saucepan over medium-high heat to 375°F (190°C); adjust heat to maintain temperature.

5. For taco shells, place 1 tortilla in taco fryer basket;** close gently. Fry tortilla ½ to 1 minute until crisp and golden. Open basket; gently remove taco shell. Drain on paper towels. Repeat with remaining tortillas.

6. Layer beef, cheese, lettuce and tomato in each taco shell. Garnish, if desired.

Makes 6 servings

**Taco fryer baskets are available in large supermarkets and in housewares stores.

Step 1. Browning beef.

Step 3. Cooking beef until most of liquid has evaporated.

Step 5. Shaping tortilla into taco shell.

Pork Burritos

2 cups (500 ml) Refried Beans
    (page 332)
    or canned refried beans
1 boneless fresh pork butt roast
    (about 2½ pounds/1.12 kg)
1 cup (250 ml) chopped white
    onion
1 carrot, sliced
1 clove garlic, minced
½ teaspoon (2 ml) salt
½ teaspoon (2 ml) ground cumin
½ teaspoon (2 ml) coriander
    seeds, lightly crushed
    Water
    Fresh Tomato Salsa (page 300)
12 flour tortillas (8-inch/20 cm
    diameter)
2 medium, firm-ripe avocados,
    pared, pitted, diced
1 cup/250 ml (4 ounces/112 g)
    shredded
    Monterey Jack cheese
    Carrot sticks, avocado slices
    and cilantro sprig for
    garnish

1. Prepare Refried Beans.

2. Place pork, white onion, sliced carrot, garlic, salt, cumin and coriander seeds in 5-quart (5 L) Dutch oven. Add just enough water to cover pork. Bring to a boil over high heat. Reduce heat to low. Cover and simmer 2 to 2½ hours until pork is tender.

3. Prepare Fresh Tomato Salsa.

4. Preheat oven to 350°F (180°C). Remove pork from Dutch oven; set aside. Strain cooking liquid through cheesecloth-lined sieve; reserve ½ cup (125 ml) liquid.

5. Place pork on rack in roasting pan. Roast 40 to 45 minutes until well browned, turning once. Let stand until cool enough to handle.

6. Trim and discard outer fat from pork. Using 2 forks, pull pork into coarse shreds. Combine pork and reserved cooking liquid in medium skillet. Heat over medium heat 5 minutes or until meat is hot and moistly coated with liquid; stir often.

7. Soften and warm tortillas. (Technique on page 285.) Reheat beans, if necessary.

8. Place about 2½ tablespoons (38 ml) beans on bottom half of 1 tortilla; spread out slightly. Layer with pork, salsa, diced avocado and cheese.

9. To form, fold right edge of tortilla up over filling; fold bottom edge over filling, then loosely roll up, leaving left end of burrito open. Garnish, if desired.

Makes 6 servings

Step 2. Adding enough water to cover pork.

Step 6. Pulling pork into coarse shreds.

Step 9. Forming burrito.

Spicy Grilled Chicken

⅓ cup (83 ml) Chili Butter (recipe
    follows)
6 boneless chicken breast halves
    (about 6 ounces/165 g each)
Cilantro sprigs for garnish
Jícama-Cucumber Salad
    (page 326) (optional)
Flour Tortillas (optional)

1. Prepare Chili Butter. Cut Chili Butter into ⅛-inch-thick (3 mm) slices. Loosen skin at one end of each chicken piece; insert 1 slice of Chili Butter under skin of each piece.

2. Preheat broiler. Place chicken, skin side down, on greased rack of broiler pan; dot with some of remaining butter. Broil chicken, 6 inches (15 cm) from heat, 10 minutes or until tops are browned. Turn chicken over; dot with more of the remaining butter. Broil 10 minutes or until browned and juices run clear.

3. To serve, top with Chili Butter, if desired. Serve with Jícama-Cucumber Salad and tortillas.

Makes 6 servings

Step 1. Placing Chili Butter under chicken skin.

Step 2. Dotting chicken with Chili Butter.

Chili Butter

1 small dried ancho chili, toasted,
    seeded, deveined, rinsed
    (technique on page 285)
1 cup (250 ml) boiling water
½ cup (125 ml) butter, softened
1 clove garlic, minced
¼ teaspoon (1 ml) dried oregano
    leaves, crushed

1. Place chili in small bowl; cover with boiling water. Let stand 1 hour.

2. Place chili and 1½ tablespoons (22 ml) soaking water in blender; process until smooth. Cool completely. Discard remaining soaking water.

3. Beat butter in small bowl with electric mixer until fluffy. Beat in garlic and oregano. Gradually beat in chili mixture. Cover and refrigerate 30 minutes or until firm. Spoon butter in a strip onto plastic wrap; enclose in plastic wrap and roll back and forth to form smooth 1-inch-thick (2.5 cm) roll. Refrigerate until firm.

Makes about ⅔ cup (187 ml)

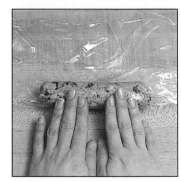

Chili Butter: Step 3. Rolling butter mixture into log.

Chicken Mole

3 small dried pasilla chilies, toasted, seeded, deveined, rinsed (technique on page 285)

3 small dried mulato chilies, toasted, seeded, deveined, rinsed (technique on page 285)

1½ cups (375 ml) boiling water

¼ cup (62.5 ml) sesame seeds

3 whole cloves

1 piece cinnamon stick (about 1 inch/2.5 cm)

¼ teaspoon (1 ml) whole coriander seeds

⅛ teaspoon (0.5 ml) whole anise seeds

¼ cup (62.5 ml) vegetable oil

¼ cup (62.5 ml) whole unblanched almonds

¼ cup (62.5 ml) raisins

6 whole chicken legs, thighs attached (about 3 pounds/1.3 kg)

¼ teaspoon (1 ml) salt

½ cup (125 ml) coarsely chopped white onion

2 cloves garlic

1 tablespoon (15 ml) tomato paste

1½ ounces (42 g) Mexican chocolate

1 cup (250 ml) chicken broth

Tomato wedges and cilantro sprigs for garnish

Green Rice Pilaf (page 330) (optional)

1. Place pasilla and mulato chilies in medium bowl; cover with boiling water. Let stand 1 hour.

2. Toast sesame seeds in dry, heavy skillet over medium heat 2 minutes or until golden, stirring frequently. Remove from skillet.

3. Combine cloves, cinnamon stick, coriander seeds and anise seeds in same skillet; toast over medium heat 20 to 30 seconds until they start to change color and become fragrant, stirring frequently. Remove from skillet.

4. Heat oil in 12-inch (30 cm) skillet over medium heat until hot. Add almonds. Cook and stir 2 to 3 minutes until brown. Remove with slotted spoon; drain on paper towels.

5. Add raisins. Cook and stir 30 seconds or until puffed. Remove with slotted spoon.

6. Sprinkle chicken with salt. Cook in same skillet over medium heat 10 minutes or until browned, turning once. Remove to plate. Remove all but 2 tablespoons (30 ml) oil from skillet.

continued on page 312

Step 1. Covering chilies with boiling water.

Step 2. Toasting sesame seeds.

Step 4. Browning almonds.

Chicken Mole, continued

7. Place raisins in blender; process until finely ground. Coarsely chop almonds; add to blender. Process until finely ground. Add onion and garlic to blender; process until finely ground.

8. Process 2 tablespoons (30 ml) sesame seeds with on/off pulses in electric spice grinder to fine powder. Add to blender.

9. Process clove mixture in grinder to fine powder; add to blender.

10. Add chilies, ⅓ cup (83 ml) of the soaking water and the tomato paste to blender; process until smooth. If mixture is too thick, add just enough of the remaining soaking water, 1 teaspoon (5 ml) at a time, until blender blade can spin. Discard remaining soaking water.

11. Coarsely chop chocolate using a sharp knife.

12. Reheat oil in skillet over medium heat until hot. Reduce heat to medium-low. Add chili mixture. Cook and stir 5 minutes. Add chocolate; cook and stir 2 minutes or until melted. Gradually stir in broth. Cook and stir 5 minutes.

13. Return chicken to skillet. Reduce heat to low. Cover and simmer 45 minutes or until chicken is tender and juices run clear, turning chicken occasionally. Sprinkle remaining sesame seeds over chicken just before serving. Garnish, if desired. Serve with Green Rice Pilaf.

Makes 6 servings

Step 7. Adding onion to raisin mixture.

Step 10. Processed chili mixture.

Step 12. Cooking mole sauce.

Chilies Rellenos

Tomato Sauce (page 314)
8 fresh poblano or Anaheim
   chilies
Picadillo Filling (page 314)
Vegetable oil
⅓ cup (83 ml) all-purpose flour
5 eggs, separated
¼ teaspoon (1 ml) cream of
   tartar
¼ teaspoon (1 ml) salt
Pimiento-stuffed green olives
   for garnish

1. Prepare Tomato Sauce.

2. Roast, peel, seed and devein chilies, leaving stems intact and taking care not to break chilies. (Technique on pages 284-285.)

3. Prepare Picadillo Filling.

4. Carefully spoon about ¼ cup (62.5 ml) Picadillo Filling into each chili; press chilies firmly between hands to ease out air and to close.

5. Preheat oven to 250°F (120°C). Heat 1 inch (2.5 cm) oil in deep, heavy skillet over medium-high heat to 375°F (190°C); adjust heat to maintain temperature. Line baking sheet with paper towels.

6. Roll each chili in flour to coat lightly; pat off excess. Reserve remaining flour, about ¼ cup (62.5 ml).

7. Beat egg whites, cream of tartar and salt in large bowl with electric mixer at high speed until soft peaks form. Beat egg yolks in medium bowl with electric mixer at medium speed until thick and lemon colored. Gradually beat reserved flour into egg yolks until smooth. Fold ¼ of egg whites into yolk mixture; fold in remaining egg whites until blended.

8. To coat each chili with egg batter, grasp stem; support bottom of chili with fork. Dip into batter to coat; let excess drain off.

continued on page 314

Step 4. Spooning filling into chilies.

Step 6. Rolling chili in flour.

Step 8. Coating chili with egg batter.

Chilies Rellenos, continued

9. Immediately slip chili into oil. Fry 4 minutes or until deep gold, turning once. Remove with slotted spatula; drain on paper towels. Keep warm in oven.

10. Reheat Tomato Sauce over medium heat. Spoon sauce on plates; arrange chilies on plates. Garnish, if desired.

Makes 4 servings

Tomato Sauce

1½ pounds (675 g) tomatoes, peeled, seeded (technique on page 290)
1 medium white onion, chopped
1 clove garlic, chopped
2 tablespoons (30 ml) vegetable oil
1½ cups (375 ml) chicken broth
½ teaspoon (2 ml) dried thyme leaves, crushed
¼ teaspoon (1 ml) salt

1. Place tomatoes, onion and garlic in blender; process until smooth.

2. Heat oil in deep, large skillet over medium heat until hot. Add tomato mixture; cook and stir 5 minutes.

3. Stir broth, thyme and salt into skillet. Bring to a boil over high heat. Reduce heat to medium-low. Cook and stir 10 to 15 minutes until sauce has thickened slightly. Remove from heat; set aside.

Makes about 2 cups (500 ml)

Picadillo Filling

1 tablespoon (15 ml) vegetable oil
¼ cup (62.5 ml) slivered almonds
¾ pound (337 g) ground beef
¼ cup (62.5 ml) finely chopped white onion
1 large tomato, peeled, seeded, finely chopped (technique on page 290)
1 tablespoon (15 ml) tomato paste
1 clove garlic, minced
2 tablespoons (30 ml) raisins
2 tablespoons (30 ml) thinly sliced pimiento-stuffed green olives
1 tablespoon (15 ml) cider vinegar
1 teaspoon (5 ml) dark brown sugar
¼ teaspoon (1 ml) salt
¼ teaspoon (1 ml) ground cinnamon
⅛ teaspoon (0.5 ml) ground cumin
⅛ teaspoon (0.5 ml) ground cloves

1. Heat oil in large skillet over medium heat. Add almonds; cook and stir 2 to 3 minutes until golden. Remove; drain on paper towels.

2. Crumble beef into skillet. Brown beef 5 minutes; stir often. Add onion; cook and stir 4 minutes or until softened. Add tomato, tomato paste and garlic. Cook and stir 2 minutes. Stir in remaining ingredients except almonds. Cover and simmer over low heat 15 minutes.

3. Uncover skillet; cook over medium-low heat 3 minutes until most of liquid has evaporated. Skim and discard fat. Stir in almonds. Let stand until cool enough to handle.

Makes about 2 cups (500 ml)

Step 9. Frying chilies.

Picadillo Filling: Step 1. Toasting almonds.

Picadillo Filling: Step 2. Stirring spices into ground beef mixture.

Fajitas

2 beef skirt steaks (about 1 pound/450 g each)
2 cloves garlic, divided
3 tablespoons (45 ml) vegetable oil, divided
2 tablespoons (30 ml) *plus* 1 to 2 teaspoons (5 to 10 ml) fresh lime juice, divided
Dash ground black pepper
½ cup (125 ml) minced white onion
2 large tomatoes, seeded, finely chopped (technique on page 290)
2 small green bell peppers, roasted, peeled, seeded, deveined, finely chopped (technique on pages 284-285)
2 tablespoons (30 ml) minced cilantro
1 fresh serrano chili, minced
Refried Beans (page 332) (optional)
Flour tortillas (8-inch/20 cm diameter) (optional)

1. Place steaks between pieces of plastic wrap. Pound with flat side of meat mallet to ¼-inch (6 mm) thickness. Cut each steak crosswise into halves.

2. Pound 1 garlic clove with meat mallet to crush into coarse shreds. Combine with 2 tablespoons (30 ml) oil, 2 tablespoons (30 ml) lime juice and black pepper in large shallow glass baking dish. Add steaks, turning to coat with marinade. Marinate in refrigerator 30 minutes.

3. Mince remaining garlic clove. Cook and stir onion and garlic in remaining 1 tablespoon (15 ml) oil in medium skillet over medium heat 3 to 4 minutes until onion is softened. Remove from heat.

4. Stir in tomatoes, bell peppers, cilantro and chili. Season to taste with remaining lime juice. Let stand, covered, at room temperature.

5. Prepare coals for grill.* Remove steaks from marinade; pat dry with paper towels. Discard marinade. Grill 6 inches (15 cm) from heat 3 minutes for medium-rare or until desired doneness is reached, turning once.

6. Reheat beans, if necessary. If not freshly made, soften and warm tortillas. (Technique on page 285.)

7. Serve steaks with tomato relish, Refried Beans and tortillas.

Makes 4 servings

*Steaks can be cooked on lightly oiled, well-seasoned heavy griddle or large skillet. Heat over medium heat until very hot. Cook steaks in single layer on griddle 3 minutes for medium-rare or until desired doneness is reached, turning once.

Step 1. Pounding meat to ¼-inch (6 mm) thickness.

Step 4. Stirring cilantro into tomato relish.

Chili

2 tablespoons (30 ml) vegetable
  oil
2 pounds (900 g) ground chuck,
  coarse chili grind or
  regular grind
2 cups (500 ml) finely chopped
  white onions
1 or 2 dried de árbol chilies
2 cloves garlic, minced
1 teaspoon (5 ml) ground cumin
½ to 1 teaspoon (2 to 5 ml) salt
¼ teaspoon (1 ml) ground cloves
1 can (28 ounces/785 g) whole
  peeled tomatoes,
  undrained, coarsely
  chopped
½ cup (125 ml) fresh orange
  juice
½ cup (125 ml) tequila or water
¼ cup (62.5 ml) tomato paste
1 tablespoon (15 ml) grated
  orange peel
  Lime wedges and cilantro
  sprigs for garnish

1. Heat oil in deep, 12-inch (30 cm) skillet over medium-high heat until hot. Crumble beef into skillet. Brown beef 6 to 8 minutes, stirring to separate meat. Reduce heat to medium. Add onions. Cook and stir 5 minutes until onions are softened.

2. Crush chilies into fine flakes in mortar with pestle. Add chilies, garlic, cumin, salt and cloves to skillet. Cook and stir 30 seconds.

3. Stir in tomatoes, orange juice, tequila, tomato paste and orange peel. Bring to a boil over high heat. Reduce heat to low. Cover and simmer 1½ hours, stirring occasionally.

4. Uncover skillet. Cook chili over medium-low heat 10 to 15 minutes until thickened slightly, stirring frequently. Ladle into bowls. Garnish, if desired.

Makes 6 to 8 servings

Step 1. Browning ground beef.

Step 2. Crushing chilies in mortar with pestle.

Step 3. Stirring orange peel into tomato mixture.

Grilled Chili-Marinated Pork

3 tablespoons (45 ml) ground
    seeded dried pasilla chilies
1 teaspoon (5 ml) coarse or
    kosher salt
½ teaspoon (2 ml) ground cumin
2 tablespoons (30 ml) vegetable
    oil
1 tablespoon (15 ml) fresh lime
    juice
3 cloves garlic, minced
2 pounds (900 g) pork
    tenderloin or thick boneless
    loin pork chops, trimmed
    of fat
Shredded romaine lettuce
    (optional)
Radishes for garnish

1. Mix chilies, salt and cumin in small bowl. Stir in oil and lime juice to make smooth paste. Stir in garlic.

2. Butterfly pork by cutting lengthwise about ⅔ of the way through, leaving meat in one piece; spread meat flat.

3. Cut tenderloin crosswise into 8 equal pieces. *Do not cut chops into pieces.*

4. Place pork between pieces of plastic wrap. Pound with flat side of meat mallet to ¼-inch (6 mm) thickness.

5. Spread chili paste on both sides of pork pieces to coat evenly. Place in shallow glass baking dish. Marinate, covered, in refrigerator 2 to 3 hours.

6. Prepare coals for grill or preheat broiler. Grill or broil pork 6 inches (15 cm) from heat 8 to 10 minutes for grilling or 6 to 7 minutes for broiling, turning once. Serve on lettuce-lined plate. Garnish, if desired.

Makes 6 to 8 servings

Step 2. Butterflying pork roast.

Step 3. Cutting pork roast into 8 equal pieces.

Step 4. Pounding meat to ¼-inch (6 mm) thickness.

Red Snapper in Chili-Tomato Sauce

6 red snapper fillets (8 to 10 ounces/225 to 280 g each)
¼ teaspoon (1 ml) salt
⅛ teaspoon (0.5 ml) pepper
⅓ cup (83 ml) all-purpose flour
¼ cup (62.5 ml) olive oil
3 cloves garlic, sliced
2 medium white onions, cut lengthwise into thin slivers
1½ pounds (675 g) fresh plum tomatoes, peeled, seeded, finely chopped (technique on page 290)
½ cup (125 ml) tomato juice
¼ cup (62.5 ml) fresh lime juice
¼ cup (62.5 ml) sliced pimiento-stuffed green olives
1 or 2 pickled jalapeño chilies, seeded, finely chopped
1 tablespoon (15 ml) drained capers
1 bay leaf
Fresh bay leaves and lime slices for garnish
Boiled, quartered new potatoes with fresh dill (optional)

1. Sprinkle fish with salt and pepper. Coat both sides of fish with flour; shake off excess.

2. Heat oil in 12-inch (30 cm) skillet over medium heat. Add garlic; cook and stir 2 to 3 minutes until golden. Remove garlic with slotted spoon; discard.

3. Place fillets in single layer in skillet without crowding. Cook over medium heat 4 minutes or until fillets are light brown, turning once. Remove to plate. Repeat with remaining fillets.

4. Add onions. Cook and stir 4 minutes or until onions are softened. Stir in tomatoes, tomato juice, lime juice, olives, chilies, capers and bay leaf. Bring to a boil over high heat. Reduce heat to low. Cover and simmer 15 minutes.

5. Add any accumulated juices from fillets on plate to skillet. Increase heat to medium-high. Cook, uncovered, 2 to 3 minutes until thickened, stirring frequently. Remove and discard bay leaf.

6. Return fillets to skillet. Spoon sauce over fillets. Reduce heat to low. Cover; simmer 3 to 5 minutes until fillets flake easily when tested with a fork. Garnish, if desired. Serve with potatoes.

Makes 6 servings

Step 1. Coating fish with flour.

Step 2. Removing garlic from skillet.

Step 4. Stirring in remaining sauce ingredients.

Baked Shrimp with Chili-Garlic Butter

1½ pounds (675 g) medium raw
   shrimp in shells
½ cup (125 ml) butter
¼ cup (62.5 ml) vegetable oil
8 cloves garlic, finely chopped
1 to 3 dried de árbol chilies,
   coarsely crumbled*
1 tablespoon (15 ml) fresh lime
   juice
¼ teaspoon (1 ml) salt
   Green onion tops, slivered,
   for garnish

*For milder flavor, seed some or all of
the chilies.

1. Preheat oven to 400°F (200°C). Shell and devein shrimp, leaving tails attached; rinse and drain well.

2. Heat butter and oil in small skillet over medium heat until butter is melted and foamy. Add garlic, chilies, lime juice and salt. Cook and stir 1 minute. Remove from heat.

3. Arrange shrimp in even layer in shallow 2-quart (2 L) gratin pan or baking dish. Pour hot butter mixture over shrimp.

4. Bake shrimp 10 to 12 minutes until shrimp turn pink and opaque, stirring once. Do not overcook or shrimp will be dry and tough. Garnish, if desired.

Makes 4 servings

Step 1. Removing shells from shrimp.

Step 2. Adding seasonings to melted butter.

Step 3. Pouring butter mixture over shrimp.

Jícama-Cucumber Salad

1 jícama (1¼ to 1½ pounds/560
    to 675 g)*
1 small cucumber, unpared
½ cup (125 ml) very thinly
    slivered mild red onion
2 tablespoons (30 ml) fresh lime
    juice
½ teaspoon (2 ml) grated lime
    peel
1 clove garlic, minced
¼ teaspoon (1 ml) salt
⅛ teaspoon (0.5 ml) crumbled
    dried de árbol chili
3 tablespoons (45 ml) vegetable
    oil
    Leaf lettuce
    Red onion slivers and lime
    wedges for garnish

*Or, substitute Jerusalem artichokes.
Cut pared artichokes lengthwise into
halves; cut halves crosswise into thin
slices.

1. Pare jícama. Cut lengthwise into 8 wedges; cut wedges crosswise into ⅛-inch-thick (3 mm) slices.

2. Cut cucumber lengthwise in half; scoop out and discard seeds. Cut halves crosswise into ⅛-inch-thick (3 mm) slices.

3. Combine jícama, cucumber and onion in large bowl; toss lightly to mix.

4. Combine lime juice, lime peel, garlic, salt and chili in small bowl. Gradually add oil, whisking continuously, until dressing is thoroughly blended.

5. Pour dressing over salad; toss lightly to coat. Cover and refrigerate 1 to 2 hours to blend flavors.

6. Serve salad in lettuce-lined salad bowl. Garnish, if desired.

Makes 6 servings

Step 1. Cutting jícama crosswise into ⅛-inch-thick (3 mm) slices.

Step 2. Removing seeds from cucumber half.

Step 5. Pouring dressing over salad.

Zesty Zucchini-Chick Pea Salad

3 medium zucchini (about
6 ounces/165 g each)
½ teaspoon (2 ml) salt
5 tablespoons (75 ml) white
vinegar
1 clove garlic, minced
¼ teaspoon (1 ml) dried thyme
leaves, crushed
½ cup (125 ml) olive oil
1 cup (250 ml) drained canned
chick peas
½ cup (125 ml) sliced pitted ripe
olives
3 green onions, minced
1 canned chipotle chili in adobo
sauce, drained, seeded,
minced
1 ripe avocado, pitted, pared,
cut into ½-inch (1.5 cm)
cubes
⅓ cup (83 ml) crumbled feta *or*
3 tablespoons (45 ml)
grated Romano cheese
1 head Boston lettuce, cored,
separated into leaves
Sliced tomatoes and cilantro
sprigs for garnish

1. Cut zucchini lengthwise into halves; cut halves crosswise into ¼-inch-thick (6 mm) slices. Place slices in medium bowl; sprinkle with salt. Toss to mix. Spread zucchini on several layers of paper towels. Let stand at room temperature 30 minutes to drain.

2. Combine vinegar, garlic and thyme in large bowl. Gradually add oil, whisking continuously until dressing is thoroughly blended.

3. Pat zucchini dry; add to dressing. Add chick peas, olives and onions; toss lightly to coat. Cover and refrigerate at least 30 minutes or up to 4 hours, stirring occasionally.

4. Add chili to salad just before serving. Stir gently to mix. Add avocado and cheese; toss lightly to mix.

5. Serve salad in lettuce-lined shallow bowl or plate. Garnish, if desired.
Makes 4 to 6 servings

Step 1. Draining zucchini on paper towels.

Step 2. Whisking oil into vinegar mixture.

Step 4. Adding avocado and cheese to salad.

Green Rice Pilaf

2 tablespoons (30 ml) vegetable oil

1 cup (250 ml) raw long-grain white rice (not converted)

¼ cup (62.5 ml) finely chopped white onion

2 fresh poblano or Anaheim chilies, roasted, peeled, seeded, deveined, chopped (technique on pages 284-285)

6 thin green onions, thinly sliced

1 clove garlic, minced

¼ teaspoon (62.5 ml) salt

¼ teaspoon (62.5 ml) ground cumin

1¾ cups (437 ml) chicken broth

1½ cups (375 ml) shredded queso Chihuahua or Monterey Jack cheese

⅓ cup (83 ml) coarsely chopped cilantro

Cilantro sprig for garnish

1. Preheat oven to 375°F (190°C). Heat oil in large skillet over medium heat until hot. Add rice. Cook and stir 2 minutes or until rice turns opaque.

2. Add white onion; cook and stir 1 minute. Stir in chilies, green onions, garlic, salt and cumin; cook and stir 20 seconds.

3. Stir in broth. Bring to a boil over high heat. Reduce heat to low. Cover and simmer 15 minutes or until rice is almost tender.*

4. Remove skillet from heat. Add 1 cup (250 ml) cheese and chopped cilantro; toss lightly to mix. Transfer to greased 1½-quart (1.5 L) baking dish; top with remaining ½ cup (125 ml) cheese.

5. Bake, uncovered, 15 minutes or until rice is tender and cheese topping is melted. Garnish, if desired.

Makes 4 to 6 servings

*For plain green rice, complete recipe from this point as follows: Cook rice in skillet 2 to 4 minutes more until tender. Stir in chopped cilantro just before serving; omit cheese.

Step 2. Stirring chilies, onions and seasonings into rice mixture.

Step 3. Mixing broth into rice mixture.

Step 4. Tossing cheese with rice mixture.

Refried Beans

8 ounces (225 g) dried red, pink or pinto beans (1⅓ cups/333 ml)
4½ cups (1.12 L) cold water
⅓ cup (83 ml) *plus* 1 tablespoon (15 ml) vegetable shortening or vegetable oil, divided
1 small white onion, sliced
1½ teaspoons (7 ml) salt
1 small white onion, finely chopped
1 small clove garlic, minced

1. Rinse beans thoroughly in sieve under cold running water, picking out any debris or blemished beans.

2. Place beans, water, 1 tablespoon (15 ml) shortening and sliced onion in 3-quart (3 L) saucepan. Bring to a boil over high heat. Reduce heat to low. Cover and simmer 1½ hours or just until beans are tender, not soft.

3. Stir in salt. Cover and simmer over very low heat 30 to 45 minutes until beans are very soft. Do not drain.*

4. Heat remaining ⅓ cup (83 ml) shortening in heavy, large skillet over high heat until very hot. Add chopped onion and garlic. Reduce heat to medium. Cook and stir 4 minutes or until onion is softened.

5. Increase heat to high. Add 1 cup (250 ml) undrained beans. Cook and stir, mashing beans with bean or potato masher.

6. As beans begin to dry, add another 1 cup (250 ml) undrained beans. Cook and stir, mashing beans with bean or potato masher. Repeat until all beans and cooking liquid have been added and mixture is a coarse purée. Adjust heat as needed to prevent beans from sticking and burning. Total cooking time will be around 20 minutes.

7. Beans may be served as a side dish or used as an ingredient for another recipe.

Makes about 2 cups (500 ml)

*Flavor is improved if beans are prepared to this point, then refrigerated, covered, overnight before completing recipe.

Step 1. Rinsing beans.

Step 5. Mashing beans.

Step 6. Adding cooking liquid to mashed beans.

Flour Tortillas

2 cups (500 ml) all-purpose
    flour
½ teaspoon (2 ml) salt
¼ cup (62.5 ml) vegetable
    shortening
½ cup (125 ml) warm water

1. Combine flour and salt in medium bowl. Rub shortening into flour with fingertips until mixture has fine, even texture. Stir in water until dough forms.

2. Knead dough on floured surface 2 to 3 minutes until smooth and elastic. Wrap in plastic wrap. Let stand 30 minutes at room temperature.

3. Knead dough a few times. Divide evenly into 8 pieces for 10-inch (25 cm) tortillas or 12 pieces for 8-inch (20 cm) tortillas. Shape pieces into balls; cover with plastic wrap to prevent them from drying out.

4. Using rolling pin, roll out each dough ball on floured surface, turning over frequently, into 8- or 10-inch (20 or 25 cm) circle. Stack each tortilla between sheets of waxed paper.

5. Heat ungreased heavy griddle or skillet over medium-high heat until a little water sprinkled on surface dances. Carefully lay 1 tortilla on griddle; cook 20 to 30 seconds until top is bubbly and bottom is flecked with brown spots. Turn tortilla over; cook 15 to 20 seconds until flecked with brown spots. If tortilla puffs up while second side is cooking, press it down gently with spatula. Remove tortilla to foil.

6. Cook remaining tortillas as directed in step 5. If griddle becomes too hot, reduce heat to prevent burning. Stack cooked tortillas and cover with foil until all are cooked. Use immediately or wrap in foil and keep warm in 250°F (120°C) oven up to 30 minutes. Tortillas are best when fresh, but can be wrapped in foil and refrigerated up to 3 days or frozen up to 2 weeks. Reheat in 350°F (180°C) oven 10 minutes before using.

Makes 8 (10-inch/25 cm) or
12 (8-inch/20 cm) tortillas

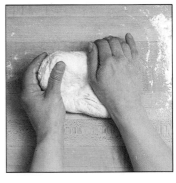

Step 2. Kneading dough.

Step 4. Rolling dough into circle.

Step 5. Pressing tortilla down to flatten puffed area.

Corn Tortillas

2 cups (500 ml) masa harina
1 to 1¼ cups (250 to 312 ml)
     warm water
   Corn Tortilla Chips (page 335)

1. Cut 2 (7-inch/17.5 cm) squares from heavy-duty plastic bag. Combine masa harina and 1 cup (250 ml) water in medium bowl. Add remaining water, 1 tablespoon (15 ml) at a time, until a smooth stiff dough is formed.

2. Test consistency of dough by rolling 1 piece dough into 1¾-inch (4.3 cm) ball; flatten slightly. Place ball on piece of plastic on lower plate of tortilla press, slightly off-center away from handle.* Cover with second piece of plastic; press down firmly with top of press to make 6-inch (15 cm) tortilla. Peel off top piece of plastic; invert tortilla onto hand and peel off second piece of plastic. If edges are cracked or ragged, dough is too dry; mix in water, 1 to 2 teaspoons (5 to 10 ml) at a time, until dough presses out with smooth edges. If tortilla sticks to plastic, dough is too wet; mix in masa harina, 1 tablespoon (15 ml) at a time, until dough no longer sticks when pressed.

3. When dough has correct consistency, divide evenly into 12 pieces for 6-inch (15 cm) tortillas or 24 pieces for 4-inch (10 cm) tortillas. Shape pieces into balls; cover with plastic wrap to prevent them from drying out.

4. Press out tortillas as directed in step 2, stacking between sheets of plastic wrap or waxed paper.

Step 1. Adding water, 1 tablespoon (15 ml) at a time, to dough.

Step 2. Flattening dough in tortilla press.

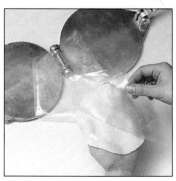

Step 2. Testing texture of flattened dough.

5. Heat ungreased heavy griddle or skillet over medium-high heat until a little water sprinkled on surface dances. Carefully lay 1 tortilla on griddle; cook 30 seconds or until edges begin to dry out. Turn tortilla over; cook 45 seconds to 1 minute until dry and lightly flecked with brown spots. Turn tortilla over again; cook first side 15 to 20 seconds more until dry and light brown. During last stage of cooking, tortilla may puff up; do not press down. Remove tortilla to kitchen towel; it will be slightly stiff, but will soften as it stands.

6. Cook remaining tortillas as directed in step 5. If griddle becomes too hot, reduce heat to prevent burning. Stack cooked tortillas and keep wrapped in towel until all are cooked. Use immediately or wrap in foil and keep warm in 250°F (120°C) oven up to 30 minutes. Tortillas are best when fresh, but can be wrapped in foil and re-frigerated up to 3 days or frozen up to 2 weeks. Reheat in 350°F (180°C) oven 10 minutes before using.

Makes 12 (6-inch/15 cm) or 24 (4-inch/10 cm) tortillas

*A tortilla press works best, but if necessary, you can press with bottom of pie plate or heavy skillet.

Corn Tortilla Chips

**12 corn tortillas (6-inch/15 cm diameter), preferably day old
Vegetable oil
½ to 1 teaspoon (2 to 5 ml) salt**

1. If tortillas are fresh, let stand, uncovered, in single layer on wire rack 1 to 2 hours to dry slightly.

2. Stack 6 tortillas; cutting through stack, cut tortillas into 6 or 8 equal wedges. Repeat with remaining tortillas.

3. Heat ½ inch (1.25 cm) oil in deep, heavy, large skillet over medium-high heat to 375°F (190°C); adjust heat to maintain temperature.

4. Fry tortilla wedges in a single layer 1 minute or until crisp, turning occasionally. Remove with slotted spoon; drain on paper towels. Repeat until all chips have been fried. Sprinkle chips with salt.

Makes 6 to 8 dozen chips

Note: Tortilla chips are served with salsa as a snack, used as the base for nachos and used as scoops for guacamole, other dips or refried beans. They are best eaten fresh. but can be stored, tightly covered, in cool place 2 or 3 days. Reheat in 350°F (180°C) oven a few minutes before serving.

Step 5. Cooking tortilla.

Corn Tortilla Chips: Step 2. Cutting tortillas into chips.

Corn Tortilla Chips: Step 4. Frying chips.

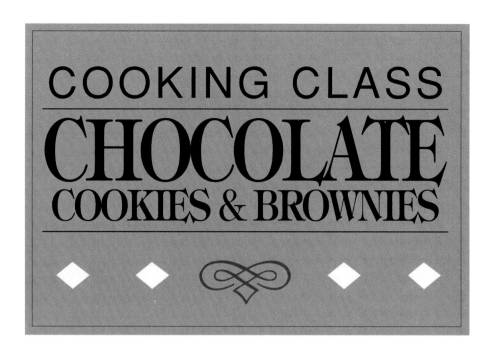

COOKING CLASS
CHOCOLATE
COOKIES & BROWNIES

338   CLASS NOTES

340   QUICK AS A WINK

348   CHIPS GALORE

358   FAMILY FAVORITES

378   BROWNIES

386   EXTRA SPECIAL

Special Treat No-Bake Squares *(page 360)*

CLASS NOTES

Melt-in-your-mouth cookies made with heavenly chocolate is an unbeatable combination. In this section, we teach you the basic techniques to prepare and bake delectable chocolate cookies and brownies. For those who would like to expand their cookie baking skills, we've also included easy-to-follow directions for special touches, such as pinwheel, cut-out and checkerboard cookies.

TYPES OF COOKIES

There are five basic types of cookies: bar, drop, refrigerator, rolled and shaped. These types are determined by the consistency of the dough and how it is formed into cookies.

Bar Cookies: Always use the pan size called for in the recipe. Using a different size will affect the cookies' texture; a smaller pan will give a more cakelike texture and a larger pan will give a drier texture.

Drop Cookies: Cookies that are uniform in size and shape will finish baking at the same time. To easily shape drop cookies into a uniform size, use an ice cream scoop with a release bar. The bar usually has a number on it indicating the number of scoops that can be made from one quart of ice cream. The handiest size for cookies is a #80 or #90 scoop. This will yield about one rounded teaspoonful of dough for each cookie.

Refrigerator Cookies: Always shape the dough into rolls before chilling. Shaping is easier if you first place the dough on a piece of waxed paper or plastic wrap. Before

chilling, wrap the rolls securely in plastic wrap or air may cause the dough to dry out.

Use gentle pressure and a back-and-forth sawing motion with a sharp knife when slicing the rolls; this helps the cookies keep their nice round shape. Rotating the roll while slicing also keeps one side from flattening.

Rolled Cookies: Chill the cookie dough before rolling for easier handling. Remove only enough dough from the refrigerator to work with at one time. Save any trimmings and reroll them all at once to prevent the dough from becoming tough.

Shaped Cookies: These cookies can be simply hand-shaped into balls or crescents or forced through a cookie press into more complex shapes.

If the recipe calls for a cookie press, do not shape the cookies by hand unless the recipe states that you may do so. The consistency of the dough was created to work in a cookie press.

When using a cookie press, if your first efforts are not successful, just place the dough back into the cookie press.

TYPES OF CHOCOLATE

Unsweetened Chocolate: Also called bitter or baking chocolate, this is pure chocolate with no sugar or flavorings added. It is used in baking and is packaged in individually wrapped l-ounce (28 g) squares.

Bittersweet Chocolate: This is pure chocolate with some sugar added.

Bittersweet chocolate is available in l-ounce (28 g) squares or in bars. If unavailable, substitute half unsweetened chocolate and half semisweet chocolate.

Semisweet Chocolate: This is pure chocolate combined with some sugar and extra cocoa butter. It is sold in a variety of forms, including l-ounce (28 g) squares, bars, chips and chunks.

Milk Chocolate: This is pure chocolate with sugar, extra cocoa butter and milk solids added. It is available in various shapes—bars, chips, stars, etc.

Sweet Cooking Chocolate: This is pure chocolate combined with extra cocoa butter and sugar. It is available in bars.

White Chocolate: This is not considered real chocolate since most or all of the cocoa butter has been removed and replaced with another vegetable fat. White chocolate is available in chips and bars.

Unsweetened Cocoa: This is formed by extracting most of the cocoa butter from pure chocolate and grinding the remaining chocolate solids into a powder. Since most of the cocoa butter is removed, it is low in fat.

GENERAL GUIDELINES

Take the guesswork out of cookie baking by practicing the following techniques:

• Read the recipe before you begin.

• Remove butter, margarine and cream cheese from the refrigerator to soften, if necessary.

- Toast and chop nuts, peel and slice fruit and melt chocolate before preparing the dough.
- Measure all the ingredients accurately. Assemble them as directed in the recipe.
- When making bar cookies or brownies, use the pan size specified in the recipe. Prepare the pans according to the recipe directions. Adjust oven racks and preheat the oven. Check oven temperature for accuracy with an oven thermometer.
- Follow recipe directions and baking times. Check doneness with the test given in the recipe.

MEASURING INGREDIENTS

Dry Ingredients: Always use standardized "dry" measuring spoons and "dry" measuring cups. Fill the correct measuring spoon or cup to overflowing and level it off with a metal spatula.

Use "dry" measures to measure flour, brown sugar, granulated sugar, peanut butter, chocolate chips, sour cream, yogurt, nuts, dried fruit, coconut, chopped fresh fruit, preserves and jams.

When measuring flour, lightly spoon it into a measuring cup, then level it off. Do not tap or bang the measuring cup as this will pack the flour.

When measuring brown sugar, pack the sugar by pressing it into the cup. It should be the shape of the cup when turned out.

Liquid Ingredients: Use a standardized glass or plastic measuring cup ("liquid" measuring cup) with a pouring spout. Place the cup on a flat surface and fill to

the desired mark. Check measurement at eye level.

When measuring sticky liquids, such as honey and molasses, grease the measuring cup or spray it with non-stick cooking spray to make removal easier.

BAKING

The best cookie sheets to use are those with no sides or up to two short sides. They allow the heat to circulate easily during baking and promote even browning.

For even baking and browning place only one cookie sheet at a time in the center of the oven. If the cookies brown unevenly, rotate the cookie sheet from front to back halfway through the baking time.

When baking more than one sheet of cookies at a time, rotate them from top to bottom halfway through the baking time.

For best results, use shortening or a nonstick cooking spray to grease cookie sheets. Or, just line the cookie sheets with parchment paper; it eliminates cleanup, bakes the cookies more evenly and allows them to cool right on the paper instead of on wire racks.

Allow cookie sheets to cool between batches, as the dough spreads if placed on a hot cookie sheet.

To avoid overbaking cookies, check them at the minimum baking time. If more time is needed, watch carefully to make sure they don't burn. It is usually better to slightly underbake than to overbake cookies.

Many cookies should be removed from cookie sheets immediately

after baking and placed in a single layer on wire racks to cool. Fragile cookies may need to cool slightly on the cookie sheet before removing to wire racks to cool completely. Bar cookies and brownies may be cooled and stored right in the baking pan.

STORAGE

Unbaked cookie dough can usually be refrigerated for up to one week or frozen for up to six weeks. Label dough with baking information for convenience.

Store soft and crisp cookies separately at room temperature to prevent changes in texture and flavor. Keep soft cookies in airtight containers. If they begin to dry out, add a piece of apple or bread to the container to help them retain moisture. If crisp cookies become soggy, heat undecorated cookies in a 300°F (150°C) oven for 3 to 5 minutes.

Store cookies with sticky glazes, fragile decorations and icings in single layers between sheets of waxed paper. Bar cookies and brownies may be stored in their own baking pans. Cover with foil or plastic wrap when cool.

As a rule, crisp cookies freeze better than soft, moist cookies. Rich, buttery bar cookies and brownies are exceptions to this rule since they freeze extremely well. Baked cookies can be frozen in airtight containers or freezer bags for up to three months. Meringue-based cookies do not freeze well and chocolate-dipped cookies may discolor if frozen. Thaw cookies and brownies unwrapped at room temperature.

Quick Chocolate Softies

1 package (18.25 ounces/510 g)
    devil's food chocolate cake
    mix
⅓ cup (83 ml) water
¼ cup (62.5 ml) butter or
    margarine, softened
1 large egg
1 cup (250 ml) large vanilla
    baking chips
½ cup (125 ml) coarsely
    chopped walnuts

1. Preheat oven to 350°F (180°C). Lightly grease cookie sheets.

2. Combine cake mix, water, butter and egg in large bowl. Beat with electric mixer at low speed until moistened, scraping down side of bowl once. Increase speed to medium; beat 1 minute, scraping down side of bowl once. (Dough will be thick.) Stir in chips and walnuts with mixing spoon until well blended.

3. Drop heaping *teaspoonfuls* of dough 2 inches (5 cm) apart (for smaller cookies) or heaping *tablespoonfuls* of dough 3 inches (7.5 cm) apart (for larger cookies) onto prepared cookie sheets.

4. Bake 10 to 12 minutes or until set. Let cookies stand on cookie sheets 1 minute. Remove cookies with spatula to wire racks; cool completely.

5. Store tightly covered at room temperature or freeze up to 3 months.

*Makes about 2 dozen large or
4 dozen small cookies*

Preparation time: 15 minutes

Step 1. Lightly greasing cookie sheet.

Step 3. Placing heaping teaspoonfuls of dough on cookie sheet.

Step 4. Removing cookies to wire rack.

Peanut Butter Chocolate Chippers

1 cup (250 ml) creamy or
   chunky peanut butter
1 cup (250 ml) firmly packed
   light brown sugar
1 large egg
¾ cup (187 ml) milk chocolate
   chips
   Granulated sugar

1. Preheat oven to 350°F (180°C).

2. Combine peanut butter, brown sugar
and egg in medium bowl with mixing
spoon until well blended. Add chips; mix
well.

3. Roll heaping tablespoonfuls of dough
into 1½-inch (3.75 cm) balls. Place balls 2
inches (5 cm) apart on *ungreased* cookie
sheets.

4. Dip table fork into granulated sugar;
press criss-cross fashion onto each ball,
flattening to ½-inch (1.25 cm) thickness.

5. Bake 12 minutes or until set. Let
cookies stand on cookie sheets 2 minutes.
Remove cookies with spatula to wire
racks; cool completely.

6. Store tightly covered at room
temperature or freeze up to 3 months.
Makes about 2 dozen cookies

Preparation time: 10 minutes

Step 3. Rolling dough into
1½-inch (3.75 cm) balls.

Step 4. Pressing fork into dough
to form criss-cross pattern.

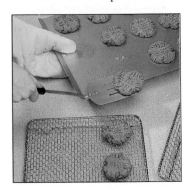

Step 5. Removing cookies to
wire racks.

Chocolate Chip Macaroons

2½ cups (625 ml) flaked coconut
⅔ cup (167 ml) mini semisweet
    chocolate chips
⅔ cup (167 ml) sweetened
    condensed milk
1 teaspoon (5 ml) vanilla

1. Preheat oven to 350°F (180°C). Grease cookie sheets; set aside.

2. Combine coconut, chips, milk and vanilla in medium bowl; stir with mixing spoon until well blended.

3. Drop rounded teaspoonfuls of dough 2 inches (5 cm) apart onto prepared cookie sheets.

4. Press dough gently with back of spoon to flatten slightly.

5. Bake 10 to 12 minutes or until light golden brown. Let cookies stand on cookie sheets 1 minute. Remove cookies with spatula to wire racks; cool completely.

6. Store tightly covered at room temperature. These cookies do not freeze well.

Makes about 3½ dozen cookies

Preparation time: 10 minutes

Step 1. Greasing cookie sheet with nonstick cooking spray.

Step 3. Placing rounded teaspoonfuls of dough on cookie sheet.

Step 4. Pressing dough to flatten slightly.

No-Fuss Bar Cookies

24 graham cracker squares
1 cup (250 ml) semisweet
    chocolate chips
1 cup (250 ml) flaked coconut
¾ cup (187 ml) coarsely
    chopped walnuts
1 can (14 ounces/390 g)
    sweetened condensed milk

1. Preheat oven to 350°F (180°C). Grease 13 x 9-inch (32.5 x 22.5 cm) baking pan; set aside.

2. Place graham crackers in food processor. Process until crackers form fine crumbs. Measure 2 cups (500 ml) crumbs.

3. Combine crumbs, chips, coconut and walnuts in medium bowl; stir to blend. Add milk; stir with mixing spoon until blended.

4. Spread batter evenly into prepared baking pan.

5. Bake 15 to 18 minutes or until edges are golden brown. Let pan stand on wire rack until completely cooled. Cut into 2¼ x 2¼-inch (5.5 x 5.5 cm) bars.

6. Store tightly covered at room temperature or freeze up to 3 months.
Makes 20 bars

Preparation time: 10 minutes

Step 2. Processing graham crackers in food processor to form fine crumbs.

Step 4. Spreading batter in pan.

Step 5. Cutting into bars.

Ultimate Chippers

2½ cups (625 ml) all-purpose flour
1 teaspoon (5 ml) baking soda
½ teaspoon (2 ml) salt
1 cup (250 ml) butter or margarine, softened
1 cup (250 ml) packed light brown sugar
½ cup (125 ml) granulated sugar
2 large eggs
1 tablespoon (15 ml) vanilla
1 cup (250 ml) semisweet chocolate chips
1 cup (250 ml) milk chocolate chips
1 cup (250 ml) vanilla chips
½ cup (125 ml) coarsely chopped pecans (optional)

1. Preheat oven to 375°F (190°C).

2. Place flour, baking soda and salt in medium bowl; stir to combine.

3. Beat butter, brown sugar and granulated sugar in large bowl with electric mixer at medium speed until light and fluffy, scraping down side of bowl once. Beat in eggs and vanilla, scraping down side of bowl once. Add flour mixture. Beat at low speed, scraping down side of bowl once.

4. Stir in chips and pecans with mixing spoon.

5. Drop heaping teaspoonfuls of dough 2 inches (5 cm) apart onto *ungreased* cookie sheets.*

6. Bake 10 to 12 minutes or until edges are golden brown. Let cookies stand on cookie sheets 2 minutes. Remove cookies with spatula to wire racks; cool completely.

7. Store tightly covered at room temperature or freeze up to 3 months.
Makes about 6 dozen cookies

*Or, use a small ice cream scoop (#90) filled with dough and pressed against side of bowl to level.

Step 3. Scraping down side of bowl.

Step 5. Placing dough on cookie sheet with ice cream scoop.

Step 7. Storing cookies.

Chocolate Chip Shortbread

½ cup (125 ml) butter,* softened
½ cup (125 ml) sugar
1 teaspoon (5 ml) vanilla
1 cup (250 ml) all-purpose flour
¼ teaspoon (1 ml) salt
½ cup (2 ml) mini semisweet
    chocolate chips

*For best flavor, do not substitute margarine for butter.

1. Preheat oven to 375°F (190°C).

2. Beat butter and sugar in large bowl with electric mixer at medium speed until light and fluffy, scraping down side of bowl occasionally. Beat in vanilla. Add flour and salt. Beat at low speed, scraping down side of bowl once. Stir in chips with mixing spoon.

3. Divide dough in half. Press each half into *ungreased* 8-inch (20 cm) round cake pan.

4. Bake 12 minutes or until edges are golden brown. Score shortbread with sharp knife, taking care not to cut completely through shortbread. Make 8 wedges per pan.

5. Let pans stand on wire racks 10 minutes. Invert shortbread onto wire racks; cool completely. Break into wedges.

6. Store tightly covered at room temperature or freeze up to 3 months.

Makes 16 cookies

Step 3. Pressing dough into cake pan.

Step 4. Scoring into wedges.

Step 5. Breaking into wedges.

Banana Chocolate Chip Softies

1 ripe, medium banana
1¼ cups (312 ml) all-purpose
    flour
1 teaspoon (5 ml) baking
    powder
½ teaspoon (2 ml) salt
⅓ cup (83 ml) butter or
    margarine, softened
⅓ cup (83 ml) granulated sugar
⅓ cup (83 ml) firmly packed
    light brown sugar
1 large egg
1 teaspoon (5 ml) vanilla
1 cup (250 ml) milk chocolate
    chips
½ cup (125 ml) coarsely
    chopped walnuts (optional)

1. Preheat oven to 375°F (190°C). Lightly grease cookie sheets.

2. Peel banana and place in small bowl. Mash enough banana with fork to measure ½ cup (125 ml). Set aside.

3. Place flour, baking powder and salt in small bowl; stir to combine.

4. Beat butter, granulated sugar and brown sugar in large bowl with electric mixer at medium speed until light and fluffy, scraping down side of bowl once. Beat in banana, egg and vanilla, scraping down side of bowl once. Add flour mixture. Beat at low speed until well blended, scraping down side of bowl once.

5. Stir in chips and walnuts with mixing spoon. (Dough will be soft.)

6. Drop rounded teaspoonfuls of dough 2 inches (5 cm) apart onto prepared cookie sheets.

7. Bake 9 to 11 minutes or until edges are golden brown. Let cookies stand on cookie sheets 2 minutes. Remove cookies with spatula to wire racks; cool completely.

8. Store tightly covered at room temperature. These cookies do not freeze well.

Makes about 3 dozen cookies

Step 2. Mashing banana with fork.

Step 4. Adding flour mixture to butter mixture.

Step 6. Placing rounded teaspoonfuls of dough on cookie sheet.

Kids' Favorite Jumbo Chippers

2¼ cups (562 ml) all-purpose
    flour
1 teaspoon (5 ml) baking soda
¾ teaspoon (3.7 ml) salt
1 cup (250 ml) butter or
    margarine, softened
¾ cup (187 ml) granulated sugar
¾ cup (187 ml) packed brown
    sugar
2 large eggs
1 teaspoon (5 ml) vanilla
1 package (12 ounces/337 g)
    mini baking semi-sweet
    chocolate candies
1 cup (250 ml) peanut butter
    flavored chips

1. Preheat oven to 375°F (190°C).

2. Place flour, baking soda and salt in medium bowl; stir to combine.

3. Beat butter, granulated sugar and brown sugar in large bowl with electric mixer at medium speed until light and fluffy, scraping down side of bowl once. Beat in eggs and vanilla, scraping down side of bowl once. Add flour mixture. Beat at low speed until well blended, scraping down side of bowl once.

4. Stir in candies and chips with mixing spoon.

5. Drop heaping tablespoonfuls of dough 3 inches (7.5 cm) apart onto *ungreased* cookie sheets.

6. Bake 10 to 12 minutes or until edges are golden brown. Let cookies stand on cookie sheets 2 minutes. Remove cookies with spatula to wire racks; cool completely.

7. Store tightly covered at room temperature or freeze up to 3 months.

Makes 3 dozen jumbo cookies

Step 3. Scraping down side of bowl.

Step 5. Placing heaping tablespoonfuls of dough on cookie sheet.

Step 6. Removing cookies to wire rack.

Orange-Walnut Chippers

½ cup (125 ml) all-purpose flour
¼ teaspoon (1 ml) baking soda
¼ teaspoon (1 ml) salt
½ cup (125 ml) butter or
    margarine, softened
1 cup (250 ml) packed light
    brown sugar
1 large egg
1 tablespoon (15 ml) orange
    peel
1½ cups (375 ml) uncooked
    quick-cooking or
    old-fashioned oats
1 cup (250 ml) semisweet
    chocolate chips
½ cup (125 ml) coarsely
    chopped walnuts

1. Preheat oven to 375°F (190°C). Lightly grease cookie sheets; set aside.

2. Place flour, baking soda and salt in small bowl; stir to combine.

3. Beat butter and sugar in large bowl with electric mixer at medium speed until light and fluffy, scraping down side of bowl once. Beat in egg and orange peel, scraping down side of bowl once. Add flour mixture. Beat at low speed, scraping down side of bowl once.

4. Stir in oats with mixing spoon. Stir in chips and nuts.

5. Drop teaspoonfuls of dough 2 inches (5 cm) apart onto prepared cookie sheets.

6. Bake 10 to 12 minutes or until golden brown. Let cookies stand on cookie sheets 2 minutes. Remove cookies with spatula to wire racks; cool completely.

7. Store tightly covered at room temperature or freeze up to 3 months.

Makes about 3 dozen cookies

Step 1. Lightly greasing cookie sheet.

Step 5. Placing teaspoonfuls of dough on cookie sheet.

Step 6. Removing cookies to wire rack.

Double-Dipped Chocolate Peanut Butter Cookies

1¼ cups (312 ml) all-purpose
     flour
½ teaspoon (2 ml) baking
     powder
½ teaspoon (2 ml) baking soda
½ teaspoon (2 ml) salt
½ cup (125 ml) butter or
     margarine, softened
     Granulated sugar
½ cup (125 ml) packed light
     brown sugar
½ cup (125 ml) creamy or
     chunky peanut butter
1 large egg
1 teaspoon (5 ml) vanilla
1½ cups (375 ml) semisweet
     chocolate chips
3 teaspoons (15 ml) shortening,
     divided
1½ cups (375 ml) milk chocolate
     chips

1. Preheat oven to 350°F (180°C). Place flour, baking powder, baking soda and salt in bowl; stir.

2. Beat butter, ½ cup (125 ml) granulated sugar and brown sugar in large bowl with electric mixer at medium speed until light and fluffy, scraping down side of bowl once. Beat in peanut butter, egg and vanilla, scraping down side of bowl once. Gradually stir in flour mixture with mixing spoon, blending well.

3. Roll heaping tablespoonfuls of dough into 1½-inch (4 cm) balls. Place balls 2 inches (5 cm) apart on *ungreased* cookie sheets. (If dough is too soft to roll into balls, refrigerate 30 minutes.)

4. Dip table fork into granulated sugar; press criss-cross fashion onto each ball, flattening to ½-inch (1.25 cm) thickness.

5. Bake 12 minutes or until set. Let cookies stand on cookie sheets 2 minutes. Remove cookies with spatula to wire rack; cool completely.

6. Melt semisweet chocolate chips and 1½ teaspoons (8 ml) shortening in top of double boiler over hot, not boiling, water. Dip one end of each cookie one third the way up in chocolate; place on waxed paper. Let stand until chocolate is set, about 30 minutes.

7. Melt milk chocolate chips with 1½ teaspoons (8 ml) shortening in top of double boiler over hot, not boiling, water. Dip opposite end of each cookie one third the way up in chocolate; place on waxed paper. Let stand until chocolate is set, about 30 minutes.

8. Store cookies between sheets of waxed paper at cool room temperature or freeze up to 3 months.

*Makes about 2 dozen 3-inch
(7.5 cm) cookies*

Step 4. Pressing fork into dough to form a criss-cross pattern.

Step 7. Dipping cookie one third the way into melted chocolate.

Special Treat No-Bake Squares

Crust
- ½ cup (125 ml) butter or margarine
- ¼ cup (62.5 ml) granulated sugar
- ¼ cup (62.5 ml) unsweetened cocoa powder
- 1 large egg
- ¼ teaspoon (1 ml) salt
- 1½ cups (375 ml) graham cracker crumbs (about 18 graham crackers)
- ¾ cup (187 ml) flaked coconut
- ½ cup (125 ml) chopped pecans

Filling
- ⅓ cup (83 ml) butter or margarine, softened
- 1 package (3 ounces/85 g) cream cheese, softened
- 1 teaspoon (5 ml) vanilla
- 1 cup (250 ml) powdered sugar

Glaze
- 2 ounces (56 g) dark sweet or bittersweet chocolate candy bar, broken into ½-inch (1.25 cm) pieces
- 1 teaspoon (5 ml) butter or margarine

1. Line 9-inch (22.5 cm) square pan with foil, shiny side up, allowing 2-inch (5 cm) overhang on sides. (The overhang allows cookie to be lifted out of pan for easier cutting.) Or, lightly grease pan. Set aside.

2. For crust, combine ½ cup (125 ml) butter, granulated sugar, cocoa, egg and salt in medium saucepan. Cook over medium heat, stirring constantly, until mixture thickens, about 2 minutes.

3. Remove from heat; stir in graham cracker crumbs, coconut and pecans. Press evenly into prepared pan.

4. For filling, beat ⅓ cup (83 ml) butter, cream cheese and vanilla in small bowl with electric mixer at medium speed until smooth, scraping down side of bowl once. Gradually beat in powdered sugar. Spread over crust; refrigerate 30 minutes.

5. For glaze, combine candy bar and 1 teaspoon (5 ml) butter in small resealable plastic freezer bag; seal bag. Microwave at HIGH 50 seconds. Turn bag over; microwave at HIGH 40 to 50 seconds or until melted. Knead bag until candy bar is smooth. (Technique on page 374.)

6. Cut off very tiny corner of bag; drizzle chocolate over filling. Refrigerate until firm, about 20 minutes.

7. Remove bars from pan, using foil. Cut into 1½-inch (3.75 cm) squares. Store tightly covered in refrigerator.

Makes 25 squares

Step 4. Spreading filling over crust.

Step 6. Drizzling chocolate over filling.

Choco Cheesecake Squares

⅓ cup (83 ml) butter or margarine, softened
⅓ cup (83 ml) packed light brown sugar
1 cup (250 ml) *plus* 1 tablespoon (15 ml) all-purpose flour, divided
½ cup (125 ml) chopped pecans (optional)
1 cup (250 ml) semisweet chocolate chips
1 package (8 ounces/225 g) cream cheese, softened
¼ cup (62.5 ml) granulated sugar
1 large egg
1 teaspoon (5 ml) vanilla
1 tablespoon (15 ml) powdered sugar
1 tablespoon (15 ml) unsweetened cocoa powder

1. Preheat oven to 350°F (180°C). Grease 8-inch (20 cm) square baking pan; set aside.

2. Beat butter and brown sugar in large bowl with electric mixer at medium speed until light and fluffy, scraping down side of bowl once. Add 1 cup (250 ml) flour. Beat at low speed, scraping down side of bowl once. Stir in pecans with mixing spoon. (Mixture will be crumbly.) Press evenly into prepared pan.

3. Bake 15 minutes.

4. Place chips in 1-cup (250 ml) glass measure. Microwave at HIGH 2½ to 3 minutes or until melted, stirring after 2 minutes.

5. Beat cream cheese and granulated sugar in medium bowl with electric mixer at medium speed until light and fluffy, scraping down side of bowl once. Add remaining 1 tablespoon (15 ml) flour, egg and vanilla; beat at low speed until smooth. Gradually stir in melted chocolate, mixing well.

6. Pour cream cheese mixture over partially baked crust. Return to oven; bake 15 minutes or until set.

7. Remove pan to wire rack; cool completely. Combine powdered sugar and cocoa in cup. Place in fine-mesh strainer; sprinkle over brownies, if desired. Cut brownies into 2-inch (5 cm) squares.

8. Store tightly covered in refrigerator or freeze up to 3 months.

Makes 16 squares

Step 2. Scraping down side of bowl.

Step 4. Stirring melted chocolate chips.

Step 6. Pouring cream cheese mixture over crust.

Chocolate Caramel Pecan Bars

2 cups (500 ml) butter, softened, divided
½ cup (125 ml) granulated sugar
1 large egg
2¾ cups (687 ml) all-purpose flour
⅔ cup (167 ml) packed light brown sugar
¼ cup (62.5 ml) light corn syrup
2½ cups (625 ml) coarsely chopped pecans
1 cup (500 ml) semisweet chocolate chips

1. Preheat oven to 375°F (190°C). Grease 15 x 10-inch (37.5 x 25 cm) jelly-roll pan; set aside.

2. Beat 1 cup (250 ml) butter and granulated sugar in large bowl with electric mixer at medium speed until light and fluffy, scraping down side of bowl once. Beat in egg. Add flour. Beat at low speed, scraping down side of bowl once. Pat dough into prepared pan.

3. Bake 20 minutes or until light golden brown.

4. While bars are baking, prepare caramel topping. Combine remaining 1 cup (250 ml) butter, brown sugar and corn syrup in medium, heavy saucepan. Cook over medium heat until mixture boils, stirring frequently. Boil gently 2 minutes, without stirring. Quickly stir in pecans and spread caramel topping evenly over base. Return to oven and bake 20 minutes or until dark golden brown and bubbling.

5. Immediately sprinkle chocolate chips evenly over hot caramel. Gently press chips into caramel topping with spatula. Loosen caramel from edges of pan with a thin spatula or knife.

6. Remove pan to wire rack; cool completely. Cut into 3 x 1½-inch (7.5 x 3.7 cm) bars.

7. Store tightly covered at room temperature or freeze up to 3 months.

Makes 40 bars

Step 2. Patting dough into pan.

Step 4. Stirring pecans into hot topping.

Step 5. Pressing chips into caramel topping.

Chocolate Macaroons

2 large eggs
12 ounces (336 g) semisweet
    baking chocolate or chips
1 can (8 ounces/225 g) almond
    paste
½ cup (125 ml) powdered sugar
2 tablespoons (30 ml) all-
    purpose flour
    Powdered sugar for garnish

1. Preheat oven to 300°F (150°C). Line cookie sheets with parchment paper; set aside.

2. To separate egg whites from yolks, gently tap egg in center against hard surface, such as side of bowl. Holding a shell half in each hand, gently transfer yolk back and forth between the 2 halves. Allow white to drip down between the 2 halves into bowl. When all white has dripped into bowl, place yolk in another bowl. Transfer white to third bowl. Repeat with remaining egg. Store unused egg yolks, covered with water, in airtight container. Refrigerate up to 3 days.

3. Melt chocolate in small, heavy saucepan over low heat, stirring constantly; set aside.

4. Beat almond paste, egg whites and sugar in large bowl with electric mixer at medium speed 1 minute, scraping down side of bowl once. Beat in chocolate until well combined. Beat in flour at low speed, scraping down side of bowl once.

5. Spoon dough into pastry tube fitted with rosette tip. Pipe 1½-inch (3.7 cm) spirals 1 inch (2.5 cm) apart onto prepared cookie sheets. Pipe all cookies at once; dough will get stiff upon standing.

6. Bake 20 minutes or until set. Carefully remove parchment paper to countertop; cool completely.

7. Peel cookies off parchment paper. Place powdered sugar in fine-mesh strainer; sprinkle over cookies, if desired.

8. Store tightly covered at room temperature or freeze up to 3 months.

Makes about 3 dozen cookies

Step 2. Separating an egg.

Step 5. Piping dough onto cookie sheet.

Step 7. Removing cookies from parchment paper.

Chocolate Sugar Spritz

2 squares (1 ounce/28 g each) unsweetened chocolate, coarsely chopped
2¼ cups (562 ml) all-purpose flour
¼ teaspoon (1 ml) salt
1 cup (250 ml) butter or margarine, softened
¾ cup (187 ml) granulated sugar
1 large egg
1 teaspoon (5 ml) almond extract
½ cup (125 ml) powdered sugar
1 teaspoon (5 ml) ground cinnamon

1. Preheat oven to 400°F (200°C).

2. Melt chocolate in small, heavy saucepan over low heat, stirring constantly; set aside.

3. Combine flour and salt in small bowl; stir to combine.

4. Beat butter and granulated sugar in large bowl with electric mixer at medium speed until light and fluffy, scraping down side of bowl once. Beat in egg and almond extract, scraping down side of bowl. Beat in chocolate. Gradually add flour mixture with mixing spoon. (Dough will be stiff.)

5. Fit cookie press with desired plate (or change plates for different shapes after first batch). Fill press with dough; press dough 1 inch (2.5 cm) apart onto *ungreased* cookie sheets.

6. Bake 7 minutes or until just set.

7. Combine powdered sugar and cinnamon in small bowl. Transfer to fine-mesh strainer and sprinkle over hot cookies while they are still on cookie sheets. Remove cookies with spatula to wire racks; cool completely.

8. Store tightly covered at room temperature. These cookies do not freeze well.

Makes 4 to 5 dozen cookies

Step 4. Stirring flour into batter.

Step 5. Pressing dough onto cookie sheet.

Step 7. Sprinkling cinnamon-sugar mixture over cookies.

Two-Toned Spritz Cookies

1 square (1 ounce/28 g)
    unsweetened chocolate,
    coarsely chopped
2¼ cups (562 ml) all-purpose
    flour
¼ teaspoon (1 ml) salt
1 cup (250 ml) butter or
    margarine, softened
1 cup (250 ml) sugar
1 large egg
1 teaspoon (5 ml) vanilla

1. Melt chocolate in small, heavy saucepan over low heat, stirring constantly; set aside.

2. Place flour and salt in bowl; stir.

3. Beat butter and sugar in large bowl with electric mixer at medium speed until light and fluffy, scraping down side of bowl once. Beat in egg and vanilla, scraping down side of bowl once. Gradually add flour mixture. Beat at low speed, scraping down side of bowl once.

4. Remove and reserve 2 cups (500 ml) dough. Beat chocolate into dough in bowl until smooth. Flatten chocolate and vanilla doughs into discs; wrap in plastic wrap and refrigerate 20 minutes, or until doughs are easy to handle.

5. Preheat oven to 400°F (200°C). Unwrap vanilla dough. Roll out between 2 sheets of waxed paper to ½-inch (1.25 cm) thickness. Cut into 5 x 4-inch (12.5 x 10 cm) rectangles.

6. Unwrap chocolate dough. Place on sheet of waxed paper. Using waxed paper to hold dough, roll it back and forth to form a log about 1 inch (2.5 cm) in diameter. Cut into 5-inch-long (12.5 cm) logs.

7. Place chocolate log in center of vanilla rectangle. Wrap vanilla dough around log and fit into cookie press fitted with star disc.

8. Press dough 1½ inches (3.7 cm) apart on cold, *ungreased* cookie sheets. (Technique on page 368.)

9. Bake 10 minutes or until just set. Remove cookies with spatula to wire racks; cool completely.

10. Store tightly covered at room temperature or freeze up to 3 months.
Makes about 4 dozen cookies

Step 5. Rolling out vanilla dough.

Step 6. Rolling chocolate dough into log.

Step 7. Shaping vanilla dough around chocolate log.

Black and White Cut-Outs

2¾ cups (562 ml) *plus* 2
    tablespoons (30 ml) all-
    purpose flour, divided
1 teaspoon (5 ml) baking soda
¾ teaspoon (3.7 ml) salt
1 cup (250 ml) butter or
    margarine, softened
¾ cup (187 ml) granulated sugar
¾ cup (187 ml) packed light
    brown sugar
2 large eggs
1 teaspoon (5 ml) vanilla
¼ cup (62.5 ml) unsweetened
    cocoa powder
4 ounces (112 g) white chocolate
    baking bar, broken into
    ½-inch (1.25 cm) pieces
    Assorted decorative candies
    (optional)
4 ounces (112 g) semisweet
    chocolate chips

1. Place 2¾ cups (687 ml) flour, baking soda and salt in small bowl; stir to combine.

2. Beat butter, granulated sugar and brown sugar in large bowl with electric mixer at medium speed until light and fluffy, scraping down side of bowl once. Beat in eggs, 1 at a time, scraping down side of bowl after each addition. Beat in vanilla. Gradually add flour mixture. Beat at low speed, scraping down side of bowl once.

3. Remove half of dough from bowl; reserve. To make chocolate dough, beat cocoa into remaining dough with mixing spoon until well blended. To make vanilla cookie dough, beat remaining 2 table-spoons (30 ml) flour into reserved dough.

4. Flatten each piece of dough into a disc; wrap in plastic wrap and refrigerate about 1½ hours or until firm. (Dough may be refrigerated up to 3 days before baking.)

5. Preheat oven to 375°F (190°C).

6. Working with 1 type of dough at a time, unwrap dough and place on lightly floured surface. Roll out dough to ¼-inch (6 mm) thickness with well-floured rolling pin.

continued on page 374

Step 3. Mixing chocolate dough.

Step 4. Wrapping flattened dough in plastic wrap.

Step 6. Rolling out chocolate dough.

Black and White Cut-Outs, continued

7. Cut dough into desired shapes with cookie cutters. Place cut-outs 1 inch (2.5 cm) apart on *ungreased* cookie sheets.

8. Bake 9 to 11 minutes or until set. Let cookies stand on cookie sheets 2 minutes. Remove cookies with spatula to wire rack; cool completely.

9. For white chocolate drizzle, place baking bar pieces in small resealable plastic freezer bag; seal bag. Microwave at MEDIUM (50% power) 2 minutes. Turn bag over; microwave at MEDIUM (50% power) 2 to 3 minutes or until melted. Knead bag until baking bar is smooth.

10. Cut off very tiny corner of bag; pipe or drizzle baking bar onto chocolate cookies. Decorate as desired with assorted candies. Let stand until white chocolate is set, about 30 minutes.

11. For chocolate drizzle, place chocolate chips in small resealable plastic freezer bag; seal bag. Microwave at HIGH 1 minute. Turn bag over; microwave at HIGH 1 to 2 minutes or until melted. Knead bag until chocolate is smooth.

12. Cut off tiny corner of bag; pipe or drizzle chocolate onto vanilla cookies. Decorate as desired with assorted candies. Let stand until chocolate is set, about 40 minutes.

13. Store tightly covered at room temperature or freeze up to 3 months.
Makes 3 to 4 dozen cookies

Black and White Sandwiches: Cut out both doughs with same cookie cutter. Spread thin layer of prepared frosting on flat side of chocolate cookie. Place flat side of vanilla cookie over frosting. Drizzle either side of cookie with melted chocolate or white chocolate.

Step 7. Cutting out dough.

Step 9. Kneading white chocolate in plastic bag.

Black and White Sandwiches: Making sandwich cookies.

Old-Fashioned Ice Cream Sandwiches

2 squares (1 ounce/28 g each) semisweet baking chocolate, coarsely chopped
1½ cups (375 ml) all-purpose flour
¼ teaspoon (1 ml) baking soda
¼ teaspoon (1 ml) salt
½ cup (125 ml) butter or margarine, softened
½ cup (125 ml) sugar
1 large egg
1 teaspoon (5 ml) vanilla
Vanilla or mint chocolate chip ice cream, softened*

*One quart (1 L) of ice cream can be softened in the microwave at HIGH for about 20 seconds.

1. Place chocolate in 1-cup (250 ml) glass measure. Microwave at HIGH 3 to 4 minutes or until chocolate is melted, stirring after 2 minutes; set aside.

2. Place flour, baking soda and salt in small bowl; stir to combine.

3. Beat butter and sugar in large bowl with electric mixer at medium speed until light and fluffy, scraping down side of bowl once.

4. Beat in egg and vanilla, scraping down side of bowl once. Gradually beat in chocolate. Stir in flour mixture with mixing spoon.

5. Form dough into 2 discs; wrap in plastic wrap and refrigerate until firm, at least 2 hours. (Dough may be stored in the refrigerator up to 3 days before baking.)

6. Preheat oven to 350°F (180°C). Grease cookie sheet; set aside.

7. Unwrap 1 piece of dough. Roll out to ¼ to ⅛-inch (3 mm to 6 mm) thickness between 2 sheets of waxed paper.

continued on page 376

Step 1. Stirring melted chocolate.

Step 5. Wrapping flattened dough in plastic wrap.

Step 7. Rolling out dough between two sheets of waxed paper.

Old-Fashioned Ice Cream Sandwiches, continued

8. Remove top sheet of waxed paper; invert dough onto prepared cookie sheet.

9. Cut through dough down to cookie sheets with paring knife, forming 3 x 2-inch (7.5 x 5 cm) rectangles. Remove excess scraps of dough from edges. Add to second disc of dough and repeat rolling and scoring until dough is used up. Prick each rectangle with table fork, if desired.

10. Bake 10 minutes or until set. Let cookies stand on cookie sheet 1 minute. Cut through score marks with paring knife while cookies are still warm. Remove cookies with spatula to wire racks; cool completely.

11. Spread softened ice cream on flat side of half the cookies; top with remaining cookies.

12. Serve immediately or wrap separately in plastic wrap and freeze up to 1 month.

Makes about 8 ice cream sandwiches

Step 8. Removing top sheet of waxed paper.

Step 9. Cutting dough into rectangles.

Step 11. Spreading ice cream on cookies.

White Chocolate Chunk Brownies

4 squares (1 ounce/28 g each) unsweetened chocolate, coarsely chopped
½ cup (125 ml) butter or margarine
2 large eggs
1¼ cups (312 ml) granulated sugar
1 teaspoon (5 ml) vanilla
½ cup (125 ml) all-purpose flour
½ teaspoon (2 ml) salt
6 ounces (165 g) white baking bar, cut into ¼-inch (6 mm) pieces
½ cup (125 mm) coarsely chopped walnuts (optional)
Powdered sugar for garnish

1. Preheat oven to 350°F (180°C). Grease 8-inch (20 cm) square baking pan; set aside.

2. Melt unsweetened chocolate and butter in small, heavy saucepan over low heat, stirring constantly; set aside.

3. Beat eggs in large bowl with electric mixer at medium speed 30 seconds. Gradually add granulated sugar, beating at medium speed about 4 minutes until very thick and lemon colored.

4. Beat in chocolate mixture and vanilla. Beat in flour and salt at low speed just until blended. Stir in baking bar pieces and walnuts with mixing spoon. Spread batter evenly into prepared baking pan.

5. Bake 30 minutes or until edges just begin to pull away from sides of pan and center is set.

6. Remove pan to wire rack; cool completely. Cut into 2-inch (5 cm) squares. Place powdered sugar in fine-mesh strainer; sprinkle over brownies, if desired.

7. Store tightly covered at room temperature or freeze up to 3 months.

Makes 16 brownies

Step 3. Batter beaten to lemon color.

Step 4. Stirring in baking bar pieces.

Step 6. Sprinkling powdered sugar over brownies.

Minted Chocolate Chip Brownies

¾ cup (187 ml) granulated sugar
½ cup (125 ml) butter or margarine
2 tablespoons (30 ml) water
1 cup (250 ml) semisweet chocolate chips or mini chocolate chips
1½ teaspoons (7 ml) vanilla
1¼ cups (312 ml) all-purpose flour
½ teaspoon (2 ml) baking soda
½ teaspoon (2 ml) salt
2 large eggs
1 cup (250 ml) mint chocolate chips
Powdered sugar for garnish

1. Preheat oven to 350°F (180°C). Grease 9-inch (22.5 cm) square baking pan; set aside.

2. Combine sugar, butter and water in medium microwavable mixing bowl. Microwave at HIGH 2½ to 3 minutes or until butter is melted. Stir in semisweet chips; stir gently until chips are melted and mixture is well blended. Stir in vanilla; let stand 5 minutes to cool.

3. Place flour, baking soda and salt in small bowl; stir to combine.

4. Beat eggs into chocolate mixture, 1 at a time, with mixing spoon. Add flour mixture; mix well. Stir in mint chips. Spread batter evenly into prepared baking pan.

5. Bake 25 minutes for fudgy brownies or 30 to 35 minutes for cakelike brownies.

6. Remove pan to wire rack; cool completely. Cut into 2¼-inch (5.5 cm) squares. Place powdered sugar in fine-mesh strainer; sprinkle over brownies, if desired.

7. Store tightly covered at room temperature or freeze up to 3 months.

Makes 16 brownies

Step 2. Stirring chocolate chips in melted butter mixture.

Step 4. Beating in eggs, one at a time.

Step 6. Sprinkling powdered sugar over brownies.

Butterscotch Brownies

1 cup (250 ml) butterscotch-
    flavored chips
1 cup (250 ml) all-purpose flour
½ teaspoon (2 ml) baking
    powder
¼ teaspoon (1 ml) salt
¼ cup (62.5 ml) butter or
    margarine, softened
½ cup (125 ml) packed light
    brown sugar
2 large eggs
½ teaspoon (2 ml) vanilla
1 cup (250 ml) semisweet
    chocolate chips
1 tablespoon (15 ml)
    unsweetened cocoa powder
    for garnish

1. Preheat oven to 350°F (180°C). Lightly grease 9-inch (22.5 cm) square baking pan; set aside.

2. Melt butterscotch-flavored chips in small, heavy saucepan over low heat, stirring constantly; set aside.

3. Place flour, baking powder and salt in small bowl; stir to combine.

4. Beat butter and sugar in large bowl with electric mixer at medium speed until light and fluffy, scraping down side of bowl once. Beat in eggs, 1 at a time, scraping down side of bowl after each addition. Beat in vanilla. Beat in melted butterscotch chips. Add flour mixture. Beat at low speed until well blended, scraping down side of bowl. Spread batter evenly into prepared baking pan.

5. Bake 20 to 25 minutes or until golden brown and center is set. Remove pan from oven and immediately sprinkle chocolate chips in single layer over brownie. Let stand about 4 minutes until chocolate is melted. Spread chocolate evenly over top of brownie with thin spatula. Slightly swirl chocolate, if desired.

6. Place pan on wire rack; cool completely.

7. To garnish, place small strips of cardboard over chocolate. Place cocoa in fine-mesh strainer; sprinkle over brownie. Carefully remove cardboard. Cut brownie into 2¼-inch (5.5 cm) squares.

8. Store tightly covered at room temperature or freeze up to 3 months.

Makes 16 brownies

Step 2. Melting and stirring butterscotch chips.

Step 4. Scraping down side of bowl.

Step 5. Spreading chocolate chips over hot brownie.

Irish Brownies

1 cup (250 ml) all-purpose flour
½ teaspoon (2 ml) baking
      powder
¼ teaspoon (1 ml) salt
4 squares (1 ounce/28 g each)
      semisweet baking
      chocolate, coarsely chopped
½ cup (125 ml) butter or
      margarine
½ cup (125 ml) sugar
2 large eggs
¼ cup (62.5 ml) Irish cream
      liqueur
   Irish Cream Frosting (recipe
      follows)

1. Preheat oven to 350°F (180°C). Grease 8-inch (20 cm) square baking pan; set aside. Place flour, baking powder and salt in small bowl; stir to combine.

2. Melt chocolate and butter in medium, heavy saucepan over low heat, stirring constantly. Stir in sugar. Beat in eggs, 1 at a time, with wire whisk. Whisk in liqueur. Whisk flour mixture into chocolate mixture until just blended. Spread batter evenly into prepared baking pan.

3. Bake 22 to 25 minutes or until center is set. Remove pan to wire rack; cool completely before frosting.

4. Prepare Irish Cream Frosting. Spread frosting over cooled brownie. Chill at least 1 hour or until frosting is set. Cut into 2-inch (5 cm) squares.

5. Store tightly covered in refrigerator. These brownies do not freeze well.
Makes 16 brownies

Step 2. Whisking in eggs one at a time.

Irish Cream Frosting: Step 1. Sifting powdered sugar.

Irish Cream Frosting

   Powdered sugar
2 ounces (56 g) cream cheese
      (¼ cup/62.5 ml), softened
2 tablespoons (30 ml) butter or
      margarine, softened
2 tablespoons (30 ml) Irish cream
      liqueur

1. Sift powdered sugar with sifter or fine-mesh strainer onto waxed paper. Gently spoon into measuring cups to measure 1½ cups (375 ml).

2. Beat cream cheese and butter in small bowl with electric mixer at medium speed until smooth, scraping down side of bowl once. Beat in liqueur. Gradually beat in powdered sugar until smooth.
Makes about ⅔ cup (167 ml)

Checkerboard Bars

½ cup (125 ml) hazelnuts (2½ ounces/70 g)

4 ounces (112 g) bittersweet or semisweet chocolate candy bar, broken into pieces

2¼ cups (562 ml) all-purpose flour

½ teaspoon (2 ml) baking powder

¼ teaspoon (1 ml) salt

¾ cup (187 ml) butter or margarine, softened

¾ cup (187 ml) sugar

2 large eggs, divided

1 teaspoon (5 ml) vanilla

1. Preheat oven to 350°F (180°C). To remove skins from hazelnuts, spread hazelnuts in single layer on baking sheet. Bake 10 to 12 minutes until toasted and skins begin to flake off; let cool slightly. Wrap hazelnuts in heavy kitchen towel; rub against towel to remove as much of the skins as possible.

2. Place hazelnuts in food processor. Process using on/off pulsing action until hazelnuts are finely chopped, but not pasty.

3. Melt chocolate in small bowl set in bowl of very hot water, stirring twice. This will take about 10 minutes.

4. Place flour, baking powder and salt in medium bowl; stir to combine.

5. Beat butter and sugar in large bowl with electric mixer at medium speed until light and fluffy, scraping down side of bowl once. Beat in 1 egg and vanilla, scraping down side of bowl once. Gradually add flour mixture. Beat at low speed, scraping down side of bowl occasionally.

6. Remove and reserve 1¼ cups (312 ml) dough. Stir chocolate and nuts into remaining dough with mixing spoon. Wrap both doughs in plastic wrap and refrigerate 20 minutes.

7. Unwrap chocolate dough. Place on lightly floured surface. Roll out to ⅓-inch (8 ml) thickness with floured rolling pin. Cut dough into eight 4 x ¾-inch (10 x 3 cm) strips. Reroll scraps as necessary, until all dough has been cut into strips. Repeat process with vanilla dough.

continued on page 388

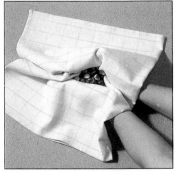

Step 1. Rubbing hazelnuts to remove skins.

Step 6. Making chocolate dough.

Step 7. Cutting dough into strips.

Checkerboard Bars, *continued*

8. To assemble, beat remaining egg in small dish with fork until frothy. Place 1 strip of chocolate dough on sheet of plastic wrap. Brush edge with egg. Place 1 strip of vanilla dough next to chocolate dough. Brush edge with egg. Repeat with 1 more chocolate strip and 1 more vanilla strip to make bottom layer. Brush top with egg.

9. Prepare second row by stacking strips on first row, alternating vanilla dough over chocolate and chocolate dough over vanilla. Brush edge of each strip and top layer with egg. Repeat with third row to complete 1 checkerboard bar. Repeat entire process with remaining dough strips to complete second checkerboard bar. Cover with plastic wrap; refrigerate 1 hour or until firm enough to slice.

10. Preheat oven to 350°F (180°C). Grease cookie sheets.

11. Unwrap checkerboard bar and cut crosswise with long, sharp knife into ¼-inch (6 mm) slices. Place 2 inches (5 cm) apart on prepared cookie sheets.

12. Bake 10 to 12 minutes or until set. Cool cookies on cookie sheets 2 minutes. Remove cookies with spatula to wire racks; cool completely.

13. Store tightly covered at room temperature or freeze up to 3 months.

Makes 2 dozen bars

Step 8. Arranging first row of checkerboard.

Step 9. Brushing edge of strip with beaten egg.

Step 11. Cutting checkerboard into ¼-inch (6 mm) slices.

Viennese Meringue Bars

½ cup (125 ml) slivered almonds
3 large eggs
1 cup (250 ml) butter or
    margarine, softened
1¼ cups (362 ml) sugar, divided
¼ teaspoon (1 ml) salt
2¼ cups (562 ml) all-purpose
    flour
1 cup (250 ml) seedless
    raspberry jam
1½ cups (375 ml) mini semisweet
    chocolate chips

1. Preheat oven to 350°F (180°C). To toast almonds, spread on baking sheet. Bake 8 to 10 minutes or until golden brown, stirring frequently. Remove almonds from pan and cool.

2. To separate egg yolks from whites, gently tap egg in center against hard surface, such as side of bowl. Holding a shell half in each hand, gently transfer yolk back and forth between the 2 halves. Allow white to drip down between the 2 halves into bowl. When all white has dripped into bowl, place yolk in another bowl. (Whites must be free of any egg yolk to reach the proper volume when beaten.) Transfer white to third bowl. Repeat with remaining eggs.

3. Store 1 egg yolk, covered with water, in airtight container for another use. Refrigerate up to 3 days.

4. Preheat oven to 350°F (180°C).

5. Beat butter and ½ cup (125 ml) sugar in large bowl with electric mixer at medium speed until light and fluffy, scraping down side of bowl once. Beat in 2 egg yolks and salt. Gradually add flour. Beat at low speed, scraping down side of bowl once.

6. With buttered fingers, pat dough evenly into *ungreased* 15 x 10-inch (37.5 x 25 cm) jelly-roll pan.

continued on page 390

Step 1. Toasting almonds.

Step 2. Separating an egg.

Step 6. Patting dough into pan.

Viennese Meringue Bars, *continued*

7. Bake 22 to 25 minutes or until light golden brown. Remove from oven; immediately spread jam over crust. Sprinkle evenly with chocolate chips.

8. To make meringue topping, beat egg whites in clean large bowl with electric mixer on high speed until foamy. Gradually beat in remaining ¾ cup (187 ml) sugar until stiff peaks form. (After beaters are lifted from egg white mixture, stiff peaks should remain on surface, and mixture will not slide around when bowl is tilted.)

9. Fold in almonds with rubber spatula by gently cutting down to bottom of the bowl, scraping up side of the bowl, then folding over top of the mixture. Repeat until almonds are evenly incorporated into the meringue.

10. Spoon meringue over chocolate mixture; spread evenly with small spatula.

11. Return pan to oven; bake 20 to 25 minutes until golden brown. Transfer pan to wire rack; cool completely. Cut into 2 x 2½-inch (5 x 6.25 cm) bars.

12. Store loosely covered at room temperature. These cookies do not freeze well.

Makes 28 bars

Step 8. Egg whites beaten to stiff peaks.

Step 9. Folding in almonds.

Step 10. Spreading meringue over base.

Cinnamon Nut Chocolate Spirals

1½ cups (375 ml) all-purpose
    flour
¼ teaspoon (1 ml) salt
⅓ cup (83 ml) butter or
    margarine, softened
¾ cup (187 ml) sugar, divided
1 large egg
1 cup (250 ml) mini semisweet
    chocolate chips
1 cup (250 ml) very finely
    chopped walnuts
2 teaspoons (10 ml) ground
    cinnamon
3 tablespoons (45 ml) butter or
    margarine, melted

1. Place flour and salt in small bowl; stir to combine. Beat softened butter and ½ cup (125 ml) sugar in large bowl with electric mixer at medium speed until light and fluffy, scraping down side of bowl once. Beat in egg. Gradually add flour mixture, mixing with mixing spoon. Dough will be stiff. (If necessary, knead dough by hand until it holds together.)

2. Roll out dough between 2 sheets of waxed paper into 12 x 10-inch (30 x 25 cm) rectangle. Remove waxed paper from top of rectangle. (Techniques on pages 375 and 376.)

3. Combine chips, walnuts, remaining ¼ cup (60 ml) sugar and cinnamon in medium bowl. Pour hot melted butter over mixture; mix well. (Chocolate will melt partially.) Spoon mixture over dough. Spread evenly with small spatula, leaving ½-inch (1.5 cm) border on long edges.

4. Using bottom sheet of waxed paper as a guide and starting at long side, tightly roll up dough jelly-roll style, removing waxed paper as you roll. Wrap in plastic wrap; refrigerate 30 minutes to 1 hour.

5. Preheat oven to 350°F (180°C). Lightly grease cookie sheets. Unwrap dough. Using dental floss or heavy thread, cut dough into ½-inch (1.5 cm) slices.* Position floss under roll; bring up ends, cross over center, and gently pull ends of thread to cut each slice. Place slices 2 inches (5 cm) apart on prepared cookie sheets.

6. Bake 14 minutes or until edges are light golden brown. Remove cookies with spatula to wire racks; cool.

7. Store tightly covered at room temperature or freeze up to 3 months.
Makes about 2 dozen cookies

*If dough is chilled longer than 1 hour, slice with a sharp, thin knife.

Step 4. Rolling up dough jelly-roll style.

Step 5. Cutting dough into ½-inch (1.25 cm) slices with dental floss.

Peek-A-Boo Apricot Cookies

4 ounces (112 g) bittersweet
   chocolate candy bar,
   broken into pieces
3 cups (750 ml) all-purpose
   flour
½ teaspoon (2 ml) baking soda
½ teaspoon (2 ml) salt
⅔ cup (167 ml) butter or
   margarine, softened
¾ cup (187 ml) sugar
2 large eggs
2 teaspoons (10 ml) vanilla
   Apricot preserves

1. Melt chocolate in small bowl set in bowl of very hot water, stirring twice. This will take about 10 minutes.

2. Place flour, baking soda and salt in medium bowl; stir to combine.

3. Beat butter and sugar in large bowl with electric mixer at medium speed until light and fluffy, scraping down side of bowl once. Beat in eggs, 1 at a time, scraping down side of bowl after each addition. Beat in vanilla and chocolate. Slowly add flour mixture. Beat at low speed, scraping down side of bowl once.

4. Divide dough into 2 rounds; flatten into discs. Wrap in plastic wrap; refrigerate 2 hours or until firm.

5. Preheat oven to 350°F (180°C). Unwrap dough; roll out to ¼- to ⅛-inch (3 to 6 mm) thickness on lightly floured surface with floured rolling pin. Cut out dough with 2½-inch-round (6.2 cm) cutter. Cut 1-inch (2.5 cm) centers out of half the circles. Remove scraps of dough from around and within circles; reserve. Place circles on *ungreased* cookie sheets. Repeat rolling and cutting with remaining scraps of dough.

6. Bake cookies 9 to 10 minutes or until set. Let cookies stand on cookie sheets 2 minutes. Remove cookies with spatula to wire rack; cool completely.

7. To assemble cookies, spread about 1½ teaspoons (8 ml) preserves over flat side of cookie circles; top with cut-out cookies to form sandwiches.

8. Store tightly covered at room temperature. These cookies do not freeze well.

Makes about 1½ dozen cookies

Step 1. Melting chocolate in a bowl set in very hot water.

Step 5. Cutting out centers from cookies.

Step 7. Assembling cookies.

Chocolate Chip Almond Biscotti

1 cup (250 ml) sliced almonds
2¾ cups (687 ml) all-purpose
   flour
1½ teaspoons (8 ml) baking
   powder
¼ teaspoon (1 ml) salt
½ cup (125 ml) butter or
   margarine, softened
1 cup (250 ml) sugar
3 large eggs
3 tablespoons (45 ml)
   almond-flavored liqueur
1 tablespoon (15 ml) water
1 cup (250 ml) mini semisweet
   chocolate chips

1. Preheat oven to 350°F (180°C). To toast almonds, spread on baking sheet. Bake 8 to 10 minutes or until golden brown, stirring frequently. Remove almonds; cool. Coarsely chop almonds with chef's knife to measure ¾ cup (187 ml).

2. Place flour, baking powder and salt in medium bowl; stir to combine.

3. Beat butter and sugar in large bowl with electric mixer at medium speed until light and fluffy, scraping down side of bowl once. Beat in eggs, 1 at a time, scraping down side of bowl after each addition. Beat in liqueur and water. Gradually add flour mixture. Beat at low speed, scraping down side of bowl occasionally. Stir in chips and almonds.

4. Divide dough into fourths. Spread each piece evenly down center of sheet of waxed paper. Using waxed paper to hold dough, roll it back and forth to form a 15-inch (37.5 cm) log. (Technique on page 370.) Wrap securely. Refrigerate about 2 hours or until firm.

5. Preheat oven to 375°F (190°C). Lightly grease cookie sheet. Unwrap and place each log on prepared cookie sheet. With floured hands, shape each log 2 inches (5 cm) wide and ½ inch (1.2 cm) thick.

6. Bake 15 minutes. Remove from oven. Cut each log with serrated knife into l-inch (2.5 cm) diagonal slices. Place slices, cut side up, on cookie sheet; bake 7 minutes. Turn cookies over; bake 7 minutes or until cut surfaces are golden brown and cookies are dry. Remove cookies with spatula to wire racks; cool.

7. Store tightly covered at room temperature or freeze up to 3 months.

Makes about 4 dozen cookies

Step 5. Shaping log on cookie sheet.

Step 6. Cutting into diagonal slices.

Cardamom-Chocolate Sandwiches

1½ cups (375 ml) all-purpose
    flour
  1 teaspoon (5 ml) ground
    cardamom
  ½ teaspoon (2 ml) baking soda
  ½ teaspoon (2 ml) salt
  ¾ cup (187 ml) butter or
    margarine, softened
  ¾ cup (187 ml) firmly packed
    light brown sugar
  ¼ cup (62.5 ml) half-and-half
  ½ cup (125 ml) milk chocolate
    chips
  2 tablespoons (30 ml) butter
  2 tablespoons (30 ml) milk
  1 cup (250 ml) sifted powdered
    sugar

1. Place flour, cardamom, baking soda and salt in small bowl; stir to combine.

2. Beat ¾ cup (187 ml) butter and brown sugar with electric mixer at medium speed until light and fluffy, scraping down side of bowl once. Beat in half-and-half, scraping down side of bowl once. Gradually add flour mixture. Beat at low speed, scraping down side of bowl once.

3. Spoon dough down center of sheet of waxed paper. Using waxed paper to hold dough, roll it back and forth to form a tight, smooth 10-inch (25 cm) log. (Technique on page 370.) If dough is too soft to form a tight log, refrigerate 1 hour and reroll log until smooth. Wrap securely. Refrigerate about 4 hours or until firm. (Dough may be kept refrigerated up to 3 days.)

4. Preheat oven to 375°F (190°C). Unwrap dough; cut into ¼-inch (6 mm) slices with long, sharp knife. Place 2 inches (5 cm) apart on *ungreased* cookie sheets.

5. Bake 10 to 12 minutes or until edges are golden brown and cookies are set. Let cookies stand on cookie sheets 2 minutes. Remove cookies with spatula to wire racks; cool completely.

6. For filling, place chips and 2 tablespoons (30 ml) butter in small microwavable bowl. Microwave at HIGH 1½ minutes or until melted, stirring after 1 minute. Stir in milk until smooth. Beat in powdered sugar.

7. Spread filling over bottom side of half the cookies; top with remaining cookies.

8. Store tightly covered at room temperature or freeze up to 3 months.
Makes about 1 dozen cookies

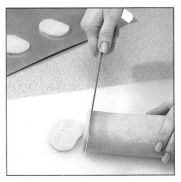
Step 4. Cutting dough into ¼-inch (6 mm) slices.

Step 7. Spreading filling on cookies.

Chocolate Edged Lace Cookies

⅔ cup (167 ml) ground almonds
½ cup (125 ml) butter
½ cup (125 ml) sugar
⅓ cup (83 ml) all-purpose flour
2 tablespoons (30 ml) heavy
    cream
¼ teaspoon (1 ml) salt
4 ounces (112 g) dark sweet or
    bittersweet chocolate candy
    bar, broken into pieces

1. Preheat oven to 375°F (190°C). Grease cookie sheets well; set aside.

2. Spread ground almonds onto baking sheet. Bake 5 minutes or until light golden brown and fragrant.

3. Combine butter, sugar, flour, cream and salt in medium, heavy saucepan. Add almonds; cook over medium heat, stirring constantly, about 5 minutes or until butter melts and small bubbles form around sides of saucepan. Remove from heat; stir well.

4. Drop rounded teaspoonfuls of batter 6 inches (15 ml) apart onto prepared cookie sheets. (Bake only 4 cookies per sheet.)

5. Bake 6 to 8 minutes or until cookies are deep golden brown around edges. Let cookies stand on cookie sheet 2 minutes. Remove cookies with spatula to wire rack;* cool.

6. Melt chocolate in small, heavy saucepan over low heat, stirring constantly. Tilt saucepan to pool chocolate at one end; dip edge of each cookie in chocolate, turning cookie slowly so entire edge is tinged with chocolate.

7. Let cookies stand on waxed paper until chocolate is set.

8. Store tightly covered at room temperature. Do not freeze.
Makes about 2½ dozen cookies

*For tuile-shaped cookies, balance a wooden spoon over two cans of the same height. Working quickly while cookies are still hot, drape the cookies over the handle of the spoon so that both sides hang down and form a taco shape; cool completely. Dip both edges of cookies into chocolate .

Step 4. Placing teaspoonfuls of batter on cookie sheet.

Step 6. Dipping edge of cookie in melted chocolate.

Tuile-shaped cookies: Shaping cookies.

COOKING CLASS
CAKES

404   CLASS NOTES

406   THE CLASSICS

414   THE CHOCOLATE
       COLLECTION

428   FULL-O-FRUIT

436   POTPOURRI

Black Forest Cake *(page 417)*

CLASS NOTES

Nothing beats the tantalizing aroma and luscious flavor of a home-baked cake. Whether it's a light, delicate angel food cake or a decadently rich devil's food cake, many of the preparation principles remain the same. The following information on cake basics is sure to provide you with all you'll need to make your next cake presentation one that will win you raves!

CAKE BASICS

Cakes are divided into two categories according to what makes them rise. Butter cakes rely primarily on baking powder or baking soda for height, while sponge cakes depend on the air trapped in the eggs during beating.

Some cake recipes specifically call for cake flour, which contains less protein than all-purpose flour and produces a more tender cake. Because of its delicate nature, cake flour often needs to be sifted before it is measured and added to the cake batter.

Butter Cakes

Butter cakes include pound cakes and yellow, white, spice and chocolate layer cakes. These cakes use butter, shortening or oil for moistness and richness and are leavened with baking powder and/or baking soda. Soften the butter first so that it mixes easily with the sugar.

Sponge Cakes

These cakes achieve their high volume from beaten eggs rather than a leavening agent like baking powder. Sponge cakes do not contain butter, oil or shortening. Angel food cakes are the most popular and are literally fat free since they use only egg whites, not yolks. Yellow sponge cakes are prepared with whole eggs. Chiffon cakes are also lightened with beaten eggs, but they are not true sponge cakes because they contain vegetable oil.

When preparing sponge cakes, be sure to beat the eggs to the proper stage; do not overbeat or underbeat them. Handle the beaten eggs gently when folding them into the other ingredients or they will lose air and volume.

PREPARING PANS

Always use the exact pan size called for in the recipe. If the pan is too large, the cake will not rise properly or brown evenly. If the pan is too small, the cake will sink in the center and the texture will be coarse; the batter may also run over the top of the pan during baking.

For butter cakes, use shiny metal pans or pans with a nonstick finish. Grease and flour the pans before mixing the cake batter so that the cake can be baked immediately.

To grease and flour cake pans, use a pastry brush, paper towel or waxed paper to apply a thin, even layer of shortening. Sprinkle flour into the greased pan; shake or tilt the pan to coat evenly with flour, then tap lightly to remove any excess.

To line pans with paper, invert pan; top with waxed paper. Press around the edge of the pan to form a crease in paper. Cut along crease to form a circle. Grease the pan. Press the paper onto the bottom of the greased pan. If the kitchen is very warm, it is helpful to refrigerate the prepared pans until you are ready to pour the batter in.

Sponge cakes are usually baked in tube pans. The center tube helps the heat circulate during baking and also supports the delicate structure of the cake. *Do not* grease the pans for sponge cakes. The ungreased pan lets the batter cling to the sides as it rises.

BAKING

Place the filled cake pan(s) in the center of a preheated oven. Oven racks may need to be set lower for cakes baked in tube pans. If two racks are used, arrange them so they divide the oven into thirds and then stagger the pans so they are not directly over each other. Avoid opening the oven door during the first half of the baking time. The oven temperature must remain constant in order for the cake to rise properly.

A butter cake is done when it begins to pull away from the sides of the pan, the top springs back when lightly touched and a cake tester or wooden pick inserted in the center comes out clean and dry. A sponge cake is done when it is delicately browned and the top springs back when lightly touched.

COOLING

After removing butter cakes from the oven, let them stand in their pans on wire racks for 10 minutes, or as the recipe directs. Run a knife around the edge of the cake to loosen it from the sides of the pan. Place a wire rack, top-side down, over the pan. Flip the rack and the pan over together and the cake should drop out onto the rack. If it does not come out, tap the bottom of the pan; the cake should come out easily. Remove the pan. Remove the paper liner from the cake if one was used. Place a second wire rack over the cake and flip both racks and the cake back over so the cake can cool top-side up. Remove the top rack.

Invert a sponge cake baked in a tube pan onto a heatproof funnel or bottle immediately after removing it from the oven. If it is cooled top side up, it will fall. Do not remove a sponge cake from the pan until it is completely cool.

FROSTING

Make sure the cake is completely cool before frosting it. Brush off any loose crumbs from the cake's surface. To keep the cake plate clean, place small strips of waxed paper under the edges of the cake; remove them after the cake has been frosted.

You will achieve a more professional look if you first apply a layer of frosting thinned with milk on the cake as a base coat to help seal in any remaining crumbs. Let this base coat dry a few minutes before covering with the final frosting. For best results, use a flat metal spatula for applying frosting. Place a mound of frosting in the center of the cake. Spread frosting across the top by pushing it out toward the sides with the spatula. Always keep the spatula on a frosted surface, because once it touches the cake surface, crumbs will mix in with the frosting. To frost sides, work from the top down, making sure the spatula only touches frosting.

STORING

Store one-layer cakes in their baking pans, tightly covered. Store two- or three-layer cakes in a cake-saver or under a large inverted bowl. If the cake has a fluffy or cooked frosting, insert a teaspoon handle under the edge of the cover to prevent an airtight seal and moisture buildup.

Cakes with whipped cream frostings or cream fillings should be stored in the refrigerator. Unfrosted cakes can be frozen for up to four months if well wrapped in plastic. Thaw in their wrappers at room temperature. Frosted cakes should be frozen unwrapped until the frosting hardens, then wrapped and sealed; freeze for up to two months. To thaw, remove the wrapping and thaw at room temperature or in the refrigerator. Cake with fruit or custard fillings do not freeze well because they become soggy when thawed.

Chiffon Cake

5 eggs
½ teaspoon (2 ml) cream of tartar
2¼ cups (562 ml) sifted all-purpose flour
1½ cups (375 ml) sugar
1 tablespoon (15 ml) baking powder
1 teaspoon (5 ml) salt
¾ cup (187 ml) water
½ cup (125 ml) vegetable oil
1 teaspoon (5 ml) vanilla
1 teaspoon (5 ml) almond extract
Strawberries, kiwifruit, star fruit, orange and whipped cream for garnish

1. Preheat oven to 325°F (160°C).

2. To separate egg yolk from white, gently tap egg in center against a hard surface, such as side of bowl. Holding shell half in each hand, gently transfer yolk back and forth between 2 shell halves. Allow white to drip down between 2 halves into medium bowl.

Step 2. Separating egg yolk from white.

3. When all white has dripped into bowl, place yolk in another bowl. Transfer white to third bowl. Repeat with remaining 4 eggs. (Egg whites must be free from any egg yolk to reach the proper volume when beaten.)

4. Add cream of tartar to egg whites. Beat with electric mixer at high speed until stiff peaks form. At this stage, stiff peaks remain on surface, and mixture does not slide when bowl is tilted. Set aside.

5. Sift together dry ingredients into large bowl. Make a well in flour mixture.

Step 5. Sifting together dry ingredients.

6. Add egg yolks; mix well. Blend in water, oil and flavorings.

7. Fold egg whites into egg yolk mixture with rubber spatula by gently cutting down to bottom of bowl, scraping up side of bowl, then folding over top of mixture. Repeat until egg whites are evenly incorporated. Pour into ungreased 10-inch (25 cm) tube pan.

Step 7. Folding in egg white mixture.

8. Bake 55 minutes. *Increase oven temperature to 350°F (180°C):* Continue baking 10 minutes or until cake springs back when lightly touched with finger.

9. Invert pan; place on top of clean empty bottle. Allow cake to cool completely in pan. Garnish, if desired.
    Makes one 10-inch (25 cm) tube cake

Carrot Cake

¾ pound (338 g) carrots
1 cup (250 ml) granulated sugar
1 cup (250 ml) packed brown sugar
1 cup (250 ml) vegetable oil
1 cup (250 ml) Polly-O® Ricotta Cheese
3 eggs
2 cups (500 ml) all-purpose flour
2 teaspoons (10 ml) baking powder
2 teaspoons (10 ml) baking soda
1 teaspoon (5 ml) salt
2 teaspoons (10 ml) ground cinnamon
½ teaspoon (2 ml) ground nutmeg
¼ to ½ cup (62.5 to 125 ml) raisins
½ cup (125 ml) chopped pineapple*
½ cup (125 ml) chopped walnuts
Cream Cheese Topping (page 410)
Additional raisins and chopped walnuts for garnish

*If using canned pineapple, use drained unsweetened pineapple.

1. Preheat oven to 350°F (180°C). Grease 10-inch (25 cm) tube pan with small amount of shortening.

2. Add 2 to 3 teaspoons (10 to 15 ml) flour to pan; gently tap side of pan to evenly coat bottom, side and center cone with flour. Invert pan and tap bottom to remove excess flour.

3. Trim ends of carrots; discard. Peel carrots. Shred with shredding disk of food processor or hand shredder. Measure 2 cups (500 ml); set aside.

4. Beat together sugars, oil and ricotta cheese in large bowl with electric mixer at medium speed until well blended.

5. Add eggs, 1 at a time, beating well after each addition.

6. Sift together flour, baking powder, baking soda, salt, cinnamon and nutmeg.

7. Remove 2 tablespoons (30 ml) flour mixture; toss with raisins in small bowl to prevent raisins from sinking in batter.

8. Gradually add flour mixture to sugar mixture. Mix until well blended.

9. Add raisins to batter with carrots, pineapple and walnuts; mix well.

continued on page 410

Step 1. Greasing tube pan.

Step 3. Shredding carrots.

Step 9. Adding raisins, carrots, pineapple and walnuts to batter.

Carrot Cake, *continued*

10. Pour batter into prepared pan, spreading evenly to edge.

11. Bake 1 hour or until wooden pick inserted in center comes out clean.

12. Cool cake in pan on wire rack 10 minutes. Loosen edge of cake with knife or flexible metal spatula. Using oven mitts or hot pads, place wire cooling rack on top of cake in pan. Turn cake and pan over so wire rack is on bottom. Gently shake cake to release from pan. Remove pan. Cool completely.

13. Prepare Cream Cheese Topping. Spread over cake just before serving. Garnish, if desired.
Makes one 10-inch (25 cm) tube cake

Cream Cheese Topping

**2 tablespoons (30 ml) butter, softened
4 ounces cream (112 g) cheese, softened
½ cup (125 ml) Polly-O® Ricotta Cheese
1 teaspoon (5 ml) vanilla
2 cups (500 ml) powdered sugar**

1. Beat together butter, cream cheese, ricotta cheese and vanilla in large bowl with electric mixer at medium speed until well blended.

2. Add powdered sugar; beat until smooth and creamy. Add additional powdered sugar, if necessary, for desired consistency.

Step 10. Pouring batter into pan.

Step 11. Testing cake for doneness with wooden pick.

Cream Cheese Topping: Step 1. Beating together butter, cream cheese, ricotta cheese and vanilla.

Boston Cream Pie

½ cup (125 ml) shortening
1 cup (250 ml) granulated sugar
1 egg
1 teaspoon (5 ml) vanilla
1¼ cups (312 ml) all-purpose
    flour
1½ teaspoons (375 ml) baking
    powder
½ teaspoon (2 ml) salt
¾ cup (187 ml) milk
    Custard Filling (page 412)
    Chocolate Glaze (page 412)

1. Preheat oven to 350°F (180°C). Grease and flour one 9-inch (22.5 cm) round cake pan. (Technique on page 422.)

2. Beat together shortening and sugar in large bowl with electric mixer at medium speed until well blended. Blend in egg and vanilla. Add combined dry ingredients alternately with milk, beating well after each addition. Pour into prepared pan.

3. Bake 35 minutes or until wooden pick inserted in center comes out clean. Cool cake in pan 10 minutes. Loosen edge of cake with knife or flexible metal spatula. Using oven mitts or hot pads, place wire cooling rack on top of cake in pan. Turn cake and pan over so wire rack is on bottom. Gently shake cake to release from pan. Remove pan. Cool completely.

4. Use ruler to measure height of cake layer. Insert wooden picks halfway up side of cake layer at 2-inch (5 cm) intervals.

5. To split layer in half, place 15- to 18-inch (37.5 to 45 cm) length of thread at far side of cake. Pull ends of thread together through cake, following line at top of wooden picks.

6. Prepare Custard Filling; set aside. Prepare Chocolate Glaze; set aside.

7. To assemble, place bottom half of cake, cut side up, on cake plate; brush off loose crumbs with hands or pastry brush. (Technique on page 422.) Spread cake layer with Custard Filling.

continued on page 412

Step 4. Using ruler to measure height of cake layer.

Step 5. Splitting cake layer in half.

Step 7. Spreading cake layer with Custard Filling.

Boston Cream Pie, continued

8. Cover with top half of cake layer. Spread top with Chocolate Glaze. Refrigerate until glaze is completely set. Store in refrigerator.
Makes one 9-inch (22.5 cm) cake

Custard Filling

⅓ **cup (83 ml) granulated sugar**
2 **tablespoons (30 ml) cornstarch**
¼ **teaspoon (62.5 ml) salt**
1½ **cups (375 ml) milk**
2 **egg yolks, slightly beaten**
2 **teaspoons (10 ml) vanilla**

1. Combine granulated sugar, cornstarch and salt in 2-quart (2 L) saucepan. Gradually stir in milk.

2. Cook over medium heat, stirring constantly, until mixture thickens and comes to a boil. Boil 1 minute, stirring constantly.

3. Gradually stir small amount of hot mixture into egg yolks; mix thoroughly.

4. Return egg yolk mixture to hot mixture in pan. Return to a boil; boil 1 minute, stirring constantly. *(Do not overcook.)*

5. Remove saucepan from heat; stir in vanilla. Cool to room temperature. Refrigerate.

Chocolate Glaze

2 **squares (1 ounce/28 g each) unsweetened chocolate**
3 **tablespoons (45 ml) butter**
1 **cup (250 ml) powdered sugar**
¾ **teaspoon (3.7 ml) vanilla**
1 **to 2 tablespoons (15 to 30 ml) hot water**

1. Combine chocolate and butter in medium saucepan; stir over low heat until melted. Remove from heat.

2. Stir in powdered sugar and vanilla. Stir in water, 1 teaspoonful (5 ml) at a time, until glaze is of desired consistency. Cool slightly.

Custard Filling: Step 2. Cooking until mixture thickens.

Custard Filling: Step 3. Adding small amount of hot mixture into egg yolks.

Chocolate Glaze: Step 1. Melting chocolate and butter.

Elegant Chocolate Log

3¼ cups (810 ml) sifted powdered
    sugar, divided
5 tablespoons (75 ml) sifted all-
    purpose flour
½ teaspoon (2 ml) salt
5 tablespoons (75 ml)
    unsweetened cocoa powder
6 eggs
¼ teaspoon (1 ml) cream of
    tartar
1¼ teaspoons (6 ml) vanilla
1 tablespoon (15 ml) water
1 square (1 ounce/28 g)
    unsweetened chocolate
12 large marshmallows *or* ¾ cup
    (187 ml) miniature
    marshmallows
1 cup (250 ml) whipping cream
2 tablespoons (30 ml)
    granulated sugar
3 to 4 tablespoons (45 to 60 ml)
    light cream
¼ cup (62.5 ml) chopped pecans

1. Preheat oven to 375°F (190°C). Grease 15 x 10 x 1-inch (37.5 x 25 x 2.5 cm) jelly-roll pan with small amount of shortening; line with waxed paper.

2. Sift together 1¾ cups (435 ml) powdered sugar, flour, salt and cocoa three times; set aside.

3. To separate egg yolk from white, gently tap egg in center against a hard surface, such as side of bowl. Holding shell half in each hand, gently transfer yolk back and forth between 2 shell halves. Allow white to drip down between 2 halves into bowl.

4. When all white has dripped into bowl, place yolk in another bowl. Transfer white to third bowl. Repeat with remaining 5 eggs. (Egg whites must be free from any egg yolk to reach the proper volume when beaten.)

5. Beat egg whites in large bowl with electric mixer at high speed until foamy. Add cream of tartar; beat until stiff peaks form. (Technique on page 420.) Set aside.

6. Beat egg yolks in separate large bowl with electric mixer at high speed until thick and lemon colored.

7. Blend in vanilla and water. Add dry ingredients; beat on medium speed until well blended. Fold in egg whites with rubber spatula by gently cutting down to bottom of bowl, scraping up side of bowl, then folding over top of mixture. Repeat until egg whites are evenly incorporated.

8. Spread batter into prepared pan.

continued on page 416

Step 1. Lining with waxed paper.

Step 3. Separating egg yolk from white.

Step 6. Beating egg yolks until thick and lemon colored.

Elegant Chocolate Log, continued

9. Bake 15 to 20 minutes or until wooden pick inserted in center comes out clean. Meanwhile, lightly dust clean dish towel with additional powdered sugar.

10. Loosen warm cake from edges of pan with spatula; invert onto prepared towel. Remove pan; carefully peel off paper.

11. Roll up cake gently, from one short end, by folding cake over and then tucking it in towel.

12. Continue rolling cake, using towel as an aid.

13. Let cake cool completely in towel on wire rack.

14. Meanwhile, unwrap chocolate; place chocolate in small heavy saucepan over *very low* heat, stirring constantly, until chocolate is just melted. (Or, place *unwrapped* chocolate in small microwavable dish. Microwave at HIGH (100% power) 1 to 2 minutes or until almost melted, stirring after each minute. Stir until smooth.) Set aside to cool.

15. If using large marshmallows, cut into smaller pieces with scissors or knife. (To prevent sticking, occasionally dip scissors or knife into small amount of cornstarch before cutting.)

16. Beat whipping cream in separate small bowl with electric mixer at high speed until thickened. Gradually add granulated sugar, beating until soft peaks form. Fold in marshmallows with rubber spatula by gently cutting down to bottom of bowl, scraping up side of bowl, then folding over top of mixture. Repeat until marshmallows are evenly incorporated.

17. Unroll cake; remove towel.

18. Spread cake with whipped cream mixture; reroll cake.

19. Combine cooled chocolate and remaining 1½ cups (375 ml) powdered sugar in small bowl. Stir in light cream, 1 tablespoonful (15 ml) at a time, until frosting is of spreading consistency. Spread on cake roll. Sprinkle cake with pecans. Refrigerate.

Makes one jelly-roll cake

Step 11. Rolling up the cake.

Step 18. Rerolling cake after spreading with whipped cream mixture.

Step 19. Spreading frosting on cake roll.

Black Forest Cake

2 cups (500 ml) *plus* 2
    tablespoons (30 ml)
    all-purpose flour
2 cups (500 ml) granulated
    sugar
¾ cup (187 ml) unsweetened
    cocoa
1½ teaspoons (8 ml) baking
    powder
¾ teaspoon (3.7 ml) baking soda
¾ teaspoon (3.7 ml) salt
3 eggs
1 cup (250 ml) milk
½ cup (125 ml) vegetable oil
1 tablespoon (15 ml) vanilla
    Cherry Topping (page 418)
    Whipped Cream Frosting
    (page 418)

1. Preheat oven to 350°F (180°C). Grease and flour two 9-inch (22.5 cm) round cake pans with small amount of shortening. (Technique on page 422.) Line bottoms with waxed paper.

2. Combine flour, granulated sugar, cocoa, baking powder, baking soda and salt in large bowl. Add eggs, milk, oil and vanilla; beat with electric mixer at medium speed until well blended. Pour evenly into prepared pans.

3. Bake 35 minutes or until wooden pick inserted in centers comes out clean. Cool layers in pans on wire racks 10 minutes. Loosen edge of cake with knife or flexible metal spatula. Using oven mitts or hot pads, place wire cooling rack on top of cake in pan. Turn cake and pan over so wire rack is on bottom. Gently shake cake to release from pan. Remove pan. Repeat with remaining cake layer. Invert layers to cool top side up. Cool completely.

4. While cake is baking, prepare Cherry Topping; set aside to cool.

5. Use ruler to measure height of each cake layer; insert wooden picks halfway up side of layer at 2-inch (5 cm) intervals.

6. With long serrated knife, split each cake layer horizontally in half, cutting along line marked with wooden picks.

7. Tear one split layer into crumbs; set aside.

8. Prepare Whipped Cream Frosting. Reserve 1½ cups (375 ml) for decorating cake; set aside.

continued on page 418

Step 1. Lining bottoms of pans with waxed paper.

Step 5. Measuring height of cake layer.

Step 6. Cutting cake layer in half.

9. Gently brush loose crumbs off top and side of each cake layer with pastry brush or hands. (Technique on page 422.)

10. To assemble, place one cake layer on cake plate. Spread with 1 cup (250 ml) Whipped Cream Frosting; top with ¾ cup (187 ml) Cherry Topping. Top with second cake layer; repeat layers of frosting and topping. Top with third cake layer.

11. Frost side of cake with remaining frosting. Gently press reserved crumbs onto frosting on side of cake.

12. Spoon reserved frosting into pastry bag fitted with star decorator tip. Pipe around top and bottom edges of cake. Spoon remaining topping onto top of cake. Store cake in refrigerator.

Makes one 3-layer cake

Cherry Topping

**2 cans (20 ounces/560 g each) tart
    pitted cherries, undrained
1 cup (250 ml) granulated sugar
¼ cup (62.5 ml) cornstarch
1 teaspoon (5 ml) vanilla**

Drain cherries, reserving ½ cup (125 ml) juice. Combine reserved juice, cherries, granulated sugar and cornstarch in 2-quart (2 L) saucepan. Cook over low heat until thickened, stirring constantly. Stir in 1 teaspoon (5 ml) vanilla. Cool; set aside.

Whipped Cream Frosting

**3 cups (750 ml) whipping cream
⅓ cup (83 ml) powdered sugar**

Chill large bowl and beaters thoroughly. Combine chilled whipping cream and powdered sugar in chilled bowl. Beat with electric mixer at high speed until stiff peaks form. To test, lift beaters from whipped cream; stiff peaks should remain on surface.

Step 11. Pressing reserved crumbs onto side of cake.

Step 12. Piping frosting on edges of cake.

Chocolate Angel Food Cake

1½ cups (375 ml) granulated
    sugar, divided
¾ cup (187 ml) sifted cake flour
¼ cup (62.5 ml) unsweetened
    cocoa powder
¼ teaspoon (1 ml) salt
12 egg whites
1½ teaspoons (8 ml) cream of
    tartar
1½ teaspoons (8 ml) vanilla
    Powdered sugar and frosting
    daisies* for garnish

*To make frosting daisies, gradually add 1 to 2 teaspoons (5 to 10 ml) milk to small amount of powdered sugar, mixing until well blended (frosting should have slightly stiff consistency). Tint with food coloring, if desired. Spoon into pastry bag fitted with star decorator tip. Pipe onto cake.

1. Preheat oven to 375°F (190°C).

2. Sift together ¾ cup (187 ml) granulated sugar with flour, cocoa and salt two times; set aside.

3. Beat egg whites in large bowl with electric mixer at medium speed until foamy.

4. Add cream of tartar; beat at high speed until soft peaks form.

5. Gradually add remaining ¾ cup (187 ml) granulated sugar, 2 tablespoons (30 ml) at a time, beating until stiff peaks form. At this stage, stiff peaks should remain on surface, and mixture does not slide when bowl is tilted. Blend in vanilla.

6. Sift about ¼ of the cocoa mixture over egg white mixture.

7. Fold cocoa mixture into batter. (Technique on page 406.) Repeat with remaining cocoa mixture. Pour into ungreased 10-inch (25 cm) tube pan.

8. Bake 35 to 40 minutes or until cake springs back when lightly touched with finger.

9. Invert pan; place on top of clean empty heatproof bottle. Allow cake to cool completely before removing from pan.

10. Turn cake, top side up, onto cake plate. Dust lightly with powdered sugar, if desired.

11. Decorate with frosting daisies, if desired.
    Makes one 10-inch (25 cm) tube cake

Step 5. Testing egg white mixture for stiff peaks.

Step 9. Inverting pan to allow cake to cool.

*Piping frosting daisies.

Tin Roof Sundae Cake

1 cup/250 ml (2 sticks) butter,
   softened
2 cups (500 ml) granulated
   sugar
4 eggs
3 cups (750 ml) all-purpose
   flour
2 teaspoons (10 ml) baking
   powder
1 cup (250 ml) milk
1 teaspoon (5 ml) vanilla
1 teaspoon (5 ml) butter
   flavoring
3 tablespoons (45 ml)
   unsweetened cocoa powder
Peanut Filling (page 424)
Chocolate Cream Frosting
   (page 424)
1 bar (2 ounces/56 g) white
   chocolate for garnish

1. Preheat oven to 350°F (180°C). Grease three 8- or 9-inch (20 or 22.5 cm) round cake pans with small amount of shortening.

2. Add 2 to 3 teaspoons (10 to 15 ml) flour to *each* pan. Gently tap side of pan to evenly coat bottom and side with flour. Invert pan and gently tap bottom to remove excess flour.

3. Beat together butter and granulated sugar in large bowl with electric mixer at high speed until light and fluffy.

4. Add eggs, 1 at a time, beating well after each addition.

5. Combine flour and baking powder in medium bowl. Add to butter mixture alternately with milk, beating well after each addition. Blend in vanilla and butter flavoring.

6. Pour ⅓ of the batter into each of two of the prepared pans.

7. Blend cocoa into the remaining batter; pour into remaining pan.

8. Bake 30 minutes or until wooden pick inserted in centers comes out clean.

9. Cool layers in pans on wire racks 10 minutes. Loosen edge of cake with knife or flexible metal spatula. Using oven mitts or hot pads, place wire rack on top of cake in pan. Turn cake and pan over so wire rack is on bottom. Gently shake cake to release from pan. Remove pan. Repeat with remaining layers. Invert layers to cool top side up. Cool completely.

10. Gently brush loose crumbs off tops and sides of cake layers with pastry brush or hands.

Step 2. Flouring the pan.

Step 6. Pouring batter into two of the pans.

Step 10. Brushing crumbs from cooling cake layers.

Tin Roof Sundae Cake, continued

11. Prepare Peanut Filling and Chocolate Cream Frosting. To assemble, place one yellow layer on cake plate; spread with ½ of the Peanut Filling.

12. Cover with chocolate layer; spread with remaining filling.

13. Top with remaining yellow cake layer. Frost with Chocolate Cream Frosting.

14. Unwrap white chocolate; place chocolate in small heavy saucepan. Heat over *very low* heat, stirring constantly, just until chocolate is melted. (Or, place *unwrapped* chocolate square in microwavable dish. Microwave at HIGH (100% power) 1 to 2 minutes or until almost melted, stirring after each minute. Stir until smooth.) Cool slightly.

15. Spoon white chocolate into pastry bag fitted with writing tip. Pipe onto cake.

Makes one 3-layer cake

Peanut Filling

½ **cup/125 ml (1 stick) butter, softened**
4 **ounces (112 g) cream cheese, softened**
2 **cups (500 ml) powdered sugar**
¾ **cup (187 ml) crunchy peanut butter**
1 **teaspoon (5 ml) vanilla**
1 **teaspoon (5 ml) butter flavoring**
⅓ **cup (83 ml) finely chopped peanuts**
1 **to 2 tablespoons (15 to 30 ml) milk (optional)**

1. Beat together butter and cream cheese in medium bowl with electric mixer at medium speed until creamy.

2. Gradually add powdered sugar, beating until fluffy.

3. Blend in peanut butter, vanilla and butter flavoring. Stir in peanuts. Add milk if necessary for desired consistency.

Chocolate Cream Frosting

2 **squares (1 ounce/28 g each) unsweetened chocolate**
4 **ounces (112 g) cream cheese, softened**
¼ **cup/62.5 ml (½ stick) butter, softened**
3 **tablespoons (45 ml) whipping cream**
1 **tablespoon (15 ml) lemon juice**
1 **teaspoon (5 ml) vanilla**
2 **cups (500 ml) powdered sugar**

1. Melt chocolate (see step 14 for directions). Set aside to cool.

2. Beat together cream cheese and butter in medium bowl with electric mixer at medium speed until creamy. Beat in whipping cream. Blend in chocolate, lemon juice and vanilla.

3. Gradually beat in powdered sugar until mixture is fluffy.

Step 12. Spreading remaining Peanut Filling.

Step 15. Piping white chocolate onto cake.

Chocolate Cream Frosting: Step 3. Beating in powdered sugar.

Chocolate Sour Cream Cake

½ cup (125 ml) boiling water
½ cup (125 ml) unsweetened
    cocoa powder
⅔ cup (167 ml) butter or
    margarine, softened
1¾ cups (437 ml) granulated
    sugar
2 eggs
1 teaspoon (5 ml) vanilla
2½ cups (625 ml) sifted cake flour
1½ teaspoons (8 ml) baking soda
½ teaspoon (2 ml) salt
1 cup (250 ml) sour cream
    Cocoa-Nut Filling (page 426)
    Fluffy Cocoa Frosting
      (page 426)
1 square (1 ounce/28 g)
    unsweetened chocolate for
    garnish
    Chocolate-Dipped
      Strawberries (page 426) and
      fresh mint leaves for garnish

1. Preheat oven to 350°F (180°C). Grease two 9-inch (22.5 cm) round cake pans with small amount of shortening.

2. Add 2 to 3 teaspoons (10 to 15 ml) flour to *each* pan. Gently tap side of pan to evenly coat bottom and side with flour. Invert pan and gently tap bottom to remove excess flour.

Step 2. Flouring the pan.

3. Gradually add boiling water to cocoa in small bowl, stirring until well blended; cool slightly.

4. Meanwhile, beat butter and granulated sugar in large bowl with electric mixer at high speed until well blended.

5. Add eggs, 1 at a time, beating well after each addition. Blend in vanilla.

Step 5. Adding eggs.

6. Combine flour, baking soda and salt in medium bowl. Add to butter mixture alternately with sour cream, beating well after each addition.

7. Add cocoa mixture to batter; beat until well blended.

8. Pour batter evenly into prepared pans.

9. Bake 35 minutes or until wooden pick inserted in centers comes out clean. Cool layers in pans on wire racks 10 minutes. Loosen edge of cake with knife or flexible metal spatula. Using oven mitts or hot pads, place wire cooling rack on top of cake in pan. Turn cake and pan over so wire rack is on bottom. Gently shake cake to release from pan. Remove pan. Repeat with remaining cake layer. Invert layers to cool top side up. Cool completely.

Step 7. Adding cocoa mixture to batter.

continued on page 426

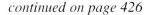

Chocolate Sour Cream Cake,
continued

10. Gently brush loose crumbs off tops and sides of cake layers with pastry brush or hands. (Technique on page 422.)

11. Prepare Cocoa-Nut Filling and Fluffy Cocoa Frosting. To assemble, place one cake layer on cake plate; spread with Cocoa-Nut Filling.

12. Top with second cake layer. Frost with Fluffy Cocoa Frosting.

13. Grate chocolate; sprinkle over cake.

14. Prepare Chocolate-Dipped Strawberries. Place on cake. Surround with mint leaves, if desired.

Makes one 2-layer cake

Cocoa-Nut Filling

½ cup (125 ml) Fluffy Cocoa
    Frosting (recipe follows)
¼ cup (62.5 ml) flaked coconut
    (optional)
¼ cup (62.5 ml) chopped nuts,
    toasted

Combine ingredients in small bowl; mix until well blended.

Fluffy Cocoa Frosting

4½ cups (1.12 L) powdered sugar
½ cup (125 ml) unsweetened cocoa
    powder
½ cup/125 ml (1 stick) butter or
    margarine, softened
5 tablespoons (75 ml) half-and-half
    or milk
1 teaspoon (5 ml) vanilla

1. Combine powdered sugar and cocoa in medium bowl; set aside.

2. Beat butter in large bowl with electric mixer at medium speed until creamy.

3. Add ½ of cocoa mixture; beat until fluffy. Blend in half-and-half and vanilla.

4. Gradually add remaining cocoa mixture, beating until frosting is of spreading consistency.

Chocolate-Dipped Strawberries

½ cup (125 ml) semisweet chocolate
    chips
1 teaspoon (5 ml) shortening
10 to 12 fresh strawberries, cleaned

1. Place chocolate chips and shortening in small microwavable bowl. Microwave at HIGH (100% power) 1½ to 3 minutes or until smooth when stirred, stirring after each minute. (Or, place in top of double boiler. Heat over hot, not boiling, water until chocolate is smooth when stirred.)

2. Dip strawberries into chocolate. Place on waxed paper-lined jelly-roll pan or cookie sheet; let stand until chocolate is set.

Step 11. Spreading cake layer with Cocoa-Nut Filling.

Step 13. Grating chocolate.

Chocolate-Dipped Strawberries: Step 2. Dipping strawberries into chocolate.

Apple Streusel Cake

¼ cup/62.5 ml (½ stick) *plus* 3 tablespoons (45 ml) butter, divided
½ cup (125 ml) packed brown sugar
1 teaspoon (5 ml) ground cinnamon
¼ teaspoon (1 ml) ground nutmeg
3 apples
2 teaspoons (10 ml) lemon juice
1⅓ cups (333 ml) sifted cake flour
¾ cup (187 ml) granulated sugar
1¾ teaspoons (437 ml) baking powder
¼ teaspoon (1 ml) salt
½ cup (125 ml) milk
1 teaspoon (5 ml) vanilla
1 egg, separated (technique on page 406)
½ cup (125 ml) chopped pecans

1. Preheat oven to 375°F (190°C).

2. Melt ¼ cup (62.5 ml) butter in 8-inch (20 cm) square baking pan. Add brown sugar and spices; mix well.

3. Peel apples. Remove cores; discard.

4. Cut apples into rings. Arrange over brown sugar mixture in bottom of pan; sprinkle with lemon juice. Set aside.

5. Combine cake flour, granulated sugar, baking powder and salt in large bowl. Cut in remaining 3 tablespoons (45 ml) butter with pastry blender until mixture resembles coarse crumbs.

6. Add milk and vanilla; beat with electric mixer at low speed until dry ingredients are moistened. Continue beating 2 minutes at medium speed. Blend in egg yolk and pecans.

7. Clean beaters of electric mixer. Beat egg white in small bowl with electric mixer at high speed until stiff peaks form. (Technique on page 420.) Gently fold egg whites into batter. Pour over apples in pan.

8. Bake 35 minutes or until wooden pick inserted in center comes out clean. Cool cake in pan on wire rack 5 minutes. Loosen edges and invert onto serving plate. Let stand 1 minute before removing pan. Serve warm.

Makes one 8-inch (20 cm) square cake

Step 3. Removing cores of apples.

Step 5. Cutting in butter.

Fresh Pear Cake

4 cups (1 L) chopped peeled
    pears
2 cups (500 ml) granulated
    sugar
1 cup (250 ml) chopped nuts
3 cups (750 ml) all-purpose
    flour
2 teaspoons (10 ml) baking soda
½ teaspoon (2 ml) salt
½ teaspoon (2 ml) ground
    cinnamon
½ teaspoon (2 ml) ground
    nutmeg
2 eggs
1 cup (250 ml) vegetable oil
1 teaspoon (5 ml) vanilla
    Powdered sugar for garnish

1. Combine pears, granulated sugar and nuts in medium bowl; mix lightly. Let stand 1 hour, stirring frequently.

2. Preheat oven to 375°F (190°C). Grease 10-inch (25 cm) fluted tube or tube pan with small amount of shortening.

3. Add 2 to 3 teaspoons (10 to 15 ml) flour to pan. Gently tap side of pan to evenly coat bottom, side and center cone with flour. Invert pan and gently tap bottom to remove excess flour.

4. Combine flour, baking soda, salt, cinnamon and nutmeg in separate medium bowl; set aside.

5. Beat eggs in large bowl with electric mixer at medium speed. Blend in oil and vanilla. Add flour mixture; mix well. Add pear mixture; stir well. Pour into prepared pan.

6. Bake 1 hour and 15 minutes or until wooden pick inserted in center comes out clean. Cool cake in pan on wire rack 10 minutes. Loosen edge of cake with knife or flexible metal spatula. Using oven mitts or hot pads, place wire cooling rack on top of cake in pan. Turn cake and pan over so wire rack is on bottom. Gently shake cake to release from pan. Remove pan. Cool completely.

7. Place cake on cake plate. Insert strips of waxed paper under cake to keep plate clean.

8. Dust lightly with powdered sugar. Remove waxed paper.
    Makes one 10-inch (25 cm) tube cake

Step 2. Greasing fluted tube pan.

Step 6. Loosening edges of cake.

Step 7. Inserting strips of waxed paper under cake.

Sunflower Lemon Cake

2 lemons
1½ cups (375 ml) sugar
1 cup (250 ml) sunflower oil
6 eggs
1⅔ cups (317 ml) *plus* 1
    tablespoon (15 ml)
    all-purpose flour, divided
2 teaspoons (10 ml) baking
    powder
¼ teaspoon (1 ml) salt
½ cup (125 ml) sunflower
    kernels
    Lemon Twist Garnish*
    Whipped cream, lemon peel
    and fresh mint leaves for
    garnish

*Lemon Twist Garnish: Cut lemon into slices, each about ¼ inch (6 mm) thick. Make one cut in each slice from center to outer edge; twist slice.

1. Preheat oven to 300°F (150°C). Grease two 9 x 5-inch (22.5 x 12.5 cm) loaf pans with small amount of shortening.

2. Add 2 to 3 teaspoons (10 to 15 ml) flour to *each* pan. Gently tap side of pan to evenly coat bottom and sides with flour. Invert pan and tap bottom to remove excess flour.

3. Finely grate colored portion of lemon peel using bell grater or hand-held grater. Measure 5 teaspoons (25 ml).

4. Beat together sugar, lemon peel and oil in large bowl with electric mixer at medium speed. Add eggs, 1 at a time, beating well after each addition.

5. Add 1⅔ cups (317 ml) flour, baking powder and salt; mix well.

6. Combine remaining 1 tablespoon (15 ml) flour and sunflower kernels in small bowl, toss lightly. Stir into batter.

7. Pour batter evenly into prepared pans.

8. Bake 1 hour or until wooden pick inserted in centers comes out clean. Cool loaves in pans on wire racks 10 minutes. Loosen edge of cake with knife or flexible metal spatula. Using oven mitts or hot pads, place wire cooling rack on top of cake in pan. Turn cake and pan over so wire rack is on bottom. Gently shake cake to release from pan. Remove pan. Cool completely. Garnish, if desired.

*Makes two 9 x 5-inch
(22.5 x 12.5 cm) loaves*

Step 2. Flouring the pan.

Step 6. Tossing sunflower kernels with flour.

*Lemon Twist Garnish: Twisting lemon slices.

Spanish Orange-Almond Cake

1 medium orange
⅓ cup (83 ml) shortening
1 cup (250 ml) *plus* 2
    tablespoons (30 ml) sugar,
    divided
1 egg
1¼ cups (312 ml) all-purpose
    flour
1½ teaspoons (8 ml) baking
    powder
½ teaspoon (2 ml) salt
¾ cup (187 ml) milk
½ cup (125 ml) sliced almonds
¼ cup (62.5 ml) orange-flavored
    liqueur
    Additional orange for garnish

1. Preheat oven to 350°F (180°C). Grease and flour 8-inch (20 cm) square or 9-inch (22.5 cm) round cake pan. (Technique on page 422.)

2. Finely grate colored portion of orange peel using bell grater or hand-held grater. Measure 4 teaspoons (20 ml) orange peel; set aside.

3. Beat together shortening and 1 cup (250 ml) sugar in large bowl with electric mixer at medium speed until light and fluffy. Add egg; beat until well blended.

4. Combine flour, baking powder and salt in medium bowl. Add to sugar mixture alternately with milk, beating well after each addition. Stir in orange peel. Pour into prepared pan; sprinkle with almonds.

5. Bake 40 to 45 minutes or until wooden pick inserted in center comes out clean.

6. Sprinkle with remaining 2 tablespoons (30 ml) sugar; drizzle with liqueur.

7. Cool cake in pan on wire rack 10 minutes. Loosen edge of cake with knife or flexible metal spatula. Using oven mitts or hot pads, place wire cooling rack on top of cake in pan. Turn cake and pan over so wire rack is on bottom. Gently shake cake to release from pan. Remove pan. Cool almond side up.

8. If desired, use citrus zester to remove colored peel, not white pith, of additional orange; sprinkle over top of cake.

*Makes one 8- or 9-inch
(20 or 22.5 cm) cake*

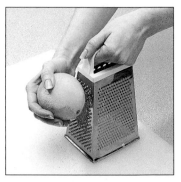

Step 2. Grating orange peel.

Step 4. Sprinkling batter with almonds.

Step 6. Drizzling cake with liqueur.

Velvety Coconut and Spice Cake

Granulated sugar
2½ cups (625 ml) all-purpose
    flour
1½ teaspoons (375 ml) baking
    powder
¾ teaspoon (3.7 ml) baking soda
½ teaspoon (2 ml) salt
1½ teaspoons (8 ml) ground
    cinnamon
¼ teaspoon (1 ml) ground cloves
¼ teaspoon (1 ml) ground
    nutmeg
¼ teaspoon (1 ml) ground
    allspice
¼ teaspoon (1 ml) ground
    cardamom
½ cup/125 ml (1 stick) butter or
    margarine, softened
½ cup (125 ml) packed brown
    sugar
4 eggs
1 teaspoon (5 ml) vanilla
1½ cups (375 ml) light cream
¼ cup (62.5 ml) molasses
1½ cups (375 ml) shredded
    coconut
⅔ cup (167 ml) orange
    marmalade
Creamy Orange Frosting
    (page 438)
Candied Orange Rose
    (page 438) and toasted
    coconut* for garnish

*To toast coconut, spread in even layer on baking sheet. Bake in preheated 350°F (180°C) oven 8 to 10 minutes or until golden brown.

1. Preheat oven to 350°F (180°C). Grease three 8-inch (20 cm) round cake pans; sprinkle with enough granulated sugar to lightly coat bottoms and sides of pans.

2. Combine flour, baking powder, baking soda, salt and spices in medium bowl; set aside.

3. Beat butter in large bowl with electric mixer at medium speed until creamy.

4. Add ½ cup (125 ml) granulated sugar and brown sugar; beat until light and fluffy.

5. Add eggs, 1 at a time, beating well after each addition. Blend in vanilla.

6. Combine light cream and molasses in small bowl. Add flour mixture to egg mixture alternately with molasses mixture, beating well after each addition.

7. Stir in shredded coconut; pour evenly into prepared pans.

8. Bake 20 minutes or until wooden pick inserted in centers comes out clean. Cool layers in pans on wire racks 10 minutes. Loosen edge of cake with knife or flexible metal spatula. Using oven mitts or hot pads, place wire cooling rack on top of cake in pan. Turn cake and pan over so wire rack is on bottom. Gently shake cake to release from pan. Repeat with remaining cake layers. Cool layers completely.

continued on page 438

Step 4. Beating in sugars until light and fluffy.

Step 6. Adding molasses mixture.

Step 7. Stirring in coconut.

Velvety Coconut and Spice Cake, continued

9. Gently brush loose crumbs off tops and sides of cake layers with pastry brush or hands. (Technique on page 422.)

10. To assemble, spread two cake layers with marmalade; stack on cake plate. Top with third layer.

11. Prepare Creamy Orange Frosting. Frost top and side of cake. Refrigerate. Garnish, if desired.

Makes one 3-layer cake

Creamy Orange Frosting

   1 package (3 ounces/85 g) cream cheese, softened
   2 cups (500 ml) sifted powdered sugar
   Few drops orange extract
   Milk (optional)

1. Beat cream cheese in large bowl until creamy. Gradually add powdered sugar, beating until fluffy. Blend in orange extract.

2. If necessary, add milk, 1 teaspoonful (5 ml) at a time, for a thinner consistency.

Candied Orange Rose

   1 cup (250 ml) granulated sugar
   1 cup (250 ml) water
   1 orange

1. Combine sugar and water in medium saucepan. Bring to a boil over medium-high heat, stirring occasionally.

2. Meanwhile, thinly peel orange with sharp knife, leaving as much membrane on orange as possible.

3. Carefully roll up peel, starting at one short end; secure with wooden pick.

4. Place on slotted spoon; add to hot sugar syrup.

5. Reduce heat to low; simmer 5 to 10 minutes or until orange rind turns translucent. Remove from syrup; place on waxed paper-lined cookie sheet to cool. Remove wooden pick.

continued on page 440

Step 10. Spreading layers with marmalade.

Candied Orange Rose: Step 2. Peeling orange.

Candied Orange Rose: Step 4. Adding rose to hot sugar syrup.

Carmel-Butter Pecan Cake

1 cup (250 ml) shortening
2 cups (500 ml) granulated
    sugar
4 eggs
3 cups (750 ml) sifted cake flour
2½ teaspoons (12 ml) baking
    powder
½ teaspoon (2 ml) salt
1 cup (250 ml) milk
1 teaspoon (2 ml) vanilla
1 teaspoon (2 ml) almond
    extract
    Caramel Filling (page 440)
    Buttercream Frosting
      (page 440)
¼ cup (60 ml) chopped pecans

Step 5. Removing cake layer to rack to cool.

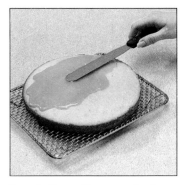

Step 6. Spreading top of cake layer with Caramel Filling.

Step 7. Making vertical strips around side of cake.

1. Preheat oven to 350°F (180°C). Grease and flour three 9-inch (22.5 cm) round cake pans. (Technique on page 422.)

2. Beat together shortening and granulated sugar in large bowl with electric mixer at medium speed until light and fluffy.

3. Add eggs, 1 at a time, beating well after each addition.

4. Sift together dry ingredients. Add to sugar mixture alternately with milk, beating well after each addition. Blend in vanilla and almond extract. Pour evenly into prepared pans.

5. Bake 20 to 25 minutes or until wooden pick inserted in centers comes out clean. Cool layers in pans on wire racks 10 minutes. Loosen edge of cake with knife or flexible metal spatula. Using oven mitts or hot pads, place wire cooling rack on top of cake in pan. Turn cake and pan over so wire rack is on bottom. Gently shake cake to release from pan. Remove pan. Repeat with remaining cake layers. Invert layers to cool top side up. Cool completely.

6. Gently brush loose crumbs off tops and sides of cake layers with pastry brush or hands. (Technique on page 422.) Prepare Caramel Filling. To assemble, spread tops of layers with filling; stack on cake plate.

7. Prepare Buttercream Frosting. To make basketweave design on side of cake, spoon ¼ to ⅓ of the frosting into pastry bag fitted with ridged decorator tip. Make vertical strips at 2-inch (5 cm) intervals around side of cake.

Caramel-Butter Pecan Cake,
continued

8. Make horizontal strip around side of cake, just below top edge. Repeat halfway down side of cake.

9. Repeat step 7, making one new strip at a point halfway between each of the strips made in step 7. (Continue to refill pastry tube with additional frosting as necessary.)

10. Make short horizontal strips, each at a point halfway between the horizontal strips made in step 8 and also at bottom of cake. Each short strip starts at the edge of one vertical strip, crosses over next vertical strip, and ends at edge of next vertical strip.

11. Replace ridged decorator tip with star tip. Pipe any remaining frosting around top of cake. Sprinkle with pecans.

Makes one 3-layer cake

Caramel Filling

3 cups (750 ml) granulated sugar, divided
¾ cup (187 ml) milk
1 egg, beaten
  Dash of salt
½ cup/125 ml (1 stick) butter, softened

1. Place ½ cup (125 ml) granulated sugar in large heavy saucepan. Cook over medium heat, stirring constantly, until sugar is light golden brown.

2. Combine remaining 2½ cups (625 ml) granulated sugar, milk, egg and salt in medium bowl; stir in butter. Add to caramelized sugar.

3. Cook over medium heat, stirring occasionally, until candy thermometer registers 230°F/130°C (15 to 20 minutes); cool 5 minutes. Stir with wooden spoon until well blended and thickened.

Buttercream Frosting

⅓ cup/83 ml (⅔ stick) butter, softened
3 cups (750 ml) sifted powdered sugar
2 tablespoons (30 ml) half-and-half
½ teaspoon (2 ml) vanilla

1. Beat butter in large bowl with electric mixer at medium speed until creamy.

2. Gradually add powdered sugar alternately with half-and-half, beating until light and fluffy. Add additional 1 tablespoon (15 ml) half-and-half if necessary for desired consistency. Stir in vanilla.

Step 8. Making horizontal strips around side of cake.

Step 9. Making additional vertical strips.

Step 10. Making short horizontal strips.

Brandy-Pecan Corn Meal Cake

1 cup/250 ml (2 sticks)
    margarine, softened
1¼ cups (312 ml) granulated
    sugar
¾ cup (187 ml) packed brown
    sugar
5 eggs
1 cup (250 ml) sour cream
½ cup (125 ml) brandy
2¼ cups (562 ml) all-purpose
    flour
½ cup (125 ml) Quaker®
    Enriched Corn Meal
2 teaspoons (10 ml) baking
    powder
1 teaspoon (5 ml) salt (optional)
1 teaspoon (5 ml) ground
    cinnamon
½ teaspoon (2 ml) ground
    nutmeg
1½ cups (375 ml) chopped pecans
    Brandy Glaze (recipe follows)
    Pecan halves for garnish

1. Preheat oven to 325°F (160°C). Generously grease and flour 10-inch (25 cm) fluted tube or tube pan with small amount of shortening.

2. Beat together margarine and sugars in large bowl with electric mixer at medium speed until light and fluffy. Add eggs, 1 at a time, beating well after each addition. Blend in sour cream and brandy.

3. Sift together dry ingredients. Add to margarine mixture, mixing until well blended. Stir in pecans. Pour into prepared pan, spreading evenly to edges.

4. Bake 65 to 70 minutes or until wooden pick inserted in center comes out clean. (Surface will appear slightly wet in center.)

5. Cool cake in pan on wire rack 10 minutes. Loosen edges and remove to rack to cool completely. (Technique on page 430.)

6. Prepare Brandy Glaze. Drizzle over cake. Garnish, if desired. Store tightly covered.
    Makes one 10-inch (25 cm) tube cake

Step 4. Testing doneness with wooden pick.

Step 6. Drizzling Brandy Glaze over cake.

Brandy Glaze

2 tablespoons (30 ml) margarine
1 cup (250 ml) sifted powdered sugar
1 to 2 teaspoons (5 to 10 ml) brandy
4 to 5 teaspoons (20 to 25 ml) milk

1. Heat margarine in medium saucepan over medium heat until melted and golden brown; cool slightly.

2. Add powdered sugar, brandy and milk; beat until smooth.

Champion Pumpkin Cake

¾ cup (187 ml) shortening
1½ cups (375 ml) granulated
    sugar
3 eggs
1½ cups (375 ml) solid-pack
    pumpkin
1 cup (250 ml) buttermilk
2¾ cups (687 ml) all-purpose
    flour
1 tablespoon (15 ml) baking
    powder
1½ teaspoons (8 ml) baking soda
½ teaspoon (2 ml) salt
1 teaspoon (5 ml) ground
    cinnamon
¼ teaspoon (1 ml) ground
    allspice
¼ teaspoon (1 ml) ground
    nutmeg
⅛ teaspoon (0.5 ml) ground
    ginger
⅛ teaspoon (0.5 ml) pumpkin
    pie spice
Snow Frosting (recipe
    follows)

1. Preheat oven to 350°F (180°C). Grease and flour two 9-inch (22.5 cm) round cake pans. (Technique on page 422).

2. Beat shortening and granulated sugar in large bowl with electric mixer at medium speed until light and fluffy. Add eggs, 1 at a time, beating after each addition. Add pumpkin and buttermilk; beat well.

3. Sift together remaining dry ingredients; add to shortening mixture. Beat well. Pour evenly into prepared pans.

4. Bake 40 to 45 minutes or until wooden pick inserted in centers comes out clean. Cool in pans on wire racks 10 minutes. Loosen edges and remove to racks to cool completely. (Technique on page 439.)

5. Gently brush loose crumbs off tops and sides of cake layers with pastry brush or hands. (Technique on page 422.) Fill and frost with Snow Frosting.

Makes one 2-layer cake

Step 1. Flouring the pan.

Step 2. Adding eggs.

Step 3. Pouring batter into pans.

Snow Frosting

½ cup (125 ml) shortening
½ cup/125 ml (1 stick) butter, softened
2 egg whites*
1 teaspoon (5 ml) vanilla
4 cups (1 L) sifted powdered sugar

1. Beat together shortening and butter in large bowl with electric mixer at medium speed until light and fluffy.

2. Add egg whites and vanilla; mix well. Gradually add powdered sugar, beating well.

*Use clean, uncracked eggs.

COOKING CLASS
DESSERTS

448   CLASS NOTES

450   PERFECT PIES

462   DAYDREAM DESSERTS

468   GLORIOUS CHOCOLATE

478   FRUIT FANTASIES

484   GRAND FINALES

Raspberry Cheesecake Blossoms *(page 482)*

CLASS NOTES

A fabulous dessert will add a special touch to any meal and this collection is sure to please. You'll marvel at the variety of desserts—cakes, pies, soufflés and mousses—and the multitude of flavors, such as vanilla, caramel, cherry, peanut butter, apple, strawberry, maple and, of course, chocolate!

Success in the kitchen is often a matter of careful organization and preparation. Before you begin a recipe, carefully read through the instructions, then gather all the ingredients and equipment. Do not make ingredient substitutions unless specifically called for in the recipe. Substitutions can alter the delicate balance of ingredients and the result may be less than perfect. Mastering the following dessert-making skills will help ensure success every time.

BAKING TIPS

• Measure all ingredients carefully and accurately. To measure flour, spoon it lightly into a dry measuring cup and level it off with a straight-edge metal spatula (do not shake it down or tap it on the counter).

• Use the pan size specified in each recipe and prepare the pan as stated. The wrong size pan may cause the dessert to burn on the edges and bottom or sink in the middle.

• Oven temperatures may vary depending on the oven model

and manufacturer, so watch your dessert carefully and check for doneness using the test given in the recipe.

PASTRY MAKING TIPS

• Cut the shortening, margarine or butter into the flour and salt using a pastry blender or two knives until the mixture forms pea-sized pieces. Add the liquid, 1 tablespoon (15 ml) at a time, tossing lightly with a fork, until the dough is just moist enough to hold together when pressed.

• If the dough is sticky and difficult to handle, refrigerate it until firm. The easiest way to roll out pastry dough without sticking is to use a rolling pin cover and pastry cloth. Lightly flour the covered rolling pin and pastry cloth before using, and handle the dough quickly and lightly. A tough pie crust is often the result of too much flour worked into the dough or overhandling.

• Roll the dough out to a ⅛-inch (3 mm) thick circle at least 1 inch (2.5 cm) larger than an inverted pie plate. To transfer dough to pie plate, place the rolling pin on one side of the dough. Gently roll the dough over the rolling pin once. Carefully lift the rolling pin and the dough, unrolling the dough over the pie plate. Ease the dough into the pie plate with fingertips and gently press into place. Be careful not to pull or stretch the dough, as this will cause it to shrink during baking.

- Often a pie crust is "baked blind," which means it is baked before the filling is added. To keep the pastry from puffing up during baking, line the crust with foil and fill it with dried beans, uncooked rice or ceramic or metal pie weights. Bake the crust until set. Remove the foil and weights and either return the crust to the oven to finish baking or cool it completely before adding filling.

BEATING EGG WHITES

- Eggs separate more easily when cold, but egg whites reach their fullest volume if allowed to stand at room temperature for 30 minutes before beating.

- When beating egg whites, always check that the bowl and beaters are completely clean and dry. The smallest trace of yolk, water or fat can prevent the whites from obtaining maximum volume. For best results, use a copper, stainless steel or glass bowl (plastic bowls may have an oily film, even after repeated washings).

- Beat the whites slowly until they are foamy, then increase the speed. Add a pinch of salt and cream of tartar at this point to help stabilize them. Do not overbeat or they will become dry and clump together.

- Beat the egg whites to the desired stage. For soft peaks, lift beaters from the egg whites; they should have droopy, but definite, peaks. For stiff peaks, lift the beaters from the egg whites; stiff peaks should remain on the surface and the mixture will not slide around when the bowl is tilted.

- Immediately fold beaten egg whites gently into another mixture so volume is not lost; never beat or stir.

DISSOLVING GELATIN

- To dissolve unflavored gelatin successfully, sprinkle one package of gelatin over $\frac{1}{4}$ cup (62.5 ml) of cold liquid in a small saucepan. Let it stand for 3 minutes to soften. Stir over low heat about 5 minutes or until the gelatin is completely dissolved.

- Run a finger over the spoon to test for undissolved gelatin granules. If it is smooth, the gelatin is completely dissolved; if it feels granular, continue heating until it feels smooth.

WHIPPING CREAM

- For best results when beating whipping or heavy cream, first chill the cream, bowl and beaters—the cold keeps the fat in the cream solid, thus increasing the volume.

- For optimum volume, beat the cream in a deep, narrow bowl. Generally 1 cup (250 ml) of cream will yield 2 cups (500 ml) of whipped cream, so be sure to choose a bowl that will accommodate the increased volume. Beat the cream until soft peaks form. To test, lift the beaters from the whipping cream; the mixture should form droopy, but definite, peaks. Do not overbeat or the cream will clump together and form butter.

Mixed Berry Pie

Classic Double Pie Crust
(page 461)
2 cups (500 ml) canned or
thawed frozen
blackberries, well drained
1½ cups (375 ml) canned or
thawed frozen blueberries,
well drained
½ cup (125 ml) canned or
thawed frozen
gooseberries, well drained
¼ cup (60 ml) sugar
3 tablespoons (45 ml)
cornstarch
⅛ teaspoon (0.5 ml) almond
extract

1. Prepare pie crust following steps 1 and 2 of Classic Double Pie Crust. Roll out and place bottom crust in pie plate following steps 3 through 6 on page 461. Cover with plastic wrap and refrigerate 30 minutes to allow dough to relax.

2. Preheat oven to 425°F (220°C).

3. Combine blackberries, blueberries and gooseberries in large bowl. Add sugar, cornstarch and almond extract; stir well.

4. Spoon into prepared pie crust. Roll out top crust following steps 3 and 4 on page 461. Place top crust over filling following step 7 on page 461.

5. Trim edge leaving ½-inch (1.25 cm) overhang. Fold overhang under so crust is even with edge of pie plate. Press between thumb and forefinger to make stand-up edge. Cut slits in crust at ½-inch (1.25 cm) intervals around edge of pie to form flaps.

6. Press l flap in toward center of pie and the next out toward rim of pie plate. Continue alternating in and out around edge of pie.

7. Pierce top crust with fork to allow steam to escape.

8. Bake 40 minutes or until crust is golden brown. Cool completely on wire rack.
Makes 6 to 8 servings

Step 4. Unrolling top crust over filling.

Step 5. Cutting slits in crust.

Step 6. Pressing flap in toward center of pie.

My Golden Harvest Apple Pie

Classic Double Pie Crust
   (page 461)
2 tablespoons (30 ml)
   all-purpose flour
2 pounds (900 g) apples
½ cup (125 ml) sugar
1 teaspoon (5 ml) ground
   cinnamon
1 teaspoon (5 ml) ground
   nutmeg
3 tablespoons (45 ml) low-sugar
   orange marmalade
2 tablespoons (30 ml) butter or
   margarine
   Milk

1. Prepare pie crust following steps 1 and 2 of Classic Double Pie Crust (page 461). Roll out and place bottom crust in pie plate following steps 3 through 6 on page 461. Cover with plastic wrap and refrigerate 30 minutes to allow dough to relax. Sprinkle crust with flour.

2. Preheat oven to 450°F (230°C).

3. Peel apples. Remove cores; discard. Thinly slice apples.

4. Combine sugar, cinnamon and nutmeg in small bowl. Layer apple slices alternately with sugar mixture in pie crust.

5. Drop marmalade by teaspoonfuls on top of apples.

6. Cut butter into 10 pieces. Place butter pieces on top of apples in pie crust.

7. Roll out top crust following steps 3 and 4 on page 461. Place top crust over filling following step 7 on page 461.

8. Trim edge leaving ½-inch (1.25 cm) overhang. Fold overhang under so crust is even with edge of pie plate.

9. To flute, place index finger on inside edge of rim, pointing toward outside of pie. Pinch crust into "V" shape between index finger and thumb of other hand. Repeat along entire edge.

10. Cut out design in top crust with paring knife. Reroll dough scraps and cut out stem and leaf shapes. Brush top crust with milk. Place shapes on pie.

11. Bake 15 minutes. *Reduce oven temperature to 375°F (190°C).* Continue baking 30 to 35 minutes or until golden brown. Cool completely on wire rack.

Makes 6 to 8 servings

Step 5. Dropping marmalade on top of apples.

Step 9. Fluting edge of pie crust.

Step 10. Cutting out stem and leaf shapes.

Norma Gene's Peanut Butter Creme Pie

Classic Single Pie Crust (page 460)
3 eggs
¾ cup (187 ml) granulated sugar, divided
3 tablespoons (45 ml) cornstarch
1 tablespoon (15 ml) all-purpose flour
⅛ teaspoon (0.5 ml) salt
3 cups (750 ml) milk
2 teaspoons (10 ml) butter or margarine
1 teaspoon (5 ml) vanilla
¾ cup (187 ml) powdered sugar
½ cup (125 ml) crunchy peanut butter
¼ teaspoon (1 ml) cream of tartar

1. Prepare pie crust following steps 1 and 2 of Classic Single Pie Crust. Roll out and place in pie plate following steps 3 through 7 on page 460.

2. Trim dough leaving ¼-inch (6 mm) overhang. Fold overhang under and press flat. Cut slits around edge of pie crust at 1-inch (2.5 cm) intervals, cutting in toward center about ½-inch (1.25 cm).

3. Fold dough flap under on a diagonal at each slit to form a point. Cover pie crust with plastic wrap and refrigerate 30 minutes to allow dough to relax.

4. Preheat oven to 425°F (220°C).

5. Pierce pie crust with fork at ¼-inch (6 mm) intervals, about 40 times.

6. Cut a square of foil about 4 inches (10 cm) larger than pie plate. Line pie crust with foil. Fill with dried beans, uncooked rice or ceramic pie weights.

7. Bake 10 minutes or until set. Remove from oven. Gently remove foil lining and beans. Return pie crust to oven and bake 5 minutes or until very light brown. Cool completely on wire rack. *Reduce oven temperature to 375°F (190°C).*

8. To separate egg yolk from white, gently tap egg in center against hard surface, such as side of bowl. Holding shell half in each hand, gently transfer yolk back and forth between the 2 shell halves. Allow white to drip down between the 2 halves into bowl. (Technique on page 474.)

Step 2. Cutting slits in crust.

Step 3. Folding dough flaps under.

Step 6. Filling lined pie crust with dried beans.

continued on page 456

Norma Gene's Peanut Butter Creme Pie, continued

9. When all the white has dripped into bowl, place yolk in another bowl. Transfer white to third bowl. Repeat with remaining 2 eggs. (Egg whites must be free from any egg yolk to reach proper volume when beaten.)

10. To make filling, stir together ½ cup (125 ml) granulated sugar, cornstarch, flour and salt. Add egg yolks and milk; beat with wire whisk until well blended. Bring to a boil over medium heat, stirring constantly. Continue cooking and stirring 2 minutes or until thick. Remove from heat. Stir in butter and vanilla.

11. Place powdered sugar in medium bowl. Cut peanut butter into powdered sugar with pastry blender or 2 knives until mixture forms pea-sized pieces.

12. Sprinkle ⅓ of peanut butter crumbs over bottom of pie crust. Spoon ½ of filling over crumbs. Sprinkle with another ⅓ of crumbs; top with remaining filling.

13. To make meringue, combine egg whites and cream of tartar in clean large bowl. Beat with electric mixer at high speed until foamy. Gradually beat in remaining ¼ cup (62.5 ml) granulated sugar until stiff peaks form. After beaters are lifted from meringue, stiff peaks should remain on surface, and mixture does not slide around when bowl is tilted. (Technique on page 420.)

14. Spread meringue over pie filling with rubber spatula, making sure it completely covers filling and touches edge of pie crust.

15. Create decorative peaks and swirls by twisting and lifting spatula while spreading meringue. Sprinkle remaining peanut butter crumbs around edge.

16. Bake 8 to 10 minutes or until meringue is golden. Cool completely on wire rack.

Makes 6 to 8 servings

Step 11. Cutting peanut butter into powdered sugar.

Step 14. Spreading meringue over pie filling.

Step 15. Creating decorative peaks and swirls.

Chocolate Hazelnut Pie

**Chocolate Hazelnut Crust
   (page 458)**
1 envelope unflavored gelatin
¼ cup (62.5 ml) cold water
**2 cups (500 ml) whipping
   cream, divided**
**1½ cups (375 ml) semisweet
   chocolate chips**
2 eggs*
**3 tablespoons (45 ml)
   hazelnut-flavoredliqueur**
1 teaspoon (5 ml) vanilla
**24 caramels, unwrapped
   Caramel Flowers for garnish
   (page 458)**

*Use clean, uncracked eggs.

1. Prepare Chocolate Hazelnut Crust; set aside.

2. Sprinkle gelatin over water in small saucepan. Let stand without stirring 3 minutes for gelatin to soften. Heat over low heat, stirring constantly, until gelatin is completely dissolved, about 5 minutes. To test for undissolved gelatin, run a finger over the spoon. If it is smooth, the gelatin is completely dissolved; if it feels granular, continue heating until it feels smooth.

3. Stir 1 cup (250 ml) whipping cream into gelatin mixture. Heat just to a boil; remove from heat. Add chocolate chips. Stir until chocolate is melted.

4. Add ½ cup (125 ml) whipping cream, eggs, liqueur and vanilla; beat well. Pour into large bowl; refrigerate about 15 minutes or until thickened.

5. Combine caramels and remaining ½ cup (125 ml) whipping cream in small saucepan. Simmer over low heat, stirring occasionally, until completely melted and smooth.

6. Pour caramel mixture into prepared crust; let stand about 10 minutes.

7. Beat thickened gelatin mixture with electric mixer at medium speed until smooth. Pour over caramel layer; refrigerate 3 hours or until firm. Garnish, if desired.

Makes 6 to 8 servings

continued on page 458

Step 2. Testing for undissolved gelatin.

Step 3. Stirring until chocolate is melted.

Step 5. Stirring until caramel is melted and smooth.

Chocolate Hazelnut Crust

¾ **cup (187 ml) hazelnuts**
30 chocolate cookie wafers
½ **cup (125 ml) melted butter or**
   margarine

1. Preheat oven to 350°F (180°C).

2. To toast hazelnuts, spread hazelnuts in single layer on baking sheet. Bake 10 to 12 minutes or until toasted and skins begin to flake off; let cool slightly. Wrap hazelnuts in heavy kitchen towel; rub towel back and forth to remove as much of the skins as possible.

3. Combine cookies and hazelnuts in food processor or blender container; process with on/off pulses until finely crushed.

4. Combine cookie crumb mixture and butter in medium bowl. Press firmly onto bottom and up side of 9-inch (22.5 cm) pie plate, forming a high rim.

5. Bake 10 minutes; cool completely on wire rack.

Caramel Flowers

6 to 8 caramels

1. Place 1 fresh, soft caramel between 2 sheets of waxed paper.

2. With rolling pin, roll out caramel to 2-inch (5 cm) oval (press down hard with rolling pin).

3. Starting at 1 corner, roll caramel into a cone to resemble a flower. Repeat with remaining caramels. Before serving, place 1 Caramel Flower on each piece of pie.

Chocolate Hazelnut Crust: Step 2. Rubbing skins off toasted hazelnuts.

Caramel Flowers: Step 2. Rolling caramel out to 2-inch (5 cm) oval.

Caramel Flowers: Step 3. Rolling caramel into a cone.

Classic Single Pie Crust

1⅓ cups (333 ml) all-purpose
    flour
½ teaspoon (2 ml) salt
½ cup (125 ml) Crisco®
    Shortening
3 tablespoons (45 ml) cold
    water

1. Combine flour and salt in large bowl. Cut in shortening using pastry blender or 2 knives until mixture forms pea-sized pieces.

2. Sprinkle with water, 1 tablespoon (15 ml) at a time. Toss with fork until mixture holds together. Press together to form a ball.

3. Press dough between hands to form 5- to 6-inch (12.5 to 15 cm) disk.

4. Lightly flour surface and rolling pin. Roll dough in short strokes, starting in middle of disk and rolling out toward edge. Rotate dough ¼ turn to right. Sprinkle more flour under dough and on rolling pin as necessary to prevent sticking. Continue to roll and rotate dough 2 to 3 more times.

5. Roll dough into ⅛-inch-thick (3 mm) circle and at least 1 inch (1.25 cm) larger than inverted pie plate.

6. Place rolling pin on 1 side of dough. Gently roll dough over rolling pin once.

7. Carefully lift rolling pin and dough. Unroll dough over pie plate. Ease dough into pie plate with fingertips. Do not stretch dough.

8. Trim crust, leaving ½-inch (1.25 cm) overhang. Fold overhang under. Flute as desired. Cover pie crust with plastic wrap and refrigerate 30 minutes to allow dough to relax.

Step 1. Cutting in shortening.

Step 3. Pressing dough into disk.

Step 5. Rolling out dough.

Classic Double Pie Crust

2 cups (500 ml) all-purpose flour
1 teaspoon (5 ml) salt
¾ cup (187 ml) Crisco® Shortening
5 tablespoons (75 ml) cold water

1. Combine flour and salt in large bowl. Cut in shortening using pastry blender or 2 knives until mixture forms pea-sized pieces.

2. Sprinkle with water, 1 tablespoon (15 ml) at a time. Toss with fork until mixture holds together. Press together to form a ball.

3. Divide dough in half. Press each half between hands to form 5- to 6-inch (12.5 to 15 cm) disk.

4. Roll out each half as described in Classic Single Pie Crust, steps 4 and 5.

5. Place rolling pin on 1 side of dough. Gently roll dough over rolling pin once.

6. Carefully lift rolling pin and dough. Unroll dough over pie plate. Ease dough into pie plate with fingertips. Do not stretch dough. Trim edge even with edge of pie crust. Cover pie crust with plastic wrap and refrigerate to allow dough to relax.

7. Add desired filling to unbaked pie crust. Moisten edge of crust with water. Lift top crust onto filled pie as described in step 5. Unroll over filling. Pierce top crust with fork to allow steam to escape.

8. Trim crust leaving ½-inch (1.25 cm) overhang. Fold overhang under bottom crust. Flute as desired.

Step 5. Lifting rolled out dough.

Step 6. Unrolling dough over pie plate.

Step 7. Unrolling top crust over filling.

Apple Butter Pound Cake

1½ cups (375 ml) granulated
    sugar
1 package (8 ounces/225 g)
    cream cheese, softened
    (technique on page 478)
½ cup (125 ml) margarine,
    softened
6 eggs
2 cups (500 ml) all-purpose
    flour
1 cup (250 ml) Quakers®
    Enriched Corn Meal
2 teaspoons (10 ml) baking
    powder
1 teaspoon (5 ml) ground
    cinnamon
¼ teaspoon (1 ml) salt (optional)
1 cup (250 ml) spiced apple
    butter
1 tablespoon (15 ml) bourbon
    whiskey (optional)
1 teaspoon (5 ml) vanilla
1 cup (250 ml) chopped pecans
    Creamy Glaze (recipe follows)

1. Preheat oven to 350°F (180°C). Grease 12-cup (3 L) Bundt pan or 10-inch (25 cm) tube pan.

2. Beat sugar, cream cheese and margarine in large bowl with electric mixer at medium speed until light and fluffy, scraping down side of bowl once.

3. Add eggs, 1 at a time, beating well after each addition.

4. Combine flour, corn meal, baking powder, cinnamon and salt in small bowl.

5. Combined apple butter, bourbon and vanilla in separate small bowl.

6. Alternately add flour mixture and apple butter mixture to cream cheese mixture. Beat at low speed until well blended, scraping down side of bowl once. Stir in pecans with wooden spoon.

7. Spoon into prepared pan; spread evenly to edge.

8. Bake 60 to 70 minutes or until cake tester or wooden skewer inserted into center comes out clean. Cool 10 minutes in pan; remove from pan to wire rack. Cool completely.

9. Prepare Creamy Glaze. Drizzle over cake from tip of spoon.
Makes 10 to 12 servings

Step 1. Greasing pan.

Step 9. Drizzling Creamy Glaze over cake.

Creamy Glaze

  1 cup (250 ml) powdered sugar
1½ teaspoons (8 ml) light corn syrup
  ¼ teaspoon (1 ml) vanilla or Bourbon
     whiskey
  4 to 5 teaspoons (20 to 25 ml) milk

Combine powdered sugar, corn syrup and vanilla in medium bowl; mix well. Add milk, 1 teaspoon (5 ml) at a time, until proper drizzling consistency is reached.

Daydream Desserts • DESSERTS 463

Chocolate Chip Cake

2 cups (500 ml) all-purpose
   flour
1 cup (250 ml) packed dark
   brown sugar
1 tablespoon (15 ml) baking
   powder
1 teaspoon (5 ml) salt
½ teaspoon (2 ml) baking soda
½ cup (125 ml) granulated sugar
½ cup (125 ml) shortening
3 eggs
1¼ cups (312 ml) milk
1½ teaspoons (7 ml) vanilla
½ cup (125 ml) semisweet
   chocolate chips, finely
   chopped
   Butterscotch Filling (recipe
   follows)
½ cup (125 ml) finely chopped
   walnuts, divided
½ cup (125 ml) semisweet
   chocolate chips
2 tablespoons (30 ml) butter
1 tablespoon (15 ml) light corn
   syrup
   Fresh raspberries and mint
   leaves for garnish

1. Preheat oven to 350°F (180°C). Grease and flour two 9-inch (22.5 cm) round baking pans. (Technique on page 424.)

2. Combine flour, brown sugar, baking powder, salt and baking soda; set aside.

3. Beat granulated sugar and shortening in large bowl with electric mixer at medium speed until light and fluffy. Add eggs, 1 at a time, beating well after each addition.

4. Beat in milk and vanilla. Add flour mixture and chopped chocolate chips; beat well. Pour into prepared pans.

5. Bake 40 to 45 minutes or until cake tester or wooden pick inserted into center comes out clean. Remove from pans to wire racks; cool.

6. Prepare Butterscotch Filling. Spread 1 cake layer with Butterscotch Filling; sprinkle with ¼ cup (62.5 ml) walnuts. Top with second cake layer.

7. Combine chocolate chips, butter and corn syrup in small saucepan. Stir over low heat until chocolate melts.

8. Pour over top of cake, allowing some to drip down side of cake. Sprinkle with remaining ¼ cup (62.5 ml) walnuts. Garnish, if desired.

Makes 8 to 10 servings

Butterscotch Filling

½ cup (125 ml) packed light brown
   sugar
2 tablespoons (30 ml) cornstarch
¼ teaspoon (1 ml) salt
½ cup (125 ml) water
1 tablespoon (15 ml) butter

Combine sugar, cornstarch and salt in saucepan. Add water; bring to a boil, stirring constantly. Boil 1 minute, stirring constantly. Stir in butter; cool.

Step 4. Pouring batter into prepared pans.

Step 6. Sprinkling walnuts over Butterscotch Filling.

Step 8. Pouring chocolate mixture over cake.

Black Walnut Fudge

4 cups (1 L) sugar
½ cup (125 ml) margarine
1 can (12 ounces/335 g)
    evaporated milk
3 tablespoons (45 ml) light corn
    syrup
1 pound (450 g) vanilla milk
    chips*
1 jar (13 ounces/363 g)
    marshmallow creme
1 cup (250 ml) chopped black
    walnuts
1 tablespoon (15 ml) vanilla

*Do not use compound chocolate or
confectioner's coating.

1. Line 13 x 9-inch (32.5 x 22.5 cm) pan with foil, leaving l-inch (2.5 cm) overhang on sides to use for handles when lifting fudge out of pan. Lightly butter foil.

2. Combine sugar, margarine, evaporated milk and corn syrup in large saucepan; stir well. Bring to a boil over medium heat, stirring just until sugar dissolves.

3. Attach candy thermometer to side of pan, making sure bulb is completely submerged in sugar mixture but not touching bottom of pan.

4. Continue heating, without stirring, until mixture reaches soft-ball stage (234°F/113°C) on candy thermometer.

5. Remove from heat and add vanilla milk chips. Stir with wooden spoon until melted. Add marshmallow creme, walnuts and vanilla, stirring well after each addition.

6. Pour into prepared pan. Score into squares by cutting halfway through fudge with sharp knife while fudge is still warm.

7. Remove from pan by lifting fudge and foil using foil handles. Place on cutting board. Cool completely. Cut along score lines into squares. Remove foil.
Makes about 3 pounds (1.35 kg)

Step 1. Lining pan with foil.

Step 3. Attaching candy thermometer to pan.

Step 6. Scoring fudge.

Chocolate Rice Pudding

2 cups (500 ml) water
1 cup (250 ml) uncooked Uncle Ben's® Converted® Brand Rice
2 tablespoons (30 ml) butter
¼ cup (62.5 ml) sugar
2 teaspoons (10 ml) cornstarch
2 cups (500 ml) milk
½ teaspoon (2 ml) vanilla
2 egg yolks
½ cup (125 ml) semisweet chocolate chips
Whipped cream
Unsweetened cocoa powder and cookies for garnish

1. Bring water to a boil in large saucepan. Stir in rice and butter. Reduce heat; cover and simmer 20 minutes. Remove from heat. Let stand covered until all liquid is absorbed, about 5 minutes.

2. Combine sugar and cornstarch in small bowl; add to hot rice in saucepan. Stir in milk.

3. Bring mixture to a boil, stirring occasionally. Boil 1 minute, stirring constantly. Remove from heat; stir in vanilla.

4. Beat egg yolks in small bowl. Stir about 1 cup (250 ml) of hot rice mixture into beaten egg yolks.

5. Stir egg yolk mixture back into remaining rice mixture in saucepan.

6. Cook rice mixture over medium heat, stirring frequently, just until mixture starts to bubble. Remove from heat; add chocolate chips and stir until melted.

7. Spoon into individual serving dishes. Refrigerate.

8. Spoon whipped cream into pastry bag fitted with large star decorator tip. Pipe onto top of each serving.

9. Sift unsweetened cocoa powder through fine-meshed strainer or sifter over each serving. Garnish, if desired.

Makes 6 servings

Step 4. Adding 1 cup (250 ml) of hot rice mixture to egg yolks.

Step 5. Adding egg yolk mixture back to rice mixture.

Step 8. Piping whipped cream onto each serving.

Orange Cappuccino Brownies

2 oranges
¾ cup (187 ml) butter
2 squares (1 ounce/28 g each)
    semisweet chocolate,
    coarsely chopped
2 squares (1 ounce/28 g each)
    unsweetened chocolate,
    coarsely chopped
1¾ cups (437 ml) sugar
1 tablespoon (15 ml) instant
    espresso powder or instant
    coffee granules
3 eggs
¼ cup (62.5 ml) orange-flavored
    liqueur
1 cup (250 ml) all-purpose flour
1 package (12 ounces/335 g)
    semisweet chocolate chips
2 tablespoons (30 ml)
    shortening

1. Preheat oven to 350°F (180°C). Grease 13 x 9-inch (32.5 x 22.5 cm) pan.

2. Finely grate colored portion of peel of 1 orange using bell grater or handheld grater. Measure 2 teaspoons (10 ml) orange peel; set aside.

3. Melt butter, chopped semisweet chocolate and unsweetened chocolate in large heavy saucepan over low heat, stirring constantly. Stir in sugar and espresso powder. Remove from heat. Cool slightly.

4. Beat in eggs, 1 at a time, with wire whisk. Whisk in liqueur and orange peel.

5. Beat flour into chocolate mixture until just blended. Spread batter evenly into prepared pan.

6. Bake 25 to 30 minutes or until center is just set. Remove pan to wire rack.

7. Meanwhile, melt chocolate chips and shortening in small, heavy saucepan over low heat, stirring constantly.

8. Immediately after removing brownies from oven, spread hot chocolate mixture over warm brownies. Cool completely in pan on wire rack. Cut into 2-inch (5 cm) squares.

9. To make orange peel garnish, remove thin strips of peel from remaining orange using citrus zester.

10. Tie strips into knots or twist into spirals. Garnish, if desired.

Makes about 2 dozen brownies

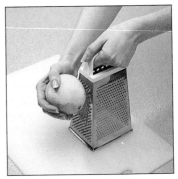

Step 2. Grating orange peel.

Step 8. Spreading chocolate mixture over warm brownies.

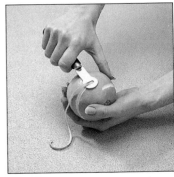

Step 9. Removing thin strips of orange peel for garnish.

Raspberry Chocolate Mousse Pie

40 chocolate wafer cookies
¼ cup (62.5 ml) butter, melted
6 squares (1 ounce/28 g each) semisweet chocolate
1¼ cups (312 ml) whipping cream
½ cup (125 ml) water
7 tablespoons (105 ml) sugar
5 egg yolks
3 tablespoons (45 ml) raspberry-flavored liqueur
   Whipped cream, fresh raspberries and mint leaves for garnish

1. Place cookies in food processor or blender container; process with on/off pulses until finely crushed.

2. Combine cookie crumbs and butter in medium bowl; mix well. Press firmly onto bottom and 1 inch (2.5 cm) up side of 9-inch (22.5 cm) springform pan.

3. Melt chocolate in top of double boiler over hot, not boiling, water. Cool.

4. Chill large bowl and beaters thoroughly. Pour chilled whipping cream into chilled bowl and beat with electric mixer at high speed until soft peaks form. To test, lift beaters from whipping cream; mixture should have droopy, but definite, peaks. Refrigerate.

5. Combine water and sugar in small saucepan. Bring to a boil over medium-high heat. Boil 1 minute. Place hot syrup in 1-cup (250 ml) glass measure.

6. Place egg yolks in large, deep, heatproof bowl. Whisk in hot syrup. Place bowl in large saucepan of hot, not boiling, water. Continue to whisk until soft peaks form. To test, lift whisk; mixture should have droopy, but definite, peaks. Remove from heat.

7. Beat mixture until cool. Stir in melted chocolate and liqueur. Stir ½ cup (125 ml) whipped cream into chocolate mixture.

8. Fold in remaining whipped cream with rubber spatula by gently cutting down to bottom of bowl, scraping up side of bowl, then folding over top of mixture. Repeat until chocolate mixture is evenly incorporated.

9. Pour into prepared crust. Refrigerate until firm, about 3 hours or overnight. To serve, remove side of pan. Garnish, if desired.

Makes 10 servings

Step 2. Pressing crumb mixture into pan.

Step 4. Testing for soft peaks.

Step 6. Whisking hot syrup into egg yolks.

Double Chocolate Bombe

5 eggs, divided*
1½ cups (375 ml) whipping
    cream, divided
1 envelope unflavored gelatin
1 package (12 ounces/335 g)
    semisweet chocolate chips
¼ teaspoon (1 ml) salt
⅓ cup (83 ml) sugar
    Chocolate Cake (page 477)
3 white chocolate baking bars
    (2 ounces/56 g each),
    divided

*Use clean, uncracked eggs.

1. Line 2-quart (2 L) bowl with plastic wrap; oil lightly.

2. To separate egg white from yolk, gently tap egg in center against hard surface, such as side of bowl. Holding shell half in each hand, gently transfer yolk back and forth between the 2 shell halves. Allow white to drip down between the 2 halves into bowl.

3. When all white has dripped into bowl, place yolk in another bowl. Transfer white to third bowl. Repeat with remaining 4 eggs. (Egg whites must be free from any egg yolk to reach the proper volume when beaten.)

4. Place egg yolks and ½ cup (62.5 ml) whipping cream in small bowl; beat slightly with fork. Sprinkle gelatin over egg yolk mixture. Let stand without stirring 5 minutes to soften.

5. Melt chocolate chips in top of double boiler over hot, not boiling, water.

6. Stir about ½ cup (125 ml) melted chocolate into egg yolk mixture.

7. Stir egg yolk mixture back into remaining chocolate in top of double boiler. Continue to heat until gelatin is completely dissolved. (Technique on page 457.)

continued on page 476

Step 1. Oiling lined bowl.

Step 2. Separating egg.

Step 5. Melting chocolate chips in top of double boiler.

Double Chocolate Bombe, *continued*

8. To make meringue, beat egg whites and salt in clean large bowl with electric mixer at high speed until foamy. Gradually beat in sugar until stiff peaks form. (After beaters are lifted from meringue, stiff peaks should remain on surface, and mixture does not slide around when bowl is tilted.)

9. Fold in chocolate mixture with rubber spatula by gently cutting down to bottom of bowl, scraping up side of bowl, then folding over top of mixture. Repeat until chocolate mixture is evenly incorporated into the meringue.

10. Beat whipping cream until soft peaks form. (Technique on page 472.)

11. Fold into chocolate mixture as described in step 9.

12. Pour into prepared bowl. Cover and refrigerate 4 hours.

13. Prepare Chocolate Cake.

14. Melt 2 bars white chocolate in small bowl set in bowl of very hot water, stirring occasionally. This will take about 10 minutes.

15. Pour onto waxed-paper-lined cookie sheet. Refrigerate until firm, about 15 minutes.

16. Cut into large triangle shapes with sharp knife.

17. Immediately lift shapes carefully from waxed paper with spatula or knife. Refrigerate until ready to use.

18. Place cake on serving plate. Unmold mousse onto cake. Remove plastic wrap. Trim edge of cake around mousse, if desired.

19. Place remaining white chocolate baking bar in small resealable plastic freezer bag. Microwave at **MEDIUM** (50% power) 2 minutes. Turn bag over; microwave at **MEDIUM** (50% power) 2 to 3 minutes or until chocolate is melted. Knead bag until chocolate is smooth.

20. Cut off very tiny corner of bag; drizzle chocolate over mousse. Refrigerate until white chocolate is set, about 30 minutes. Garnish, if desired.

Makes about 8 servings

Step 8. Testing for stiff peaks.

Step 16. Cutting white chocolate into shapes.

Step 20. Drizzling white chocolate over mousse.

Chocolate Cake

1 cup (250 ml) sugar
⅓ cup (83 ml) shortening
2 eggs
⅓ cup (83 ml) water
½ teaspoon (2 ml) vanilla
1 cup (250 ml) all-purpose flour
⅓ cup (83 ml) unsweetened
    cocoa powder
1 teaspoon (5 ml) baking soda
¼ teaspoon (1 ml) baking
    powder
¼ teaspoon (1 ml) salt

1. Preheat oven to 375°F (190°C). Grease bottom and side of 9-inch (22.5 cm) round baking pan. Add 2 to 3 teaspoons (10 to 15 ml) flour to pan. Gently tap side of pan to evenly coat bottom and side with flour.

2. Combine sugar and shortening in large bowl. Beat with electric mixer at medium speed until light and fluffy, scraping down side of bowl once. Add eggs, water and vanilla; beat well.

3. Combine flour, cocoa, baking soda, baking powder and salt in small bowl. Add to shortening mixture; beat with electric mixer at medium speed until smooth. Pour into prepared pan.

4. Bake 20 to 25 minutes or until cake tester or wooden pick inserted into center comes out clean. Cool 10 minutes in pan.

5. Loosen edge and remove to wire rack; cool completely.

Chocolate Cake: Step 1.
Coating pan with flour.

Chocolate Cake: Step 3.
Beating until smooth.

Pineapple Macadamia Cheesepie

Macadamia Nut Crust
(recipe follows)
12 ounces (335 g) cream cheese
1 can (8 ounces/225 g) Dole®
    Crushed Pineapple in Juice
1 egg
¾ cup (187 ml) plain yogurt
½ cup (125 ml) sugar
1 teaspoon (5 ml) vanilla

1. Preheat oven to 350°F (180°C). Prepare Macadamia Nut Crust.

2. Place cream cheese on opened packages on cutting board. With utility knife, cut cream cheese lengthwise into ½-inch (1.25 cm) slices. Then cut crosswise into ½-inch (1.25 cm) pieces. Let stand at room temperature until softened. (Cream cheese will be easy to push down.)

3. Drain pineapple, pressing out excess juice with back of spoon. Reserve 2 tablespoons (30 ml) pineapple. Spread remaining pineapple over prepared crust.

4. Combine cream cheese, egg, yogurt, sugar and vanilla in medium bowl; blend thoroughly. Pour cream cheese mixture over pineapple in crust.

5. Bake 20 minutes or until just set; cool completely on wire rack. Refrigerate at least 2 hours.

6. Before serving, garnish with reserved 2 tablespoons (30 ml) pineapple and additional macadamia nuts.

Makes 6 servings

Step 2. Softening cream cheese.

Step 4. Pouring cream cheese mixture over pineapple in crust.

Macadamia Nut Crust

12 graham cracker squares
1 cup (250 ml) macadamia nuts
6 tablespoons (90 ml) butter, melted
2 tablespoons (30 ml) sugar

1. Break graham crackers into large pieces Place in food processor or blender container. Add nuts. Process until finely crushed. Measure 1¾ cups (437 ml).

2. Combine crumb mixture, butter and sugar in small bowl.

3. Press firmly onto bottom and up side of 8- or 9-inch (20 or 22.5 cm) pie plate; refrigerate until firm.

Macadamia Nut Crust: Step 1. Processing crackers and nuts until finely crushed.

Ginger & Pear Tart

30 gingersnap cookies
½ cup (125 ml) chopped pecans
⅓ cup (83 ml) butter, melted
1 cup (250 ml) sour cream
¾ cup (187 ml) half-and-half
1 package (4-serving size)
　　vanilla instant pudding mix
2 tablespoons (30 ml) apricot
　　brandy
4 ripe pears*
⅓ cup (83 ml) packed dark
　　brown sugar
½ teaspoon (2 ml) ground ginger

*Or, substitute 1 (16-ounce/450 g) can
pear halves, drained and thinly sliced,
for fresh pears.

1. Preheat oven to 350°F (180°C).

2. Combine cookies and pecans in food processor or blender container; process with on/off pulses until finely crushed.

3. Combine crumb mixture and butter in medium bowl. Press firmly onto bottom and up side of 10-inch (25 cm) quiche dish or 9-inch (22.5 cm) pie plate. Bake 7 minutes; cool completely on wire rack.

4. Combine sour cream and half-and-half in large bowl. Beat until smooth. Whisk in pudding mix. Add apricot brandy. Beat until smooth.

5. Pour into prepared crust. Cover; refrigerate several hours or overnight.

6. Just before serving, preheat broiler. Peel pears with vegetable peeler. Cut pears in half lengthwise. Remove cores and seeds; discard. Thinly slice pears.

7. Arrange pear slices in overlapping circles on top of pudding mixture.

8. Combine brown sugar and ginger in small bowl. Sprinkle evenly over pears. Broil 4 to 6 minutes or until sugar is melted and bubbly. Watch carefully so sugar does not burn. Serve immediately.

Makes 6 to 8 servings

Step 3. Pressing crumb mixture into quiche dish.

Step 6. Thinly slicing pears.

Step 7. Arranging pear slices on top of pudding mixture.

Raspberry Cheesecake Blossoms

3 packages (10 ounces/280 g each) frozen raspberries, thawed

8 sheets phyllo dough*

¼ cup (62.5 ml) butter, melted

1 package (8 ounces/225 g) cream cheese, softened (technique on page 478)

½ cup (125 ml) cottage cheese

1 egg

½ cup (125 ml) *plus* 3 tablespoons (45 ml) sugar, divided

4 teaspoons (20 ml) lemon juice, divided

½ teaspoon (2 ml) vanilla

Fresh raspberries and sliced kiwifruit for garnish

*Cover with plastic wrap, then with damp kitchen towel to prevent dough from drying out.

1. Drain thawed raspberries in fine-meshed sieve over 1-cup (250 ml) glass measure. Reserve liquid.

2. Preheat oven to 350°F (180°C). Grease 12 (2½-inch/6.2 cm) muffin cups.

3. Brush melted butter onto 1 phyllo sheet. Cover with second phyllo sheet; brush with butter. Repeat with remaining sheets of phyllo.

4. Cut stack of phyllo dough in half lengthwise, then into thirds crosswise to make a total of 12 squares. Gently fit each stacked square into prepared muffin cup.

5. Place cream cheese, cottage cheese, egg, 3 tablespoons (45 ml) sugar, 1 teaspoon (5 ml) lemon juice and vanilla in food processor or blender. Process until smooth. Divide mixture evenly among muffin cups.

6. Bake 10 to 15 minutes or until lightly browned. Carefully remove from muffin cups to wire racks to cool.

7. Bring reserved raspberry liquid to a boil in small saucepan over medium-high heat. Cook until reduced to ¾ cup, (187 ml) stirring occasionally.

8. Place thawed raspberries in food processor or blender. Process until smooth. Press through fine-meshed sieve with back of spoon to remove seeds.

9. Combine raspberry purée, reduced syrup, remaining ½ cup (125 ml) sugar and 3 teaspoons (15 ml) lemon juice in small bowl. Mix well.

10. To serve, spoon raspberry sauce onto 12 dessert plates. Place cheesecake blossom on each plate. Garnish, if desired.

Makes 12 servings

Step 1. Draining raspberries.

Step 3. Brushing butter onto phyllo.

Step 4. Fitting phyllo dough into muffin cups.

Coconut Cheesecake

1 can (3½ ounces/95 g) flaked coconut (1⅓ cups/333 ml), divided
20 chocolate wafer cookies
1 cup (250 ml) finely chopped pecans
2 tablespoons (30 ml) sugar
¼ cup (62.5 ml) margarine or butter, melted
3 packages (8 ounces/225 g each) cream cheese, softened (technique on page 478)
3 eggs
2 tablespoons (30 ml) all-purpose flour
1 can (15 ounces/420 g) Coco Lopez® Cream of Coconut
Whipped cream for garnish

1. Preheat oven to 300°F (150°C).

2. To toast coconut, spread on baking sheet. Bake 4 to 6 minutes or until light golden brown, stirring frequently. Remove coconut from baking sheet and cool; set aside.

3. Place cookies in food processor or blender container; process with on/off pulses until finely crushed.

4. Combine cookie crumbs, pecans and sugar in small bowl; stir in margarine. Press firmly onto bottom of 9-inch (22.5 cm) springform pan.

5. Beat cream cheese with electric mixer at high speed until fluffy. Add eggs and flour; beat at high speed until smooth, scraping down side of bowl once. Gradually beat in cream of coconut. Stir in ¾ cup (187 ml) toasted coconut with wooden spoon.

6. Pour over crust. Bake 1 hour and 10 minutes or until cheesecake springs back when lightly touched (center will be soft). Carefully loosen cheesecake from edge of pan with spatula. Cool on wire rack; refrigerate until firm. Remove side of pan.

7. Spoon whipped cream into pastry bag fitted with star decorating tip. Pipe around edge of cheesecake. Sprinkle remaining toasted coconut inside whipped cream border.

Makes 10 to 12 servings

Step 3. Processing cookies until finely crushed.

Step 5. Adding eggs.

Step 6. Loosening cheesecake from edge of pan.

Tiramisu

Zabaglione (page 488)
⅔ cup (167 ml) whipping cream
4 tablespoons (60 ml) sugar, divided
1 pound (450 g) mascarpone cheese* (about 2¼ cups/562 ml)
⅓ cup (83 ml) freshly brewed espresso or strong coffee
¼ cup (62.5 ml) Cognac or brandy
1 tablespoon (15 ml) vanilla
3 packages (3 ounces/85 g each) ladyfingers, split
3 ounces (85 g) bittersweet or semisweet chocolate, grated
1 tablespoon (15 ml) cocoa powder
Edible flowers, such as pansies, for garnish**

*Mascarpone is available at Italian markets and some specialty stores. If unavailable, blend 2 packages (8 ounces/225 g each) softened cream cheese with ½ cup (125 ml) heavy or whipping cream and 5 tablespoons (75 ml) sour cream.

**Be sure to use only nontoxic flowers.

1. Prepare Zabaglione. Cover and refrigerate until chilled.

2. Beat cream with 2 tablespoons (30 ml) sugar in large bowl until soft peaks form. Fold in mascarpone cheese with rubber spatula by gently cutting down to bottom of bowl, scraping up side of bowl, then folding over top of mixture. Repeat until mascarpone cheese is evenly incorporated, then fold in Zabaglione. (If Zabaglione has separated, beat until well mixed before folding into mascarpone.) Refrigerate 3 hours or until chilled.

3. Combine espresso, cognac, remaining 2 tablespoons sugar and vanilla extract.

4. Layer ¼ of ladyfingers in flower-petal design in 2-quart (2 L) glass bowl with straight sides or trifle dish.

5. Generously brush ladyfingers with espresso mixture. Spoon ¼ of cheese mixture over ladyfingers to within 1 inch (2.5 cm) of side of bowl. Sprinkle with ¼ of grated chocolate.

6. Repeat layers 3 more times using remaining ladyfingers, espresso mixture and grated chocolate. (For garnish, sprinkle remaining ¼ of grated chocolate around edge of dessert, if desired.)

continued on page 488

Step 2. Folding Zabaglione into whipped cream mixture.

Step 4. Layering ladyfingers.

Step 5. Brushing ladyfingers with espresso mixture.

Tiramisu, continued

7. Sift cocoa powder over top with fine-meshed sieve or sifter. Cover and refrigerate at least 30 minutes or until chilled. Garnish, if desired.

Makes 8 to 10 servings

Zabaglione

5 egg yolks
¼ cup (62.5 ml) sugar
½ cup (125 ml) marsala, divided
¼ cup (62.5 ml) dry white wine

1. Place egg yolks in top of double boiler; add sugar. Beat with electric mixer at medium speed until mixture is pale yellow and creamy.

2. Place water in bottom of double boiler. Bring to a boil over high heat; reduce heat to low. Place top of double boiler over simmering water.

3. For custard, gradually beat ¼ cup (62.5 ml) marsala into egg yolk mixture with electric mixer. Beat 1 minute. Gradually beat in remaining ¼ cup (62.5 ml) marsala and white wine.

4. Continue cooking custard over gently simmering water 6 to 10 minutes until mixture is fluffy and thick enough to form soft mounds when dropped from beaters, beating constantly and scraping bottom and side of pan frequently. (Watch carefully and *do not overcook*, or custard will curdle.) Immediately remove top of double boiler from water. Whisk custard briefly.***

Makes 4 servings

***Zabaglione can be served as its own recipe. Pour into 4 individual serving dishes. Serve immediately with fresh berries and/or cookies.

Step 7. Sifting cocoa powder over Tiramisu.

Zabaglione: Step 3. Adding marsala to egg yolk mixture.

Zabaglione: Step 4. Beating custard until soft mounds form.

Chocolate Mousse Espresso with Hazelnut Brittle

⅔ cup (167 ml) hazelnuts
2 envelopes Knox® Unflavored Gelatine
¾ cup (187 ml) sugar, divided
4 teaspoons (20 ml) instant espresso coffee powder
2¾ cups (687 ml) milk
12 squares (1 ounce/28 g each) semisweet chocolate
1½ cups (375 ml) whipping cream
45 chocolate wafer cookies
Hazelnut Brittle (page 490) for garnish

1. Preheat oven to 350°F (180°C).

2. To toast hazelnuts, spread hazelnuts in single layer on baking sheet. Bake 10 to 12 minutes or until toasted and skins begin to flake off; let cool slightly. Wrap hazelnuts in heavy kitchen towel; rub towel back and forth to remove as much of the skins as possible. Set aside.

3. Combine gelatine with ½ cup (125 ml) sugar and coffee powder in medium saucepan. Stir in milk. Let stand without stirring 3 minutes for gelatine to soften. Heat over low heat, stirring constantly, until gelatine is completely dissolved, about 5 minutes. To test for undissolved gelatine, run a finger over the spoon. If it is smooth, the gelatine is completely dissolved; if it feels granular, continue heating until it feels smooth.

4. Add chocolate and continue heating over low heat, stirring constantly, until chocolate is melted. Using wire whisk, beat until chocolate is thoroughly blended. Pour into large bowl and refrigerate, stirring occasionally. Chill until mixture mounds slightly when dropped from spoon. Remove from refrigerator.

5. Chill large bowl and beaters thoroughly. Pour chilled whipping cream and remaining ¼ cup (62.5 ml) sugar into chilled bowl and beat with electric mixer at high speed until soft peaks form. To test, lift beaters from whipping cream; mixture should have droopy, but definite, peaks. Reserve ½ cup (125 ml) for garnish.

Step 2. Rubbing skins off hazelnuts.

Step 4. Testing gelatin mixture.

Step 5. Testing for soft peaks.

continued on page 490

Chocolate Mousse Espresso with Hazelnut Brittle, continued

6. Fold remaining whipped cream into gelatine mixture with rubber spatula by gently cutting down to bottom of bowl, scraping up side of bowl, then folding over top of mixture. Repeat until whipped cream is evenly incorporated into gelatine mixture.

7. Place cookies and hazelnuts in food processor or blender container; process with on/off pulses until finely crushed.

8. Alternately layer gelatine mixture with cookie crumb mixture in dessert dishes. Refrigerate at least 30 minutes. Garnish with whipped cream and Hazelnut Brittle.

Makes about 10 servings

Hazelnut Brittle

1 cup (250 ml) hazelnuts
1½ cups (375 ml) sugar

1. Grease baking sheet.

2. Toast and skin hazelnuts as described in step 1 of main recipe. Coarsely chop hazelnuts.

3. Place 1½ cups (375 ml) sugar in large heavy skillet over medium heat. As sugar begins to melt, gently tilt skillet until sugar is completely melted and golden brown.

4. Stir in hazelnuts. Quickly pour mixture onto prepared baking sheet; do not spread.

5. Let stand until cooled and hardened. Break into pieces.

Step 7. Processing cookies and hazelnuts until finely crushed.

Hazelnut Brittle: Step 3. Melting sugar.

Hazelnut Brittle: Step 4. Pouring mixture onto prepared baking sheet.

COOKING CLASS
HOLIDAY
RECIPES

494   CLASS NOTES

496   APPETIZERS &
         BEVERAGES

510   ENTRÉES

524   SIDE DISHES

546   DESSERTS

Roast Turkey with Pan Gravy *(page 510)*

CLASS NOTES

Whether you plan on dazzling your family and friends with a spectacular holiday meal, or are simply bringing a scrumptious dessert or savory vegetable to another's home, the recipes in this section will make whatever you serve special.

CARVING

Carving may seem like a formidable task. However, with the following guidelines and illustrations you'll learn to carve the main attraction like a pro.

General Guidelines

- Allow enough time before serving not only for cooking the meat, but for stand time and carving.

- A stand time of 10 to 20 minutes is recommended for large cuts of meat, such as roasts, turkeys and whole chickens. Stand time allows the meat to finish cooking. Meat is easier to carve after standing. If meat is carved immediately out of the oven, it loses more of its flavorful juices.

- The temperatures given for removing meat and poultry from the oven are 5° (2.4°C) to 10°F (4.8°C) lower than the standard final temperatures. This is because the temperature continues to rise during the stand time.

- During the stand time, put the finishing touches on the salad and side dishes. This is also a good time to make the gravy.

- Unless you are planning on carving at the table, place the meat on a large cutting board with a well at one end to hold the juice. (Or, place a cutting board inside a baking sheet. The juice will collect in the baking sheet.) Use a long, sharp carving knife to slice the meat and a long-handled meat fork to steady the meat.

- While you are carving the meat, warm the bread in the oven.

Boneless Roasts

Boneless beef, pork and lamb roasts are easy to carve. Hold the roast steady with a long-handled meat fork. With the knife held perpendicular to the cutting board, cut across the grain into thin uniform slices. Cut the slices between ¼ to ½ inch (6 mm and 1.25 cm) thick.

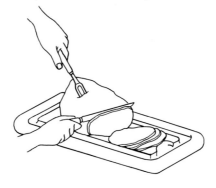

Standing Beef Rib Roast

For added stability when carving standing rib roast, cut a wedge-shaped slice from the large end of the roast so that the meat will sit flat on the cutting board.

Insert a long-handled meat fork below the top rib. Slice across the top of roast toward the rib bone. This roast can be sliced between ½ to ¾ inch (1.25 to 1.8 cm) thick.

With the tip of the knife, cut along the rib bone to release the slice of meat.

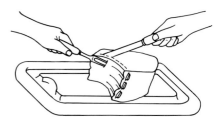

To remove the meat slice, slide the knife blade under the cut slice of meat. Holding it steady with a meat fork, lift the slice and place it on a platter.

Bone-in Leg of Lamb

For stability, place the leg of lamb on its side on the cutting board with the shank bone facing away from you. Cut two or three lengthwise slices from the section of the meat facing you. This will allow the meat to sit flat on the cutting board.

Turn the roast up so that it sits on the cut area. Hold the roast steady with a long-handled meat fork inserted into the meat opposite the shank bone. Holding the knife perpendicular to the cutting board and starting by the shank bone, cut across the grain into uniform, thin slices. Cut the slices between ¼ to ½ inch (6 mm to 1.25 cm) thick.

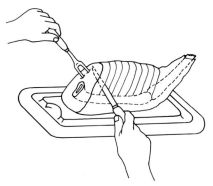

When you reach the aitch bone, release the slices by cutting under them along the leg bone.

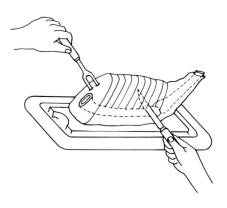

Roast Turkey

To start carving roast turkey, remove the leg; hold the drumstick and cut the skin with a carving knife between the thigh and the body of the turkey to the joint. Pull the leg away from the body of the turkey and cut through the joint at the backbone.

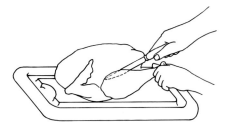

To separate the drumstick from the thigh, place the leg on the cutting board skin side up. Cut through at the joint.

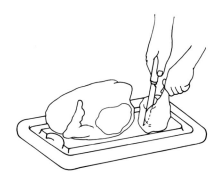

At this point, the drumstick may be served as it is or cut into slices. To slice the drumstick, hold the drumstick at an angle, bony side up. Cut down into ¼-inch (6 mm) slices. Rotate the drumstick as you cut. Remove and discard the large tendons.

To cut the thigh into slices, turn the thigh skin side down. Cut along the length of the bone, then turn skin side up and cut the meat across the grain.

To remove the wings, insert a long-handled meat fork into the turkey to hold it steady. Cut down between the wing and the body of the turkey with a carving knife. Pull the wing out and cut through the joint.

To remove the breast meat, insert a long-handled meat fork into the turkey to hold it steady. At the base of the breast meat, make a horizontal cut across the breast to the bone. Cut the slices with straight even strokes down to the horizontal cut. At that point, the slices will fall free.

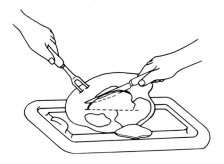

Three Mushroom Ratatouille

1 package (3½ ounces/100 g)
   fresh shiitake mushrooms*
1 small tomato
   Fresh parsley
1 tablespoon (15 ml) olive oil
1 large onion, chopped
   (technique on page 543)
4 cloves garlic, minced
   (technique on page 543)
1 package (8 ounces/225 g)
   button mushrooms,
   chopped
1 package (6 ounces/170 g)
   crimini mushrooms,
   chopped
1 cup (250 ml) chicken broth
2 tablespoons (30 ml) grated
   Parmesan cheese
3 pita breads (6 inches/15 cm
   each)
   Fresh Italian parsley for
   garnish

*Or, substitute 1 ounce (28 g) dried
black Chinese mushrooms. Place dried
mushrooms in small bowl: cover with
warm water. Soak 20 minutes to soften.
Drain; squeeze out excess moisture.
Prepare as directed in step 1.

1. Remove stems from shiitake mushrooms; discard stems. Chop caps with utility knife.

2. Cut tomato into halves. Remove stem. Scrape out seeds with spoon. Chop enough tomato into small pieces with chef's knife to measure ½ cup (125 ml).

3. To chop fresh parsley, place parsley in l-cup (250 ml) measuring cup. Snip enough parsley with kitchen scissors to measure 2 tablespoons (30 ml). Set aside.

4. Preheat broiler. Heat oil in large skillet over medium heat until hot. Add onion and garlic. Cook 5 minutes, stirring occasionally. Add all 3 types of mushrooms. Cook 5 minutes more, stirring often.

5. Add chicken broth. Bring to a boil. Cook about 10 minutes or until liquid is absorbed. Remove from heat. Stir in tomato, chopped parsley and cheese. Spoon into bowl.

6. Meanwhile, split each pita bread horizontally in half. Stack halves; cut the stack into 6 wedges. Arrange wedges in single layer on baking sheet. Broil 4 inches (10 cm) from heat 1 to 3 minutes or until wedges are toasted.

7. Arrange toasted pita bread triangles and warm dip in basket. Garnish, if desired.

Makes about 2¼ cups (562 ml)

Step 1. Chopping mushroom caps.

Step 3. Snipping parsley with scissors to measure 2 tablespoons (30 ml).

French-Style Pizza Bites (Pissaladière)

2 tablespoons (30 ml) olive oil
1 medium onion, thinly sliced
1 medium sweet red pepper, cut into 3-inch-long (7.5 cm) strips
2 cloves garlic, minced (technique on page 543)
⅓ cup (83 ml) pitted ripe olives, each cut into thin wedges
1 can (10 ounces/280 g) refrigerated pizza crust dough
¾ cup/187 ml (3 ounces/85 g) finely shredded Swiss or Gruyère cheese

1. Position oven rack to lowest position. Preheat oven to 425°F (220°C). Grease large baking sheet; set aside.

2. Heat oil until hot in medium skillet over medium heat. Add onion, pepper and garlic. Cook and stir 5 minutes until vegetables are crisp-tender. Stir in olives. Remove from heat; set aside.

3. Remove dough from can and pat into 16 x 12-inch (40 x 30 cm) rectangle on prepared baking sheet.

4. Arrange vegetables over dough rectangle. Sprinkle with cheese. Bake 10 minutes. With long spatula, loosen crust from baking sheet. Slide crust onto oven rack. Bake 3 to 5 minutes more until golden brown.

5. Slide baking sheet under crust to remove crust from rack. Transfer to cutting board. Cut dough crosswise into eight 1¾-inch- (4.3 cm) wide strips. Cut dough diagonally into ten 2-inch-wide (5 cm) strips, making diamond pieces. Serve immediately.

Makes about 24 servings (2 diamonds per serving)

Step 3. Patting dough into 16 x 12-inch (40 x 30 cm) rectangle on baking sheet.

Step 4. Sliding crust onto oven rack.

Step 5. Cutting dough into diamond-shaped pieces.

Coconut Fish Bites

1 cup (250 ml) flaked coconut
½ cup (125 ml) unsalted peanuts
1 egg
1 tablespoon (15 ml) soy sauce
¼ teaspoon (1 ml) salt
⅓ cup (83 ml) cornstarch
1 pound (450 g) firm white fish
    (orange roughy, haddock
    or cod fish), cut into 1-inch
    pieces
    Dipping Sauce (recipe
    follows)
1 quart (1 L) vegetable oil for
    deep frying
    Lemon wedges and fresh
    celery leaves for garnish

1. Place coconut and peanuts in food processor. Process using on/off pulsing action until peanuts are ground.

2. Combine egg, soy sauce and salt in 9-inch (22.5 cm) pie plate; set aside. Place cornstarch on waxed paper. Place coconut mixture on another piece of waxed paper.

3. Toss fish cubes in cornstarch until well coated. Add to egg mixture; toss until coated. Lightly coat with coconut mixture. Refrigerate until ready to cook.

4. Prepare Dipping Sauce; set aside.

5. Heat oil in heavy 3-quart (3 L) saucepan over medium heat until deep-fat thermometer registers 365°F (185°C). Fry fish, a few pieces at a time, 4 to 5 minutes or until golden brown and fish cubes flake easily when tested with fork. Adjust heat to maintain temperature. (Allow temperature of oil to return to 365°F/ 185°C between each batch.) Drain well. Serve with sauce. Garnish, if desired.

Makes about 24 appetizers

Step 1. Ground coconut and peanut mixture.

Step 5. Frying fish.

Dipping Sauce

    1 can (8 ounces/225 g) sliced peaches,
        undrained
    2 tablespoons (30 ml) packed brown
        sugar
    2 tablespoons (30 ml) ketchup
    1 tablespoon (15 ml) vinegar
    1 tablespoon (15 ml) soy sauce
    2 teaspoons (10 ml) cornstarch

1. Combine ingredients in food processor. Process using on/off pulsing action until peaches are chopped.

2. Bring sauce mixture to a boil in 1-quart (1 L) saucepan over medium heat; boil 1 minute until thickened, stirring constantly. Pour into serving bowl; set aside. (Sauce can be served warm or cold.)

Makes about 1¼ cups (312 ml)

Cheese & Sausage Bundles

Salsa (recipe follows)
¼ pound (112 g) bulk hot Italian pork sausage
1 cup/250 ml (4 ounces/112 g) shredded Monterey Jack cheese
1 can chopped green chili peppers, drained on paper towels
2 tablespoons (30 ml) finely chopped green onion (about 1 large)
40 wonton wrappers
1 quart (1 L) vegetable oil for deep frying

1. Prepare Salsa. Set aside; keep warm. Brown sausage in small skillet over medium-high heat 6 to 8 minutes; stir to separate meat. Drain drippings.

2. Combine sausage, cheese, peppers and onion in medium bowl. Spoon 1 round teaspoon (5 ml) sausage mixture near 1 corner of wonton wrapper. Brush opposite corner with water.

3. Fold over corner; roll up jelly-roll style.

4. Moisten both ends of roll with water. Bring ends together to make a "bundle"; overlapping ends slightly; firmly press to seal. Repeat with remaining filling and wonton wrappers.

5. Heat oil in heavy 3-quart (3 L) saucepan over medium heat until deep-fat thermometer registers 365°F (185°C). Fry bundles, a few at a time, about 1½ minutes or until golden. Adjust heat to maintain temperature. (Allow temperature of oil to return to 365°F/185°C between frying each batch.) Drain on paper towels. Serve hot with Salsa.

Makes 40 appetizers

Step 3. Rolling up wonton wrapper jelly-roll style.

Step 4. Bringing ends together to form a bundle.

Salsa

1 can (16 ounces/450 g) whole tomatoes, undrained
2 tablespoons (30 ml) olive oil
2 tablespoons (30 ml) chopped green onion
2 cloves garlic, minced (technique on page 543)
3 tablespoons (45 ml) chopped cilantro or parsley (technique on page 496)

Combine tomatoes with juice and oil in food processor. Process until tomatoes are chopped. Pour into l-quart (1 L) saucepan. Stir in green onion and garlic. Bring to a boil over medium heat. Cook, uncovered, 5 minutes. Remove from heat. Stir in cilantro.

Makes 1¾ cups (438 ml)

Pesto-Cheese Logs

⅓ cup (83 ml) walnuts
1 package (8 ounces/225 g) cream cheese, softened
⅓ cup (83 ml) refrigerated pesto sauce (about half of 7-ounce/195 g package)
2 ounces (56 g) feta cheese, crumbled (about ⅓ cup/83 ml)
2 teaspoons (10 ml) cracked black pepper
2 tablespoons (30 ml) finely shredded carrot
2 tablespoons (30 ml) chopped fresh parsley (technique on page 496)
Assorted crackers
Carrot slivers, parsley and fresh thyme for garnish

1. Preheat oven to 350°F (180°C). To toast walnuts, spread in single layer on baking sheet. Bake 8 to 10 minutes or until golden brown, stirring frequently. Remove walnuts from sheet and cool.

2. Place walnuts in food processor. Process using on/off pulsing action until walnuts are ground, but not pasty. Remove from food processor; set aside.

3. Place cream cheese, pesto sauce and feta cheese in food processor. Process until cheese mixture is smooth.

4. Spread ¾ cup (187 ml) cheese mixture on sheet of waxed paper and form 4-inch-long (10 cm) log. Wrap waxed paper around cheese mixture. Repeat with remaining cheese mixture.

5. Refrigerate logs, at least 4 hours, until well chilled. Roll each chilled log back and forth to form 5-inch (12.5 cm) log.

6. Combine walnuts and black pepper on 1 sheet of waxed paper. Unwrap 1 log and roll it in nut mixture to coat.

7. Combine carrot and parsley on another sheet of waxed paper. Unwrap remaining log and roll in carrot mixture to coat.

8. Serve immediately or wrap and refrigerate up to a day before serving. To serve, thinly slice log and serve with crackers. Garnish, if desired.

Makes 2 logs

Note: If you prefer, you may coat each log with ¼ cup (62.5 ml) chopped parsley instead of walnuts, pepper and carrot.

Step 2. Ground nuts.

Step 5. Rolling chilled log back and forth to form 5-inch (12.5 cm) log.

Step 6. Rolling log in walnut-pepper mixture.

Viennese Coffee

1 cup (250 ml) heavy cream, divided
1 teaspoon (5 ml) powdered sugar
1 bar (3 ounces/85 g) bitter-sweet or semisweet chocolate
3 cups (750 ml) strong freshly brewed hot coffee
¼ cup (62.5 ml) crème de cacao or Irish cream (optional)
Reserved chocolate shavings

1. Chill bowl, beaters and cream before whipping. Place ⅔ cup (167 ml) cream and sugar into chilled bowl. Beat with electric mixer at high speed until soft peaks form. To test, lift beaters from mixture; mixture should have droopy, but definite peaks. *Do not overbeat.*

2. Cover and refrigerate up to 8 hours. If mixture has separated slightly after refrigeration, whisk lightly with a wire whisk before using.

3. To make chocolate shavings for garnish, place waxed paper under chocolate. Holding chocolate in one hand, make short, quick strokes across chocolate with vegetable peeler; set aside. Break remaining chocolate into pieces.

4. Place remaining ⅓ cup (83 ml) cream in heavy, small saucepan. Bring to a simmer over medium-low heat. Add chocolate pieces; cover and remove from heat. Let stand 5 minutes or until chocolate is melted; stir until smooth.

5. Add hot coffee to chocolate mixture. Heat on low heat just until bubbles form around the edge of pan and coffee is heated through, stirring frequently. Remove from heat; stir in crème de cacao.

6. Pour into 4 warmed mugs. Top with whipped cream. Garnish with chocolate shavings.
Makes about 3½ cups (875 ml), 4 servings

Step 1. Testing whipped cream mixture for soft peaks.

Step 3. Making chocolate shavings.

Step 5. Heating coffee mixture.

Hot Mulled Cider

1 orange
1 lemon
12 whole cloves
6 cups (1.5 L) apple cider
⅓ cup (83 ml) sugar
3 cinnamon sticks
12 whole allspice berries
   Additional cinnamon sticks
      and citrus strips for garnish

1. Pierce 6 evenly spaced holes around orange and lemon with point of wooden skewer.

2. Insert whole cloves into the holes.

3. Cut a slice out of the orange to include all of the cloves. Cut the remainder of orange into thin slices with utility knife. Repeat procedure with lemon.

4. Combine orange slices, lemon slices, cider, sugar, 3 cinnamon sticks and allspice in medium saucepan. Bring just to a simmer over medium heat. *Do not boil.* Reduce heat to low; cook 5 minutes.

5. Pour cider through fine-mesh strainer into mugs. Discard fruit and seasonings. Garnish, if desired.
   Makes 6 cups (1.5 L), 6 servings

Step 1. Piercing orange with wooden skewer.

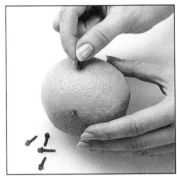

Step 2. Inserting whole cloves into orange.

Step 5. Pouring cider through strainer into mug.

Roast Turkey with Pan Gravy

1 fresh or thawed frozen turkey (12 to 14 pounds/5.4 to 6.3 kg),* reserve giblets and neck (discard liver or reserve for another use)
Sausage-Cornbread Stuffing (page 540) or your favorite stuffing (optional)
2 cloves garlic, minced (technique on page 543) (optional)
½ cup (125 ml) butter, melted
Turkey Broth with Giblets (page 512)
1 cup (250 ml) dry white wine or vermouth
3 tablespoons (45 ml) all-purpose flour
Salt and freshly ground black pepper

*A 12- to 14-pound (5.4 to 6.3 kg) turkey should take 2 to 3 days to thaw in the refrigerator. *Do not thaw at room temperature.*

1. Preheat oven to 450°F (230°C). Rinse turkey; pat dry with paper towels.

2. Prepare stuffing, if desired.

3. Stuff body and neck cavities loosely with stuffing, if desired.

4. Fold skin over openings and close with skewers. Tie legs together with cotton string or tuck through skin flap, if provided. Tuck wings under turkey.

5. Place turkey on meat rack in shallow roasting pan. If desired, stir garlic into butter. Insert meat thermometer in thickest part of thigh not touching bone. Brush ⅓ of butter mixture evenly over turkey.

6. Place turkey in oven and immediately turn temperature down to 325°F (160°C). Roast 18 to 20 minutes per pound for unstuffed turkey or 22 to 24 minutes per pound for stuffed turkey, brushing with butter mixture after 1 hour and then after 1½ hours. Baste with pan juices every hour of roasting. (Total roasting time should be 4 to 5 hours.) If turkey is overbrowning, tent with foil. Turkey is done when internal temperature reaches 180°F (87°C) and legs move easily in sockets.

7. While turkey is roasting, prepare Turkey Broth with Giblets.

continued on page 512

Step 4. Tucking wings under turkey.

Step 5. Inserting meat thermometer.

Step 6. Basting turkey with pan juices.

Roast Turkey with Pan Gravy, continued

8. Transfer turkey to cutting board; tent with foil. Let stand 15 minutes while preparing gravy.

9. Pour off and reserve all juices from roasting pan. To deglaze the pan, pour wine into pan. Place over burners and cook over medium-high heat, scraping up browned bits and stirring constantly 2 to 3 minutes or until the mixture has reduced by about half.

10. Spoon off ⅓ cup (83 ml) fat from pan drippings;** discard any remaining fat. Place ⅓ cup (83 ml) fat in large saucepan.

11. Add flour; cook over medium heat 1 minute, stirring constantly. Slowly stir in the 3 cups (750 ml) Turkey Broth, the defatted turkey drippings from the roasting pan and the deglazed wine mixture from the roasting pan.

12. Cook over medium heat 10 minutes, stirring occasionally. Stir in reserved chopped giblets; heat through. Season with salt and pepper to taste.

13. Carve turkey with carving knife. (Techniques on page 495.)

Makes 12 servings and 3½ cups (875 ml) gravy

**Or, substitute ⅓ cup (83 ml) butter or margarine for turkey fat.

Creamy Turkey Gravy: Stir in 1 cup (250 ml) heavy cream with giblets; proceed as recipe directs. Makes 4½ cups (1.12 L) gravy.

Turkey Broth with Giblets

Reserved giblets and neck from turkey (discard liver or reserve for another use)
4 cups (1 L) water
1 can (about 14 ounces/390 g) chicken broth
1 medium onion, cut into quarters
2 medium carrots, coarsely chopped or sliced
4 large parsley sprigs
1 bay leaf
1 teaspoon (5 ml) dried thyme leaves, crushed
10 whole black peppercorns

1. For broth, combine giblets and neck, water and chicken broth in 3-quart (3 L) saucepan. Bring to a boil over high heat; skim off any foam.

2. Stir in onion, carrots, parsley, bay leaf, thyme and peppercorns. Reduce heat to low. Simmer, uncovered, 1½ to 2 hours, stirring occasionally. (If liquid evaporates too quickly, add additional ½ cup/125 ml water.) Cool to room temperature.

3. Strain broth; set aside. If broth measures less than 3 cups (750 ml), add water to equal 3 cups (750 ml) liquid. If broth measures more than 3 cups (750 ml), bring to a boil and heat until liquid is reduced to 3 cups (750 ml).

4. Remove meat from neck and chop giblets finely; set aside.

5. Broth may be prepared up to 1 day before serving. Cover giblets and broth separately and refrigerate.

Makes 3 cups (750 ml)

Step 9. Deglazing pan.

Step 10. Spooning off ⅓ cup (83 ml) fat from drippings.

Turkey Broth with Giblets: Step 3. Straining broth.

Prime Rib with Yorkshire Pudding and Horseradish Cream Sauce

3 cloves garlic, minced (technique on page 543)
1 teaspoon (5 ml) freshly ground black pepper
3-rib standing beef roast, trimmed* (about 6 to 7 pounds/2.7 to 3.15 kg)
Yorkshire Pudding (page 514)
Horseradish Cream Sauce (page 514)

*Ask meat retailer to remove the chine bone for easier carving. Fat should be trimmed to ¼-inch (6 mm) thickness.

1. Preheat oven to 450°F (230°C). Combine garlic. and pepper; rub over surfaces of roast.

2. Place roast, bone side down, (the bones take the place of a meat rack) in shallow roasting pan. Insert meat thermometer in thickest part of roast, not touching bone or fat. Roast 15 minutes.

3. *Reduce oven temperature to 325°F (160°C)*: Roast 20 minutes per pound (450 g) or until internal temperature is 120° (58°C) to 130°F (63°C) for rare, 135° (65°C) to 145°F (70°C) for medium.

4. Meanwhile, prepare Yorkshire Pudding and Horseradish Cream Sauce.

5. When roast has reached desired temperature, transfer to cutting board; tent with foil. Let stand in warm place 20 to 30 minutes to allow for easier carving. Temperature of roast will continue to rise about 10°F (4.8°C) during stand time.

6. Reserve ¼ cup (62.5 ml) drippings from roasting pan. Immediately after roast has been removed from oven, *increase oven temperature to 450°F (230°C).*

7. While pudding is baking, carve roast with carving knife. (Techniques on page 494.) Serve with Yorkshire Pudding and Horseradish Cream Sauce.

Makes 6 to 8 servings

continued on page 514

Step 2. Inserting meat thermometer.

Step 5. Tenting roast with foil during stand time.

Step 6. Reserving ¼ cup (62.5 ml) drippings.

Yorkshire Pudding

1 cup (250 ml) milk
2 eggs
½ teaspoon (2 ml) salt
1 cup (250 ml) all-purpose flour
¼ cup (62.5 ml) reserved drippings
    from roast or unsalted butter

1. Process milk, eggs and salt in food processor or blender 15 seconds. Add flour; process 2 minutes. Let batter stand in food processor at room temperature 30 minutes to 1 hour. (This lets the flour fully absorb liquid for a more tender pudding.)

2. Place drippings in 9-inch (22.5 cm) square baking pan. Place in 450°F (230°C) oven 5 minutes. (Use oven mitt when removing pan from oven as pan will be very hot.)

3. Process batter another 10 seconds; pour into hot drippings. *Do not stir.*

4. Immediately return pan to oven. Bake 20 minutes. *Reduce oven temperature to 350°F (180°C)*; bake 10 minutes until pudding is golden brown and puffed. Cut into squares.

Makes 6 to 8 servings

Horseradish Cream Sauce

1 cup (250 ml) heavy cream
⅓ cup (83 ml) prepared
    horseradish, undrained
2 teaspoons (10 ml) balsamic or red
    wine vinegar
1 teaspoon (5 ml) dry mustard
¼ teaspoon (1 ml) sugar
⅛ teaspoon (0.5 ml) salt

1. Chill large bowl, beaters and cream before whipping. Pour cream into chilled bowl and beat with electric mixer at high speed until soft peaks form. To test, lift beaters from cream; mixture should have droopy, but definite peaks. *Do not overbeat.*

2. Combine horseradish, vinegar, mustard, sugar and salt in medium bowl.

3. Fold whipped cream into horseradish mixture by gently cutting down to bottom of bowl, scraping up side of bowl, then folding over top of mixture. Repeat until whipped cream is evenly incorporated into horseradish mixture. Cover and refrigerate at least 1 hour. Sauce may be made up to 8 hours before serving.

Makes about 1½ cups (375 ml)

Yorkshire Pudding: Step 3.
Pouring batter into hot drippings.

Horseradish Cream Sauce:
Step 1. Testing whipped
cream mixture for soft peaks.

Chicken Wellington

6 large boneless skinless
   chicken breast halves
   (about 6 ounces/170 g *each*)
¾ teaspoon (3.7 ml) salt, divided
¼ teaspoon (1 ml) freshly
   ground black pepper,
   divided
¼ cup (62.5 ml) butter or
   margarine, divided
12 ounces (335 g) mushrooms
   (button or crimini), finely
   chopped
½ cup (125 ml) finely chopped
   shallots or onion
2 tablespoons (30 ml) port wine
   or cognac
1 tablespoon (15 ml) fresh
   thyme leaves *or* 1 teaspoon
   (5 ml) dried thyme leaves,
   crushed
1 package (17¼ ounces/485 g)
   frozen puff pastry, thawed
1 egg, separated
1 tablespoon (15 ml) country-
   style Dijon-style mustard
1 teaspoon (5 ml) milk

1. Sprinkle chicken with ¼ teaspoon (1 ml) salt and ⅛ teaspoon (0.5 ml) pepper. Melt 2 tablespoons (30 ml) butter in large skillet over medium heat until foamy. Cook 3 chicken breast halves 6 minutes until golden brown on both sides. (Center will be springy.) Transfer to plate. Cook remaining chicken; cool slightly.

2. Melt remaining 2 tablespoons (30 ml) butter in skillet over medium heat until foamy. Add mushrooms and shallots. Cook and stir 5 minutes or until mushrooms release their liquid. Add wine, thyme, remaining ½ teaspoon (2 ml) salt and ⅛ teaspoon (0.5 ml) pepper; simmer 10 to 12 minutes or until liquid evaporates, stirring frequently. Cool.

3. Roll out each pastry sheet to 15 x 12-inch (37.5 x 30 cm) rectangle on lightly floured surface. Cut each into three 12 x 5-inch (30 x 12.5 cm) rectangles. Cut off small amount of pastry from corners to use as decoration, if desired.

4. Beat egg white in cup; brush over pastry rectangles. Place 1 cooled chicken breast on one side of each pastry rectangle. Spread ½ teaspoon (2 ml) mustard over each chicken breast, then spread with ¼ cup (62.5 ml) cooled mushroom mixture.

5. Fold opposite half of pastry rectangle over chicken. Fold edge of bottom dough over top, pressing edges together to seal. Place on ungreased baking sheet.

6. Beat yolk and milk in cup; brush over surface of pastry. Decorate with pastry scraps, if desired, then brush again with yolk mixture. Cover loosely with plastic wrap. Refrigerate until cold 1 to 4 hours before baking.

7. Preheat oven to 400°F (200°C). Re-move plastic wrap; bake chicken 25 to 30 minutes or until deep golden brown and chicken is 160°F (77°C). Garnish, if desired.

Makes 6 servings

Step 4. Spreading mushroom mixture over chicken.

Step 5. Pressing edges of dough together to seal.

Step 6. Decorating with pastry scraps.

Brisket of Beef

**1 whole well-trimmed beef
   brisket (about 5 pounds/
   2.25 kg)**
**4 cloves garlic, minced
   (technique on page 543)**
**½ teaspoon (2 ml) freshly
   ground black pepper**
**2 large onions, peeled and cut
   into ¼-inch (6 mm) slices**
**1 bottle (12 ounces/375 ml) chili
   sauce**
**¾ cup (187 ml) beef broth, beer
   or water**
**2 tablespoons (30 ml)
   Worcestershire sauce**
**1 tablespoon (15 ml) packed
   brown sugar**

l. Preheat oven to 350°F (180°C). Place brisket, fat side up, in shallow roasting pan. Spread garlic evenly over brisket; sprinkle with pepper.

2. Separate onions into rings; arrange over brisket. Combine chili sauce, broth, Worcestershire sauce and sugar; pour over brisket and onions.

3. Cover with heavy-duty foil or roasting pan lid.

4. Roast 2 hours. Turn brisket over; stir onions into sauce and spoon over brisket. Cover; roast 1 to 2 hours more or until fork-tender. (The roasting time depends on thickness of brisket and quality of meat.)

5. Transfer brisket to cutting board. Tent with foil; let stand 10 minutes.

6. At this point, the brisket may be covered and refrigerated up to 1 day before serving. To reheat brisket, cut diagonally into thin slices with carving knife. Place brisket slices and juice in large skillet. Cover and heat over medium-low heat until heated through.

7. Stir juices in roasting pan. Spoon off and discard fat from juices. (Juices may be thinned to desired consistency with water or thickened by simmering, uncovered, in saucepan.)

8. Carve brisket *diagonally* across grain into thin slices with carving knife. Spoon juices over brisket.

Makes 10 to 12 servings

Variation: If desired, stir red boiling potatoes, cut carrots, parsnips or turnips into juices during last hour of cooking time.

Step 1 . Spreading garlic over brisket.

Step 2. Pouring chili sauce mixture over brisket and onions.

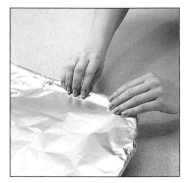

Step 3. Covering pan with heavy-duty foil.

Glazed Pork Tenderloin

2 whole well-trimmed pork
    tenderloins (about 1½
    pounds/675 g)
½ cup (125 ml) currant jelly or
    canned jellied cranberry
    sauce
1 tablespoon (15 ml) bottled
    grated horseradish,
    drained
½ cup (125 ml) chicken broth
¼ cup (62.5 ml) Rhine or other
    sweet white wine
    Salt and pepper to taste
    (optional)

1. Preheat oven to 325°F (160°C).

2. Place tenderloins on meat rack in shallow roasting pan.

3. Combine jelly and horseradish in microwavable dish or small saucepan. Heat at HIGH 1 minute or over low heat on rangetop until jelly is melted; stir well. Brush half of mixture over tenderloins.

4. Roast 30 minutes; turn tenderloins over. Brush with remaining jelly mixture. Continue to roast 30 to 40 minutes depending on thickness of tenderloins or until thermometer registers 160°F (77°C).* Remove thermometer and check temperature of other tenderloin.

5. Transfer tenderloins to cutting board; tent with foil. Let stand 10 minutes.

6. Remove meat rack from roasting pan. To deglaze the pan, pour broth and wine into pan. Place over burners and cook over medium-high heat, stirring frequently and scraping up any browned bits, 4 to 5 minutes or until sauce is reduced to ½ cup (125 ml).

7. Strain sauce through a fine-mesh strainer; season to taste with salt and pepper, if desired.

8. Carve tenderloins into thin slices with carving knife. (Technique on page 494.) Serve with sauce.

Makes 6 servings

*Since pork tenderloins are so thin, the most accurate way to measure internal temperature is with an instant read thermometer, which has a narrower stem than a standard meat thermometer. Insert thermometer into thickest part of tenderloin. Do not leave thermometer in tenderloin during roasting since thermometer is not ovenproof.

Step 6. Deglazing pan.

Step 7. Pouring sauce through strainer.

Roast Leg of Lamb

3 tablespoons (45 ml) coarse-
    grained mustard
2 cloves garlic, minced*
    (technique on page 543)
1½ teaspoons (8 ml) rosemary
    leaves, crushed
½ teaspoon (2 ml) freshly
    ground black pepper
1 leg of lamb, well-trimmed,
    boned, rolled and tied
    (about 4 pounds/1.8 kg)
    Mint jelly (optional)

*For a more intense garlic flavor inside
the meat, cut garlic into slivers. Cut
small pockets at random intervals
throughout roast with tip of sharp
knife; insert garlic slivers.

1. Preheat oven to 400°F (200°C).
Combine mustard, garlic, rosemary and
pepper. Rub mustard mixture over surface
of lamb. At this point lamb may be
covered and refrigerated up to 24 hours
before roasting.

2. Place roast on meat rack in shallow
foil-lined roasting pan. Insert meat
thermometer in thickest part of roast.

3. Roast 15 minutes. *Reduce oven
temperature to 325°F (160°C)*; roast 20
minutes per pound until roast registers
150°F (72°C) for medium.

4. Transfer roast to cutting board; tent
with foil. Let stand 10 minutes before
carving. Temperature of roast will
continue to rise 5° (2.4°C) to 10°F (4.8°C)
during stand time.

5. Cut strings with scissors; discard. Carve
roast into thin slices with carving knife.
(Technique on page 494.) Serve with mint
jelly, if desired.

Makes 6 to 8 servings

Bone-in Roast Leg of Lamb: Prepare as
directed above, except roast a 5- to 6-
pound (2.25 to 2.7 kg) bone-in leg of lamb
25 minutes per pound (450 g). After stand
time, carve roast into thin slices with
carving knife. (Technique on page 495.)

*Inserting garlic slivers into
lamb.

Step 1. Rubbing mustard
mixture over lamb.

Step 2. Inserting meat
thermometer.

Orange-Glazed Carrots

Fresh ginger (optional)
1 pound (450 g) fresh or frozen baby carrots, thawed
⅓ cup (83 ml) orange marmalade
2 tablespoons (30 ml) butter
2 teaspoons (10 ml) Dijon-style mustard

1. Peel small piece of fresh ginger with vegetable peeler or sharp knife. Grate enough ginger with ginger grater or finest side of box-shaped grater to measure ½ teaspoon (2 ml). Set aside.

2. To cook carrots, heat 1 inch (2.5 cm) lightly salted water in 2-quart (2 L) saucepan over high heat to a boil. Immediately add carrots. Return to a boil. Reduce heat to low. Cover and simmer 10 to 12 minutes for fresh carrots (8 to 10 minutes for frozen carrots) or until crisp-tender.

3. Drain well; return carrots to pan.

4. Stir in marmalade, butter, mustard and ginger. Simmer, uncovered, over medium heat 3 minutes until carrots are glazed, stirring occasionally.

5. At this point, carrots may be transferred to a microwavable casserole dish with lid. Cover and refrigerate up to 8 hours before serving. To reheat, microwave at HIGH 4 to 5 minutes or until hot.

Makes 6 servings

Note: Recipe may be doubled to serve 10 to 12.

Step 1. Grating fresh ginger with ginger grater.

Step 2. Testing doneness.

Step 4. Stirring in remaining ingredients.

Brussels Sprouts in Mustard Sauce

1½ pounds (675 g) fresh Brussels
    sprouts*
1 tablespoon (15 ml) butter or
    margarine
⅓ cup (83 ml) chopped shallots
    or onion
⅓ cup (83 ml) half-and-half
1½ tablespoons (22 ml) tarragon
    Dijon-style mustard** or
    Düsseldorf mustard
¼ teaspoon (1 ml) salt
⅛ teaspoon (0.5 ml) freshly
    ground black pepper *or*
    ground nutmeg
1½ tablespoons (22 ml) grated
    Parmesan cheese (optional)

*Or, substitute 2 (10-ounce/280 g)
packages frozen Brussels sprouts for
fresh Brussels sprouts. Omit steps 1, 2
and 3. Cook according to package
directions; drain and rinse as directed
in step 4.

**Or, substitute 1½ tablespoons (22
ml) Dijon-style mustard plus ½
teaspoon (2 ml) dry tarragon leaves,
crushed, for tarragon Dijon-style
mustard.

1. Cut stem from each Brussels sprout and pull off outer bruised leaves.

2. For faster, more even cooking, crosshatch core by cutting an "X" deep into the stem end of each Brussels sprout with paring knife. If some Brussels sprouts are larger than others, cut large Brussels sprouts lengthwise into halves.

3. Use a large enough saucepan to allow Brussels sprouts to fit in a single layer. Bring 2 quarts (2 L) salted water to a boil in saucepan. Add Brussels sprouts; return to a boil. Boil, uncovered, 7 to 10 minutes or until almost tender when pierced with fork.

4. Drain in colander. Rinse under cold water to stop cooking; drain thoroughly.

5. Melt butter in same saucepan over medium heat until foamy. Add shallots; cook 3 minutes, stirring occasionally. Add half-and-half, mustard, salt and pepper. Simmer 1 minute until thickened.

6. Add drained Brussels sprouts; heat about 1 minute or until heated through, tossing gently with sauce.

7. At this point, Brussels sprouts may be covered and refrigerated up to 8 hours before serving. Reheat in saucepan over low heat. Or, place in microwavable covered dish and reheat in microwave oven at HIGH 3 minutes until hot.

8. Just before serving, sprinkle with cheese, if desired.

Makes 4 cups (1 L), 6 to 8 servings

Step 1. Pulling off outer bruised leaves.

Step 2. Cutting an "X" in stem end of Brussels sprouts.

Broccoli with Red Pepper and Shallots

2 bunches fresh broccoli (about
   2¼ pounds/1 kg)
1 large red bell pepper
3 large shallots (3 ounces/85 g)
   or 1 small onion
2 teaspoons (10 ml) margarine
   or butter
½ teaspoon (2 ml) salt
¼ teaspoon (1 ml) freshly
   ground black pepper
¼ cup (62.5 ml) sliced almonds,
   toasted* (optional)

*To toast almonds, see toasting walnut directions on page 504, step 1.

1. Trim leaves from broccoli stalks. Trim ends of stalks. Cut broccoli into flowerets by removing the heads to include a small piece of stem. Peel stalks, then cut into l-inch (2.5 cm) pieces.

2. To cook broccoli, heat 2 quarts (2 L) lightly salted water in 3-quart (3 L) saucepan over high heat to a boil. Immediately add broccoli. Return to a boil. Boil, uncovered, 3 to 5 minutes until bright green and tender. Drain broccoli in colander. Rinse under cold water; drain thoroughly.

3. Rinse bell pepper under cold running water. To seed pepper, stand on end on cutting board. Cut off sides in 3 to 4 lengthwise slices with utility knife. (Cut close to, but not through stem.) Discard stem and seeds. Scrape out any remaining seeds. Rinse inside of pepper under cold running water, then cut into short thin strips.

4. Remove papery outer skin from shallots. Cut off root end. Cut shallots into thin slices.

5. At this point, vegetables may be wrapped separately and refrigerated up to 6 hours before cooking.

6. Melt margarine in 12-inch (30 cm) nonstick skillet over medium heat. Add bell pepper and shallots. Cook 3 minutes, stirring occasionally. Add broccoli to skillet. Cook 4 to 6 minutes, stirring occasionally. Sprinkle with salt and black pepper; mix well. Garnish with almonds, if desired.

Makes 6 cups (1.5 L), 6 to 8 servings

Step 1. Cutting stalks into l-inch (2.5 cm) pieces.

Step 3. Cutting sides off bell pepper.

Step 4. Cutting root end from shallot.

Sweet Potato Gratin

3 pounds (1.35 kg) sweet
    potatoes (about 5 large)
½ cup (125 ml) butter or
    margarine, divided
¼ cup (62.5 ml) *plus* 2
    tablespoons (30 ml) packed
    light brown sugar, divided
2 eggs
⅔ cup (167 ml) orange juice
2 teaspoons (10 ml) ground
    cinnamon, divided
½ teaspoon (2 ml) salt
¼ teaspoon (1 ml) ground
    nutmeg
⅓ cup (83 ml) all-purpose flour
¼ cup (62.5 ml) uncooked
    old-fashioned oats
⅓ cup (83 ml) chopped pecans
    or walnuts

1. Bake sweet potatoes until tender in preheated 350°F (180°C) oven 1 hour. Or, pierce sweet potatoes several times with fork and place on microwavable plate. Microwave at HIGH 16 to 18 minutes, rotating and turning over sweet potatoes after 9 minutes. Let stand 5 minutes.

2. While sweet potatoes are hot, cut lengthwise into halves. Scrape hot pulp from skins into large bowl.

3. Beat ¼ cup (62.5 ml) butter and 2 tablespoons (30 ml) sugar into sweet potatoes with electric mixer at medium speed until butter is melted. Beat in eggs, orange juice, 1½ teaspoons (8 ml) cinnamon, salt and nutmeg, scraping down side of bowl once. Beat until smooth. Pour mixture into 1½-quart (1.5 L) baking dish or gratin dish; smooth top.

4. For topping, combine flour, oats, remaining ¼ cup (62.5 ml) sugar and remaining ½ teaspoon (2 ml) cinnamon in medium bowl. Cut in remaining ¼ cup (62.5 ml) butter with pastry blender or 2 knives until mixture becomes coarse crumbs. Stir in pecans.

5. Sprinkle topping evenly over sweet potatoes.

6. At this point, Sweet Potato Gratin may be covered and refrigerated up to 1 day. Let stand at room temperature 1 hour before baking.

7. Preheat oven to 350°F (180°C).

8. Bake 25 to 30 minutes or until sweet potatoes are heated through. For a crisper topping, broil 5 inches (12.5 cm) from heat 2 to 3 minutes or until golden brown.
Makes 6 to 8 servings

Step 2. Scraping sweet potato from skins into bowl.

Step 3. Beating sweet potato mixture until smooth.

Step 4. Cutting butter into topping mixture.

Potato Latkes

2 large *or* 3 medium baking
    (russet) potatoes (about
    1¾ pounds/790 g)
1 large onion (8 ounces/225 g)
2 eggs
¼ cup (62.5 ml) matzo meal
¾ teaspoon (3.7 ml) salt
¼ teaspoon (1 ml) freshly
    ground black pepper
2 tablespoons (30 ml) vegetable
    oil, divided
    Applesauce (optional)
    Sour cream (optional)

1. To prepare potatoes, remove skins with vegetable peeler.

2. Shred potatoes and onion with shredding disc of food processor or shred by hand using a box-shaped grater.

3. Place potato mixture in large bowl. Add eggs, matzo meal, salt and pepper; mix well.

4. Heat 1 tablespoon (15 ml) oil in large nonstick skillet over medium-low heat until hot. Drop potato mixture by level ¼ cupfuls (62.5 ml) into skillet.

5. Use back of spatula to flatten potato mixture into 3½-inch (9 cm) patties, about ½ inch (1.2 cm) thick.

6. Cook about 4 minutes per side or until golden brown. Transfer to ovenproof platter lined with paper towels.

7. Keep warm in 200°F (96°C) oven while preparing remaining latkes. Add remaining 1 tablespoon (15 ml) oil as needed. Serve warm with applesauce or sour cream. Garnish as desired.

Makes about 18 latkes

Step 2. Shredding potatoes in food processor.

Step 4. Dropping potato mixture by ¼ cupfuls (62.5 ml) into hot oil.

Step 5. Flattening potato mixture into patties with back of spatula.

Low-Calorie Mashed Potatoes

**2 pounds (900 g) medium red
 boiling potatoes
4 large cloves garlic, peeled
¾ cup (187 ml) cultured
 buttermilk
 (1½% fat)
½ teaspoon (2 ml) salt
¼ teaspoon (1 ml) freshly
 ground black pepper
2 tablespoons (30 ml) chopped
 chives for garnish**

1. To prepare potatoes, remove skins with vegetable peeler. Cut into chunks.

2. Place potatoes and garlic in large saucepan. Add enough water to cover; bring to a boil over high heat. Reduce heat to medium. Simmer, uncovered, 20 to 30 minutes or until potatoes are fork-tender; drain.

3. Place potatoes and garlic in medium bowl. Mash with potato masher or beat with electric mixer at medium speed until smooth.* Add buttermilk, salt and pepper. Stir with fork until just combined. Garnish, if desired.

Makes 4 cups (1 L), 8 servings

*For a smoother texture, force potatoes through potato ricer or food mill into medium bowl. Finish as directed in step 3.

Buttery Mashed Potatoes: Follow directions given above. In step 3, add 1 tablespoon (15 ml) butter or margarine to potatoes along with buttermilk, salt and pepper.

Step 1. Cutting potatoes into chunks.

Step 2. Placing potatoes in saucepan.

*Forcing potatoes through ricer.

Mixed Greens with Raspberry Vinaigrette

½ cup (125 ml) walnut pieces
1 shallot
⅓ cup (83 ml) vegetable oil
2½ tablespoons (38 ml) raspberry vinegar
½ teaspoon (2 ml) salt
½ teaspoon (2 ml) sugar
Romaine lettuce leaves
Spinach leaves
Red leaf lettuce leaves
1 cup (250 ml) red seedless grapes, halved

1. Preheat oven to 350°F (180°C). To toast walnuts, spread in single layer on baking sheet. Bake 6 to 8 minutes or until lightly golden brown, stirring frequently. Remove walnuts from baking sheet and cool. Coarsely chop with chef's knife; set aside.

2. Remove papery outer skin from shallot. Cut off root end. Finely chop enough shallot with chef's knife to measure 1 tablespoon (15 ml).

3. Place oil, vinegar, shallot, salt and sugar in small bowl or small jar with lid. Whisk together or cover and shake jar until mixed. Cover; refrigerate up to 1 week.

4. Wash greens separately in several changes of cold water. Drain well and if necessary pat with paper towels to remove excess moisture. Or, spin in salad spinner to remove moisture.

5. Discard any wilted or bruised leaves. Cut or tear off stems if they are woody.

6. Tear enough romaine lettuce into bite-sized pieces to measure 2 packed cups (500 ml). Tear enough spinach into bite-sized pieces to measure 2 packed cups (500 ml). Tear enough red leaf lettuce into bite-sized pieces to measure 2 packed cups (500 ml).

7. Combine greens, grapes and cooled walnuts in large bowl. Just before serving, add dressing; toss well to coat.

Makes 6 to 8 servings

Step 2. Cutting root end from shallot.

Step 4. Spinning greens in salad spinner to remove moisture.

Step 6. Packing romaine lettuce into measuring cup.

Cranberry-Apple Chutney

1 package (12 ounces/335 g)
    fresh or frozen cranberries
    (about 3½ cups/875 ml)
2 medium Granny Smith apples
1 medium onion
1¼ cups (312 ml) granulated
    sugar
½ cup (125 ml) water
½ cup (125 ml) golden raisins
½ cup (125 ml) packed light
    brown sugar
¼ cup (62.5 ml) cider vinegar
1 teaspoon (5 ml) ground
    cinnamon
1 teaspoon (5 ml) ground ginger
⅛ teaspoon (0.5 ml) ground
    cloves
⅛ teaspoon (0.5 ml) ground
    allspice
½ cup (125 ml) walnuts or
    pecans, toasted* and
    chopped (optional)

*To toast walnuts, see directions on page 504, step 1.

1. Wash cranberries and pick through, discarding any stems or withered cranberries.

2. Peel apples with vegetable peeler. Cut into quarters; remove stems and cores with sharp knife. Cut apples into ¼-inch (6 mm) pieces. Cut enough to make 2 cups (500 ml).

3. To chop onion, peel skin. Cut onion in half through root with utility knife. Place cut side down on cutting board. Holding knife horizontally, make cuts parallel to board, almost to root end. Next, cut onion vertically into thin slices, holding onion with fingers to keep its shape, then turn onion and cut crosswise to root end. (The closer the cuts are, the finer the onion is chopped.) Repeat with remaining onion half.

4. Combine granulated sugar and water in heavy 2-quart (2 L) saucepan. Cook over high heat until boiling. Boil gently 3 minutes.

5. Add cranberries, apples, onion, raisins, brown sugar, vinegar, cinnamon, ginger, cloves and allspice. Bring to a boil over high heat. Reduce heat to medium. Simmer, uncovered, 20 to 25 minutes or until mixture is very thick, stirring occasionally. Cool; stir in walnuts, if desired.

6. Cover and refrigerate up to 2 weeks before serving.
    Makes about 3½ cups (833 ml) without walnuts or 4 cups (1 L) with walnuts

Note: This chutney makes a wonderful appetizer when spooned over cream cheese spread on melba rounds.

Step 2. Cutting apples into ¼-inch (6 mm) pieces.

Step 3. Chopping onion.

Sausage-Cornbread Stuffing

1 recipe day-old Cornbread*
   (page 542)
8 ounces (112 g) bulk pork
   sausage (regular or spicy)
½ cup (125 ml) butter or
   margarine
2 medium onions, chopped
   (technique on page 543)
2 cloves garlic, minced
   (technique on page 543)
2 teaspoons (10 ml) dried sage
1 teaspoon (5 ml) poultry
   seasoning
¾ to 1¼ cups (187 to 312 ml)
   chicken broth
   Sage leaves for garnish

*Or, substitute 1 package (16 ounces/
450 g) prepared dry cornbread crumbs
for homemade cornbread. Omit step 1.

1. Preheat oven to 350°F (180°C). Crumble cornbread coarsely. Crumble enough to make 6 cups (1.5 L). Spread evenly in 15 x 10-inch (37.5 x 25 cm) jelly-roll pan. Bake 20 to 25 minutes or until dry.

2. Brown sausage in large skillet over medium-high heat until no longer pink, stirring to crumble meat. Drain sausage on paper towels; set aside. Wipe skillet with paper towels to remove grease.

3. Melt butter in same skillet over medium heat until foamy. Cook onions and garlic in butter 10 minutes until onions are softened. Stir in sage and poultry seasoning; cook 1 minute more.

4. Combine cornbread crumbs, sausage and onion mixture in large bowl.

5. *If stuffing is to be cooked in a turkey,* drizzle ¾ cup (187 ml) broth over stuffing; toss lightly until evenly moistened. Stuff body and neck cavities loosely with stuffing. Stuffing may be prepared up to 1 day before using. *Do not stuff the turkey until just before you are ready to roast it.* Roast according to directions given on page 510 or according to instructions given with turkey.

continued on page 542

Step 1. Spreading cornbread crumbs in pan.

Step 2. Stirring sausage to crumble.

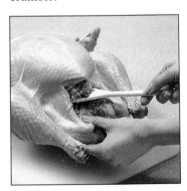

Step 5. Stuffing turkey.

**Sausage-Cornbread Stuffing,
continued**

6. *If stuffing is to be cooked separately,*
drizzle 1¼ cups (312 ml) broth over
stuffing; toss stuffing lightly until
evenly moistened. Transfer to 3-quart
(3 L) casserole.

7. At this point, Sausage-Cornbread
Stuffing may be covered and
refrigerated up to 1 day before baking.

8. Preheat oven to 350°F (180°C).

9. Bake 45 minutes (55 to 60 minutes if
refrigerated) or until heated through.
For a drier stuffing, uncover during last
15 minutes of baking. Garnish, if
desired.

Makes 12 cups (3 L) stuffing

Cornbread

1¼ cups (312 ml) yellow cornmeal
¾ cup (187 ml) all-purpose flour
2 tablespoons (30 ml) sugar
1 tablespoon (15 ml) baking
  powder
¾ teaspoon (3.7 ml) salt
1 egg
1 cup (250 ml) milk
3 tablespoons (45 ml) butter or
  margarine, melted and cooled

1. Preheat oven to 425°F (220°C).
Grease 9-inch (22.5 cm) square baking
pan; set aside.

2. Combine cornmeal, flour, sugar,
baking powder and salt in medium
bowl. Combine egg, milk and butter in
4-cup (1 L) measure; add to cornmeal
mixture. Stir just until dry ingredients
are moistened. Pour into prepared pan.

3. Bake 20 to 25 minutes or until
golden brown and wooden toothpick
inserted in center comes out clean. Cool
completely on wire rack.

4. Cornbread may be prepared up to 2
days before using as stuffing. Cover; let
stand at room temperature.
Makes 6 cups (1.5 L) cornbread crumbs

Cornbread: Step 2. Adding milk
mixture to dry ingredients.

Cornbread: Step 3. Testing
doneness of cornbread with
wooden toothpick.

Wild Rice Mushroom Stuffing

½ cup (125 ml) uncooked wild
    rice
6 ounces (170 g) fresh
    mushrooms*
1 large onion
1 clove garlic
    Day-old French bread (about
    4 ounces/112 g)
½ cup (125 ml) butter or
    margarine
½ teaspoon (2 ml) rubbed sage
½ teaspoon (2 ml) dried thyme
    leaves, crushed
½ teaspoon (2 ml) salt
¼ teaspoon (1 ml) freshly
    ground black pepper
1 cup (250 ml) chicken broth
½ cup (125 ml) coarsely
    chopped pecans
    Thyme sprigs for garnish

*Or, substitute 1½ cups (375 ml) fresh
sliced shiitake mushroom caps for 3
ounces (85 g) fresh mushrooms.

1. Rinse and cook rice according to
package directions; set aside.

2. Wipe mushrooms clean with damp
kitchen towel or paper towel. Cut thin
piece from stem; discard. With paring
knife, cut mushrooms into slices to
measure 3 cups (750 ml).

3. To chop onion, peel skin. Cut onion in
half through root with utility knife. Place
cut side down on cutting board. Holding
knife horizontally, make cuts parallel to
board, almost to root end. Next, cut onion
vertically into thin slices, holding onion
with fingers to keep its shape, then turn
onion and cut crosswise to root end. (The
closer the cuts are, the finer the onion is
chopped.) Repeat with remaining onion
half.

4. To mince garlic, trim ends of garlic
cloves. Slightly crush clove under flat side
of chef's knife blade; peel away skin.
Chop garlic with chef's knife until garlic
is in uniform fine pieces. Set aside.

continued on page 544

Step 2. Wiping mushroom
with damp kitchen towel.

Step 3. Chopping onion.

Step 4. Crushing garlic to
remove skin.

Wild Rice Mushroom Stuffing,
continued

5. Cut French bread with a serrated knife into ½-inch (1.25 cm) slices. Stack a few of the slices. Cut lengthwise into ½-inch-wide (1.25 cm) strips, then cut crosswise to form ½-inch (1.25 cm) cubes. Cut enough bread to measure 4 cups (1 L).

6. Spread bread cubes in single layer on baking sheet. Broil 5 to 6 inches (12.5 to 15 cm) from heat 4 minutes or until lightly toasted, stirring after 2 minutes; set aside.

7. Heat butter in large skillet over medium heat until foamy. Add onion and garlic. Cook and stir 3 minutes. Add mushrooms; cook 3 minutes, stirring occasionally. Add sage, ½ teaspoon (2 ml) thyme, salt and pepper. Add cooked rice; cook 2 minutes, stirring occasionally. Stir in broth. Add pecans and toasted bread cubes; toss lightly.

8. Transfer to 1½-quart (1.5 L) casserole.

9. At this point, Wild Rice Mushroom Stuffing may be covered and refrigerated up to 8 hours before baking.

10. Preheat oven to 325 °F (160°C).

11. Cover with casserole lid or foil. Bake 40 minutes (50 minutes if refrigerated) or until heated through. Garnish, if desired.

Makes 6 to 8 servings

Step 5. Cutting French bread into cubes.

Step 6. Spreading bread cubes on baking sheet.

Step 7. Tossing bread cubes with broth mixture.

Praline Pumpkin Tart

1¼ cups (312 ml) all-purpose
    flour
  1 tablespoon (15 ml) granulated
    sugar
  ¾ teaspoon (3.7 ml) salt, divided
  ¼ cup (62.5 ml) vegetable
    shortening
  ¼ cup (62.5 ml) butter or
    margarine
  2 to 4 tablespoons (30 to 60 ml)
    cold water
  1 can (16 ounces/450 g)
    pumpkin
  1 can (13 ounces/365 g)
    evaporated milk (1½ cups/
    375 ml)
  2 eggs
  ⅔ cup (167 ml) packed brown
    sugar
  1 teaspoon (5 ml) ground
    cinnamon
  ½ teaspoon (2 ml) ground ginger
  ¼ teaspoon (1 ml) ground cloves
    Praline Topping (page 548)
    Sweetened Whipped Cream
    (page 550)
    Additional cinnamon and
    pecans halves for garnish

1. For crust, combine flour, granulated sugar and ¼ teaspoon (1 ml) salt in large bowl. Cut in shortening and butter using pastry blender or 2 knives until mixture forms pea-sized pieces.

2. Sprinkle flour mixture with water, 1 tablespoon (15 ml) at a time. Toss with fork until mixture holds together. Press together to form ball. Wrap in plastic wrap. Refrigerate about 1 hour or until chilled.

3. Remove plastic wrap. Flatten dough into 5- to 6-inch (12.5 to 15 cm) disc. Lightly flour surface and rolling pin. Roll dough in short strokes starting in the middle of the disc rolling out toward the edge using rolling pin. Rotate dough ¼ turn to the right. Sprinkle more flour under dough and on rolling pin as necessary to prevent sticking. Continue to roll and rotate dough 2 to 3 more times. Roll out dough to ⅛-inch (3 mm) thickness.

4. Trim dough to 1 inch (2.5 cm) larger than inverted 10-inch (25 cm) tart pan with removable bottom or 1½ inches (3.7 cm) larger than inverted 9-inch (22.5 cm) pie plate. Place rolling pin on one side of dough. Gently roll dough over rolling pin once.

5. Carefully lift rolling pin and dough, unrolling dough over tart pan. Ease dough into tart pan with fingertips. Do not stretch dough. Cut dough even with edge of tart pan. (Roll and flute edge of dough in pie plate.)

6. Cover tart crust with plastic wrap and refrigerate 30 minutes to relax dough.

7. Preheat oven to 400°F (200°C).

continued on page 548

Step 3. Rolling out dough.

Step 4. Rolling dough over rolling pin.

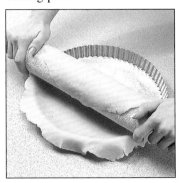

Step 5. Unrolling dough over tart pan.

Praline Pumpkin Tart, continued

8. To blind bake tart crust, pierce tart crust with tines of fork at ¼-inch (6 mm) intervals, about 40 times.

9. Cut a square of foil about 4 inches (10 cm) larger than tart pan. Line tart pan with foil. Fill with dried beans, uncooked rice or ceramic pie weights.

10. Bake 10 minutes or until set. Remove from oven. Gently remove foil lining and beans. Return to oven and bake 5 minutes or until very light brown. Cool completely on wire rack. (If using beans or rice, save to use again for blind baking. The beans or rice are no longer usable in recipes.)

11. For filling, preheat oven to 400°F (200°C). Beat pumpkin, milk, eggs, brown sugar, 1 teaspoon (5 ml) cinnamon, remaining ½ teaspoon (2 ml) salt, ginger and cloves in large bowl with electric mixer at low speed. Pour into cooled tart crust. Bake 35 minutes.

12. Prepare Praline Topping. Sprinkle topping over center of tart leaving 1½-inch (3.75 cm) rim around edge of tart.

13. Bake 15 minutes more or until knife inserted 1 inch (2.5 cm) from center comes out clean.

14. Cool completely on wire rack. Prepare Sweetened Whipped Cream and spoon into decorating bag with fluted tip. Pipe whipped cream around edge of pie, making decorative edge. Sprinkle additional cinnamon over whipped cream. Garnish with pecan halves.

Makes 8 servings

Praline Topping

⅓ **cup (83 ml) packed brown sugar**
⅓ **cup (83 ml) chopped pecans**
⅓ **cup (83 ml) uncooked quick-cooking oats**
1 **tablespoon (15 ml) butter or margarine, softened**

Place sugar, pecans and oats in small bowl. Cut in butter with pastry blender or 2 knives until crumbs form.

Step 8. Piercing crust with tines of fork.

Step 9. Filling foil liner with dried beans.

Step 13. Testing doneness with knife.

Rich Chocolate Truffle Cake

2 packages (8 ounces/225 g
    each) semisweet chocolate
    (16 squares)
1½ cups (375 ml) butter or
    margarine
1 cup (250 ml) sugar
½ cup (125 ml) light cream
6 large eggs
2 teaspoons (10 ml) vanilla
    Chocolate Curls (page 550)
    Chocolate Glaze (page 550)
    Sweetened Whipped Cream
    (page 550)
    Mint leaves for garnish

1. Preheat oven to 350°F (180°C). Line bottom of 9-inch (22.5 cm) springform pan with foil, tucking foil edges under bottom. Attach springform side. Bring foil up around side of pan. Grease foil-lined bottom and side of pan with butter; set aside.

2. Heat chocolate, butter, sugar and cream in heavy 2-quart (2 L) saucepan over low heat until chocolate melts and mixture is smooth, stirring frequently. Remove from heat.

3. Beat eggs and vanilla in large bowl with wire whisk until frothy. Slowly whisk in warm chocolate mixture until well blended. *Do not vigorously beat mixture.* You do not want to incorporate air into the mixture.

4. Pour batter into prepared pan. Bake 45 minutes or until wooden toothpick inserted about 1 inch (2.5 cm) from edge comes out clean and center is set. Cool cake completely in pan on wire rack.

5. Prepare Chocolate Curls; refrigerate.

6. When cake is cool, carefully remove side of springform pan. Leave cake on bottom of pan. Wrap cake in foil. Refrigerate until well chilled, at least 4 hours or overnight.

7. Prepare Chocolate Glaze. Unwrap cake. Remove from bottom of pan and place upside-down on cake plate. Surround cake with waxed paper strips.

8. Spread top and side of cake with warm glaze, using metal spatula. Remove waxed paper after glaze sets.

continued on page 550

Step 1. Lining bottom of pan with foil.

Step 4. Testing doneness of cake with wooden toothpick.

Step 7. Placing waxed paper strips around edge of plate.

**Rich Chocolate Truffle Cake,
continued**

9. Prepare Sweetened Whipped Cream. Spoon cream mixture into decorating bag with medium star tube. Pipe cream around edge of cake.

10. Garnish piped cream with Chocolate Curls. Refrigerate until serving. Just before serving, garnish with mint leaves.

Makes 16 to 20 servings

Chocolate Curls

1 square (1 ounce/28 g) chocolate, coarsely chopped
1 teaspoon (5 ml) vegetable shortening

1. Place chocolate and shortening in l-cup (250 ml) glass measure. Microwave at HIGH about 1½ minutes or until melted, stirring after every 30 seconds of cooking.

2. Pour melted chocolate onto back of baking sheet, marble slab or other heat-resistant flat surface. Quickly spread chocolate into a very thin layer with metal spatula. Refrigerate about 10 minutes or until firm, but still pliable.

3. When chocolate is just firm, use small straight-edge metal spatula or paring knife. Holding spatula at a 45° angle, push spatula firmly along baking sheet, under chocolate, so chocolate curls as it is pushed. (If chocolate is too firm to curl, let stand a few minutes at room temperature. Refrigerate if it becomes too soft.)

4. Using small skewer or toothpick, transfer curls to waxed paper. Store in cool, dry place until ready to use.

Chocolate Glaze

1 cup (250 ml) semisweet chocolate chips
2 tablespoons (30 ml) butter or margarine
3 tablespoons (45 ml) half-and-half
2 tablespoons (30 ml) light corn syrup

Heat chocolate chips and butter in heavy l-quart (1 L) saucepan over low heat, stirring frequently. Remove from heat. Stir in half-and-half and corn syrup until smooth.

Makes about 1¼ cups (312 ml)

Sweetened Whipped Cream

1 cup (250 ml) heavy cream
2 tablespoons (30 ml) powdered sugar
½ teaspoon (2 ml) vanilla

Chill large bowl, beaters and cream thoroughly. Place cream, sugar and vanilla into chilled bowl and beat with electric mixer at high speed until soft peaks form. To test, lift beaters from whipping cream; mixture should have droopy, but definite peaks. *Do not overbeat.* Refrigerate.

Makes about 2 cups (500 ml)

Step 9. Piping cream around edge of cake.

Sweetened Whipped Cream: Testing whipped cream mixture for soft peaks.

Linzer Torte

½ cup (125 ml) whole almonds, toasted*
1½ cups (375 ml) all-purpose flour
1 teaspoon (5 ml) ground cinnamon
¼ teaspoon (1 ml) salt
¾ cup (187 ml) granulated sugar
½ cup (125 ml) butter or margarine
½ teaspoon (2 ml) grated lemon peel
1 egg
¾ cup (187 ml) raspberry or apricot jam
  Powdered sugar

*To toast almonds, see toasting walnuts directions page 504, step 1.

1. Place almonds in food processor. Process using on/off pulsing action until almonds are ground, but not pasty.

2. Preheat oven to 375°F (190°C).

3. Combine flour, almonds, cinnamon and salt in medium bowl; set aside.

4. Beat granulated sugar, butter and lemon peel in large bowl using electric mixer at medium speed about 5 minutes or until light and fluffy, scraping down side of bowl once. Beat in egg until well blended.

5. Beat in flour mixture at low speed until well blended. Spoon ⅔ of dough onto bottom of 10-inch (25 cm) tart pan with removable bottom. Pat dough evenly over bottom and up side of pan. Spread jam over bottom of dough.

6. Roll remaining ⅓ of dough on lightly floured surface with lightly floured rolling pin into 10 x 6-inch (25 x 15 cm) square. Cut dough into 10 x ½-inch (25 x 1.25 cm) strips using a pizza wheel or sharp knife.

7. Arrange 4 to 5 strips of dough lengthwise across jam. Arrange another 4 to 5 strips of dough crosswise across top. Press ends of dough strips into edge of crust.

8. Bake 25 to 35 minutes or until crust is golden brown. Cool completely in pan on wire rack. Remove torte from pan. Cut into wedges. Sprinkle with powdered sugar.

9. Store, tightly covered, at room temperature 1 to 2 days.

Makes 12 servings

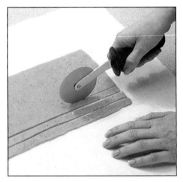
Step 6. Cutting dough into strips with pizza wheel.

Step 7. Arranging strips in a lattice pattern on torte.

Individual Orange Soufflés

Nonstick cooking spray
3 oranges
1½ tablespoons (22 ml)
    cornstarch
3 tablespoons (45 ml) orange-
    flavored liqueur
6 egg whites
⅛ teaspoon (0.5 ml) salt
6 tablespoons (90 ml)
    granulated sugar
1½ tablespoons (22 ml) sliced
    almonds (optional)
1½ tablespoons (22 ml) powdered
    sugar (optional)

1. Preheat oven to 450°F (230°C). Spray 6 individual soufflé dishes (8 to 10 ounces/20 to 25 cm each) with cooking spray. Place dishes on jelly-roll pan; set aside.

2. Grate colored portion (not with pith) of orange peel using box-shaped grater or hand-held grater. Grate enough orange peel to equal 1½ teaspoons (8 ml).

3. Cut peel and membrane from oranges; section oranges over 1-quart (1 L) saucepan. Dice oranges. There will be 1½ cups (375 ml) juice and pulp.

4. Stir in cornstarch until smooth. Cook and stir over medium heat until mixture comes to a boil and thickens slightly. Remove from heat. Stir in liqueur and reserved orange peel.

5. Beat egg whites and salt with electric mixer at high speed in large bowl until soft peaks form. To test, lift beaters from egg whites; mixture should have droopy, but definite peaks.

6. Gradually beat in granulated sugar, 1 tablespoon (15 ml) at a time, until stiff peaks form and sugar is dissolved. After beaters are lifted from egg white mixture, stiff peaks should remain on top, and when bowl is tilted, mixture will not slide around.

7. Fold ¼ of egg white mixture into orange mixture, using rubber spatula or wire whisk. Then, fold all of orange mixture into remaining egg white mixture. Spoon into prepared dishes. Sprinkle with almonds, if desired.

8. Immediately bake 12 to 15 minutes or until soufflés are puffed and browned. Sprinkle with powdered sugar, if desired. Serve immediately.

Makes 6 servings

Step 5. Testing egg white mixture for soft peaks.

Step 6. Testing egg white mixture for stiff peaks.

Step 7. Folding egg white mixture into orange mixture.

Rugelach

1½ cups (375 ml) all-purpose
    flour
¼ teaspoon (1 ml) salt
¼ teaspoon (1 ml) baking soda
½ cup butter (125 ml) or
    margarine
1 package (3 ounces/85 g)
    cream cheese, softened
⅓ cup (83 ml) *plus* ¼ cup (62.5
    ml) granulated sugar,
    divided
1 teaspoon (5 ml) grated lemon
    peel, divided
1 cup (250 ml) ground toasted
    walnuts (technique on page
    504) or 1 cup (250 ml)
    whole almonds
1 teaspoon (5 ml) ground
    cinnamon
2 tablespoons (30 ml) honey
1 tablespoon (15 ml) lemon
    juice
    Powdered sugar

1. Place flour, salt and baking soda in small bowl; combine. Beat butter, cream cheese, ⅓ cup (83 ml) granulated sugar and ½ teaspoon (2 ml) lemon peel in large bowl with electric mixer at medium speed about 5 minutes or until light and fluffy, scraping down once.

2. Gradually add flour mixture. Beat at low speed until well blended, scraping down side of bowl once.

3. Form dough into 3 (5-inch/12.5 cm) discs; wrap in plastic wrap and refrigerate until firm, about 2 hours.

4. Preheat oven to 375°F (190°C). Grease 2 cookie sheets; set aside. Combine walnuts, remaining ¼ cup (62.5 ml) granulated sugar and cinnamon in medium bowl; set aside. Combine honey, remaining ½ teaspoon (2 ml) lemon peel and lemon juice in small bowl; set aside.

5. Working with 1 piece of dough at a time, unwrap and place dough on lightly floured surface. Roll out dough with lightly floured rolling pin to 10-inch (25 cm) circle. Keep remaining dough refrigerated.

6. Brush with ⅓ of honey mixture. Sprinkle with ⅓ of nut mixture. Lightly press nut mixture into dough.

7. Cut circle into 12 triangles with pizza cutter or sharp knife. Beginning with wide end of triangle, *tightly* roll up, jelly-roll style. Place cookies 1 inch (2.5 cm) apart on prepared cookie sheets.

8. Repeat with 2 remaining dough pieces and filling ingredients. Bake 10 to 12 minutes or until lightly golden. Let cookies stand on cookie sheets 1 minute. Remove cookies to wire rack; cool. Sprinkle with powered sugar. Store tightly covered.

Makes 3 dozen

Step 5. Rolling out dough.

Step 6. Sprinkling nut mixture over dough.

Step 7. Rolling up dough jelly-roll style.

Gingerbread Bears

3½ cups (875 ml) all-purpose
    flour
  2 teaspoons (10 ml) ground
    cinnamon
1½ teaspoons (8 ml) ground
    ginger
  1 teaspoon (5 ml) salt
  1 teaspoon (5 ml) baking soda
  1 teaspoon (5 ml) ground
    allspice
  1 cup (250 ml) butter or
    margarine, softened
  1 cup (250 ml) firmly packed
    brown sugar
  1 teaspoon (5 ml) vanilla
 ⅓ cup (83 ml) molasses
  2 eggs
    Assorted cookie nonpareils
      and colored sugar
      (optional)
    Prepared creamy or gel-type
      frostings in tubes (optional)
    Assorted candies and grated
      chocolate (optional)

1. Place flour, cinnamon, ginger, salt, baking soda and allspice in medium bowl; stir to combine. Set aside.

2. Beat butter, sugar and vanilla in large bowl with electric mixer at medium speed about 5 minutes or until light and fluffy, scraping down side of bowl once. (Mixture will not be completely smooth.) Beat in molasses and eggs until well blended, scraping down side of bowl once.

3. Beat in flour mixture at low speed until well blended. Divide dough into 3 equal pieces. Flatten each piece of dough into a disc; wrap in plastic wrap. Refrigerate at least 2 hours or up to 24 hours.

4. Preheat oven to 350°F (180°C). Grease large cookie sheets; set aside.

5. Working with 1 piece of dough at a time, place dough on lightly floured surface. Roll out dough with lightly floured rolling pin to ⅛-inch (3 mm) thickness. Keep remaining dough refrigerated.

6. Cut out dough with 3-inch (7.5 cm) bear-shaped cookie cutters. Place cookies 1 inch (2.5 cm) apart on prepared cookie sheets. Roll pieces of dough scraps into balls and ropes to make eyes, noses and to decorate bears. Decorate bears with nonpareils, if desired.

7. Bake 10 minutes or until bottoms of cookies are golden brown. Let stand on cookie sheet 1 minute. Remove cookies with spatula to wire rack; cool.

8. Pipe or spread frosting on cooled cookies to decorate. Decorate with assorted nonpareils, colored sugar, assorted candies and/or grated chocolate. Store tightly covered at room temperature.
Makes about 3½ dozen cookies

Step 5. Rolling out dough.

Step 6. Cutting out dough with cookie cutter.

Step 8. Decorating bears.

COOKING CLASS
GARNISHES

562 CLASS NOTES

564 FRUIT

572 VEGETABLE

582 SWEET

590 MISCELLANEOUS

Clockwise from top left: Butter Shapes
(page 594), Tortilla Cups *(page 595)* and
Pastry Cutouts *(page 593)*

CLASS NOTES

Making food look as good as it tastes is a goal of many cooks. Yet, many hesitate to add the special finishing touch that can make all the difference. If this sounds like you, this is just what you've been looking for. This section offers more than 30 creative garnish ideas sure to add that professional look to whatever you serve.

Page through this colorful selection of garnishes and discover just how simple it is to transform common ingredients such as carrots, apples, gumdrops and chocolate into that extra-special accent. For example, bell pepper triangles can add much-needed excitement to grilled meats. Or, delight your dinner guests with their own elegant caramel rose. Need some help enticing little ones into eating their good-for-you salad? Zucchini butterflies are sure to guarantee a clean plate. And finally, nothing is more irresistible than a decadent cheesecake topped with an array of luscious chocolate leaves.

The easy-to-follow step-by-step directions and how-to photographs included with each garnish make this section as much fun to page through as it is easy to use. Whether a novice in the kitchen or an experienced cook, you'll surprise everyone—even yourself—with the professional results. To further assist you, our handy glossary lists many of the kitchen tools you'll need in order to re-create each of these eye-catching garnishes. And, to make your life even easier, we've included some time-saving tricks of the trade to further ensure foolproof results every time.

What's more, each garnish includes a list of possible applications for the occasion at hand—whether it's the fanciest dinner, a children's birthday party or a casual outdoor barbecue.

If you enjoy cooking and presenting eye-catching dishes, then this section is sure to provide you with hours of enjoyment. With a little practice, you'll soon be duplicating with ease those fabulous garnishes seen in the finest restaurants and bakeries. So, grab your tools and get ready to garnish—there's no limit to your creativity.

SELECT THE RIGHT GARNISH

When choosing a garnish, pick one that enhances and complements the color and texture of the food. Use a bright garnish to perk up a light-colored food. Accent a soft-textured food with a crisp garnish.

Be sure to consider the size of the garnish as well. Team a large garnish with a tray or large platter of food. If the food contains a mixture of ingredients, keep the garnish simple.

Remember, garnishes should enhance, not overshadow or hide the food's beauty and flavor.

BEFORE YOU START

Look for fruits and vegetables that are evenly shaped, blemish-free and at the right stage of ripeness. In general, the firmer the fruit or vegetable, the easier it is to work with and the longer the finished garnish will stay fresh and attractive.

Be sure the knives you use are sharp. A sharp knife allows you to make precise cuts because it doesn't need to be pushed or forced. Sharpen your knives yourself with a sharpening steel or have a cutlery store sharpen them for you.

MAKE GARNISHES AHEAD

Whenever possible, make garnishes before you get involved in the final tasks of meal preparation. When you're giving a party, you won't have much time for creating garnishes at the last minute. (Be sure to store the finished garnish properly and add it to the food just before serving.)

• Most vegetable garnishes may be made ahead, then placed in airtight containers or wrapped in clear plastic wrap and refrigerated until the next day.

• To keep fruit garnishes fresh, wrap them in clear plastic wrap and store them in the refrigerator. When working with apples or other fruits that darken when cut, generously brush the cut surfaces of the fruit with lemon juice before wrapping and refrigerating.

• Place garnishes that need to dry or firm-up in a cool, dry place for several hours or overnight.

• For extra crispness, let chilled garnishes stay in the ice water an extra hour or two. Or, thoroughly drain the garnishes, then wrap in plastic wrap and refrigerate overnight.

TOOLS FOR GARNISHING

Just as you rely on the equipment in your kitchen to help you turn out a good meal, you'll also need a few tools to create spectacular garnishes. Here are some of the most common items:

Apple cutter/corer: This wheel-shaped gadget is great for cutting vegetables, such as carrots, as well as apples.

Broiler pan: For best results when broiling high-fat foods, such as bacon, make sure the pan you use has a rack with grooves or holes that allow the fat to drip down into a lower pan.

Brushes: Standard pastry brushes work for most garnishing, but for precise or delicate chores, a child's small paintbrush is best.

Butter curler and butter paddles: Both of these help you shape butter. Use the curler to form delicate butter curls and the paddles for butter balls.

Citrus stripper: Use this tool to cut a thin strip of peel from citrus fruit or other fresh produce.

Cutting board: No matter what type of cutting board you have, be sure to keep it clean. Clean it with soap and water, then disinfect it with a mild solution of chlorine bleach and hot water after every use.

Decorating bag or parchment cone: Use these items for piping designs and other cake-decorating tasks.

Decorating tips: The tips you'll use most often are writing tips, star tips, rose tips and leaf tips. Start out by purchasing one of each type. Then add to your collection whenever you need an additional tip for a new garnish.

Deep-fat-frying thermometer: Be sure to use the type of thermometer that is designed to measure the high temperatures of cooking oil used in frying.

Doilies and stencils: These are used for transferring designs to the tops of cakes, cheesecakes and other desserts.

Grapefruit knife: The jagged edges on this knife come in handy for many garnishing tasks.

Hand grater: A grater with at least one section for fine pieces and another section for larger shreds is the most practical.

Hors d'oeuvre cutters or small cookie cutters: These are sold in most cookware shops. Choose the shapes you think you'll use most often.

Knives: Sharp knives are a must. The knives you'll use most often are a *chef's knife* for cutting large items, such as watermelons; a *utility knife* for medium-sized foods, such as pineapples or cantaloupes; and a *paring knife* for all-purpose cutting.

Melon baller: This handy tool comes in a variety of sizes. The one that's the most versatile is the l-inch- (2.5 cm) diameter size.

Scissors: A small pair is ideal for snipping small items, such as green onion tops. Kitchen scissors or poultry shears are better for large, tough jobs.

Skewers and toothpicks: For garnishing, keep a supply of wooden toothpicks as well as 6- and 10-inch (15 and 25 cm) wooden skewers on hand. Occasionally you may need a metal skewer. Choose one about 8 inches (20 cm) long.

Sturdy zipper-style plastic food storage bag: For piping, select a bag with a self-closing seal that is typically used for freezing. The extra weight of this type of bag makes the task easier.

Vegetable peeler: The swivel-type works best—just make sure it's sharp.

Wire strainer or sieve: This bowl-shaped tool made from wire mesh is great for sifting or sprinkling powdered sugar or cocoa over foods as well as for draining foods.

Sugared Fruit

At holiday time, spruce up tortes, fruitcakes or steamed puddings with a cascade of sugared grapes or cranberries.

For a cocktail party, arrange trays of sliced cheeses and smoked sausage. Trim the trays with an assortment of sugared fruit.

Grapes (in small clusters), cranberries, bing cherries and/or blueberries
Egg white
Sugar
Small nontoxic leaves (optional)

EQUIPMENT:
Paper towels
Small bowl
Fork
Small, clean paintbrush or pastry brush
Waxed paper
Teaspoon

1. Wash fruit. Gently blot dry with paper towels or let air-dry on paper towels.

2. Beat egg white in small bowl with fork until foamy.

3. Brush egg white onto each piece of fruit with paintbrush or pastry brush, coating all sides of fruit thinly and evenly.

4. Place fruit on waxed paper that has been covered with sugar. Sprinkle a light even coating of sugar over fruit with teaspoon. If any areas are not coated, repeat layers of egg white and sugar.

5. Let sugared fruit stand at room temperature until coating is dry. Trim with nontoxic leaves, if desired.

Step 2. Beating egg white.

Step 3. Brushing fruit with egg white.

Step 4. Sprinkling fruit with sugar.

Scored Citrus Slices

A couple of scored citrus slices along with a sprig of fresh parsley make an eye-catching garnish for your favorite fish.

Trim a Waldorf salad or any other fruit salad by tucking a border of scored orange slices around the edge of the salad.

To make a bowl of punch look party-special, float scored citrus slices in a citrus-based punch or sangria.

Drop half of a scored orange slice into a mug and fill it with hot spiced cider—wonderful on cold winter days!

Lemon, lime, orange or grapefruit

EQUIPMENT:
Citrus stripper or grapefruit
    spoon
Cutting board
Paring knife

1. Cut groove in peel of fruit with citrus stripper or tip of grapefruit spoon, cutting lengthwise from stem end to other end. Continue to cut grooves about ¼ to ½ inch (6 mm to 1.25 cm) apart until completely around fruit.

2. Place fruit on cutting board; thinly slice crosswise with paring knife.

Step 1. Cutting grooves in peel.

Step 2. Cutting fruit into slices.

Cherry Flowers

Dress up a molded cherry salad by spooning a little vanilla yogurt over each serving and centering a maraschino cherry flower on top.

Add a hint of color to individual servings of rice pudding by trimming each one with a red cherry flower and a small mint sprig.

For Christmas gift-giving, drizzle your favorite homemade breads, coffeecakes or cookies with powdered-sugar icing. Then decorate them with red and green candied-cherry flowers.

Maraschino cherry or candied cherry
Tiny piece of candied fruit or peel (optional)

EQUIPMENT:
Cutting board
Paring knife

1. Place cherry on cutting board. Cut cherry into 6 wedges with paring knife, being careful to leave bottom ⅓ of cherry uncut.

2. Use tip of knife to gently pull cherry segments out to resemble flower petals.

3. If desired, place tiny piece of candied fruit or peel in center of flower.

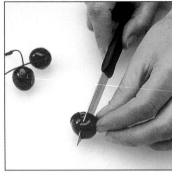

Step 1. Partially cutting through cherry to make wedges.

Step 2. Separating wedges to resemble flower.

Lemon/Lime Butterflies

Having a Mexican fiesta? Garnish each dinner plate with a lemon or lime butterfly and your guests will say "olé!"

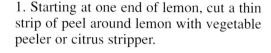

Add a flourish to baked cod or halibut by serving each portion with a delicate lemon butterfly.

Get the kids to eat their vegetables by topping each serving with a lemon or lime butterfly.

Lemon

EQUIPMENT:
Vegetable peeler or citrus stripper
Cutting board
Paring knife

1. Starting at one end of lemon, cut a thin strip of peel around lemon with vegetable peeler or citrus stripper.

2. Repeat, starting at other end.

3. Place both strips on cutting board. Using paring knife, cut peel into very thin strips, each about 1 inch (2.5 cm) long.

4. Place lemon on cutting board. Cut off ends at place where peel has been stripped; discard ends. Thinly slice remaining lemon crosswise.

5. Cut each slice into thirds.

6. To make each butterfly, arrange 2 lemon wedges on desired food or plate, with points of wedges touching at center.

7. To make antennae, carefully place 2 strips of peel where pieces touch.

Lime Butterfly Variation: Substitute lime for lemon; continue as directed.

Step 1. Cutting strip of peel.

Step 3. Cutting peel into thin strips.

Step 5. Cutting slice into thirds.

Step 7. Adding antennae.

Strawberry Fans

Strawberry shortcake, one of America's all-time favorite desserts, is made extra-special when it's sporting a dollop of whipped cream and a strawberry fan.

Make cream puffs, eclairs or neapolitans all the more irresistible by tucking a strawberry fan or two into the base of each pastry before you serve it.

Nothing beats the summer doldrums like a strawberry shake made with fresh strawberries and topped with a strawberry fan.

Strawberries with tops attached

EQUIPMENT:
Cutting board
Paring knife

1. Place strawberry on cutting board with pointed end facing you.

2. Make 4 or 5 lengthwise cuts from pointed end of strawberry not quite to stem end, using paring knife.

3. Fan slices apart slightly, being careful to keep all slices attached to cap. Place on plate or food to secure in position.

Step 2. Partially slicing strawberry.

Step 3. Fanning strawberry.

Melon Balls with Leaves

Create a decorative border of melon balls and leaves around the base of a cheese ball or molded fruit salad.

For a light dessert, arrange melon balls and leaves on individual dessert plates. Drizzle with strawberry or raspberry purée. Serve with macaroons or butter cookies.

For a summertime buffet, dress up platters of cold sliced ham and turkey with clusters of melon balls and leaves.

Top an ice cream pie or frozen mousse dessert with a grouping of melon balls and leaves.

Honeydew melon and/or cantaloupe

EQUIPMENT:
Cutting board
Chef's knife
Large spoon
Paring knife
Toothpick
Melon baller
Waxed paper

1. Place melon on cutting board; cut in half lengthwise with chef's knife. Scoop out seeds with spoon; discard seeds.

2. To make leaves, cut several thin slices from 1 melon half. Peel slices with paring knife; discard peel.

3. Cut leaf shapes out of slices with paring knife. (Small leaves should be about ⅝ inch (1.5 cm) long and ¾ inch (1.8 cm) wide. Large leaves should be about 1½ inches (3.75 cm) long and ⅝ inch (1.5 cm wide.)

4. Score vein pattern in leaves, using tip of toothpick.

5. To make melon balls, place cup of melon baller against flesh of another melon half. Press firmly on melon baller to cut into flesh. Rotate melon baller until cup faces up. Remove melon baller; invert onto waxed paper to remove melon ball. Repeat to make additional melon balls.

6. Place leaf on desired food or plate. Nestle melon balls against end of leaf.

Step 2. Peeling melon slices.

Step 3. Cutting out leaf shapes.

Step 4. Scoring pattern in leaves.

Step 5. Making melon balls.

Apple Cups

For an inventive presentation, mound carrot-raisin salad into apple cups; serve on a bed of lemon leaves or leaf lettuce.

❧

As a first course for breakfast or brunch, serve a fresh fruit medley in apple cups.

❧

When the breakfast menu features a basket of bagels, serve whipped cream cheese in an apple cup right alongside.

Apple
Orange or lemon juice

EQUIPMENT:
Cutting board
Paring knife
Grapefruit spoon or metal
    teaspoon
Pastry brush

1. If necessary to get apple to stand level, place apple on its side on cutting board and cut a thin slice from bottom of apple with paring knife.

2. For sawtooth edge, hold knife at a 45° angle and pierce middle of apple with tip of knife; insert knife halfway into side of apple. Form upside-down "V" by making a second cut, inserting knife halfway into apple to end of first cut. Repeat cutting "V"s until completely around apple. Carefully separate apple halves.

3. Using grapefruit spoon or teaspoon, remove centers from apple halves, leaving ½-inch-thick (1.25 cm) shells.

4. Using pastry brush, brush insides of apple cups generously with orange or lemon juice to prevent browning.

Step 1. Cutting thin slice from bottom of apple.

Step 2. Making sawtooth cut around apple.

Step 3. Hollowing out center of apple.

Lime/Lemon Wedges

Float lime and/or lemon wedges in a bowl of citrus punch.

For an easy yet elegant dessert, place scoops of lime sherbet in pretty glasses; trim each serving with a lime or lemon wedge and a sprig of mint.

Arrange two or three lime or lemon wedges in the center of a key lime or other citrus-based cream pie.

Perk up a bowl of buttered rice or rice pilaf with a lemon wedge garnish.

Lime

EQUIPMENT:
Cutting board
Paring knife

1. Place lime on cutting board; cut in half lengthwise with paring knife.

2. Place fruit half, cut side down, on cutting board. Working in center of the top of fruit, cut out a thin, shallow wedge from fruit, being careful not to cut all the way into fruit. Remove wedge; set aside.

3. Using a gentle sawing motion, continue cutting progressively larger wedges (each ⅛ inch/3 mm larger than the last) for a total of 4 or 5 wedges. Remove each wedge as it is cut.

4. Repeat with remaining half of fruit.

Lemon Wedge Variation: Substitute lemon for lime; continue as directed.

Step 2. Cutting shallow wedge from fruit.

Step 3. Cutting progressively larger wedges.

Zucchini/Summer Squash Flowers

Bring a heaping platter of spaghetti and meatballs to the table complete with a zucchini flower or two.

Accent the center of a spinach or broccoli quiche with a zucchini or summer squash flower.

For an elegant Oriental appetizer, arrange one or two egg rolls on a dish with side-by-side pools of sweet-and-sour and mustard sauces. Round out the dish with a zucchini or summer squash flower

Zucchini

EQUIPMENT:
Cutting board
Paring knife
Vegetable peeler
Wooden toothpicks

1. Place zucchini on its side on cutting board. Cut off both ends with paring knife; discard ends.

2. Cut thin lengthwise slices from zucchini with vegetable peeler, making sure there is green peel on both sides of each strip. Continue cutting slices until you reach seeds.

3. Turn zucchini, leaving about ½ inch (1.25 cm) of green peel. Repeat cutting of slices. Repeat turning and cutting once more.

4. Cut ends off slices with paring knife to make even.

5. Make cuts about 1/16 inch (1.5 mm) apart along 1 long edge of each slice, cutting almost to opposite edge.

6. Roll up each slice from 1 short end.

7. Insert small piece of wooden toothpick through each base to secure rolls.

8. Set flowers upright; spread slightly to open.

Summer Squash Variation: Substitute yellow summer squash for zucchini; continue as directed.

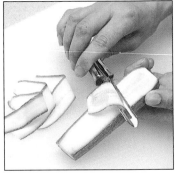

Step 2. Slicing zucchini.

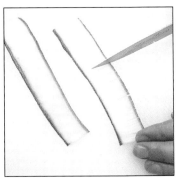

Step 5. Cutting along side of slice.

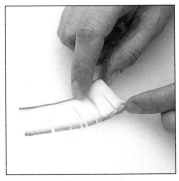

Step 6. Rolling up slice.

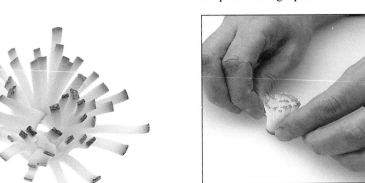

Step 7. Securing flower with toothpick.

Bell Pepper Triangles

Float a bell pepper triangle or two on the top of your favorite creamy soup.

Create an attractive accent for steaks or chops by making bell pepper triangles using green, red and yellow peppers. Arrange a triangle of each color on each dinner plate along with the meat.

Serve an appetizer dip with pepper triangles instead of chips.

To dress up main-dish salads, arrange four or five pepper triangles on individual salad plates; top with a scoop of tuna or chicken salad.

Green, red and/or yellow bell pepper
Bowl of ice water (optional)

EQUIPMENT:
Cutting board
Paring knife

1. Stand bell pepper, stem side up, on cutting board. Cut a slice, about ¼ inch (6 mm) thick, off each side of pepper with paring knife. Remove membrane and seeds; discard.

2. Cut each pepper slice into a rectangle 1¼ inches (3 cm) long and ¾ inch (1.8 cm) wide.

3. Starting ⅓ of the way from 1 long side of each rectangle, cut down remaining length of rectangle, ending ¼ inch (6 mm) from other end. Turn rectangle around; repeat on other side.

4. To make each triangle, hold the 2 outer corners of a rectangle and bring both corners to center.

5. Overlap ends to secure. If desired, place triangles in ice water to crispen. Remove; drain well.

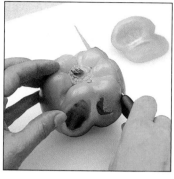

Step 1. Cutting off sides of pepper.

Step 3. Making cuts in rectangle.

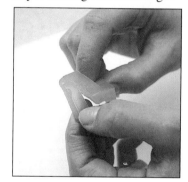

Step 4. Twisting cut rectangle to shape into triangle.

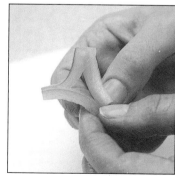

Step 5. Overlapping ends to secure triangle.

Carrot Stars

Coax the children into eating their carrots by cutting the carrots into stars rather than simple sticks or rounds.

Create colorful canapés by spreading crackers or party rye bread slices with your favorite cheese spread. Top with carrot stars.

Frost the top of a molded vegetable salad with a thin layer of whipped cream cheese. Decorate with carrot stars.

Large carrots

EQUIPMENT:
Vegetable peeler
Cutting board
Paring knife
Citrus stripper (optional)

1. Peel carrot with vegetable peeler. Place carrot on cutting board. Cut off carrot with paring knife where carrot begins to have a diameter of less than ½ inch (1.25 cm); discard thin end. Cut off stem end of carrot; discard. Standing carrot on wide flat end, cut a thin lengthwise slice from 1 side of carrot piece.

2. Repeat 4 more times, turning carrot slightly after each cut, to make a pentagon shape with 5 equal sides.

3. Cut a groove in center of each flat side using citrus stripper or tip of vegetable peeler.

4. Cut carrot crosswise into thin slices with paring knife to form stars.

Step 1. Cutting first thin lengthwise slice from carrot.

Step 2. Cutting carrot into pentagon shape.

Step 3. Cutting groove in each flat side.

Green Onion/Celery Curls

To make a chilled pasta main dish look elegant, serve it on your prettiest salad plates with a green onion or celery curl on the side.

Tuck a green onion curl in a bowl of barbecue sauce and let your guests use it to slather on additional sauce for their cooked ribs or barbecued beef sandwiches.

No Oriental meal is complete without a heaping bowl of rice. Dress up the bowl with a delicate celery or green onion curl.

Green onion or celery rib
Bowl of cold water
Bowl of ice water

EQUIPMENT:
Cutting board
Paring knife

1. **For green onion curl,** place green onion on cutting board. Cut off roots with paring knife; discard roots. Cut onion crosswise into 1 (3-inch/7.5 cm) piece, leaving about 1½ inches (3.75 cm) of both the white onion and green top portions.

2. Make lengthwise cut from white end of onion almost to center of piece; repeat to slice end into thin slivers.

3. Place onion in cold water (*not ice water*). Let stand 30 seconds or until ends curl slightly. Remove from water; drain well.

4. **For celery curl,** trim ends from celery rib; cut into 3-inch (7.5 cm) pieces. Cut each piece lengthwise in half. Cut into slivers as directed in step 2 above. Place in ice water and refrigerate until ends curl.

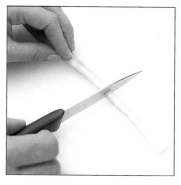

Step 1. Cutting 3-inch (7.5 cm) piece from onion.

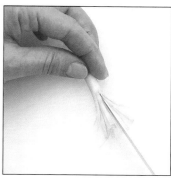

Step 2. Cutting end of onion into slivers.

Step 4. Cutting end of celery into slivers.

Radish Fans

Add radish fans to your next tossed green salad.

Team a radish fan with some fresh basil leaves—use to trim a dinner plate of chicken cacciatore.

For a party, dress up a plate of nachos with a radish fan along with a sprig of parsley.

Large radish
Bowl of ice water

EQUIPMENT:
Cutting board
Paring knife

1. Place radish on cutting board. Cut off top and bottom tip of radish with paring knife; discard.

2. Cut parallel ⅛-inch-thick (1.5 mm) crosswise slices about ¾ of the way into radish, making sure not to cut all the way through radish.

3. Place radish in ice water. Place in refrigerator several hours or until radish fans out. Remove; drain well.

Step 1. Cutting off ends of radish.

Step 2. Partially cutting radish into thin slices.

Bell Pepper Cup

Use a pepper cup in place of a bowl when serving creamy dips or guacamole. Or, use it to hold celery and carrot sticks as an edible centerpiece.

For an inventive presentation, fill pepper cups with single servings of tuna, egg or ham salad. Serve on a bed of red-tipped romaine.

Mold individual servings of tomato aspic in pepper cups. Serve them as a first course topped with mayonnaise or sour cream.

Large red, green or yellow bell pepper

EQUIPMENT:
Cutting board
Paring knife

1. Place bell pepper on cutting board. Cut about ½ inch (1.25 cm) around stem with paring knife; discard stem.

2. Remove and discard membrane and seeds.

3. Wash pepper under cold running water. Invert to drain completely.

4. If necessary, cut a thin slice off bottom of pepper to create flat surface. Stand pepper up. Fill as desired.

Step 1. Removing stem end of pepper.

Step 2. Removing membrane and seeds.

Step 4. Cutting off bottom of pepper to make level.

Tomato Roses

A delicate tomato rose is just the thing to spark up a simple bowl of cottage cheese.

Is fettucine Alfredo your idea of culinary bliss? Make it a notch better by adding a tomato rose.

When serving a large whole fish, add a little color to the platter with tomato roses.

Firm, ripe tomato
Tiny fresh mint leaves (optional)

EQUIPMENT:
Cutting board
Paring knife

1. Place tomato on cutting board. Remove core from tomato with paring knife.

2. Cut a very thin slice from bottom of tomato; discard slice.

3. Starting at top of tomato, peel tomato with knife by cutting a continuous narrow strip of peel in a spiral fashion horizontally around entire tomato, using a gentle sawing motion.

4. Place strip, either flesh or peel side up, on cutting board. Starting at end of strip where you started cutting, wrap strip around itself to form a coil.

5. Tuck end of strip underneath coil to secure. Tuck 2 or 3 mint leaves at base of tomato rose, if desired.

Step 1. Removing core from tomato.

Step 3. Peeling tomato.

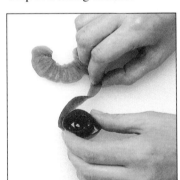

Step 4. Rolling peel into coil.

Step 5. Tucking end of strip under coil to secure.

Fluted Mushrooms

Combine one or two fluted mushrooms with a sprig of watercress to trim dinner plates when you serve London broil or other beef dishes.

Cap the ends of chicken kabobs with fluted mushrooms.

Garnish your favorite pâté with several fluted mushrooms.

Large fresh white mushroom cap
Small bowl of lemon juice

EQUIPMENT:
Clean, damp cloth
Paper towel
Cutting board
Paring knife

1. Gently wipe mushroom clean with damp cloth or rinse lightly with water. Gently pat dry with paper towel. Place mushroom on cutting board. Remove or trim stem with paring knife; discard.

2. With paring knife held at a 45° angle, begin at top center of mushroom cap and cut a thin curved groove to edge of cap. Turn mushroom. Continue cutting out curved grooves, making a total of 6 to 8 evenly spaced thin grooves.

3. Once all cuts have been made, carefully remove each triangular-shaped piece with tip of knife; discard.

4. To help keep fluted mushroom from turning brown, dip into lemon juice.

Step 2. Cutting grooves in mushroom cap.

Step 3. Removing wedges from grooves.

Zucchini/Summer Squash Butterflies

A dish of plain sliced tomatoes can be a thing of beauty when it's accented by a zucchini butterfly.

Layer zucchini butterflies with orange slices—a perfect complement to a platter of roast duck.

Gently slip zucchini butterflies on top of bowls of seafood bisque.

Small to medium zucchini
Bowl of ice water (optional)
Alfalfa sprouts or bean sprouts

EQUIPMENT:
Cutting board
Paring knife
Fork

1. Place zucchini on cutting board. Cut off both ends with paring knife; discard ends.

2. To score zucchini, draw tines of fork lengthwise down zucchini. Repeat scoring all around zucchini.

3. About ⅛ inch (3 mm) from 1 end of zucchini, make a crosswise cut about ⅔ of the way into zucchini. About ⅛ inch (3 mm) from this cut, make another crosswise cut all the way through zucchini.

4. Place slices, cut side down, on cutting board. Trim uncut side of slice about ⅛ inch (3 mm) in from edge to form a flat base.

5. To open wings, stand slice on flat base; gently spread rounded sides apart. (If desired, place slices in ice water to soften so wings can be spread further apart. Remove; drain well.) Repeat to make additional butterflies.

6. Position each butterfly on desired food or plate. To make antennae, tuck 2 sprouts into 1 end of each butterfly.

Summer Squash Variation: Substitute yellow summer squash for zucchini; continue as directed.

Step 2. Scoring zucchini.

Step 3. Slicing zucchini.

Step 4. Trimming slices to form base.

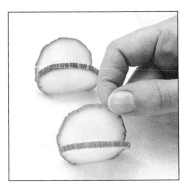

Step 5. Spreading wings.

Chili Flowers

Spruce up a plate of nachos or a layered Mexican dip with a couple of chili flowers.

Ladle up heaping bowls of gumbo or your favorite main-dish soup or stew and tuck a chili flower in at the side.

A chili flower is the perfect garnish for just about anything Oriental. How about trying it with sweet-and-sour pork?

Small red, yellow or green chili
pepper or jalapeño pepper
Bowl of ice water

EQUIPMENT:
Cutting board
Paring knife
Plastic or rubber gloves

1. Place pepper on cutting board. Cut off narrow tip with paring knife; discard tip. *(Because oils from hot peppers can burn your skin, wear plastic or rubber gloves when working with peppers.)*

2. For each flower start at tip of 1 pepper and make thin, lengthwise cut toward stem, making sure not to cut all the way through stem end. Repeat making lengthwise cuts all around pepper.

3. Rinse pepper under cold running water to remove seeds.

4. Place pepper in ice water. Refrigerate several hours or until pepper opens. Remove from water; drain well.

Step 1. Cutting off tip of pepper.

Step 2. Making lengthwise cuts in pepper.

Step 3. Rinsing pepper to remove seeds.

Chocolate Shapes

For a truly sensational dessert, fan several slices of poached apple, peach or pear in a pool of stirred custard. Top with chocolate shape.

Nothing's better than fresh strawberry pie, you say? How about fresh strawberry pie decorated with a chocolate shape?

For a quick finish to cream puffs or eclairs, top each frosted pastry with a chocolate shape.

Unsweetened, semisweet or milk chocolate (squares or bars)

EQUIPMENT:
Cutting board
Paring knife
Glass measuring cup
Small saucepan
Rubber spatula
Small zipper-style plastic food storage bag
Kitchen scissors
Waxed paper

1. Place chocolate on cutting board; shave it into small pieces with paring knife.

2. Place shavings in measuring cup. Fill saucepan ¼ full (about 1 inch/2.5 cm deep) with warm *(not hot)* water. Place measuring cup in water to melt chocolate, stirring frequently with rubber spatula until smooth. *(Be careful not to get any water into chocolate.)* Remove measuring cup from saucepan. Let chocolate cool slightly.

3. Fill plastic bag about ½ full with melted chocolate.

4. Seal bag securely. Cut small corner off bottom of plastic bag with scissors.

5. Position sealed end of bag in your writing hand. Position fingers near opening of bag; place other hand under bag to guide it.

6. While gently squeezing bag, guide opening just above waxed paper to pipe chocolate in a steady flow, making a variety of small shapes. Stop squeezing and then lift bag at end of each shape. Create flowers, hearts, Christmas trees, lattice shapes or any lacy pattern.

7. Let shapes stand in cool, dry place until chocolate is firm. *(Do not chill in refrigerator.)* Gently peel shapes off waxed paper. Store in cool, dry place until ready to use.

Step 1. Shaving chocolate.

Step 3. Filling bag with melted chocolate.

Step 4. Cutting small corner off bottom of bag.

Step 6. Making shapes.

Sifted Cocoa/Sugar Designs

A light dusting of powdered sugar brings out the best in spice cake, gingerbread or your favorite cheesecake.

An unfrosted nut torte just cries out for a powdered-sugar or cocoa-powder design.

Cheesecake, torte or cake
**Unsweetened cocoa powder or
    powdered sugar**

EQUIPMENT:
Kitchen scissors
Waxed paper
Doily with large pattern
Large spoon
Fine-mesh sieve
Skewers or toothpicks

1. With scissors, cut waxed paper into strips, each 2 to 3 inches (5 to 7.5 cm) wide and 5 to 6 inches (12.5 to 15 cm) long. Tuck strips under dessert on serving plate to keep plate clean while dusting with cocoa powder or powdered sugar.

2. Place doily on top of cheesecake, torte or cake.

3. Spoon cocoa powder or powdered sugar into sieve. (Cocoa powder works well for light-colored desserts; powdered sugar is best for dark-colored desserts.)

4. Holding sieve over dessert, gently tap sieve with hand to sift cocoa powder or sugar in an even layer over entire surface.

5. Carefully remove waxed paper strips from around bottom edge of dessert. Remove doily from top of dessert with skewer or toothpick.

6. **For paper strips variation,** omit doily. Cut clean sheets of paper into 8 to 10 strips, each strip ½ to ¾ inch (1.25 to 1.8 cm) wide and long enough to fit across top of surface you wish to cover. Arrange paper strips in crisscross pattern on top of cake, torte or cheesecake. Continue as directed in steps 3 through 5.

Step 2. Placing doily on dessert.

Step 4. Sifting cocoa over doily.

Step 5. Removing doily.

Step 6. Arranging paper strips on top of dessert.

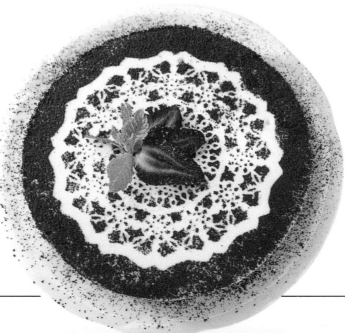

Feathered Icings

For truly elegant brownies or other bar cookies, frost them first with one color of frosting, then feather in a contrasting color of frosting.

Celebrate the holidays with feathered icings tinted to reflect the colors of the season—red and green for Christmas, red and white for Valentine's Day or pink and yellow for Easter. The choices are endless!

For added excitement, use two different colors of contrasting icing. For example, red and blue feathered icings on a cake spread with white frosting is perfect for any of the patriotic holidays.

Desired icing
Cake, brownies or cookies
Desired icing of a contrasting color

EQUIPMENT:
Narrow metal spatula or small knife
Parchment cone or decorating bag (for icing)
Kitchen scissors (optional)
Decorator writing tip (No. 2, 3 or 4)
Tablespoon

1. Spread desired icing over a cake, brownies or cookies of your choice using a metal spatula or knife.

2. If using a parchment cone, cut about ½ inch (1.25 cm) off bottom point of cone with scissors. Position writing tip into opening in decorating bag or parchment cone. (If necessary, cut larger opening in parchment to get tip to fit.)

3. Fill bag or cone about half full with contrasting icing using tablespoon. Squeeze down frosting from open end of bag or cone. Place open end of bag or cone in palm of your writing hand. Position fingers near opening of bag or near tip of cone. Position other hand under bag or cone to guide tip.

4. Hold bag or cone at a 45° angle just above food. While gently squeezing bag, guide tip to pipe line across top of iced cake or cookie. When you reach end of line, stop squeezing and then lift bag. Repeat to pipe parallel lines.

5. Holding knife or spatula at right angle to parallel lines, draw knife through lines at regular intervals, always pulling utensil in the *same* direction.

6. Or, for a different look, draw knife through every other line in *opposite* directions.

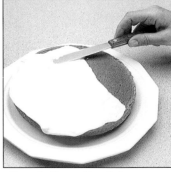

Step 1. Spreading icing on top of cake.

Step 4. Making parallel lines on top of cake.

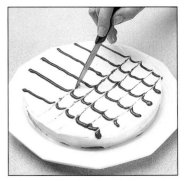

Step 5. Feathering frosting in *same* direction.

Step 6. Feathering frosting in *opposite* directions.

Chocolate Cutouts

For your child's next birthday party, place a chocolate cutout alongside each serving of cake. Have the child help you by choosing the cookie or hors d'oeuvre cutter shapes they like best.

Whip up treats for a Halloween party by topping orange-frosted cupcakes with tiny chocolate cutouts just before serving.

Semisweet chocolate (squares or bars)
Shortening

EQUIPMENT:
Cutting board
Paring knife
Glass measuring cup
Small saucepan
Rubber spatula
Baking sheet, pan or dish, marble slab or other heat-resistant flat surface
Waxed paper
Metal spatula
Hors d'oeuvre or small cookie cutters

1. Prepare melted chocolate as directed in Chocolate Leaves (page 587, steps 1 through 3). Let chocolate cool slightly.

2. Line baking sheet with waxed paper. Pour melted chocolate onto prepared baking sheet; quickly spread chocolate into a thin layer (⅛ to ¼ inch/3 mm to 6 mm thick) with metal spatula.

3. Let stand in cool, dry place until chocolate is just firm. *(Do not chill in refrigerator.)* Cut chocolate into shapes with hors d'oeuvre or cookie cutters, placing cutters as close together as possible.

4. Carefully remove cutouts with metal spatula. Store in cool, dry place until ready to use.

Note: For ease in cutting chocolate cutouts, slightly warm hors d'oeuvre or cookie cutters with hands before cutting.

Step 2. Spreading chocolate onto baking sheet.

Step 3. Cutting out shapes.

Step 4. Removing cutouts.

Gumdrop Bow

Festive green and red gumdrop bows add a hint of Christmas sparkle to frosted quick bread loaves. Try them on banana, date, orange or pumpkin breads.

Embellish a molded gelatin salad with a gumdrop bow in a matching or contrasting color.

Adorn the top of Boston cream pie with a pretty orange gumdrop bow.

Sugar
8 to 10 small gumdrops

EQUIPMENT:
Cutting board
Rolling pin
Paring knife

1. Sprinkle sugar on cutting board. To make a gumdrop strip, flatten 8 to 10 gumdrops with your thumb. Place, with ends overlapping slightly, on sugared board in 2 rows of 4 to 5 gumdrops each. Sprinkle gumdrops with additional sugar.

2. Roll flattened gumdrops into a 6 x 3-inch (15 x 7.5 cm) strip with rolling pin, turning strip over frequently to coat with sugar.

3. Trim edges of gumdrop piece with paring knife; discard edges. Cut remaining piece into ½-inch-wide (1.25 cm) strips.

4. Cut two 3-inch (7.5 cm) lengths, four 2½-inch (6 cm) lengths and one 1½-inch (3.75 cm) length from strips.

5. To assemble bow, fold both 3-inch (7.5 cm) lengths in half to form 2 loops; place end to end to form base of bow. Press ends together to secure.

6. Fold over 2 of the 2½-inch (6 cm) lengths; place end to end on top of first loops, pressing gently to secure.

7. Wrap 1½-inch (3.75 cm) length crosswise around center of bow to conceal ends of loops. Press gently to secure.

8. Trim ends of remaining two 2½-inch (6 cm) lengths at an angle with knife. Place these lengths under center of bow in an upside-down "V" to make ends of bow. Press gently to attach to bow.

Step 1. Placing flattened gumdrops in overlapping rows.

Step 2. Rolling out gumdrops to flatten completely.

Step 5. Placing 2 loops together to form base of bow.

Step 7. Making center of bow.

Chocolate Leaves

To show off your favorite chocolate cake, place it on a pedestal cake stand. Tuck chocolate leaves around the base of the cake to create an eye-catching border.

For a dramatic cheesecake presentation, arrange three chocolate leaves in the center of your favorite cheesecake. Top the leaves with a rose of your choice—either real or one made from caramels, icing or gumdrops.

Wind up a festive meal with a light, yet elegant, dessert. Place a scoop of lemon ice or orange sherbet in a fancy dessert dish. Then add a chocolate leaf or two to each serving.

Semisweet chocolate (squares or bars)
Shortening
Nontoxic leaves, such as rose, lemon or camellia

EQUIPMENT:
Cutting board
Paring knife
Glass measuring cup
Small saucepan
Rubber spatula
Paper towels
Small, clean paintbrush or pastry brush
Waxed paper

1. Place chocolate on cutting board; shave it into small pieces with paring knife (see Chocolate Shapes, page 582, step 1).

2. Place shavings in measuring cup. Add shortening. (Use 1 teaspoon/5 ml of shortening for every 2 ounces/56 g of chocolate.)

3. Fill saucepan ¼ full (about 1 inch/2.5 cm deep) with warm *(not hot)* water. Place measuring cup in water to melt chocolate, stirring frequently with rubber spatula until smooth. *(Be careful not to get any water into chocolate.)*

4. Wash leaves; dry well with paper towels. Brush melted chocolate onto underside of each leaf with paintbrush or pastry brush, coating leaf thickly and evenly. Repeat brushing with a second coating of chocolate, if desired, for a sturdier leaf.

5. Carefully wipe off any chocolate that may have run onto front of leaf.

6. Place leaves, chocolate side up, on waxed paper. Let stand in cool, dry place until chocolate is firm. *(Do not chill in refrigerator.)*

7. When chocolate is firm, carefully peel leaves away from chocolate; chill until ready to use.

Step 3. Melting chocolate.

Step 4. Brushing leaves with melted chocolate.

Step 5. Wiping excess chocolate off front sides of leaves.

Step 7. Separating leaves.

Caramel Roses

Crown your favorite frosted layer cake with a nosegay of caramel roses.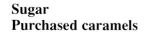

For an extra-special dessert top petits fours with caramel roses. Serve arranged on a spectacular dessert plate.

Set off a luscious caramel flan with a caramel rose.

Sugar
Purchased caramels

EQUIPMENT:
Cutting board
Teaspoon
Rolling pin
Paring knife

1. Sprinkle sugar on cutting board with teaspoon. Unwrap 3 caramels; place on sugared board. Sprinkle with additional sugar.

2. Roll each caramel into an oval (about $1/16$ inch/1.5 mm thick) with rolling pin, turning oval over frequently to coat with sugar. Cut each oval in half crosswise with paring knife.

3. To make center of rose, start at 1 side of a half oval and roll up to form a bud shape.

4. To make petals, shape another half oval, straight side down, around bud. Press petal to bud to secure; flare top edge slightly to resemble petal.

5. Repeat with remaining half ovals to shape additional petals, overlapping petals slightly.

6. Place rose on its side; trim off base with knife so rose will sit flat.

Step 2. Cutting ovals in half.

Step 3. Rolling half oval to form bud of rose.

Step 4. Placing first petal around bud.

Step 5. Forming additional petals.

Chocolate Curls

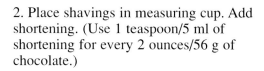

Create a halo of chocolate curls on top of your favorite frosted layer cake or cheesecake.

For an easy after-dinner treat, top cups of coffee with dollops of whipped cream and chocolate curls.

Dust chocolate curls with powdered sugar. Then use them to add a festive touch to chocolate pie or pudding.

Make brownies extra special by frosting them with vanilla buttercream frosting Then top each brownie with a chocolate curl.

Semisweet chocolate (squares or bars)
Shortening

EQUIPMENT:
Cutting board
Paring knife
Glass measuring cup
Small saucepan
Rubber spatula
Baking pan or dish, marble slab or other heat-resistant flat surface
Metal spatula
Small metal pancake turner or cheese cutter
Small skewer or toothpick
Waxed paper

1. Place chocolate on cutting board; shave it into small pieces with paring knife.

2. Place shavings in measuring cup. Add shortening. (Use 1 teaspoon/5 ml of shortening for every 2 ounces/56 g of chocolate.)

3. Fill saucepan ¼ full (about 1 inch/2.5 cm deep) with warm (*not hot*) water. Place measuring cup in water to melt chocolate, stirring frequently with rubber spatula until smooth. (*Be careful not to get any water into chocolate.*) Remove measuring cup from saucepan. Let chocolate cool slightly.

4. Pour melted chocolate onto back of baking pan. Quickly spread chocolate into a thin layer (about ¼ inch/6 mm thick) with metal spatula.

5. Let stand in cool, dry place until chocolate is firm. (*Do not chill in refrigerator.*) When chocolate is just firm, use small metal pancake turner, cheese cutter or paring knife to form curls. Hold pancake turner, cutter or knife at a 45° angle and scrape chocolate into a curl.

6. Using small skewer or toothpick, transfer curl to waxed paper. Store in cool, dry place until ready to use.

Step 1. Shaving chocolate.

Step 4. Spreading melted chocolate.

Step 5. Scraping chocolate into curls.

Step 6. Transferring curls.

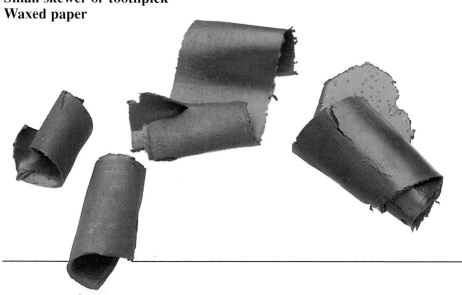

Bacon Curls

Dress up wedges of quiche with bacon curls.

Use a cluster of bacon curls to decorate the top of a tossed salad or a baked casserole.

For a quick appetizer or snack, spread melba rounds or party rye bread slices with your favorite cheese spread. Top each with a bacon curl.

Bacon slices*

EQUIPMENT:
Cutting board
Paring knife
6- to 8-inch (15 to 20 cm) metal
    skewers
Broiler pan
Fork
Paper towels

*Each bacon slice makes 3 curls.

1. Place bacon slices on cutting board. Cut each slice crosswise into 3 pieces with paring knife.

2. Loosely roll up bacon pieces; thread about ½ inch/1.25 cm apart on metal skewers.

3. Place skewers, 1½ to 2 inches (3.75 to 5 cm) apart, on unheated rack of broiler pan. Position under preheated broiler so rack is about 5 inches (12.5 cm) from heat source. Broil 4 to 6 minutes or until bacon is crisp, turning every 2 minutes. Cool. Carefully remove curls from skewers with fork. Drain on paper towels; cool completely.

Step 1. Cutting bacon.

Step 2. Threading bacon onto skewers.

Step 3. Removing curls from skewers.

Piped Cream Cheese

Squiggle cream cheese over thin slices of smoked salmon on crackers or bagel chips for the perfect accent.

Decorate whole cooked roasts by piping cream cheese in a diamond pattern over top of meat.

Pipe softened cream cheese onto your favorite gelatin salad.

Squeeze a dollop of cream cheese onto cooked steaks or hot roast beef slices.

Whipped cream cheese
Fresh dill (optional)

EQUIPMENT:
Large zipper-style plastic food
storage bag
Large spoon
Kitchen scissors

1. Fill plastic bag about ½ full with cream cheese using spoon. Seal bag securely. Cut small piece off bottom corner of bag with kitchen scissors.

2. Position sealed end of bag in your writing hand. Position fingers near opening of bag; place other hand under bag.

3. **For squiggles and lines,** hold plastic bag at a 45° angle about ¼ inch (6 mm) from surface of food. While gently squeezing bag, guide bag to create desired design. At end of each squiggle or line, stop squeezing bag and lift away from food. Trim with fresh dill weed, if desired.

4. **For puffs and dollops,** hold plastic bag at a 90° angle. Position opening just above food and gently squeeze, lifting bag slightly while squeezing. When puff or dollop is desired size, stop squeezing and lift up bag. Trim with fresh dill, if desired.

Step 1. Cutting small corner off bottom of bag.

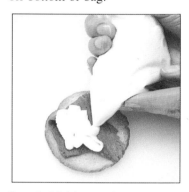

Step 3. Making squiggles.

Step 4. Making puffs.

Egg Chicken

Decorate a platter of baked ham with a family of egg chickens.

Make breakfast "eggstra" special for your toddlers by serving them egg chickens.

Serving a chef's salad for dinner? Why not top it with an egg chicken?

Red, green or yellow bell pepper
Ripe olive slice
Hard-cooked egg, shell removed

EQUIPMENT:
Cutting board
Paring knife

1. Place bell pepper on cutting board. Cut lengthwise in half with paring knife. Remove stem, membrane and seeds; discard. Cut one 2 x 1½-inch (5 x 3.75 cm) rectangle from each pepper half.

2. For tail, trim both long sides of 1 pepper rectangle at an angle. Make zigzag cuts along wide end of same rectangle.

3. Cut remaining pepper rectangle in half lengthwise. For chicken's comb, cut zigzag edge along 1 long side of 1 rectangle half. If desired, trim comb to make proportional to egg.

4. Cut a small triangle from remaining rectangle half for beak; set aside.

5. For eyes, cut 2 tiny pieces from olive slice; set aside.

6. To assemble egg chicken, cut a long thin lengthwise slice from egg with paring knife; discard. Place egg, cut side down, on cutting board.

7. Cut a horizontal slit in wide end of egg. Insert tail, peel side up, into slit. Cut a lengthwise slit in top of narrow end of egg; insert chicken's comb into slit.

8. Cut a hole in front of narrow end of egg; insert beak. Position an olive piece on either side of beak for eyes.

Step 2. Cutting zigzag cuts on tail.

Step 3. Trimming comb.

Step 6. Cutting slice from bottom of egg.

Step 7. Inserting tail and comb into egg.

Pastry Cutouts

To make a simple mincemeat pie sensational, arrange a ring of star-shaped cutouts on top pie crust before baking.

For a quick alternative to a lattice-top pie, cut out several diamonds or scalloped rounds from pastry dough instead of dough strips. Arrange cutouts in a decorative pattern over pie filling before baking.

Need a fun project to keep the kids busy? Let them cut out fanciful shapes from rolled-out pastry dough. Sprinkle cutouts with cinnamon-sugar and bake on cookie sheets. The kids will love eating their creations with applesauce, pudding or ice cream.

All-purpose flour
Pastry for pie crust
Milk
Sugar
Water

EQUIPMENT:
Pastry cloth
Rolling pin
Rolling pin cover (optional)
Hors d'oeuvre cutters, cookie
  cutters or paring knife
Baking sheet
Metal spatula
Small pastry brush
Wire rack
Pancake turner

1. Sprinkle pastry cloth lightly with flour. Place pastry on floured cloth; roll to about ⅛-inch (3 mm) thickness with rolling pin. (To minimize pastry sticking to rolling pin, use rolling pin with cover.)

2. Cut into desired shapes using hors d'oeuvre cutters, cookie cutters or paring knife.

3. **To decorate baked single-crust pie,** transfer pastry cutouts to baking sheet with metal spatula. Use tip of paring knife to decorate cutouts with design, if desired. Brush cutouts with milk using pastry brush; sprinkle with sugar.

4. Bake cutouts at 425°F/220°C (or at temperature given in pastry recipe) until golden brown. Transfer to wire rack with pancake turner; cool. Arrange baked cutouts on top of pie filling.

5. **To decorate unbaked double-crust pie,** remove cutouts from pastry cloth with metal spatula. Use pastry brush to brush back side of cutouts with water. Arrange cutouts, moistened side down, on top crust of pie.

6. Cut slits in top crust with paring knife as part of design.

7. Or, cut slits along edge of cutouts. Brush crust and cutouts with milk; sprinkle with sugar. Bake as directed in pie recipe.

Step 3. Decorating cutouts with desired pattern.

Step 4. Placing cutouts on pie.

Step 6. Cutting slits in crust.

Step 7. Cutting slits around edge of cutouts.

Butter Shapes

Top a stack of piping hot pancakes with two or three butter curls.

At your next buffet, instead of ordinary butter pats, place butter balls in a pretty glass bowl filled with crushed ice. Serve alongside a basket of hot muffins or biscuits.

For a hearty winter meal, top off bowls of steaming oyster stew with elegant seasoned butter rounds.

Bowl of hot water
Sticks of butter or margarine, chilled
Bowl of ice water
Chopped fresh herbs, crushed dried herbs *or* minced fresh garlic

EQUIPMENT:
Butter curler (for butter curls)
Butter paddles (for butter balls)
Cutting board
Paring knife
Small bowl
Metal teaspoon
Waxed paper

1. **For butter curls**, place butter curler in hot water. Starting at far end of 1 butter stick, pull curler firmly across top of butter. Place finished curl in ice water. Repeat for desired amount of curls, dipping curler into hot water before starting each curl.

2. **For butter balls**, place butter paddles in ice water until cold. Place 1 butter stick on cutting board; cut into ½-inch (1.25 cm) pieces with paring knife.

3. Using fingers, shape butter pieces into balls. Chill until firm, if necessary.

4. Roll each ball between scored sides of paddles, moving paddles in small circles in opposite directions. Place finished butter balls in ice water.

5. **For seasoned butter,** allow 1 butter stick to stand at room temperature until softened. Place butter in small bowl. Add herbs or garlic; stir with spoon until well blended. (Use about 1 teaspoon/5 ml fresh herbs or ¼ to ½ teaspoon/1 to 2 ml dried herbs or minced garlic for each stick [½ cup/125 ml] butter.) Place butter mixture on waxed paper; shape into a roll. Wrap with waxed paper; chill until firm.

6. To serve, slice butter roll into rounds with paring knife. Or, use seasoned butter roll to make butter curls or balls.

Step 1. Pulling butter curler across stick of butter.

Step 3. Rolling butter into balls.

Step 4. Rolling balls between paddles.

Step 5. Wrapping herbed butter in waxed paper to chill.

Tortilla Cups

Tortilla cups make great holders for guacamole, salsa or your favorite dip.

Fill tortilla cups with coleslaw or your favorite pasta salad for the perfect accent to a summer meal of grilled burgers.

For a refreshing salad, fill tortilla cups with fresh fruit pieces and drizzle with poppy seed dressing.

During the holidays, fashion small tortilla cups to hold cranberry sauce. Place filled cups around turkey on serving platter.

Cooking oil
6- or 7-inch (15 or 17.5 cm) flour
    tortillas

EQUIPMENT:
Large heavy saucepan
Deep-fat-frying thermometer
Oven mitts (optional)
Ladle
Long metal tongs
Paper towels

1. Pour 3 inches (7.5 cm) of cooking oil into large heavy saucepan. Attach deep-fat-frying thermometer, with bulb in oil, to side of saucepan. (Make sure bottom of thermometer does not touch bottom of pan.) Heat oil until thermometer registers 360°F (185°C).

2. Carefully place tortillas, one at a time, in hot oil. With ladle, hold tortilla down in center to form a cup. Cook tortilla until crisp and golden.

3. Empty oil from ladle; remove ladle from saucepan. Remove tortilla cup from hot oil with tongs.

4. Invert tortilla cup; drain upside down on paper towels. Repeat for desired number of tortilla cups.

Step 2. Frying tortilla.

Step 3. Removing tortilla cup from hot oil.

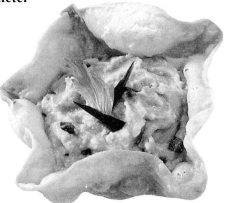

INDEX

A

Almonds
Almond Chicken, 220
browning in skillet, 310
Chocolate Chip Almond Biscotti, 396
Spanish Orange-Almond Cake, 434
toasting in oven, 389
Angel Hair Pasta with Red Chili Sauce, 65
Antipasto with Marinated Mushrooms, 242
Appetizers (see also **Dips & Spreads;**
Snacks)
Antipasto with Marinated Mushrooms, 242
Barbecued Pork, 206
Cheese & Sausage Bundles, 502
Cheesy Chorizo Wedges, 286
Chilled Seafood Lasagna with Herbed
Cheese, 18
Chinese Vegetable Rolls, 28
Coconut Fish Bites, 500
Corn Tortilla Chips, 335
Egg Champignons, 20
French-Style Pizza Bites, 498
Hors d'Oeuvre Rolls, 203
Hot 'n' Honeyed Chicken Wings, 40
Marinated Mushrooms, 244
Nachos Olé, 288
Pesto-Cheese Logs, 504
Pot Stickers, 200
Red & Green Salsa, 286
Scallops à la Schaller, 44
Scampi, 16
Shrimp Mold, 42
Shrimp Toast, 198
Spinach-Cheese Triangles, 22
Three Mushroom Ratatouille, 496
Turkey-Cheese Surprises, 38
Venetian Canapés, 240
Apple Butter Pound Cake, 462
Apples
Apple Cups, 570
Apple Curry Chicken, 162
Apple Streusel Cake, 428
Cranberry-Apple Chutney, 538
Hot Mulled Cider, 508
Lagoon Chicken Salad, 156

Apples, *continued*
My Golden Harvest Apple Pie, 452
removing stem, core and seeds, 156
Stuffed Chicken with Apple Glaze, 192
Sweet Potato and Apple Casserole, 134
Apricot Cookies, Peek-A-Boo, 394
Artichokes
Pasta Salad in Artichoke Cups, 55
preparing leaf tips, 55
scooping out choke, 56
testing for doneness, 55
Asparagus
Asparagus Chicken with Black Bean
Sauce, 218
Asparagus Wreath, 92
peeling stems, 92
Avocados
Chicken Avocado Boats, 174
Chicken Tostadas, 296
Classic Guacamole, 290
Flautas with Chicken Filling, 294
Gazpacho, 292
Pork Burritos, 306
removing pit, 174

B

Bacon
Bacon Curls, 590
Scallops à la Schaller, 44
Baked Shrimp with Chili-Garlic Butter, 324
Banana Chocolate Chip Softies, 352
Barbecued Pork, 206
Bar Cookies (*see also* **Brownies**)
Checkerboard Bars, 386
Choco Cheesecake Squares, 362
Chocolate Caramel Pecan Bars, 364
Chocolate Chip Almond Biscotti, 396
Chocolate Chip Shortbread, 350
No-Fuss Bar Cookies, 346
Special Treat No-Bake Squares, 360
Viennese Meringue Bars, 389
Basil Vinaigrette Dressing, 56
Beans
Chicken Tostadas, 296
Fresh Lima Beans in Onion Cream, 96
fresh, shelling, 96

Beans, *continued*
Green Bean Bundles, 94
Minestrone alla Milanese, 248
Refried Beans, 332
Zesty Zucchini-Chick Pea Salad, 328
Beef (*see also* **Beef, Ground**)
Beef Chimichangas, 298
Beef Enchiladas, 301
Beef with Cashews, 212
Beef with Peppers, 214
Brisket of Beef, 518
Fajitas, 316
Picadillo Filling, 314
pounding to ¼-inch (6 mm) thickness, 316
Prime Rib with Yorkshire Pudding
and Horseradish Cream Sauce, 513
roasts, inserting thermometer, 513
Spicy Beef Tacos, 304
Beef, Ground
Beef Oriental, 74
browning, 318
Chili, 318
Four-Meat Filling, 256
Four-Meat Ravioli, 255
Quick Beef Soup, 58
Spetzque, 84
Spinach Lasagna, 261
Bell Pepper Cup, 577
Bell Pepper Triangles, 573
Beverages
Hot Mulled Cider, 508
Viennese Coffee, 506
Bittersweet Farm Chicken, 178
Black and White Cutouts, 372
Black Forest Cake, 417
Black Walnut Fudge, 466
Bone-in Roast Leg of Lamb, 522
Boston Cream Pie, 411
Brandy Glaze, 442
Brandy-Pecan Corn Meal Cake, 442
Breads, Quick
Cornbread, 542
Corn Tortillas, 334
Flour Tortillas, 333
Southwestern Snack Squares, 32
Breads, Yeast
Cheesy Onion Focaccia, 25
doubled in bulk, 26
kneading, 26
proofing, 25
Brisket of Beef, 518
Broccoli
Broccoli with Red Pepper and
Shallots, 528
Chinese Vegetable Rolls, 28
cutting stalks, 70
Pasta and Broccoli, 70

Broccoli, *continued*
peeling stems, 98
steaming, 70
Vegetable Rings on Broccoli Spears, 98
Broth-Simmered Brussels Sprouts, 100
Brownies
Butterscotch Brownies, 382
Irish Brownies, 384
Minted Chocolate Chip Brownies, 380
Orange Cappuccino Brownies, 470
White Chocolate Chunk Brownies, 378
Brussels Sprouts
Broth-Simmered Brussels Sprouts, 100
Brussels Sprouts in Mustard Sauce, 526
preparing, 100
testing for doneness, 100
Buttercream Frosting, 440
Butterscotch Brownies, 382
Butterscotch Filling, 464
Butter Shapes, 594
Buttery Mashed Potatoes, 534

C
Cabbage
Chicken Chow Mein, 222
Long Soup, 210
Minestrone alla Milanese, 248
removing core, 210
shredding, 248
Cakes
Apple Butter Pound Cake, 462
Apple Streusel Cake, 428
Black Forest Cake, 417
Boston Cream Pie, 411
Brandy-Pecan Corn Meal Cake, 442
brushing crumbs from layers, 422
Caramel-Butter Pecan Cake, 439
Carrot Cake, 408
Champion Pumpkin Cake, 444
Chiffon Cake, 406
Chocolate Angel Food Cake, 420
Chocolate Cake, 477
Chocolate Chip Cake, 464
Chocolate Sour Cream Cake, 425
dividing batter between pans, 422
Elegant Chocolate Log, 414
flouring pan, 422
Fresh Pear Cake, 430
greasing and lining jelly-roll pan, 414
greasing tube pan, 408
measuring layers, 411
Rich Chocolate Truffle Cake, 549
Spanish Orange-Almond Cake, 434
splitting layers, 411
Sunflower Lemon Cake, 432
testing for doneness, 410
Tin Roof Sundae Cake, 422
Velvety Coconut and Spice Cake, 436

Calorie-Wise Dill Chicken, 176
Candied Orange Rose, 438
Caponata-Style Fettuccine, 110
Caramel
  Caramel-Butter Pecan Cake, 439
  Caramel Filling, 440
  Caramel Flowers, 458
  Caramel Roses, 588
  Chocolate Caramel Pecan Bars, 364
  Chocolate Hazelnut Pie, 457
Cardamom-Chocolate Sandwiches, 398
Carrots
  Carrot Cake, 408
  Carrot Stars, 574
  cutting into julienne strips, 102
  Orange-Glazed Carrots, 524
  Pollo alla Firènze, 186
  Savory Matchstick Carrots, 102
  shredding, 408
  testing for doneness, 524
Carving
  bone-in leg of lamb, 493
  boneless roast, 494
  roast turkey, 495
  standing rib beef roast, 494
Cauliflower
  Chinese Vegetable Rolls, 28
  Crumb-Topped Snowball, 104
  preparing, 104
Celery Curls, 575
Champion Pumpkin Cake, 444
Checkerboard Bars, 386
Cheese
  Antipasto with Marinated
    Mushrooms, 242
  Apple Butter Pound Cake, 462
  Beef Chimichangas, 298
  Beef Enchiladas, 301
  Beef Oriental, 74
  Carrot Cake, 408
  Cheese & Sausage Bundles, 502
  Cheesy Chorizo Wedges, 286
  Cheesy Onion Focaccia, 25
  Cheesy Sun Crisps, 34
  Chicken and Walnut Salad Athena, 160
  Chicken Breasts Sautéed with Sun-Dried
    Tomatoes, 190
  Chicken Tostadas, 296
  Chilled Seafood Lasagna with Herbed
    Cheese, 18
  Classic Chicken Marsala, 266
  Classic Fettuccine Alfredo, 252
  Coconut Cheesecake, 484
  cream cheese, softening, 478
  Cream Cheese Topping, 410
  Flautas with Chicken Filling, 294
  Green Rice Pilaf, 330
  Homemade Pizza, 271
  Nachos Olé, 288

Cheese, *continued*
  Pasta and Broccoli, 70
  Pesto-Cheese Logs, 504
  Pineapple Macadamia Cheesepie, 478
  Piped Cream Cheese, 591
  Pork Burritos, 306
  Raspberry Cheesecake Blossoms, 482
  Shrimp in Angel Hair Pasta Casserole, 80
  Southwestern Snack Squares, 32
  Spetzque, 84
  Spicy Beef Tacos, 304
  Spinach-Cheese Triangles, 22
  Spinach Gnocchi, 274
  Spinach Lasagna, 261
  Taco Dip, 30
  Tiramisu, 486
  Turkey-Cheese Surprises, 38
  Veal Parmesan, 264
Cherries
  Cherry Flowers, 566
  Cherry Topping, 418
Chicken
  Almond Chicken, 220
  Apple Curry Chicken, 162
  Asparagus Chicken with Black Bean
    Sauce, 218
  Bittersweet Farm Chicken, 178
  Calorie-Wise Dill Chicken, 176
  Chicken and Walnut Salad Athena, 160
  Chicken Avocado Boats, 174
  Chicken Breasts Sautéed with Sun-Dried
    Tomatoes, 190
  Chicken Chow Mein, 222
  Chicken Mole, 310
  Chicken Picante, 168
  Chicken Tostadas, 296
  Chicken Wellington, 516
  Chicken with Fruit and Mixed
    Mustards, 188
  Classic Chicken Marsala, 266
  Coconut Chicken with Fresh Chutney, 184
  cooked, chopping, 78
  cooked, deboning, 156
  cooked, dicing, 156
  cooked, shredding, 153
  Curried Chicken Rolls, 182
  Flautas with Chicken Filling, 294
  Forty-Clove Chicken Filice, 164
  Four-Meat Filling, 256
  Four-Meat Ravioli, 255
  Fresh Gazpacho Chicken, 172
  grilling, 78
  Hot 'n' Honeyed Chicken Wings, 40
  Hot Chinese Chicken Salad, 154
  Lagoon Chicken Salad, 156
  Laguna Beach Pecan Chicken Breasts, 180
  Olympic Seoul Chicken, 166
  Pollo alla Firènze, 186
  raw, chopping, 50

Chicken, *continued*
raw, cutting up whole, 151
raw, deboning, 222
raw, disjointing whole, 150
raw, flattening breasts, 150
raw, skinning, 150
raw, skinning and deboning breasts, 152
Rick's Good-as-Gold Chili, 170
Spicy Grilled Chicken, 308
Stuffed Chicken with Apple Glaze, 192
Sweet Garlic with Chicken Pasta, 78
testing for doneness, 50
Thai Chicken Fettuccine Salad, 50
Chiffon Cake, 406
Chili
Chili, 318
Rick's Good-as-Gold Chili, 170
Chili Butter, 308
Chilies Rellenos, 313
Chili Flowers, 581
Chilled Seafood Lasagna with Herbed
Cheese, 18
Chilly Cucumber Soup, 14
Chinese Vegetable Rolls, 28
Choco Cheesecake Squares, 362
Chocolate (*see also* **Brownies; Chocolate**
Chips; Cocoa)
Cardamom-Chocolate Sandwiches, 398
Checkerboard Bars, 386
Choco Cheesecake Squares, 362
Chocolate Cream Frosting, 424
Chocolate Curls, 550, 589
Chocolate Cutouts, 585
Chocolate-Dipped Strawberries, 426
Chocolate Edged Lace Cookies, 400
Chocolate Glaze, 412, 550
Chocolate Hazelnut Crust, 458
Chocolate Hazelnut Pie, 457
Chocolate Leaves, 587
Chocolate Macaroons, 366
Chocolate Mousse Espresso with Hazelnut
Brittle, 489
Chocolate Rice Pudding, 468
Chocolate Shapes, 582
Chocolate Sugar Spritz, 368
Double Chocolate Bombe, 474
Double-Dipped Chocolate Peanut Butter
Cookies, 358
Elegant Chocolate Log, 414
grating, 426
melting in double boiler, 474
melting in microwave, 375
melting over hot water, 394
Old-Fashioned Ice Cream Sandwiches, 375
Peek-A-Boo Apricot Cookies, 394
Quick Chocolate Softies, 340
Raspberry Chocolate Mousse Pie, 472
Rich Chocolate Truffle Cake, 549

Chocolate, *continued*
shaving, 506
Two-Toned Spritz Cookies, 370
Viennese Coffee, 506
Chocolate Angel Food Cake, 420
Chocolate Cake, 477
Chocolate Caramel Pecan Bars, 364
Chocolate Chips (*see also* **Chocolate**)
Banana Chocolate Chip Softies, 352
Chocolate Caramel Pecan Bars, 364
Chocolate Chip Almond Biscotti, 396
Chocolate Chip Cake, 464
Chocolate Chip Macaroons, 344
Chocolate Chip Shortbread, 350
Cinnamon Nut Chocolate Spirals, 392
Kids' Favorite Jumbo Chippers, 354
Minted Chocolate Chip Brownies, 380
No-Fuss Bar Cookies, 346
Orange-Walnut Chippers, 356
Peanut Butter Chocolate Chippers, 342
Ultimate Chippers, 348
Viennese Meringue Bars, 389
Chocolate Cream Frosting, 424
Chocolate Curls, 550, 589
Chocolate Cutouts, 585
Chocolate-Dipped Strawberries, 426
Chocolate Edged Lace Cookies, 400
Chocolate Glaze, 412, 550
Chocolate Hazelnut Crust, 458
Chocolate Hazelnut Pie, 457
Chocolate Leaves, 587
Chocolate Macaroons, 366
Chocolate Mousse Espresso with
Hazelnut Brittle, 489
Chocolate Rice Pudding, 468
Chocolate Shapes, 582
Chocolate Sour Cream Cake, 426
Chocolate Sugar Spritz, 368
Chutney-Squash Circles, 140
Cinnamon Nut Chocolate Spirals, 392
Cioppino, 245
Clams
Cioppino, 245
cooking, 245
Fresh Seafood and Linguine Salad, 52
scrubbing, 245
Classic Chicken Marsala, 266
Classic Double Pie Crust, 461
Classic Fettuccine Alfredo, 252
Classic Guacamole, 290
Classic Pesto with Linguine, 250
Classic Polenta, 278
Classic Single Pie Crust, 460
Cob Corn in Barbecue Butter, 106
Cocoa
Black and White Cutouts, 372
Black Forest Cake, 417
Chocolate Angle Food Cake, 420
Chocolate Cake, 477

Cocoa, *continued*
Chocolate Sour Cream Cake, 425
Cocoa-Nut Filling, 426
Elegant Chocolate Log, 414
Fluffy Cocoa Frosting, 426
Sifted Cocoa Designs, 583
Special Treat No-Bake Squares, 360
Tin Roof Sundae Cake, 422
Coconut
Chocolate Chip Macaroons, 344
Cocoa-Nut Filling, 426
Coconut Cheesecake, 484
Coconut Chicken with Fresh Chutney, 184
Coconut Fish Bites, 500
No-Fuss Bar Cookies, 346
Velvety Coconut and Spice Cake, 436
Cookies (*see also* **Bar Cookies; Brownies**)
Banana Chocolate Chip Softies, 352
Black and White Cutouts, 372
Cardamom-Chocolate Sandwiches, 398
Chocolate Chip Macaroons, 344
Chocolate Edged Lace Cookies, 400
Chocolate Macaroons, 366
Chocolate Sugar Spritz, 368
Cinnamon Nut Chocolate Spirals, 392
cutting out dough, 374
dipping in chocolate, 358
Double-Dipped Chocolate Peanut Butter
    Cookies, 358
Gingerbread Bears, 558
Kids' Favorite Jumbo Chippers, 354
Old-Fashioned Ice Cream Sandwiches, 375
Orange-Walnut Chippers, 356
Peanut Butter Chocolate Chippers, 342
Peek-A-Boo Apricot Cookies, 394
Quick Chocolate Softies, 340
rolling out dough, 370
rolling out dough between waxed
    paper, 375
Rugelach, 556
storing, 348
Two-Toned Spritz Cookies, 370
Ultimate Chippers, 348
using a cookie press, 368
Corn
Cob Corn in Barbecue Butter, 106
Corn and Tomatillo Salsa, 108
cutting kernels from cob, 108
preparing, 106
Spetzque, 84
Cornbread, 542
Corn Tortilla Chips, 335
Corn Tortillas, 334
Crabmeat
Crabmeat with Herbs and Pasta, 68
Fish Rolls with Crab Sauce, 226
picking out shells, 68
Shrimp Mold, 42

Cranberry-Apple Chutney, 538
Cream Cheese Topping, 410
Creamed Pearl Onions, 118
cream, whipping, 472
Creamy Glaze, 462
Creamy Orange Frosting, 438
Creamy Turkey Gravy, 512
Crisp Zucchini Ribbons, 144
Crumb-Topped Snowball, 104
Crusts
Chocolate Hazelnut Crust, 458
Classic Double Pie Crust, 461
Classic Single Pie Crust, 460
cutting in shortening, 460
cutting slits in crust, 450
fluting crust, 452
Macadamia Nut Crust, 478
rolling out dough, 460
Cucumbers
Chilly Cucumber Soup, 14
Fresh Gazpacho Chicken, 172
Jícama-Cucumber Salad, 326
Peas with Cukes 'n' Dill, 124
peeling, 172
seeding, 14
Curry
Apple Curry Chicken, 162
Curried Chicken Rolls, 182
Custard Filling, 412

D
Desserts (*see also* **Bar Cookies; Brownies;
    Cakes; Cookies; Pies; Puddings &
    Mousses; Tarts**)
Coconut Cheescake, 484
Double Chocolate Bombe, 474
Individual Orange Soufflé, 554
Linzer Torte, 552
Raspberry Cheesecake Blossoms, 482
Tiramisu, 486
Dipping Sauce, 500
Dips & Spreads
Classic Guacamole, 290
Taco Dip, 30
Double Chocolate Bombe, 474
Double-Dipped Chocolate Peanut Butter
    Cookies, 358

E
Eggplant
Caponata-Style Fettuccine, 110
Ratatouille-Stuffed Pepper Halves, 128
Eggs
Egg Champignons, 20
Egg Chicken, 592
hard-cooking, 20
Saucy Mediterranean Frittata, 82
separating, 62
whites, beating, 220

Elegant Chocolate Log, 414
Exotic Mushroom Soup, 115

F
Fajitas, 316
Feathered Icings, 584
Fillings
 Butterscotch Filling, 464
 Caramel Filling, 440
 Cocoa-Nut Filling, 426
 Custard Filling, 412
 Peanut Filling, 424
 Picadillo Filling, 314
Fish (*see also* **Clams; Crabmeat; Mussels;**
 Scallops; Shrimp; Squid)
 Chilled Seafood Lasagna with Herbed
 Cheese, 18
 Cioppino, 245
 Coconut Fish Bites, 500
 Fish Rolls with Crab Sauce, 226
 Red Snapper in Chili-Tomato Sauce, 322
Flautas with Chicken Filling, 294
Flour Tortillas, 333
Fluffy Cocoa Frosting, 426
Fluted Mushrooms, 579
Forty-Clove Chicken Filice, 164
Four-Meat Filling, 256
Four-Meat Ravioli, 255
French-Style Pizza Bites, 498
Fresh Gazpacho Chicken, 172
Fresh Lima Beans in Onion Cream, 96
Fresh Pear Cake, 430
Fresh Seafood and Linguine Salad, 52
Fresh Tomato Salsa, 300
Fried Calamari with Tartar Sauce, 268
Fried Noodles, 234
Fried Rice, 232
Frostings, Glazes & Icings
 Brandy Glaze, 442
 Buttercream Frosting, 440
 Chocolate Cream Frosting, 424
 Chocolate Glaze, 412, 550
 Creamy Glaze, 462
 Creamy Orange Frosting, 438
 Feathered Icings, 584
 Fluffy Cocoa Frosting, 426
 Irish Cream Frosting, 384
 Snow Frosting, 444
 Whipped Cream Frosting, 418
Fruit (*see also individual listings*)
 Chicken with Fruit and Mixed
 Mustards, 188
 Coconut Chicken with Fresh Chutney, 184
 Lagoon Chicken Salad, 156
 Larry's Pineapple Hula Salad, 158
 Melon Balls with Leaves, 569
 melon, making balls, 188

Fruit, *continued*
 melon, peeling, 569
 Mixed Berry Pie, 450
 Mixed Greens with Raspberry
 Vinaigrette, 536
 Sugared Fruit, 564
Fudge, Black Walnut, 466
Fusilli Pizzaiolo, 72

G
Garlic
 chopping, 166
 crushing, 58
 Garlic Croutons, 292
 Garlic-Onion Sauce, 64
Gazpacho, 292
Gelatin
 dissolving, 457
 softening, 42
 unmolding, 42
Ginger
 chopping, 212
 Ginger & Pear Tart, 480
 Gingerbread Bears, 558
 grating, 40
Glazed Pork Tenderloin, 520
Glazes (*see* **Frostings, Glazes & Icings**)
Golden Harvest Apple Pie, 452
Golden Tomato Soup, 12
Green Bean Bundles, 94
Green Onion Curls, 206, 575
Green Rice Pilaf, 330
Grilled Chili-Marinated Pork, 320
Gumdrop Bow, 586

H
Harvest-Time Popcorn, 36
Hazelnut Brittle, 490
Homemade Angel Hair Pasta with Classic
 Tomato Sauces, 258
Homemade Fettuccine, 252
Homemade Pizza, 271
Hors d'Oeuvre Rolls, 203
Horseradish Cream Sauce, 514
Hot 'n' Honeyed Chicken Wings, 40
Hot Chinese Chicken Salad, 154
Hot Mulled Cider, 508

I
Icings (*see* **Frostings, Glazes & Icings**)
Individual Orange Soufflés, 554
Irish Brownies, 384
Irish Cream Frosting, 384

J
Jícama-Cucumber Salad, 326

K
Kids' Favorite Jumbo Chippers, 354

L

Lagoon Chicken Salad, 156
Laguna Beach Pecan Chicken Breasts, 180
Lamb
    Bone-in Roast Leg of Lamb, 522
    inserting thermometer, 522
    Roast Leg of Lamb, 522
Larry's Pineapple Hula Salad, 158
Lemon
    juicing, 164
    Lemon Butterflies, 567
    Lemon Wedges, 571
    making twists, 432
    removing peel, 164
    Scored Citrus Slices, 565
    Sunflower Lemon Cake, 432
Lettuce
    drying in spinner, 536
    tearing leaves, 536
Lime
    juicing, 168
    Lime Butterflies, 567
    Lime-Cumin Dressing, 296
    Lime Wedges, 571
Linzer Torte, 552
Lo Mein Noodles with Shrimp, 224
Long Soup, 210
Low-Calorie Mashed Potatoes, 534

M

Macadamia Nut Crust, 478
Ma Po Bean Curd, 228
Marinated Mushrooms, 244
Melon Balls with Leaves, 569
Minestrone alla Milanese, 248
Minted Chocolate Chip Brownies, 380
Mixed Berry Pie, 450
Mixed Greens with Raspberry Vinaigrette, 536
Mocha
    Chocolate Mousse Espresso with Hazelnut Brittle, 489
    Orange Cappuccino Brownies, 470
    Viennese Coffee, 506
Mushrooms
    Antipasto with Marinated Mushrooms, 242
    Chicken Wellington, 516
    cleaning caps, 115
    Egg Champignons, 20
    Exotic Mushroom Soup, 115
    Fluted Mushrooms, 579
    Fusilli Pizzaiolo, 72
    Marinated Mushrooms, 244
    Pollo alla Firénze, 186
    Ratatouille-Stuffed Pepper Halves, 128
    removing stems, 214
    Sweet Garlic with Chicken Pasta, 78
    Three Mushroom Ratatouille, 496
    Wild Rice Mushroom Stuffing, 543

Mussels
    debearding, 52
    Fresh Seafood and Linguine Salad, 52
My Golden Harvest Apple Pie, 452

N

Nachos Olé, 288
Neapolitan Sauce, 260
Neptune's Spaghetti Squash, 138
No-Fuss Bar Cookies, 346
Norma Gene's Peanut Butter Creme Pie, 454
Nuts (*see also* **Almonds; Peanuts; Pecans; Walnuts**)
    Beef with Cashews, 212
    Chocolate Hazelnut Crust, 458
    Chocolate Hazelnut Pie, 457
    Chocolate Mousse Espresso with Hazelnut Brittle, 489
    Cocoa-Nut Filling, 426
    grinding, 504
    Harvest-Time Popcorn, 36
    Hazelnut Brittle, 490
    hazelnuts, rubbing skins, 386
    Macadamia Nut Crust, 478
    Pineapple Macadamia Cheesepie, 478
    toasting in skillet, 250

O

Oats
    Cheesy Sun Crisps, 34
    Orange-Walnut Chippers, 356
Old-Fashioned Ice Cream Sandwiches, 375
Olympic Seoul Chicken, 166
Onions
    blanching, 118
    Cheesy Onion Focaccia, 25
    chopping, 22, 58
    Creamed Pearl Onions, 118
    Fresh Lima Beans in Onion Cream, 96
    Garlic-Onion Sauce, 64
    Green Onion Curls, 575
    Onions Baked in Their Papers, 120
    Spinach-Garlic Pasta with Garlic-Onion Sauce, 62
    Two-Onion Pork Shreds, 216
Orange
    Bittersweet Farm Chicken, 178
    Candied Orange Rose, 438
    Creamy Orange Frosting, 438
    grating peel, 40
    Individual Orange Soufflés, 554
    making twists, 38
    Orange Cappuccino Brownies, 470
    Orange-Glazed Carrots, 524
    Orange-Walnut Chippers, 356
    removing peel, 178
    Scored Citrus Slices, 565
    Spanish Orange-Almond Cake, 434
    Wilted Spinach Mandarin, 136

P

Papaya
  dicing, 158
  peeling, 158
parsley, mincing, 22
Parsnip Patties, 122

Pasta
  Almond Chicken, 220
  Angel Hair Pasta with Red Chili Sauce, 65
  Beef Oriental, 74
  Beef with Peppers, 214
  Caponata-Style Fettuccine, 110
  Chicken Chow Mein, 222
  Chilled Seafood Lasagna with Herbed
    Cheese, 18
  Classic Fettuccine Alfredo, 252
  Classic Pesto with Linguine, 250
  Crabmeat with Herbs and Pasta, 68
  cutting dough with knife, 250
  cutting dough with pasta machine, 66
  Four-Meat Ravioli, 255
  Fresh Seafood and Linguine Salad, 52
  Fried Noodles, 234
  Fusilli Pizzaiolo, 72
  Homemade Angel Hair Pasta with Classic
    Tomato Sauces, 258
  Homemade Fettuccine, 252
  kneading dough by hand, 64
  kneading dough in pasta machine, 65
  Lo Mein Noodles with Shrimp, 224
  Pasta and Broccoli, 70
  Pasta Salad in Artichoke Cups, 55
  Quick Beef Soup, 58
  Saucy Mediterranean Frittata, 82
  Shrimp in Angel Hair Pasta Casserole, 80
  Spetzque, 84
  Spinach-Garlic Pasta with Garlic-Onion
    Sauce, 62
  Spinach Gnocchi, 274
  Spinach Lasagna, 261
  Sunday Supper Stuffed Shells, 76
  Sweet Garlic with Chicken Pasta, 78
  Thai Chicken Fettuccine Salad, 50
  Vermicelli, 235
  Zucchini-Tomato-Noodle Soup, 60
Pastry Cutouts, 593

Peanut Butter
  Double-Dipped Chocolate Peanut Butter
    Cookies, 358
  Kids' Favorite Jumbo Chippers, 354
  Norma Gene's Peanut Butter Creme Pie, 454
  Peanut Butter Chocolate Chippers, 342
  Peanut Filling, 424

Peanuts
  Peanut Filling, 424
  Tin Roof Sundae Cake, 422

Pears
  Fresh Pear Cake, 430
  Ginger & Pear Tart, 480

Peas
  Beef Oriental, 74
  Peas with Cukes 'n' Dill, 124
  removing string from pods, 126
  Sesame Snow Peas, 126
  shelling, 124
  Spetzque, 84

Pecans
  Apple Butter Pound Cake, 462
  Brandy-Pecan Corn Meal Cake, 442
  Caramel-Butter Pecan Cake, 439
  Coconut Cheesecake, 484
  grinding, 180
  Laguna Beach Pecan Chicken Breasts, 180
  Praline Topping, 548
Peek-A-Boo Apricot Cookies, 394

Peppers
  Beef with Peppers, 214
  bell, cutting off sides, 72
  Bell Pepper Cup, 577
  Bell Pepper Triangles, 573
  bell, pulling out stem and seeds, 98
  bell, scraping out seeds, 128
  bell, slicing into rings, 98
  Broccoli with Red Pepper and
    Shallots, 528
  chilies, cleaning, 285
  chilies, roasting, 284
  chilies, scraping out seeds, 66
  Chili Flowers, 581
  Ratatouille-Stuffed Pepper Halves, 128
  Vegetable Rings on Broccoli Spears, 98
Pesto-Cheese Logs, 504
Picadillo Filling, 314

Pies (*see* **also Crusts; Tarts**)
  Chocolate Hazelnut Pie, 457
  Mixed Berry Pie, 450
  My Golden Harvest Apple Pie, 452
  Norma Gene's Peanut Butter Creme
    Pie, 454
  Pineapple Macadamia Cheesepie, 478
  Raspberry Chocolate Mousse Pie, 472

Pineapple
  Larry's Pineapple Hula Salad, 158
  Pineapple Macadamia Cheesepie, 478
Piped Cream Cheese, 591
Pizza, Homemade, 271
Pizzaiola Sauce, 260
Plum Tomato Sauce, 256
Pollo alla Firénze, 186

Pork (*see also* **Sausage**)
  Barbecued Pork, 206
  butterflying, 320
  Chicken Chow Mein, 222
  Four-Meat Filling, 256
  Four-Meat Ravioli, 255
  Fried Rice, 232
  Glazed Pork Tenderloin, 520
  Grilled Chili-Marinated Pork, 320

Pork, *continued*
    Hors d'Oeuvre Rolls, 203
    Long Soup, 210
    Ma Po Bean Curd, 228
    Pork Burritos, 306
    Pot Stickers, 200
    pounding to ¼-inch (6 mm) thickness, 320
    Sunday Supper Stuffed Shells, 76
    Two-Onion Pork Shreds, 216
    Wonton Soup, 208
Potatoes (*see also* **Sweet Potatoes**)
    Buttery Mashed Potatoes, 534
    forcing through ricer, 534
    Low-Calorie Mashed Potatoes, 534
    Potato Latkes, 532
    Scalloped Red Skin Potatoes, 130
    Sweet Potato and Apple Casserole, 134
    Swiss Rosti Potatoes, 132
Pot Stickers, 200
powdered sugar, sifting, 384
Praline Pumpkin Tart, 546
Praline Topping, 548
Prime Rib with Yorkshire Pudding and
    Horseradish Cream Sauce, 513
Puddings & Mousses
    Chocolate Mousse Espresso with Hazelnut
        Brittle, 489
    Chocolate Rice Pudding, 468
Pumpkin
    Champion Pumpkin Cake, 444
    Praline Pumpkin Tart, 546

Q
Quick Beef Soup, 58
Quick Chocolate Softies, 340

R
Radish Fans, 576
Raspberries
    Raspberry Cheesecake Blossoms, 482
    Raspberry Chocolate Mousse Pie, 472
    Viennese Meringue Bars, 389
Ratatouille-Stuffed Pepper Halves, 128
Red & Green Salsa, 286
Red Chili Sauce, 66, 302
Red Snapper in Chili-Tomato Sauce, 322
Refried Beans, 332
Reuben-Stuffed Kohlrabies, 112
Rice
    Chocolate Rice Pudding, 468
    Fried Rice, 232
    Green Rice Pilaf, 330
    Lagoon Chicken Salad, 156
    Risotto alla Milanese, 276
    Shrimp Mold, 42
    Steamed Rice, 234
    Wild Rice Mushroom Stuffing, 543
Rich Chocolate Truffle Cake, 549
Rick's Good-as-Gold Chili, 170

Risotto alla Milanese, 276
Roast Leg of Lamb, 522
Roast Turkey with Pan Gravy, 510
Rugelach, 556

S
Salad Dressings
    Basil Vinaigrette Dressing, 56
    Lime-Cumin Dressing, 296
Salads, Main-Dish
    Chicken and Walnut Salad Athena, 160
    Fresh Seafood and Linguine Salad, 52
    Hot Chinese Chicken Salad, 154
    Lagoon Chicken Salad, 156
    Larry's Pineapple Hula Salad, 158
    Thai Chicken Fettuccine Salad, 50
Salads, Side-Dish
    Jícama-Cucumber Salad, 326
    Mixed Greens with Raspberry Vinaigrette,
        536
    Pasta Salad in Artichoke Cups, 55
    Zesty Zucchini-Chick Pea Salad, 52
Salsas
    Corn and Tomatillo Salsa, 108
    Fresh Tomato Salsa, 300
    Red & Green Salsa, 286
    Salsa, 502
Sauces
    Creamy Turkey Gravy, 512
    Dipping Sauce, 500
    Garlic-Onion Sauce, 64
    Horseradish Cream Sauce, 514
    Neapolitan Sauce, 260
    Pizzaiola Sauce, 260
    Plum Tomato Sauce, 256
    Red Chili Sauce, 66, 302
    Sweet and Sour Sauce, 204
    Tartar Sauce, 270
    Tomato Sauce, 82, 314
    Turkey Broth with Giblets, 512
Saucy Mediterranean Frittata, 82
Sausage
    Beef Chimichangas, 298
    Cheese & Sausage Bundles, 502
    Cheesy Chorizo Wedges, 286
    chorizo, removing casing, 286
    Four-Meat Filling, 256
    Four-Meat Ravioli, 255
    Sausage-Cornbread Stuffing, 540
Savory Matchstick Carrots, 102
Scalloped Red Skin Potatoes, 130
Scallops
    Neptune's Spaghetti Squash, 138
    Scallops à la Schaller, 44
Scampi, 16
Scored Citrus Slices, 565
sesame seeds, toasting, 310
Sesame Snow Peas, 126

Shellfish (*see* **Clams; Crabmeat; Mussels; Scallops; Shrimp; Squid**)
Shrimp
Baked Shrimp with Chili-Garlic Butter, 324
Chicken Chow Mein, 222
Cioppino, 245
deveining, 16
Fried Rice, 232
Hors d'Oeuvre Rolls, 203
Lo Mein Noodles with Shrimp, 224
Neptune's Spaghetti Squash, 138
removing shells, 16
Scampi, 16
Shrimp in Angel Hair Pasta Casserole, 80
Shrimp Mold, 42
Shrimp Toast, 198
Wonton Soup, 208
Sifted Cocoa/Sugar Designs, 583
Snacks
Cheesy Sun Crisps, 34
Corn Tortilla Chips, 335
Harvest-Time Popcorn, 36
Southwestern Snack Squares, 32
Snow Frosting, 444
Soufflés, Individual Orange, 554
Soups (*see also* **Chili**)
Chilly Cucumber Soup, 14
Cioppino, 245
Exotic Mushroom Soup, 115
Gazpacho, 292
Golden Tomato Soup, 12
Long Soup, 210
Minestrone alla Milanese, 248
Quick Beef Soup, 58
Wonton Soup, 208
Zucchini-Tomato-Noodle Soup, 60
Southwestern Snack Squares, 32
Spanish Orange-Almond Cake, 434
Special Treat No-Bake Squares, 360
Spetzque, 84
Spicy Beef Tacos, 304
Spicy Grilled Chicken, 308
Spinach
Four-Meat Filling, 256
Four-Meat Ravioli, 255
Pollo alla Firènze, 186
removing moisture, 76
removing stems, 62
Spinach-Cheese Triangles, 22
Spinach-Garlic Pasta with Garlic-Onion Sauce, 62
Spinach Gnocchi, 274
Spinach Lasagna, 261
Sunday Supper Stuffed Shells, 76
Wilted Spinach Mandarin, 136
Squash (*see also* **Zucchini**)
Chinese Vegetable Rolls, 28
Chutney-Squash Circles, 140

Squash, *continued*
cutting into rings, 140
Green Bean Bundles, 94
Neptune's Spaghetti Squash, 138
Summer Squash Butterflies, 580
Summer Squash Flowers, 572
Squid
cleaning, 268
cutting into rings, 268
Fresh Seafood and Linguine Salad, 52
Fried Calamari with Tartar Sauce, 268
Steamed Rice, 234
Stir-Fries
Almond Chicken, 220
Asparagus Chicken with Black Bean Sauce, 218
Beef Oriental, 74
Beef with Cashews, 212
Beef with Peppers, 214
Chicken Chow Mein, 222
Lo Mein Noodles with Shrimp, 224
Ma Po Bean Curd, 228
Two-Onion Pork Shreds, 216
Zucchini Shanghai Style, 230
Strawberries
Chocolate-Dipped Strawberries, 426
Strawberry Fans, 568
Stuffed Chicken with Apple Glaze, 192
Stuffings
Sausage-Cornbread Stuffing, 540
Wild Rice Mushroom Stuffing, 543
Sugar Designs, Sifted, 583
Sugared Fruit, 564
Sunday Supper Stuffed Shells, 76
Sunflower Lemon Cake, 432
Sweet and Sour Sauce, 204
Sweetened Whipped Cream, 550
Sweet Garlic with Chicken Pasta, 78
Sweet Potatoes
Sweet Potato and Apple Casserole, 134
Sweet Potato Gratin, 530
Swiss Rosti Potatoes, 132

T
Tabbouleh in Tomato Cups, 142
Taco Dip, 30
Tartar Sauce, 270
Tarts
Ginger & Pear Tart, 480
Praline Pumpkin Tart, 546
Techniques
almonds, browning in skillet, 310
almonds, toasting in oven, 389
apple, removing stem, core and seeds, 156
artichokes, preparing, 55
artichokes, scooping out choke, 56
artichokes, testing for doneness, 55
asparagus, peeling stems, 92
avocado, removing pit, 174

Techniques, *continued*

beans, fresh, shelling, 96
beef, ground, browning, 318
beef, pounding to ¼-inch (6 mm) thickness, 316
beef roast, inserting thermometer, 513
broccoli, cutting stalks, 70
broccoli, peeling stems, 98
broccoli, steaming, 70
Brussels sprouts, preparing, 100
Brussels sprouts, testing for doneness, 100
cabbage, removing core, 210
cabbage, shredding, 248
cakes, brushing crumbs from layers, 422
cakes, dividing batter between pans, 422
cakes, flouring pans, 422
cakes, greasing and lining jelly-roll pan, 414
cakes, greasing tube pan, 408
cakes, measuring layers, 411
cakes, splitting layers, 411
cakes, testing for doneness, 410
carrots, cutting into julienne strips, 102
carrots, shredding, 408
carrots, testing for doneness, 524
carving, bone-in leg of lamb, 495
carving, boneless roasts, 494
carving, roast turkey, 495
carving, standing rib beef roast, 494
cauliflower, preparing, 104
celery, cutting diagonally, 74
cheese, cream, softening, 478
chicken, cooked, chopping, 78
chicken, cooked, dicing, 156
chicken, cooked, removing bones, 156
chicken, cooked, shredding, 153
chicken, grilling, 78
chicken, raw, chopping, 50
chicken, raw, cutting up whole, 151
chicken, raw, deboning, 222
chicken, raw, disjointing whole, 150
chicken, raw, flattening breasts, 150
chicken, raw, skinning, 150
chicken, raw, skinning and deboning
    breasts, 152
chicken, testing for doneness, 50
chives, snipping, 224
chocolate, grating, 426
chocolate, melting in double boiler, 474
chocolate, melting in microwave, 375
chocolate, melting over hot water, 394
chocolate, shaving, 506
chorizo, removing casing, 286
clams, cooking, 245
clams, scrubbing, 245
cookies, dipping in chocolate, 358
cookies, rolling dough into balls, 342
cookies, rolling out dough, 370
cookies, rolling out dough between waxed
    paper, 375
cookies, storing, 348

Techniques, *continued*

cookies, using a cookie press, 368
corn, cutting kernels from cob, 108
corn, preparing, 106
crabmeat, picking out shells, 68
cream, whipping, 472
crusts, cutting in shortening, 460
crusts, cutting slits in, 450
crusts, fluting, 452
crusts, rolling out dough, 460
cucumber, peeling, 172
cucumber, seeding, 14
deglazing pan, 512
dough, yeast, doubled in bulk, 26
dough, yeast, kneading, 26
eggs, hard-cooking, 20
eggs, separating, 62
egg whites, beating, 220
garlic, chopping, 166
garlic, crushing, 58
gelatin, dissolving, 457
gelatin, softening, 42
gelatin, unmolding, 42
ginger, chopping, 212
ginger, grating, 40
hazelnuts, rubbing skins to remove, 386
julienne strips, cutting into, 102
lamb, inserting thermometer, 522
lemon, juicing, 164
lemon, making twists, 432
lemon, removing peel, 164
lettuce, drying in spinner, 536
lettuce, tearing leaves, 536
lime, juicing, 168
melon, making balls, 188
melon, peeling, 569
mushrooms, cleaning caps, 115
mushrooms, removing stems, 214
mussels, debearding, 52
nuts, grinding, 504
nuts, toasting in skillet, 250
onion, blanching, 118
onion, chopping in food processor, 22
onion, chopping with knife, 58
orange, grating peel, 40
orange, making twists, 38
orange, removing peel, 178
pan, deglazing, 512
papaya, dicing, 158
papaya, peeling, 158
parsley, mincing, 22
pasta, cutting dough with knife, 250
pasta, cutting dough with pasta
    machine, 66
pasta, kneading dough by hand, 64
pasta, kneading dough in pasta machine, 65
peas, removing string from pods, 126
peas, shelling, 124
pecans, grinding, 180

Techniques, *continued*
peppers, bell, cutting off sides, 72
peppers, bell, pulling out stem and seeds, 98
peppers, bell, scraping out seeds, 128
peppers, bell, slicing into rings, 98
peppers, chilies, cleaning, 285
peppers, chilies, roasting, 284
peppers, chilies, scraping out seeds, 66
pork, butterflying, 320
pork, pounding to ¼-inch (6 mm) thickness, 320
potatoes, forcing through ricer, 534
powdered sugar, sifting, 384
sesame seeds, toasting, 310
shrimp, deveining, 16
shrimp, removing shell, 16
spinach, removing moisture, 76
spinach, removing stems, 62
squash, cutting into rings, 140
squid, cleaning, 268
squid, cutting into rings, 268
tomatoes, peeling, 230
tomatoes, removing pulp and seeds, 142
tomatoes, seeding, 12
tomatoes, sun-dried, chopping, 190
turkey, basting, 510
turkey, inserting thermometer, 510
turkey, stuffing, 540
veal, pounding, 264
walnuts, toasting in skillet, 160
yeast, proofing, 25
zucchini, making ribbons, 144
Three Mushroom Ratatouille, 496
Tin Roof Sundae Cake, 422
Tiramisu, 486
Tomatoes
Chicken Breasts Sautéed with Sun-Dried Tomatoes, 190
Corn and Tomatillo Salsa, 108
Fresh Tomato Salsa, 300
Gazpacho, 292
Golden Tomato Soup, 12
Homemade Angel Hair Pasta with Classic Tomato Sauces, 258
peeling, 230
Plum Tomato Sauce, 256
Red Snapper in Chili-Tomato Sauce, 322
removing pulp and seeds, 142
seeding, 12
sun-dried, chopping, 190
Tabbouleh in Tomato Cups, 142
Tomato Roses, 578
Tomato Sauce, 82, 314
Zucchini-Tomato-Noodle Soup, 60
Toppings
Cherry Topping, 418
Cream Cheese Topping, 410
Praline Topping, 548
Sweetened Whipped Cream, 550
Tortilla Cups, 595

Turkey
basting, 510
inserting thermometer, 510
Roast Turkey with Pan Gravy, 510
stuffing, 540
Turkey-Cheese Surprises, 38
Turkey Broth with Giblets, 512
Two-Onion Pork Shreds, 216
Two-Toned Spritz Cookies, 370

U
Ultimate Chippers, 348

V
Veal
pounding, 264
Veal Parmesan, 264
Vegetable Rings on Broccoli Spears, 98
Vegetables *(see individual listings)*
Velvety Coconut and Spice Cake, 436
Venetian Canapés, 240
Vermicelli, 235
Viennese Coffee, 506
Viennese Meringue Bars, 389

W
Walnuts
Black Walnut Fudge, 466
Chicken and Walnut Salad Athena, 160
Cinnamon Nut Chocolate Spirals, 392
Orange-Walnut Chippers, 356
Rugelach, 556
toasting in skillet, 160
Whipped Cream Frosting, 418
White Chocolate Chunk Brownies, 378
Wild Rice Mushroom Stuffing, 543
Wilted Spinach Mandarin, 136
Wonton Soup, 208

Y
yeast, proofing, 25
Yogurt
Calorie-Wise Dill Chicken, 176
Laguna Beach Pecan Chicken Breasts, 180
Yorkshire Pudding, 514

Z
Zabaglione, 488
Zesty Zucchini-Chick Pea Salad, 328
Zucchini
Crisp Zucchini Ribbons, 144
making ribbons, 144
Minestrone alla Milanese, 248
Ratatouille-Stuffed Pepper Halves, 128
Zesty Zucchini-Chick Pea Salad, 328
Zucchini Butterflies, 580
Zucchini Shanghai Style, 230
Zucchini Squash Flowers, 572
Zucchini-Tomato-Noodle Soup, 60

METRIC CONVERSION CHART

VOLUME MEASUREMENTS (dry)

⅛ teaspoon = 0.5 mL
¼ teaspoon = 1 mL
½ teaspoon = 2 mL
¾ teaspoon = 4 mL
1 teaspoon = 5 mL
1 tablespoon = 15 mL
2 tablespoons = 30 mL
¼ cup = 60 mL
⅓ cup = 75 mL
½ cup = 125 mL
⅔ cup = 150 mL
¾ cup = 175 mL
1 cup = 250 mL
2 cups = 1 pint = 500 mL
3 cups = 750 mL
4 cups = 1 quart = 1 L

VOLUME MEASUREMENTS (fluid)

1 fluid ounce (2 tablespoons) = 30 mL
4 fluid ounces (½ cup) = 125 mL
8 fluid ounces (1 cup) = 250 mL
12 fluid ounces (1½ cups) = 375 mL
16 fluid ounces (2 cups) = 500 mL

WEIGHTS (mass)

½ ounce = 15 g
1 ounce = 30 g
3 ounces = 90 g
4 ounces = 120 g
8 ounces = 225 g
10 ounces = 285 g
12 ounces = 360 g
16 ounces = 1 pound = 450 g

DIMENSIONS

1/16 inch = 2 mm
⅛ inch = 3 mm
¼ inch = 6 mm
½ inch = 1.5 cm
¾ inch = 2 cm
1 inch = 2.5 cm

OVEN TEMPERATURES

250°F = 120°C
275°F = 140°C
300°F = 150°C
325°F = 160°C
350°F = 180°C
375°F = 190°C
400°F = 200°C
425°F = 220°C
450°F = 230°C

BAKING PAN SIZES

Utensil	Size in Inches/Quarts	Metric Volume	Size in Centimeters
Baking or Cake Pan (square or rectangular)	8 x 8 x 2	2 L	20 x 20 x 5
	9 x 9 x 2	2.5 L	22 x 22 x 5
	12 x 8 x 2	3 L	30 x 20 x 5
	13 x 9 x 2	3.5 L	33 x 23 x 5
Loaf Pan	8 x 4 x 3	1.5 L	20 x 10 x 7
	9 x 5 x 3	2 L	23 x 13 x 7
Round Layer Cake Pan	8 x 1½	1.2 L	20 x 4
	9 x 1½	1.5 L	23 x 4
Pie Plate	8 x 1¼	750 mL	20 x 3
	9 x 1¼	1 L	23 x 3
Baking Dish or Casserole	1 quart	1 L	—
	1½ quart	1.5 L	—
	2 quart	2 L	—